Docur

Ourse

# Documenting Ourselves

## Film, Video, and Culture

*Sharon R. Sherman*

THE UNIVERSITY PRESS OF KENTUCKY

Publication of this volume was made possible in part
by a grant from the National Endowment for the Humanities.

Scholarly publisher for the Commonwealth,
serving Bellarmine University, Berea College, Centre
College of Kentucky, Eastern Kentucky University,
The Filson Historical Society, Georgetown College,
Kentucky Historical Society, Kentucky State University,
Morehead State University, Murray State University,
Northern Kentucky University, Transylvania University,
University of Kentucky, University of Louisville,
and Western Kentucky University.
All rights reserved.

*Editorial and Sales Offices:* The University Press of Kentucky
663 South Limestone Street, Lexington, Kentucky 40508-4008
www.kentuckypress.com

10  09  08  07  06      6 5 4 3 2

Grateful acknowledgment is made to the following for permission
to reprint from copyrighted materials:
"The Boy in the Bubble," copyright © 1986 Paul Simon; "Kodachrome," copyright © 1973
Paul Simon; "Act Naturally" by Vonie Morrison and Johnny Russell, copyright © 1963
Sony/ATV Songs LLC (renewed), all rights administered by Sony/ATV Music Publishing,
8 Music Square West, Nashville, Tennessee 37203, all rights reserved, used by permission;
"Video Tape" written by Steve Goodman, copyright © 1985 Big Ears Music/Red Pajamas
Music (ASCAP)/Administered by BUG, all rights reserved, used by permission.

The Library of Congress Cataloging-in Publication Data
Sherman, Sharon R., 1943–
Documenting ourselves : film, video, and culture / Sharon R. Sherman
p.        cm.
Filmography: p.
Includes bibliographical references and index.
ISBN 0-8131-0934-5 (pbk. : alk. paper)
1. Documentary films. 2. Folklore in motion pictures. I. Title.
070.1'8—dc21                                97-23971

ISBN 978-0-8131-0934-3

# Contents

# Illustrations

*With love and thanks
to my mother, Trudy,
for her strength and inspiration,
and
to my husband, Steven,
for keeping the music going*

# Foreword

*Sharon R. Sherman has written* a unique book, long needed and destined to be an oft-cited and frequently quoted authority on its subject. The first of its kind, her volume analyzes the subject matter, conceptual underpinnings, and cinematic techniques in that large body of visual productions known as "folkloristic films." In addition, the author explores ways in which films and videos document and reveal much about ourselves as individuals (whether filmmakers or subjects), culture bearers, and members of a common species. Because folklorically oriented filmmakers have often been schooled in or influenced by other cinematic models, Sharon Sherman sets their work within the context of documentary and ethnodocumentary precursors, from the Lumière brothers to Flaherty, Vertov, Grierson, Rouch, Bateson and Mead, Gardner, the Mac-Dougalls, and Asch, among many others. Throughout her work, the author eschews the film-as-text approach in favor of conceptualizing film as individual creation and a form of communication. She derives much information about folkloristic films—reasons for making them, the choice of topics, why the films are structured in particular ways—directly from interviews with more than a dozen filmmakers. An experienced filmmaker and videographer herself, Dr. Sherman draws on her own documentary experiences, earlier writings, and extensive teaching to develop and illustrate insights in this book.

Writing in the *Journal of American Folklore* (1983), film review editor Keith Cunningham notes that some time during the 1970s there was "a flowering of what I have come to see as the 'folklore film,' a recognizable subgenre of documentary cinematography concentrating upon the traditional artistic productions and producers of culture and differing from anthropological film much as anthropology differs from folkloristics in general" (p. 123). Many of these films bear the signature of the maker, he contends, even more directly than in the case of fiction or feature films. He mentions the works of Tom Davenport, Jorge Preloran, and Les Blank. They are among the filmmakers that Sharon Sherman interviewed in the early 1970s for her Ph. D. dissertation, "The Folkloric Film" (1977), and in the early 1990s for the present book. Others are John Cohen, Pat Ferrero, Bill Ferris, Carl Fleischhauer, Bess Lomax Hawes, Judy Peiser, Mabel Preloran, Ken Thigpen, and Paul Wagner. All these and many more (such as Elizabeth Barret, John Bishop, Peggy Bulger, Michael Loukinen, Peter and Toshi Seeger as well as Sharon Sherman herself) have produced films that fall into a particular category.

What distinguishes the folkloristic film from other kinds of documentaries? As Sharon Sherman indicates, such a film is first and foremost about folklore, that is, expressive or symbolic behavior learned, taught, displayed, or utilized in situations of firsthand interaction and judged to be traditional. Folkloristic films typically dwell on one or a few interrelated genres of expressive behavior, usually among a particular network of people or in the life of an individual, such as the singing games of African American children in Los Angeles, fiddling and dancing in rural Minnesota at the turn of the century, contemporary Cajun foodways and music making in Louisiana, Halloween celebration among residents of a college town in Pennsylvania, the religious musical heritage of a family in North Carolina, traditional storytelling by a mule trader in Mississippi, or chainsaw sculpting by a man in Oregon. While the anthropological film tends to concern the non-Western world, often a folkloristic film explores the traditions of networks and individuals in industrialized societies, sometimes even an ethnic, religious, occupational, or special interest group with which the filmmaker is affiliated. But more than this, the questions addressed by the filmmaker and the theoretical perspectives relied upon to deal with these matters differentiate the folkloristic film from any other.

That the presence of certain theoretical perspectives defines folkloristic films became apparent to me recently when I previewed nearly four dozen visual productions submitted to UCLA's annual film and folklore festival. A few were sociological studies of groups with whom folklore has long been associated (e.g., Gypsies); these gave scant attention to the symbolic behavior, emphasizing social and political processes instead. Those that highlighted folklore clearly fell into three groups. One consisted of anthropological films. Concerned with ceremonies and rituals, initiation rites, folk medicine, and so on, their content intrigues folklorists. But the films inform viewers about the overall culture and social or political structure more than they deal with the particular behaviors that ostensibly are their focus. Ironically, as Sharon Sherman notes in this book, makers of such films are attracted to examples of folklore for what these similarities in human behavior reveal about us as members of the same species, but then they often distance themselves from their subjects as the Other by emphasizing cultural differences. A second group comprised art films. While they focused on graffiti, outsider art, Polynesian rituals, and other examples of folklore, these films and videos used the data as vehicles for personal, sometimes poetic, statements and a means to employ cinematic techniques as artifices calling attention to themselves and the auteurs. A third group, however, were unquestionably folkloristic. They featured an example of folklore, whether traditional Yugoslavian breadmaking, the early punk music scene in Los Angeles, handmade sweets in Little Tokyo, a masked festival in Puerto Rico, the costume art of Star Trek fans, the work songs of Gandy Dancers, or Italian American men who dance the Giglio. They recognized the historical rootedness of the lore, posing questions about its origins and developments. They sought to delineate the behavior as an expressive form or genre, noting its distinguishing features. They acknowledged the example of folklore as an aspect of culture related to other elements but always kept the behavior in the foreground when showing these interrelationships. And they recognized and addressed questions about the tradition as an aspect of human behavior related to participants' personal experiences, motivations, and interactions with others. The presence of these four perspectives, which typify the field of folkloristics itself as Robert A. Georges and I argue in *Folkloristics: An Introduction* (Indiana University Press, 1995), set this body of nineteen films apart from the other twenty-seven and rendered them appropriate for judging in a festival devoted to honoring the production of folkloristic films.

As numerous examples in this book illustrate, all folkloristic films isolate from the continuum of human experience examples of one or more forms of traditional symbolic behavior in order to call attention to them as historical artifacts, describable phenomena, elements of culture, and aspects of human behavior. Each film differs in regard to the perspective emphasized, which is apparent in Sharon Sherman's detailed discussion of numerous works. Filmic techniques also differ, she notes, because of varying conceptions of folklore (as text or performance, as group product or individual expression) as well as differences in analytical approaches. For instance, films that stress the historicity of tradition, attempt to reconstruct the past, or view folklore as text/object typically are narrated and rely on a montage of images. Those concerned with process and performance more often use sync-sound and voice-over by the subjects and are structured around events meaningful to the people whose behavior is documented and presented in the film. The choice of technique, Dr. Sherman indicates, may reveal as much about the filmmaker as do decisions regarding the content, research questions, and hypotheses presented in the film.

Films that record folkloric behaviors, events, and processes "document ourselves" in various ways, as Sharon Sherman discusses throughout this book. To mention a few, there is first the fact that folklore constitutes a universal in human behavior. Research over the past two centuries indicates that people worldwide and through recorded time narrate, play, make decorative objects, celebrate, ritualize, versify, and use figurative language (which has prompted the coining of *homo narrans, homo ludens, homo faber, homo festivus,* etc., to refer to the human species). In addition to communicating symbolically, human beings model their behavior on precedent and depend upon custom. When viewing folkloristic films depicting traditional dancing, music making, storytelling, celebrations, or someone fashioning an object, we see behavior remarkably like our own projected on the screen. "Thus," writes Sharon Sherman, "folklore films and videos offer an interpretive window for comprehending ourselves" as members of the same species. Moreover, most folkloristic films document and explore aspects of the filmmakers' own cultures and people like themselves: their own families, ethnicities, occupations, regions. Recent years have witnessed a spate of feminist, minority, and Third World films that document folklore of groups of which the filmmaker is a part as subjective statements, often as a bid for empowerment, a means of consciousness raising, a way of challenging long-standing beliefs or correcting social injustices. Professional works portray the self through subject choice, style, structure, and editing. Amateur videos and home movies that record birthday parties, weddings, ethnic gatherings, religious occasions, and similar events reveal much about the makers through the selection of what to shoot, how much to document, and the reactivity of the subjects who are on camera. The ubiquity of modern technology contributes significantly to the visual documentation of ourselves; as Dr. Sherman notes, families now videotape what the professional once would have filmed, erasing the line between the Other and the self; and many professional filmmakers follow amateurs in the home mode, using video to record such activities as customs and traditions in their own families. The long history of reflexivity in professional films, the close collaboration between makers of folkloristic films and their subjects, and the growing trend toward post vérité with its unabashed subjectivity lead to the inescapable conclusion that visual documentation, especially in the form of folkloristic filmmaking and videography, constructs the self.

Sharon Sherman's book is the first to concern itself with folkloristic films and the only work that explores in detail the act of documenting ourselves through film and video. She examines the interrelationship among assumptions, theoretical approaches, and cinematic technique evident in folkloristic films and remarked upon by the filmmakers themselves in her interviews with them. She explains and discusses at length such concepts as documentary film, ethnodocumentary, folkloristic film, cinéma vérité, and post vérité. She investigates reflexivity, ethical concerns, and the effects of filming on the maker and the subjects of the films. She writes about collaborative efforts between folklorists and professional filmmakers as well as between filmmakers and those whose activities are documented. At several junctures she confronts the long-standing debate over objectivity versus subjectivity. Her interviews with filmmakers contribute immensely to this endeavor, providing insights into the filmmakers' choice of subjects and treatment of them. For example, John Cohen comments on being an artist (painter, photographer) and musician (the New Lost City Ramblers) who was born in the 1930s. Intending to produce an album of Depression-era songs, he went to Eastern Kentucky in

1959 to learn more about traditional music as well as economic depression. The result was a film, *The High Lonesome Sound* (1963). Focusing on music as a way of maintaining dignity in adversity, its gritty black and white portrayal of poverty and hardship conveys a sense of the period in which Cohen grew up. The film's many striking and evocative images reveal his training as still photographer: a closeup of a spider on its web, a room papered with old newspapers, dogs frolicking in the mist, a hand and arm silhouetted against a window shade, and the out-of-frame, extreme closeups of traditional singer Roscoe Holcomb. Or consider Jorge Preloran's *Imaginero* (1969), which concerns a semi-reclusive creator of religious folk art in Northwestern Argentina. As presented by the Argentine-born filmmaker, Hermógenes Cayo appears isolated from his own sociocultural context, more often an on-looker than participant. A highly emotional portrait of Cayo as the isolated Everyman, the film depicts the creative individual who seeks to transcend the constraints of his milieu by turning them into inspiration for his version of perfect art. In interviews, the filmmaker tells Sharon Sherman about his own aspirations as artist. He also remarks on having been asthmatic as a youth and "always a loner." Who, then, is the film about? Cayo? Preloran? The film is also about us, the viewers, which is why we can identify with the artist as presented by the filmmaker. Folkloristic films and videos do indeed, as Sharon Sherman insists, serve in "documenting ourselves."

Michael Owen Jones

# Preface

*The subtitle of this book,* "film, video, and culture," marks out three vast areas of research that have a multitude of approaches and that encompass far-ranging areas of content. Film, for example, might include such topics as great directors (Hitchcock, Huston, Godard), film history, documentary film, feature films of a specific type (film noir, Westerns, science fiction), or the theoretical approaches often applied to film (semiotics, deconstruction, phenomenology, as but a few examples). I am not concerned with covering the specific content or the theoretical models of any one of these branches of thought but rather with analyzing the intersection of these branches and their relevance to each other.

Modern criticism to the contrary, I am not looking at film or any other aspect of communication as a "text," in the now current literary vogue of seeing everything as a possible textual "construct" capable of being analyzed or deconstructed. For anthropologists and folklorists, the text was always a construct that scholars created in order to place oral communication into a form familiar to their own trained western conventions of textuality. As they began to recognize that the text was their own creation, they abandoned it. Ironically, literary scholars, who were working with actual texts created by authors whose intent it was to create a text, became enamored of the ethnographic approach. In addition to looking beyond the texts in order to examine their significance in a wider context (author's background, history, audience), they added the notion of "text" to other communications with formal properties—in a reverse of that which had occurred in fields outside literature. In this work, I do not consider folklore or film as literature or as a text. Indeed, my vision of the movement away from the concept of folklore as text to folklore as communication, which I see as coupled with advances in fieldwork tools, caused me to formulate the ideas in this book.

My intention in this book is to satisfy the need for a critical examination of the folkloric film. I recommend ways to analyze the relation of film technique and procedure to the central subject or content "focus" of folkloric filmmakers. To illustrate why certain folkloric films are successful and how to judge the utility of film for various folkloric topics, I have grouped a number of films according to the way folklore is perceived and portrayed, and then analyzed them on the basis of the film techniques used.

I made my first film in 1970 as a graduate student in the folklore and mythology program at UCLA. Since then, I have created other films, served as film and video editor for *Western Folklore* and the *Journal of American Folklore*, and focused the majority of my research and teaching on film and folklore. I have taught for over two decades and have advised many students in the creation of their own visual projects. My publications, some of which I have incorporated here, have invariably dealt with this topic, and this book represents a culmination of my thinking about film and folklore.

For me, the most exciting aspect of writing this book has been talking with other filmmakers. For the folklorist, going out into the field is commonplace. Although this book is certainly not a fieldwork endeavor, I decided to use the interview technique to discover what others thought about film, the filmmaking process, and their own work. As a filmmaker, I was eager to learn whether other filmmakers faced the same concerns about what their films said about them and how funding, ethics, equipment, and attitudes about folklore shaped their work. In 1974-75, while completing a Ph.D. in folklore at Indiana University, I interviewed filmmakers for my dissertation. Now, having more experience as a filmmaker and taking the long vision which time provides, I have returned to and expanded upon many of the issues I raised decades ago. I have included some of the early interviews here, and I have interviewed four of the same filmmakers again. But I have based the majority of this work on interviews conducted in the 1990s with folklore filmmakers. To Les Blank, John Cohen, Tom Davenport, Pat Ferrero, Bill Ferris, Carl Fleischhauer, Bess Lomax Hawes, Judy Peiser, Jorge and Mabel Preloran, Ken Thigpen, and Paul Wagner, thank you for making film a viable part of the discipline. I greatly appreciate the time you have shared with me, your encouragement and acknowledgment of the need for a work such as this, and, perhaps more important, for revealing a part of yourselves to me and thus to a wider audience. This book is as much yours as it is mine.

Partial support for this book was provided by a grant from the Research and Sponsored Programs at the University of Oregon. My family has suffered with me through my intense film and video editing sessions over the years. Instead of seeing me coming and going from a remote editing room, they had to adjust to having me at home writing a book in their midst. My appreciation goes to my husband, Steven Zibelman, and my son, Michael, for their patience and love. I thank Letty Fotta of the folklore program at the University of Oregon for the gift of her unending secretarial skills and backing. I owe a great debt to Susan Fagan, whose editorial suggestions have once again turned a rough draft into polished prose, and to my colleague Daniel Wojcik, for careful reading and valuable advice. My friend and fellow folklorist Michael Owen Jones, who has urged me to write this book for eons, has my deepest thanks for his constant support. To Robert A. Georges, Jorge Preloran, and Richard M. Dorson, all of whom have influenced my life beyond measure, my heartfelt gratitude.

Some of the material for this book has been drawn from the following previously published articles: "Film and Folklore" in *American Folklore: An Encyclopedia,* ed. Jan H. Brunvand, 263–65 (New York: Garland Press Folklore Series, 1996); "Film Review of *Zulay, Facing the 21st Century,*" *Visual Anthropology Review* 11 (1995): 128–30; "Visions of Ourselves: Filming Folklore, Present and Future," *Western Folklore* 50 (1991): 53–63; "Double-edged Power: Historical Records of Gender and Race," *Western Folklore* 47 (1988): 217–23; "Human Documents: Folklore and the Films of Jorge Preloran," *Southwest Folklore* 6 (1985): 17–61; "Studying American Folkloric Films," in *Handbook of American Folklore*, ed. Richard M. Dorson, 441–46 (Bloomington: Indiana University Press, 1983); "Rank and File: The Visualization of Occupational Folklore and Union History," *Western Folklore* 42 (1983): 78–84; "Film and Folklore: An Inductive Teaching Method," *Southwest Folklore* 5 (1981): 11–20; "Folkloristic Filmmaking: A Preliminary Report," in *Conceptual Problems in Contemporary Folklore*, ed. Gerald Cashion, 107–16 (Bloomington, Ind.: Folklore Forum Bibliographic and Special Series, no. 12, 1974).

Many of the films discussed in this book are available for viewing at http://www.folkstreams.net.

# 1

## Folklore, Film, and Video
### In the Beginning

*These are the days of miracle and wonder*
*This is a long distance call*
*The way the camera follows us in slow-mo*
*The way we look to us all.*
    *—Paul Simon, "The Boy in the Bubble"*

*The folklore documentary* is ubiquitous. In a world bombarded by visual images, most of us have become not only receivers of the image but its manipulators as well. We take photographs, produce home movies, and shoot videotape of life's events. Often, these visual documents represent the realm of folklore: they record such events as birthday parties, weddings, ethnic gatherings, and religious occasions. At the same time, the films and videos we create reveal much about us *to* us and others.[1] As a folklorist, filmmaker, and videographer, I believe the use of film and video becomes a reflexive process of interpreting ourselves and culture.

A class in basic video production might begin with an assignment to create a short video about oneself. The second assignment asks the students to have someone else in the class make such a video about them. They will shoot and edit a project about themselves, have such a project made by another student, and shoot a video about another classmate. Thus, each student will have two tapes or "visions" of his or her life. The first assignment will capture the "self," or the self that the filmmaker wishes to reveal. The second assignment will also capture the self, revealing as much about the videographer as it does about that person's conception of the subject being portrayed. On the surface, the two videos will share the same topic; on quite another level, each video will be a self-expression of its videographer.

Through the lens, the camera metaphorically mirrors the self of the filmmaker. Folklorists and other scholars use the camera to gather and present data for their own work and advance their own theories about what they have shot; so-called amateur videographers employ video to reflect on their own life events; documentary and ethnographic filmmakers contrast with those whose behaviors they document, thus finding a path for defining themselves. All of these filmmakers address aspects of folklore in their work.

When we take out our own cameras and camcorders, we record our own folk events and personal visions as we see them—what Richard Dorson (1972b) labeled "folk history" and asked folklorists to examine over two decades ago. As viewers, we often find correspondences between our own lives and the data such films include. Folklore film confirms the experiences of people within their multiple subcultures, and viewers search within themselves for ways in which their behaviors are similar to or different from those of the persons depicted. As Paul Ricoeur has written, interpretation is, "explicitly or implicitly, self-understanding by means of understanding others" (1974:16-17). Folklore film and video highlight this interpretive function (much like feminist film demands identification with and by its female viewers as a mark of its success). Unlike documentary filmmakers, who tend to present social issues, or ethnographic filmmakers, who detail the lives of people considered to be "primitive" or "exotic" or of a culture that differs from that of the filmmaker, the folklore filmmaker works in his or her own backyard examining the lore of family, ethnicity, occupation, gender, age, or region. Films whose main purpose is to document, analyze, and present folklore offer us a means for understanding our traditional behavior.

Folklore film did not arrive on the scene full-blown, like Athena from the head of Zeus. The documentation of folklore via film began to increase as theory in folklore expanded from text to context to event and performance and as the fieldworker's tools shifted from notebooks to audio recordings and from still photography to film and video. These theoretical and technological changes are tied to historical developments, but each continues to enjoy favor as the appropriate theory or tool for the questions one is asking. Rather than wholly negating an approach or tool that preceded it (as scholars espousing new theories and inventors of more complex tools hoped), each advancement added to what was available and broadened the research possibilities. A selected history of documentary and ethnodocumentary films and their rhetorical conventions illustrates how the folklore filmmaker of today has been influenced, consciously or subconsciously, in choice of both subject matter and film style. As opposed to an exhaustive history, I detail the development of those films and techniques that are most relevant for folklorists.

Folklore film has developed from models well established in non-fiction film. Whether we prefer the romanticism of Robert Flaherty and his narrative and narrated style, the reconstruction of history offered by Ken Burns with the voices of authority combined with still photos, or the cultural overviews of many ethnographic films, as viewers or filmmakers we are affected by all the films that we have seen.

## The Early Documentary

A century ago, Louis and Auguste Lumière overcame the problems of earlier inventors by combining a successful medium for large-screen projection with rapidly moving still photographs of people in action. When their 1894 film *Workers Emerging from a Factory* was shown by means of their Cinématographe projector on December 28, 1895, at the Grand Cafe in Paris, it was the first public motion picture demonstration, although the film had already been shown at an academic meeting in March 1895. In 1894 W. K. L. Dickson produced *Record of a Sneeze,* which was, as one might imagine, a film account of a person sneezing. From 1895 until 1900, films of fact, or "actualities," captured the imagination. Running up to five minutes, films of fact focused on everyday events such as *New York in a Blizzard.* Filmmakers began to record specific events, for example, *The Kaiser Reviews His Troops* and *The Spanish Coronation.* The novelty of movement yielded to a desire to edify, and the use of the camera for documentation was explicit in these early films (see Jacobs 1979: 2-3). Film became recognized as a tool capable of recording events that could be shown again and again to those who were unable to witness those events in person. All of these films were shot in a single take, that is, in one camera run. Filmmakers, although they could stage their films if they so desired, could not edit their films to change their reportage.[2]

In 1903, the process of editing was discovered, giving filmmakers the absolute power to tamper with "reality." This ability to control images, with its inherent dangers of distortion, would create a controversy over the validity of film use in the social sciences, and discussions concerning the manner in which films are edited were frequent and often vehement. Yet editing brought with it unanticipated possibilities. Film historian Lewis Jacobs writes: "The invention of editing—representing a kind of technological quantum jump—endowed the movies with great new capabilities for controlling and manipulating the flow of time, the speed of events, and screen continuity or order. Editing propelled movies to a radical change in screen subject matter. Motion pictures, until then almost exclusively devoted to the film-of-fact's objective recording of unmanipulated actuality, now were suddenly opened up to the rearrangement and reconstruction of reality for narrative and dramatic purposes" (1979:3). Editing caused the film world to split in two. The commercial film was born, and films of fact were taken up by those who wished to advance scholarship and conduct research as well as to those who believed that reporting unstaged events was far more exciting than filming fictional plots.

Like folklorists, documentary filmmakers have generally presented human behavior occurring within societal structures to the members of that society. Such films provide insight into historical events from the community's point of view and can serve as source materials for the folklorist by providing a history of the folk on film. Documentaries also reflect the preconceptions of the filmmaker as they were used for romantic portrayals, historical reconstruction, and social statements. At the same time, documentaries encompass the full spectrum of camera technique from short single-take shots to cinéma vérité films to syntheses that blend montage and interviews with rapid shots or long takes. Furthermore, documentaries have served as both theoretical and stylistic models for the creation of films commonly called "ethnographic." These documentaries generally illustrate anthropological concerns and document different cultures to discover something about one's own culture. Because they are a type of documentary, a more accurate term for such films would be "ethno-documentary."

The folklorist has drawn on these techniques and approaches of documentary and ethnodocumentary filmmakers, and the folklorist and the filmmaker have often traveled parallel roads. Fascinated by the antiquity of oral narrative and song, fond of romanticizing the past, desirous of preserving that past for the future, and locked in to the literary models with which they were most familiar, folklorists remained firmly tied to their traditional concentration on texts and artifacts until the last few decades of the twentieth century. At the same time that folklorists were deeply involved in textual concerns, documentary filmmakers were creating their short films of fact as visual "texts" of events. Just as anthropologist Franz Boas rejected his predecessors' concepts of cultural evolution and advanced theories emphasizing the importance of cross-cultural influences to account for the similarities found in narrative, filmmaker Felix-Louis Regnault documented a Wolof pottery maker in 1895 and engaged in cross-cultural studies of movement. For other folklorists and anthropologists, for whom cultural traditions were survivals from a bygone era that were in danger of being lost in the face of industrialization, the lore had to be gathered quickly before it disappeared. Likewise, Alfred Cord Haddon used film in the Torres Straits as a form of salvage ethnology in 1898, and Edward S. Curtis reconstructed the activities of Indian tribes in the Northwest in the early 1900s.[3]

Film has always served as both a data-gathering device and a means of presenting research results. It has been used to (1) analyze motion such as gestures, proxemics, and facial expressions; (2) examine form and structure; (3) document historical events; (4) reconstruct history for the screen; (5) "preserve" so-called vanishing cultural traditions; (6) capture such activities as singing or house building; and (7) document the holistic events in which people are engaged.

## Defining Documentary

In his groundbreaking study of the Trobriand Islanders (1961), Bronislaw Malinowski chastises armchair scholars and asks readers to float over with him "to the shores of a Trobriand lagoon" where they might discover "myth as a living reality" (1954:100-101). For Malinowski and subsequent ethnographers, the text no longer existed in isolation. The idea of cultural context soon became firmly established among cultural theorists, as did Malinowski's request to "see with the native's eye," a suggestion taken up by filmmakers of a subsequent generation. At the time of Malinowski's writing, cameras were available but were in very limited use. They had not yet been adopted by anthropologists as serious fieldwork devices. In the Arctic, halfway across the world from Malinowski and the Trobriand Islands, an American mineral explorer named Robert Flaherty would create a landmark film, *Nanook of the North* (1922), unknowingly using many of the principles Malinowski espoused. A decade later, Margaret Mead and Gregory Bateson would begin shooting 16mm silent film in Bali.

That the documentary film differs in both content and analysis from the "story" or "fiction" film is widely recognized. John Grierson, whose British documentary film unit exposed social problems in the 1930s, coined the term *documentary* in 1926 in a review of Flaherty's film *Moana*. Grierson wrote, "*Moana*, being a visual account of events in the daily life of a Polynesian youth and his family, has documentary value" (1979:25; Grierson in Sussex 1975:3). From that time on, *documentary* has been a firmly established term.[4] Unlike the fiction film, the documentary film takes its content from the perceptible behavior of people in relation to their society. It does not fabricate characters or situations but lets the unrehearsed drama of daily life unfold before an audience. The analytic approach to documentary is similar to that used by researchers in the social sciences and the humanities. One begins with the raw data, analyzes it, and presents an edited interpretation to an audience of readers or viewers, who then evaluate the findings of the researcher.[5]

## Flaherty and the Romantic Documentary

The creative means that have been used to express "actuality" through film have varied over the years. Historically, the earliest documentaries are "slice of life" films. But the documentary as a distinct genre of feature-length films was invented by Flaherty, with his production of *Nanook of the North* in the early 1920s. Hailed as the father of documentary, Flaherty began his career prospecting for minerals in the Hudson Bay Territory and Baffin area of Canada. Beginning in 1910, he made five expeditions over six years. Although

1.1 Nanook rubbing his child's hands in *Nanook of the North*. The Museum of Modern Art Film Stills Archive

the deposits he found were not rich enough to justify excavation, Flaherty, through working with the Eskimos, became absorbed with their lifestyle and began an amateur ethnological diary of them. On one of his expeditions, he took along an Eyemo film camera and photographed 30,000 feet of film about Eskimo life. After editing the film, Flaherty accidentally dropped a lit cigarette on the negative, destroying it. Fortunately, he had a positive work print that he was able to project and use to obtain financial backing for another film expedition.

Flaherty recognized that his first film had focused on the picturesque. He wanted to structure his new film around the life of one man and his family. Nanook, a walrus hunter, was chosen as a typical representative of the Eskimo. In exchange for the credit line "Revillon Frères presents," Flaherty received $50,000 from the Canadian fur trading firm and took the best equipment available, including developers and a projector, so that he could process his film "in the field," view the results, ask Nanook about the validity of what he shot, and plan the next day's shooting. The film was shot in 1919 and 1920 and, once edited, was released in 1922.

*Nanook of the North* captures the struggle between Nanook and nature in Nanook's constant attempts to find food and create shelter for his family. Although the film is not structured into a plot, entailing the building of events to a climax, followed by a resolution, it does have continuity. The film is organized into scenes or episodes, and the audience sees Nanook preparing his hunting equipment for the coming winter, his fight to survive during the winter by hunting walrus and seal, and the use he makes of these animals for food and clothing.

Throughout the film Flaherty details the blinding expanse of snow and the blizzard conditions in and against which Nanook must search for food. While the scenes in which Nanook spears a walrus and harpoons a seal through the ice are striking, the blizzards and his search for shelter, which climaxes in the building of an igloo, are most memorable. These scenes have also been sharply criticized by viewers who noted that the seal which emerges after a lengthy struggle has obviously been dead for some time and that Nanook's igloo was too large when compared with those normally constructed. Obviously Flaherty had altered the "facts" to present his material. The igloo scene, for example, could not have been shot without making the dwelling large enough for camera equipment and light enough to render an image of Nanook's family retiring for the night under their furs. Despite these "distortions," *Nanook of the North* has become a classic on the basis of the *apparent* genuineness of its portrayal. Lewis Jacobs comments: "Nanook marked the advent of a type of film new to the world. Its use of environmental details and skilled continuity broke with the purely descriptive; it swept away the notion that what the camera recorded was the total reality. Flaherty proved there was another reality which the eye alone could not perceive, but which the heart and mind could discern" (1979:8).

Despite the artistic imagery of Flaherty's first film, five film distributors refused to back its release. Charles Pathé, the originator of the newsreel, finally signed a deal with Flaherty. The film, which did not seem destined for success at the Hollywood-oriented box office, opened in Paris and was instantly acclaimed a success by the viewers. While Nanook's life flickered on the screen, the real saga of Nanook's struggle against nature continued in the Arctic, and nature won. Two years after Flaherty left, Nanook died of starvation.

For folklore filmmakers, Flaherty's establishment of an expository style had little effect. Flaherty's romanticization, his focus on the individual as a representative figure for a culture, and his involvement of Nanook and the Inuit in the filming process are the elements of a filmic model that folklore documentary filmmakers emulated. In folklore films, the rural often takes precedence over the urban and the past assumes greater importance than the contemporary. John Cohen's search for Child ballads in Appalachia documented in *The High Lonesome Sound* (1963) or for carnival practices in the remote villages of the Andes, or Jorge Preloran's documentation of little known peoples in the isolated regions of Argentina, or Les Blank's depiction of rural Cajun life—all fit this pattern. Yet none of these filmmakers is locked into this standard. Indeed, they have examined contemporary activities and the urban scene as well. Often, like Flaherty, they began with a romantic stereotypic notion of the folk for their initial films and then recognized a need to broaden the definition of their work as their film corpus grew.

Just as Flaherty selected Nanook, folklore filmmakers often choose a biographical "everyman" to represent the group. Les Blank, in several films, has Marc Savoy explain aspects of being a Cajun; Jorge Preloran looks at Hermogenes Cajo as an exemplar of religious folk artists and Sixto Roman Zerda as the typical woodcutter; Bill Ferris documents James Thomas as a bluesman. But, as one might expect with the passage of time and the changes in technique and styles, folklore filmmakers have taken Flaherty's approach a step further by documenting these people as both cultural representatives and unique personalities. The subject's participation in the filming process (Flaherty 1950) is only now becoming a common means of sharing the authority for the film, as is evidenced by Zulay Saravino and Jorge and Mabel Preloran for *Zulay, Facing the Twenty-first Century* (1993). Flaherty's influence is also evident in Preloran's early films, which similarly explore the relationship between man and nature.

Flaherty continued to focus on man and nature in his film *Moana* (1926), a romantic vision of the South Sea Islanders of Samoa. Realizing that the Samoans did not have to struggle for food as Nanook had, the Flahertys abandoned their first intention to make a "southern style Nanook" and decided to focus on the subtleties of custom in Samoan life—the dances, rituals, and ceremonies. Yet this drama was thought to be too psychological to be conveyed on film. While filming, however, Flaherty found that color panchromatic film (sensitive to red tones when used in a black-and-white camera) did not distort the brown color of the Samoans. Orthochromatic film would ordinarily convert red to black in black-and-white, but the use of panchromatic rendered intricacies in shading, and telephoto lenses produced a stereoscopic image (Flaherty 1979). Because of these discoveries, the Flahertys decided to focus on the beauty of Samoan life.

*Moana* presents the carefree islanders amid scenes of surf and sunshine, catching a boar and a giant turtle, engaging in traditional dances, and preparing meals. *Moana* is an idyllic overview, although it climaxes in a torturous tattooing scene. This striking episode, however, does not depict a practice actively followed by Samoan boys. Although tattooing had functioned as an initiation ritual marking the transition into manhood, it had been discouraged by the missionaries and was no longer generally done. Nevertheless, the Flahertys convinced one of the Samoan boys to submit to the ritual. Whereas *Nanook* had concentrated on the struggle of man against nature, *Moana* portrayed man's infliction of pain upon himself in a world in which struggle did not exist. Both films dealt with fleeting lifestyles and with societies rapidly becoming westernized. Both also dealt with folklore: art, custom, ritual, dance, and foodways.

With the filming of *Man of Aran* (1934), Flaherty's focus on "primitive" or "isolated" peoples reached full distortion by re-creating for the screen a life which, in fact, no longer existed. Once again, Flaherty saw a drama of man against nature, this time a drama which he created for himself in the Aran Islands, an area surrounded by a raging sea near the western Ireland coast. As with *Nanook,* Flaherty wished to focus on one family to represent the entire community. Whereas Nanook's family had indeed been authentic, the family depicted in *Man of Aran* (as in *Moana*) was fabricated, its members chosen for their ability to photograph well (cf. Barsam 1988:36).

Many of the scenes demonstrate the harshness of life in a landscape of barren rock, constantly buffeted by high breakers crashing into the reefs with great force, sending up huge sheets of water and mist. The capture of a basking shark or sunfish constitutes the highlight of the film. Although these giant fish had once been profitably hunted for the oil obtained from their livers (two hundred gallons per shark), the sharks had not frequented the area for years. Six years prior to Flaherty's arrival, the sharks had returned, but the practice of hunting them was remembered only by one old, dying man. Flaherty was able to reconstruct an act that had not been performed for close to a hundred years! In fact, a whaling captain from Scotland was called upon to teach the men how to actually harpoon the shark. In many of the sequences the people risked their lives because of their admiration for Flaherty. For example, one character (Mikeleen) fishes off a shaky ledge hundreds of feet up on a cliff, and the men battle the sea, although most could not swim.

As with Flaherty's other films, the climax involves the fight for survival against the forces of nature. In the midst of a savage storm, the men bring their boat onto shore only to have it reclaimed by the rough sea. The curragh is smashed by the waves as the men join their anxious families, and the film ends with a final shot of the people staring out at a treacherous sea.

*Man of Aran,* one of Flaherty's greatest aesthetic accomplishments, was severely criticized for ignoring the deplorable social and economic conditions in which the Aran Islanders struggled in favor of a romantic portrayal of the outmoded struggle with monsters of the sea. Religious conflict between the Catholics and Protestants and the tenant-landlord system were considered the real enemies of the Islanders—not the sea. Yet Flaherty did not touch on these issues and was thus accused of being unresponsive to the needs of those he filmed. He also presented the staged events in the film as if they had happened in the course of daily life. Flaherty never clarified this misunderstanding. Arthur Calder-Marshall, in his analysis of Flaherty's life and films, *The Innocent Eye: The Life of Robert J. Flaherty,* remarks, "Flaherty did not give a Press conference and say, 'These are the people whom I used for a poetic presentation of the age-long struggle of Man against the Sea. The reality which I attempted was poetic and *Man of Aran* is not intended to be an actual representation of everyday life on the Aran Islands.' On the contrary, *Man of Aran* was presented as a true film of real life" (1963:163).

As with any document, in filmmaking the maker's underlying preconceptions about the data determine his or her film statement and portrayal. Flaherty, by filming a situation that had not existed for two generations (*Man of Aran*), by concentrating on those people whom he saw as primitive or isolated *(Nanook of the North, Moana, Man of Aran, Elephant Boy [1937], Louisiana Story [1948]*), must be considered a survivalist. Folklorists, anthropologists, and ethnodocumentary filmmakers (who are frequently also anthropologists or folklorists) often have believed that the ways of the "folk" or the "primitive" are dying out and that only the fieldworker's and filmmaker's rapid capture of these elements of life can "preserve" them. Instead of dealing with acculturation, urbanization, westernization, and industrialization as interesting facets of the sociological and economic problems in a rapidly changing world, the survivalist ignores contemporary events and re-creates the "simple, rustic" life of a romanticized past. Filmmakers who imitated Flaherty's neo-Rousseauean "romantic documentaries" made the conflict of man against nature their central theme.[6]

## City Symphonies

For other filmmakers, especially in France and Germany, the documentary continued the "slice of life" approach that had predated Flaherty in the early 1900s. The so-called continental realists began to shoot and edit overviews of city life. Not wishing to seek out the unusual or exotic in faraway places, these documentarians relished the rhythms and tempos created by anonymous urban dwellers as they went to work. Shots of people walking along roads, working in factories, and sweeping their porches, trains speeding toward the city, and even empty streets made up the "city symphonies." *Rien que les heures* [Nothing but the Hours] (1926), Alberto Cavalcanti's detailing of the upper and lower classes of Paris, and Walter Ruttmann's *Berlin: The Symphony of a Great City* (1927) are the most outstanding examples. The subjects of their shots added to the tempo and were further paralleled with the rhythm of their editing, which produced a montage of recurring patterns. Thus, these filmmakers became intigued with the cinematic shots of various aspects of city life and work, and strung the shots together to make films that emphasized the form of film itself but did not reveal people's characters, thoughts, or aspirations. Such films had no analytical statement to make, and they generated few thought-provoking ideas. Like the folklorist who focuses on various house types and admires the aesthetic forms without regard to the function they have for the inhabitants, the city symphonies looked at structure and tempo without examining the urban experience. The films are merely montages of images that gave the audience a feeling of the life force of the city. Yet in terms of today's viewing of such films, the images, like house structures, provide a document of a historical era. The buildings, the people, the vehicles, the clothing styles, and even the selection of images and the cinematic style are now historical documents in and of themselves.

## Vertov's Montage

Soviet filmmakers were also preoccupied with the camera's ability to document life. Dziga Vertov believed that the camera offered an objective means to report events. In his development of the kino-eye theory, he argued that the camera eye had powers beyond that of the human eye and, hence, was superior: "The eye lives and moves in time and space, perceiving and recording impressions in a way quite different from the human eye. It is not necessary for it to have a particular stance or to be limited in the number of movements to be observed per second. The movie camera is better. We cannot make our eyes better than they have been made, but the movie camera we can perfect forever" (Geduld 1967:83).

The camera was seen to have limitless capabilities. Instead of viewing a dance, for example, from the theatrical point of view of the audience, it could illustrate movements between, around, and behind dancers. Yet the cameraperson was not to attempt creativity. The film was to be unbiased and totally realistic in intent. Only in the editing stages could the filmmaker make a personal statement. This approach worked well for observational newsreel footage, which could then be edited in montage to show the distinctions that the filmmaker wished to convey—his own reporting of the events.

*The Man with a Movie Camera* (1928) best demonstrates Vertov's theories of the kino-eye. Vertov presents the viewer with a day in Moscow, similar to the city symphonies. At the same time, he points out how the raw material will be used. The film opens with a camera pointed at the audience. A small cameraman superimposed on the top of the camera begins to take the audience's picture. Vertov then shows the moviegoers entering the theater, taking their seats, and watching the opening of the film. At this point Vertov's montage of city life begins. Thus, the audience is instantly aware of the message that the kino-eye is meant to see all. Throughout the film an eye is intercut with the scenes to repeat that this is a film, not a "reality." Vertov matches the rhythm of the images with his editing technique. People awaken slowly, the city begins to show signs of life, and shots of these subjects remain on the screen for a fairly long time. At the height of the day when activities are more quickly paced, Vertov cuts the shots to a few seconds, rapidly editing disparate scenes together to point out his own view of their relatedness. Vertov even shows himself editing to reveal the film as a form.

The world is made up of chaos, for Vertov, and the filmmaker's job is to bring meaningful order to life by showing the masses what is not ordinarily apparent. Like Lévi-Strauss's idea of bricolage out of which the bricoleur shapes the message, Vertov believed that editing the data of everyday life would bring about a new understanding.[7] Vertov's vision of the revolutionary uses to which film could be put was expressed in his newsreel series *Kino-Pravda* (film truth). These newsreels, although focused on unrehearsed events occurring in society, were subjectively edited to convey ideology to the proletarians.

Vertov's fast-paced montage technique is also evident in his later work. *Three Songs of Lenin* (1934) uses both synchronous and nonsynchronous sound, old archival materials, early newsreel footage, interviews with Lenin, and shots of workers viewing the body of Lenin lying in state spliced together to create an overall tribute to him. The soundtrack uses folksongs to structure the images compiled by Vertov over seventeen years. Thus, folksong texts are the organizing principle, and folklore filmmakers most interested in texts will (often unknowingly) employ the techniques of montage inspired by Vertov.

Accused of concentrating on form rather than content by the Stalinists of the 1930s, Vertov lost favor with his government. But his influence can best be seen today in the work of such avant-garde filmmakers as Jean-Luc Godard. In addition, Vertov's kino-eye, which must "document from life" to create "film truth," is the precursor of cinéma verité (film truth), a technique made popular in the 1960s with the advent of portable sync-sound equipment.

As Bill Nichols (1991) observes, Vertov establishes "the reflexive mode," showing the viewer the means by which representation is achieved. But unlike Flaherty and Rouch, who tried to incorporate the reactions of those being documented, Vertov's film "truth" is solely the filmmaker's own truth as he or she constructs it. These two approaches, that of Vertov and that of Flaherty, dominate documentary practices today. Neither praxis is easily bounded or that distinctive, except perhaps in terms of form. Whereas those who "play with" form are overtly providing viewers with their vision, other filmmakers still present their own stamp of authority while deluding themselves into thinking they are allowing their subjects to shape the film. Although one might suppose that because Flaherty tried to include his subjects' input, he was reproducing the natives' attitudes, his methods for *Man of Aran* and *Moana* indicate otherwise. Vertov, despite his domination of the film, does reveal how his authority is constructed. Whereas both styles underscore how subjective film is, Vertov's work is more blatant about the impossibility of objectivity. In folklore film, the montage structure employed in such films as Ferris's Yale series and Blank's food films provides a means for discovering what the filmmaker thinks about the subject being documented. Thus, analyzing how filmmakers apply form to content offers a method for revealing their intent, as I discuss in chapters 2 and 3.

## Grierson and the British School: Films of Occupational Groups

Opposed to the romanticization of the past as presented by Flaherty, and the concentration on form evidenced by Vertov, John Grierson believed that the main intent of the documentary was the "creative treatment of reality." Like Vertov, Grierson thought that film had a social purpose, and he demanded that film inform the citizens of actual or needed social programs so that film would function as a means of communicating issues for social reform. Grierson is instructive for folklorists in his depiction of occupational groups. In 1928, the Empire Marketing Board, a British government agency established to oversee all aspects of food production and distribution, created the EMB Film Unit (Hardy 1966:16-17, Rotha 1963:96). Grierson, as the unit's director, became the most influential force in British documentary by guiding a number of filmmakers. Unlike Vertov, Grierson stressed function over form. Yet those films made by the British documentarians were definitely propagandist in intent (cf. Morris 1987). The desire was to create a more educated citizenry who would be involved in the decisions of a democracy. As Paul Rotha points out, documentaries "could be used to bridge the many gaps that exist between group and group in modern society" (1963: 206). This goal is important for today's folklore filmmakers who often use film as a means of communicating the traditional attitudes and beliefs of one group to another.

Rather than being descriptive by compiling images without analysis, the British school of filmmaking presented a problem and either offered solutions or evoked a desire in the viewer to provide a solution. Preceding Marshall McLuhan's ideas concerning the media revolution by four decades, Grierson saw a decline in print orientation and believed that films represented the new medium by which citizens might receive information.

The British documentary, which up to the 1930s sought to reveal the strange and unusual in far-off locales, now focused the camera inward on the problems of the "average" person and analyzed the situation of individuals in occupations and the importance of national and local issues and institutions.[8] These films all reflected what Rotha has termed "descriptive" or "journalist" documentaries whose aim is "an honest effort to report, describe or delineate a series of events, or the nature of a process, or the workings of an organization on the screen" (1963:176). This comment almost could serve as a characterization of folklore studies by adding the word *traditional* to the events and processes and by adding the notion of *folk* to that of an occupation or organization.[9]

## Nationalism

In the United States, *The Plow that Broke the Plains* (1936), a film made by Pare Lorentz concerning soil erosion and dust bowl farmers, was the first documentary to be produced for the U.S. government (under the auspices of the Resettlement Administration). Lorentz also obtained government sponsorship from the Farm Security Administration of the Agriculture Department to produce *The River* in 1937. The film details the use of technology to explain the necessity of building dams on the tributaries of the Mississippi River. The film was so well received that the U.S. government hired Lorentz to direct a new agency, the U.S. Film Service, in 1938.

One of its first films was *Power and the Land* (1940) by Joris Ivens, which concerned the lack of electrical power and running water on many farms in America. Unlike the fairly objective picture of conditions provided in *The River*, the narration in *Power and the Land* is overly romantic in depicting farm life. Although presented in a subjective fashion, the film is an interesting documentary in terms of the times, because it reflects the feelings of nationalism that were developing as the United States watched the war building up in Europe. *The Fight for Life* (1941) by Lorentz and *The Land* (1941) by Flaherty were also made under government sponsorship. But Congress, wary of New Deal establishments, soon voted the U.S. Film Service out of existence.

During World War II, as well as the period leading up to the actual declaration of war, various propaganda films were made by government branches to encourage Americans to join in the war effort and enlist for service. The Office of War Information and various armed services recognized the dramatic uses of documentary footage and began making training films (Griffith in Rotha 1963:344-45).

Motion pictures were able to record battles, the landing of battalions, and secret airways and munitions supply areas. Such informational films were then reviewed as a means of improving military plans. In addition, such footage was often used as newsreels to communicate information to members of the armed

1.2  Hitler walks amid a massed rally at Nuremberg in *Triumph of the Will.*
MOMA/FSA

services. These newsreels were later shown in feature film houses to the general public to keep the populace abreast of war developments around the world.

As historical documents, the propaganda films of World War II are most notable for attempting to convince the people of various countries that their national cause was just. The idea of nationalism had, of course, informed the work of early folklorists, such as William Thoms and the Brothers Grimm. Moreover, the depiction of one nation by another is significant for a study both in stereotyping and in how filmmakers reveal their ideological selves. An early classic example is Leni Riefenstahl's *Triumph of the Will* (1935). A favorite of Hitler and a silent film actress, Riefenstahl became famous for her spectacular staging of the 1934 Nazi Party Congress at Nuremberg. Using thirty-six cameras, Riefenstahl carefully selected and arranged her shots of the events (which were intentionally set up with the cameras in mind) to demonstrate Hitler's charisma and to urge viewers to become devoted to Nazi ideology. Walking down a broad aisle flanked by thousands of Nazis, Hitler reviews his troops while music by Wagner builds the drama. Powerful in impact, *Triumph of the Will* is a propagandist pageant. The event that it "documents" is a camera setup. Yet it emerged as a tribute to Hitler that served the aim of convincing uncommitted Germans to join the Nazi Party. *Olympiad* (1938), Riefenstahl's film of the 1936 Olympics, was also used to document Nazi Aryan supremacy. This aim backfired, however, when such athletes as the black American Jesse Owens walked off with numerous gold medals.

Americans who were reluctant to join in the war or enlist for service because of their isolationist ideas were also influenced by propagandist films. "Why We Fight," a series of seven films produced by Frank Capra, then a lieutenant colonel, gave Americans facts about the Japanese, Italian, and German invasions. Folklorists will find the romantic-nationalism overtones in such films familiar. Despite their drawbacks, the films provide data about the war and give today's audiences a view of the problems that were being discussed in the 1940s. The importance of the series was stressed by the army. The first five films were required viewing for all soldiers before they went overseas (Mac-Cann 1979:218).

Another war film, *The Battle of San Pietro* (1944-45), made by John Huston, glorified the American forces, but because it depicted the true violence of war it was later suppressed as being too realistic for general viewing. Like Capra's *War Comes to America* (1945), *The Battle of San Pietro* used actual war footage, which was then interspersed with reconstructions. Initiated with Flaherty, reconstruction was further established as a way to "document" history. A number of filmmakers would continue this practice, and televised reenactments of amateur video would exploit it.

## Romanticism to Realism

Following the tremendous scope and flurry of filmmaking during the war, the documentary filmmaker who had enjoyed wartime governmental support now returned to independent filmmaking or sought sponsorship, and nationalism gave way to a returning romanticism. Flaherty's *Louisiana Story,* for example, was financed solely by the Standard Oil Company at a cost of $258,000. As he had done in his earlier film work, Flaherty steeped himself in the cultural milieu, this time living, shooting, and editing his footage on location in the Louisiana bayous for a year. His focus for this film was a Cajun boy who witnesses the construction of an oil rig in a swampy area near his home. Although Flaherty seemed to have abandoned his earlier topic of man against nature, he was still occupied with it. Sun and shade filter through the trees of the bayou and reflect dreamily on the water's surface as a menacing alligator glides among the lily pads. Thus man-and-nature is the central theme, although nature is less of a threat than it was for Nanook or the Aran Is-

1.3 *Louisiana Story.* MOMA/FSA

landers. A romantic film, *Louisiana Story* seems to suggest that the forces of industrialization can coexist with nature and be understood by a "backwoods" family. This film is a fascinating contrast to Les Blank's folklore films on the Cajuns; some of Blank's films continue to perpetuate the romanticism of Flaherty, yet they do so in a celebratory fashion that shows the richness of Cajun life.

Lacking the sense of purpose that dominated the war years and faced with an era of economic prosperity, social analysis as a subject was not as keenly needed as it had been before the war. Unlike the demand for change urged in the films of the 1930s, most of the films of the 1950s were informative, such as Jacques Cousteau's undersea document, *The Silent World* (1956), and Bert Haanstra's *Glass* (1958), which compared modern and traditional glassmaking. Lionel Rogosin's *On the Bowery* (1957) posed questions still plaguing filmmakers. In this look at life on skid row, the filmmakers "cast" men from the Bowery who would portray their own lifestyle. Yet the film was scripted and the filmmakers used hidden cameras inside bars so that they could blend in with the patrons. Shortly after the filming, the "star" died. The filmmakers felt remorse at using others for their own purposes and became acutely aware that, despite their involvement, they were able to "escape" from the Bowery (Sufrin 1979 [1955-56]:315). This film foregrounds the notion of the subject as the Other. The 1950s also marked an increase in the anthropological use of film for documenting ethnography, as well as the proliferation of television documentaries, such as *The Murrow-McCarthy Debate* (1954). The documentary filmmaker as investigator reaches prominence and the occupational group continues to be significant as exemplified by Edward R. Murrow's *Harvest of Shame* (1960), an investigative film produced by CBS on the plight of migratory workers in the United States. Today, many documentarians depend on television broadcasting for their audience and for their support (from such sponsors as the Corporation for Public Broadcasting).

## Shifting Paradigms: Film and Folklore

Folklorists, linguists, anthropologists, literary scholars, historians, and others sought a way to document human behavior rather than study the relics or texts constructed from that behavior. As with many of the changes wrought by the 1960s, the emphasis in folklore moved to a more dynamic model for viewing folklore and other cultural creations. Scholars created new conceptual frameworks that posed new questions. One of the primary problems for those interested in studying folklore was to find a suitable methodology that would serve as a tool for the new inquiries concerning function, communication, interaction, taste, and aesthetics. Advances in documentary film aided the search.

Documentary filmmakers constantly sought to improve their equipment. They could shoot in the field with "wild sound," or sound recorded separately from the camera that could not be synched up with the image. They then imposed a soundtrack on their finished creations, usually with music, sound-over of peoples' comments, and/or a narrator to explain the action—much in the style of Flaherty. Such was the methodology of Gregory Bateson and Margaret Mead, who used film to observe events occurring within a culture to generate hypotheses concerning the culture as a whole. While Malinowski was working on a functional analysis in the Trobriand Islands and examining cultural practices in context, Mead and Bateson would depict one event—the witch play among the Balinese in *Trance and Dance in Bali* (shot before World War II, released in 1952), for example—to make assumptions about the behavior of the culture in general.

Despite the questions raised by this kind of "representational" film, the event as a model for documentation as developed from anthropological inquiries would eventually become a major theoretical paradigm in folklore. Although seminal articles by Robert A. Georges (1969), Barbara Kirshenblatt-Gimblett (1975), Barre Toelken (1976 [1969]), and the folklorists of "Toward

New Perspectives" (Paredes and Bauman 1971) set new directions for the study of folklore as behavior, folklore filmmakers lagged behind. Malinowski's work and Alan Dundes's article "Texture, Text, and Context" (1964) set the tone for films that asked how the study of folklore forms, such as narratives and songs, would gain from the dimension of visuals. For example, Bess Lomax Hawes's *Pizza Pizza Daddy-O* (1969) showed a group of children's songs in context, Bill Ferris's *I Ain't Lying* (1975) emphasized texts in context, and Jorge Preloran's short films on ritual and ceremony, shot in the early sixties, described ritual in cultural context (Sherman 1985).

In part, the reluctance of folklorists to see folklore as event, interaction, and communication—as opposed to a textual "thing"—was based on a long-established reliance on studying folklore as object and the film industry's slow progress in creating a portable sync-sound camera unit that would force folklorists to see folklore differently. However, as the technology improved, some folklorists converted to documentary film as a methodology.

The decade of the 1960s is the touchstone for change, at least for members of my generation. Folklorists and the literary New Critics who had concentrated on texts and their content now became enamored of structuralism, an analytic mode derived from Russian formalist and folklorist Vladimir Propp and exemplified in his 1928 book, *Morphology of the Folktale*. This work was not translated until 1958 nor was it widely recognized until 1968, when a special American Folklore Society edition was published. Vertov's and Propp's work grow out of the same school. Both of these formalists became extremely influential in the 1960s: one had a renewed influence on film; the other on folklore, literature, and anthropology. Propp's syntagmatic structuralism was joined by a paradigmatic one developed by anthropologist Claude Lévi-Strauss to study mythology, a topic central to folklore as a discipline from its inception. Developing into a strong belief in shared signification systems in which language determined a constructed meaning, structuralism favored form at the expense of studying the human element. The 1960s changed that attitude. The development of ethnographies of speaking grew out of semiotics and led to work in folklore on performance; in literary theory, J. L. Austin's *How to Do Things with Words* (1962) demonstrates how language is a performance. In film, the omniscient filmmaker gives way to the speakers who now perform and construct their own world for the camera.

## Cinéma Vérité

The social turmoil of the 1960s brought the documentary back into serious perspective as a medium that could detail and comment on changes occurring in society from the point of view of those being documented. For the first time since World War II, documentary film reached new levels of production. A change in consciousness and culture occurred with the escalation of the Vietnam War; the assassinations of John F. Kennedy, Robert Kennedy, and Martin Luther King Jr.; the urban and campus riots; and the increased availability of drugs. The 1960s were a time of turbulence constantly shadowed by the growing antiwar and civil rights movements. All these events, including daily scenes of wartime activities, exploded on television news programs in millions of American homes. The instant transmission of news events and the ability to shoot such events on the spot without extensive camera crews was made possible with new portable synchronous sound equipment—an unprecedented landmark in the history of motion pictures, that led to the development of the cinéma vérité style.[10]

The first use of the term *cinéma vérité* (truth film) in the 1960s is generally credited to Jean Rouch, a French anthropological filmmaker who, with Edgar Morin, filmed *Chronicle of a Summer* in 1960 with the new portable equipment. Rouch intentionally used the term as a tribute to Vertov, whose style influenced French filmmakers. Rouch and Morin interviewed people about their lives on the streets of Paris and later shot the interviewees' reactions to seeing themselves on film. The filmmakers interacted with the people during the filming and appeared in the film. Rouch believed the presence of the filmmaker made a difference and should be openly admitted. His style was to be closely emulated at UCLA by Mark McCarty in his theories of observational cinema, which were made apparent in *The Village,* a document of a small Irish town shot in 1968 (see McCarty 1975).

In America, cinéma vérité was developed at the same time by Drew Associates. Their first effort resulted in *Primary* (winner of the 1960 Flaherty Award), a film about the Wisconsin Democratic primary race between Hubert Humphrey and John F. Kennedy. American filmmakers often called their approach "direct cinema" to distinguish their format from their French counterparts. Whereas Rouch followed in Vertov's footsteps, the Americans were influenced by Flaherty. Richard Leacock, a member of the film team, discussed the new film development and the changes in perspective and technique that cinéma verité or direct cinema created:

> Having grown up in the documentary film tradition of Flaherty, Grierson, Elton, et al., I believed that we should go out into the real world and record the way it really is. Without sound we were limited largely to processes— this is how we fish, this is how we blow glass, make boats, build dams, etc. With the advent of sound, far from being freed we were paralyzed by the complexity and size of equipment. We still went out to the real world and proceeded to destroy, by our own impact, the very thing we went to record.

> After much experimenting and some wonderful failures, we managed to put together a portable, quiet synch-sound camera and recorder in 1960. *Primary* was the first film that our group (Bob Drew, Pennebaker, Al Maysles, Mccartney-Filgate and myself) made where the new equipment worked; where two people made up a whole film unit; where we could walk in and out of situations without lights, tripods, cables and all the other impediments that had shackled us before.
>
> We now subjected ourselves to a rather rigid set of rules. If we missed something, never ask anyone to repeat it. Never ask any questions. Never interview. We rarely broke them and when we did we regretted it. [Levin 1971:195-96]

Cinéma vérité gave the impression of film objectivity. Most camera crews would not, as Leacock states, ask anyone to repeat any action or statement. This "rule" meant that one had to capture events as they were occurring without any intrusion or attempt at restructuring situations. In America, rather than interview people, the crew merely documented their actions; because the sound was synchronous with the action, cinéma vérité seemed to let the people speak for themselves.

Stylistically, the portability of the equipment allowed the camera crew to film almost "from the inside" of an event and thus gave the audience a feel for "being there." Because events were totally unrehearsed and the film team did not know what would happen at any given time, the zoom lens would often be focused on a person or an interaction at a point when the cameraman thought something important *might* happen when, in fact, nothing significant occurred. Furthermore, cinéma verité films of the 1960s included soft focus shots and running, blurred, and shaky shots because events such as antiwar demonstrations and urban riots were too turbulent to predict, and camera crews often had to run to keep up with the action. These events necessitated the invention of the Steadi-cam, now used throughout the film industry. Prior to the Steadi-cam's development, cinéma vérité often came to be associated with a style of filmmaking that was cruder and less sophisticated than studio-made films and early documentaries. Like folk art, this apparent aesthetic weakness, however, did not prove to be a drawback. Quite the contrary, it somehow added to the notion that one was seeing the unvarnished truth, providing a raw vision of the real thing.

The uniqueness of the new filmmaking style led to its adoption by producers of many different types of films. In fiction or theatrical films, the cinéma vérité style was used, for example, by John Cassavetes in *Faces* (1968) and *Woman under the Influence* (1974), and Haskell Wexler mixed actual footage of the confrontation between demonstrators and the police at the 1968 Democratic Convention in Chicago into his fictional feature, *Medium Cool* (1969). Jean-Luc Godard used direct interviewing and left the Nagra tape recorder visible in the frame in many of his features. Woody Allen's *Zelig* (1983) mimics documentary, as does his film *Husbands and Wives* (1992) with its handheld camera style. Vérité is parodied in *This Is Spinal Tap* (1984), Rob Reiner's film satire, in which a filmmaker endeavors to make a documentary about a heavy metal British band.[11]

Cinéma vérité was the principal style for Frederick Wiseman, whose overviews of life affected by public institutions for both those who work in them and those who confront them were realized in such films as *Titicut Follies* (1967) about the Bridgewater, Massachusetts, State Hospital for the Criminally Insane (directed by Wiseman, but shot by the well-known ethno-documentary filmmaker John Marshall); *High School* (1968), a portrait of Northeastern High School in Philadelphia from both sides of the desk, reexamined in *High School II* (1995); *Law and Order* (1969), on the Kansas City police department; *Hospital* (1970); *Welfare* (1975), an analysis of the government welfare system; *Meat* (1976), regarding a meat packing plant, and *The Store* (1983), about Neiman Marcus. Wiseman has enjoyed considerable air play for his films, most of which have been telecast. These films are all quite long, running between 75 minutes (*High School*) and three hours (*Welfare*).

Wiseman has a knack for capturing human behavior that we would not normally expect to occur before the eye of a camera (until the advent of the portable videocamera). For example, scenes in *Law and Order* include one policeman strangling a prostitute and another bashing a black youth's head against a car hood. The widely broadcast videotape of Rodney King being beaten in 1990 by Los Angeles police officers (whose acquittal touched off the Los Angeles riots of 1992) demonstrates how such events may be documented by today's videographers who are now able to catch what was previously hidden. Although Wiseman presents the ugly workings of public institutions (a man being shunted from one office to another in *Welfare*, for example), he also tries to provide a balance by shooting the complexities and actualities of running such institutions, depicting both the good and the bad aspects. Totally unnarrated, using sync-sound, Wiseman's films epitomize the cinéma vérité style by letting the participants express themselves. In his editing style, however, Wiseman shows his own thoughts on the subject. In *Model* (1980), Wiseman covers the shooting of a television commercial in long takes with location sound. The ad, shown in completed form at the end of Wiseman's film, contrasted with Wiseman's cinéma vérité, illustrates the problem of representation (especially of women) and the exploitive power of film. In Wiseman's film, we see the model as a human being; in the commercial, she becomes an object.

For documentary filmmakers, cinéma vérité was the predominant style, especially for those who had been members of Drew Associates. Richard

Leacock, for example, made *Happy Mother's Day* (1963), an account of the birth of quintuplets (which was reedited for TV by ABC). Donn Alan Pennebaker filmed Bob Dylan's concert tour of England, *Don't Look Back* (1967). *Yanki No!* (1960), concerning the Castro revolution in Cuba, was shot by Al Maysles and Richard Leacock. (Because of its controversial topic, it was taken out of distribution shortly after completion.) *Monterey Pop* (1968), a filmed concert featuring Janis Joplin and Jimi Hendrix (which enjoyed success in first-run theaters) was the joint undertaking of Pennebaker, Leacock, and Maysles. Another successful rock film, *Gimme Shelter* (1970), which documented a murder at a Rolling Stones concert in Altamont, California, was made by Albert and David Maysles and Charlotte Zwerin. In *Gimme Shelter*, the line between cinéma vérité and reflexive film is blurred and the style is already evolving into what I call "postvérité." The filmmakers use a vérité style but cut back and forth to Rolling Stones lead singer Mick Jagger watching the screen on an editing table, presumably as the film is being cut. As he studies the image, it opens up and we are "in" the film again. After a time, the screen narrows and we are back in the editing room. Here the film draws attention to itself in a Vertovian manner, and preshadows the frequent image tumbling of Music Television (MTV) videos and the illusion of objectivity and display of that illusion in such films as Madonna's *Truth or Dare* (1991).

Relying heavily on folksongs as a narrative thread, Barbara Kopple's *Harlan County, U.S.A.* (1976) exemplifies the underlying issue of whether cinéma vérité presents the "truth" objectively or is used to politicize. Shot between 1973 and 1976, this film documents the struggle of coal miners in Brookside, Kentucky, who decided to join the United Mine Workers of America (UMWA) and subsequently went on strike to win a contract from the Eastover Mining Company. Kopple includes early photos of men and children working in the mines, interviews with victims of black lung disease, and shots of previous strikes to place this particular historical moment in perspective.

Although Kopple's initial intent was to document the Arnold Miller versus Tony Boyle election for UMWA president, the issues of the Harlan strike—safety standards, a living wage, medical insurance, decent housing, and the right to organize—took precedence (Mills 1977). Footage of the 1969 Jock Yablonski/Tony Boyle campaigns for union leadership and the murders of Yablonski, his wife, and daughter, followed by Boyle's indictment for the crime, demonstrate the volatility of the situation within the union itself and the complexity of union politics. But Kopple's focus is on the immediate strike. With sync-sound scenes, she puts the viewer on the picket line, where the camera is attacked by the strike breakers, and she places us inside meetings of the strikers, where they ask if she'll be on the picket line in the morning.

Kopple also creates a villain, a "scab" foreman who wields a gun and points it at the camera, and a heroine, a striker's wife who helps organize the women (Crowdus 1979: 564-65).

Using folksongs that recall the strikes of "bloody Harlan" in the 1930s, Kopple dramatizes today's struggle and links it to the past with powerful impact. The film is stylistically cinéma vérité, but subjective in its one-sided camera and editing selections. One of the most effective documentaries of the 1970s, *Harlan County, U.S.A.* won an Academy Award for best feature-length documentary and acquired national theatrical release. A sympathetic portrait of the miners' plight, the film highlights the debate over the use of cinéma vérité as a political tool.

## Postvérité: Documentary as an Art Form

Kopple's use of interviews and dramatic structuring indicate that the "rules" of which Leacock spoke were being broken. As filmmakers sought to give their subjects a voice, they increasingly relied on the interview as a means of communicating ideas. Those who presented themselves gave way to the expert witness who stood in for the filmmaker. Anthropologist Jay Ruby comments: "While 'voice of God' narration was declared *déclassé,* it was replaced by talking head 'expert witnesses.' The offscreen voice of authority simply moved into the frame. Subtitled with their pedigree, authorities continued to tell us the 'truth.' 'Talking heads' became a documentary cliché—the boring mainstay of television news and documentaries, thus dulling the impact of the method" (1992:48).

The reaction was to replace these speakers by returning to those who had lived the events about which the experts were pontificating. The interactions and performances of those caught by the eye of the cinéma vérité stylist were often reduced to historical reminiscences interspersed with archival news footage. Ruby points out that we know nothing about the interviewing situation, nor do we know if the interviews were conducted to complement found footage or if the footage was located to support the interviews. For Ruby, the films have no analysis; if the speakers experienced these events, then presumably their versions must be accepted. He points out the fallacy of this thinking: "What people say about themselves is data to be interpreted, not the truth" (Ruby 1992:49). *Eyes on the Prize* (1987), the acclaimed series on the civil rights movement, uses this approach, as does *Making Sense of the Sixties* (1991), *"We Shall Overcome"* (1988), and *Union Maids* (1976). The contemporary television documentary increasingly relies on the interview combined with historical footage.

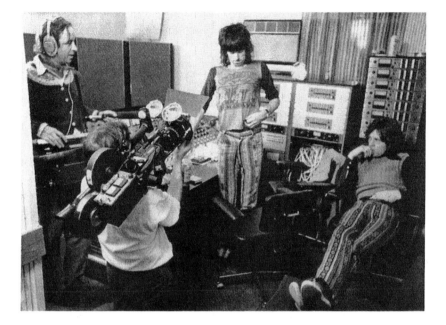

1.4 *Gimme Shelter.* MOMA/FSA

Another stylistic change announcing a new twist to cinéma vérité of the 1960s was the spiraling use of multiple cameras and sophisticated editing in postproduction. *Woodstock* (1970), Michael Wadleigh's film document of the concert that brought 400,000 people together as a community, marked an upbeat ending to a decade. In sharp contrast, *Gimme Shelter* showed the darker side of the counterculture and signaled the philosophical closing of the decade. Made in the same year, both films also signal the partial closing of a door on cinéma vérité. In *Gimme Shelter,* flashbacks confuse what is "real"; in *Woodstock,* an observational camera style is fused with split-screen images, sound mixes, and rhythmic shots chosen for their balance with the soundtrack. The long takes disappear into edited rhythms, and the interview occupies a central role.

Cinéma vérité gave folklorists the first real opportunity to document events from beginning to end and to allow fieldwork tools to match newer theoretical perspectives. Sync-sound filming became the rage. At last, the people being studied could speak for themselves in sync sound and give their own functional analyses without the imposition of a narrator or scholar. The focus on the individual shown in such films as the Maysles's *Salesman* (1969), which pictured the life of a door-to-door Bible salesman, and *Showman* (1962), a portrait of movie mogul Joseph E. Levine; Wolf Koenig and Roman Kroiter's *Lonely Boy* (1961), about teenage idol Paul Anka; and D. A. Pennebaker's film on Bob Dylan, *Don't Look Back* (1967), became examples for folklorists of how filmmakers might document individuals to arrive at the "truth." Folklore filmmakers such as Bill Ferris in his film on James Thomas, Jorge Preloran on Cochengo Miranda and Hermogenes Cayo, and Les Blank on Lightnin' Hopkins, for example, followed this biographical model begun by Flaherty and made "objective" by cinéma vérité.

The problem was that cinéma vérité did not provide "the answer" that many folklore filmmakers wanted. If anything, it raised more questions. We have edited our films to suit our theories. Those films which seem most suitable for documentary in general and folklore in particular acknowledge their power to seemingly represent experience *and* reveal the means by which they do so. Such films go beyond the ideals of cinéma vérité into the openly subjective realm of postvérité. They show film as art and tell how film is phantasm.

Film theorists have investigated many issues that folklorists need to consider. For example, Sergei Eisenstein's now classic essay, "A Close-up View," described "long shot" film theory as that which dealt with film "in context." "Medium shot" looked at the human scale of the film, and "close-up" theory broke the film down into its parts (much like folklorists' use of context, individual, and text). Thus, the opposition became one of form (what the film is) versus function (how the film affects us), akin to texualism and functionalism in folklore. Documentary filmmakers were presumed to always engage in realism. But, as Godard demonstrated, no film can actually show us reality. Films make a statement, and that statement is the filmmaker's (as proponents of the *auteur* theory were quick to point out). Filmmakers sought a level of analysis beyond that of *mise-en-scène* versus montage and realism versus expressionism. They searched for whether or not film was honest in its own right, *as a film,* and whether filmmakers were engaged in a process of communication between filmmaker and viewer. Likewise, folklorists and anthropologists began to look at their relationships with their "informants" and examine the process of what Robert Georges and Michael Owen Jones refer to as "people studying people" (1980). How did our behavior as fieldworkers and as filmmakers, and our subjects' reactions to us and our hypotheses, shape the scholarly or filmic conclusions we reached?

Today, reflexivity has become an important topic for scholars in the human sciences. Sol Worth and John Adair attempted to address this problem by allowing the Navajo to film themselves (1972), but the films "lost something in the translation," at least for me, because as a non-Navajo, I "read" their films with non-Navajo eyes. I once saw an audience of scholars and students (with the exception of one person other than me) exit the theater during a showing of Hopi filmmaker Victor Masayesva Jr.'s award-winning *Itam Hakim Hopiit* (1984).[12] As an art form, with its system of symbols and signs, film must have meanings shared by the filmmaker and the audience. Creating a dialogue between subjects and the filmmaker is surely a postvérité means of communicating a shared reality.

Researchers deluded themselves when they believed that cinema vérité would communicate objectively to audiences. The long takes became tedious because everyone became used to a tigher editing style. Indeed, today fifteen-second commercials and the rapidity of television editing have made viewers accustomed to video shots as brief as two seconds in duration (MTV addicts are accustomed to one-second shots) and to six- and seven-second long shots in film (which take longer to "read"). One reason old films look "old" to us is that the shots are long. Viewers reacted to overly narrated films in which film-makers created their vision, and they welcomed films that would not impose an outsider's view of a culture. Many scholars, filmmakers, and viewers believed that cinéma vérité allowed the people to speak for themselves; it had no narration. But the camera still had to be turned on and off by the cameraperson and pointed in the direction where that person thought the "real" action was. Once edited, the film could easily become a personal statement. Robert Gardner's *Rivers of Sand* (1974), made with the new technology, demonstrated that unnarrated films held our attention because we could relate to the people as human beings rather than as objects. But Gardner's cutting style proved that he had a message of his own to communicate about the human condition in general. Similarly, Wiseman, with his portraits of American institutions, lets viewers know in no uncertain terms what he thinks of his subjects by his framing devices and juxtaposition of images. Sync-sound cinéma vérité was not only "art." It was art masquerading as objectivity—a very clever illusion. Thus, postvérité films, like tricksters, reveal the illusion.

## Documentary Films as Expressions of the Self: Feminist, Minority, and Third World Films

The subjective nature of postvérité is highlighted by the use of film and video as tools of power by minorities, Third World peoples, and women—those whose images have been most frequently denigrated. Their films often connote cultural differences through folkloric content as well as style. For example, *Itam Hakim, Hopiit*, despite some of the problems experienced by Anglo audiences, has been lauded as replicating/creating a mythic dimension with its surrealistic, colorized images that match the storytelling of Macaya, who tells an emergence story, a Bow Clan tale in the first person, and an account of the

Spanish occupation of the Hopi Southwest. Marlon Riggs, in *Tongues Untied* (1989), displays the world of gay black men in San Francisco from an insider's perspective. Moreover, its subjective camera breaks the conventions of an "objective" reporting style that Riggs employed for *Ethnic Notions* (1987), which examined the stereotyping of African Americans in popular culture and artifacts. Whereas *Ethnic Notions* received air play on PBS, *Tongues Untied* was banned by numerous PBS affiliates, not only for the stated reasons about its content but also for its subversion of the expository "unbiased" style demanded by PBS. Like New Journalism, postvérité films have a perspective that is unabashedly subjective.

Third World filmmakers manipulate expectations about the Other by evoking their own cultural codes. Trinh T. Minh-ha combines Third World and feminist perspectives. In *Surname Viet Given Name Nam* (1989), she reenacts interviews conducted with women in Vietnam by having the interviews acted out by Vietnamese women who live in the United States. The oppression of women in Vietnamese culture and issues of representation are her main topics, and the film turns the interviews inside out stylistically, breaking with established film conventions to make a statement about portrayal. Like the work of Masayesva, Trinh Minh-ha's work does not always "translate" (an issue which she addresses in her writing [1989]) because of cultural as well as gender differences. Julia Lesage explores a similar problem for the reception of Latin American cinema by North American viewers (1982). Teshome Gabriel has noted that the aesthetics and cinematic practices of Third World filmmakers form an alternative film culture (1985, 1989). Gabriel has also argued that black Diasporan cinema reflects black nomadism and rejects the Eurocentric aesthetic, forming a new voice for marginalized peoples (1988).

Feminist film unravels women's images as objects for the gaze of men (Mulvey 1985) or women whose voices and experiences have been controlled by men, thus marking them as Other. As Lesage points out, the stories of women "function aesthetically in reorganizing women viewers' expectations derived from patriarchal narratives and in initiating a critique of these narratives" (1978:515). Women gained greater access to film school during the late 1960s and began claiming their sense of self through film. Their films, which initially resulted from the women's movement and served as tools for consciousness-raising, documented the lives of ordinary women whose stories had been ignored by the male-dominated film industry. These feminist filmmakers often stretched the limits of documentary film practice by personalizing their work and presenting their tales through experimental editing.

Here again, folkloric style and content prevail in the documentaries made by women. For *Not a Love Story* (1981), filmmaker Bonnie Klein and her companion, ex-stripper Linda Lee Tracy, use their own "fieldwork" experiences and conduct interviews with people in the pornography business to construct a journey narrative out of their personal responses to pornography. Klein demonstrates that, for women, what is personal is political (cf. Erens 1988). In *Clotheslines* (1981), Roberta Cantow blends the narratives of women who discuss the memories of their mothers evoked by doing the laundry, the ways in which husbands were recalled as clothes were ironed, and the stories generated by hanging the laundry on the clothesline. The garments not only serve as a topic for narratives—from sexy underwear that caused women to speculate about the wearer's love life to sheets of Irish linen on stretcher bars that indicated a women's expertise with fine fabrics—they also seem to whisper to themselves as they flutter in the breeze (an effect that Cantow creates). Cantow connects the experiences of women who wash clothes on rocks in streams with those who use Laundromats to indicate the international bond of a gender. She reveals the folding of laundry as a folk art—a shared knowledge and a shared aesthetic. One woman brags about arranging her linen closet well to please herself and make her friends envious. Her pride in her accomplishment strikes a familiar note with many female viewers. Cantow's work gives one of women's everyday life practices, or what Hermann Bausinger refers to as *alltägsleben* (1990), a heightened significance by documenting it on film. She demonstrates that domestic work is an art, and she does so by incorporating visual montage and a voice-over amalgam of female expression.

Feminist films often document folklore. Much of women's art, for example, is folk art. Quilt films are numerous. Ritual processes and ceremonies and family events that both celebrate and break the boundaries of the traditional domestic realm of women become central themes in the films created by women. Many women's issues are addressed via the home movie/videotape, which explores family folklore, as I discuss in chapter 7. Feminist films are frequently narrated by women. For example, using personal experience narratives as the core of *Home Economics: A Documentary of Suburbia* (1994), Jenny Cool portrays the cost of the American dream. She discovers a lifestyle pressurized by societal expectations and a commuter culture. Interviews with women in a housing development outside Los Angeles unveil the destructive effect of suburbia on the family. Another look at women's concerns, *Union Maids*, presents its argument through a fairly typical style of juxtaposing on-camera interviews with archival footage. Three women discuss the role of women as workers and their part in union organizing. As I have noted elsewhere (Sherman 1983), the film follows the standard conventions of the talking head/history approach. Nevertheless, it does draw on oral history and women's approaches to life's experiences, lending itself to feminist issues and marking it as part of folk history.

## The Documentary as Folk History

In the United States, for the most part, cinéma vérité films were used to tell the stories of the "other people." With postvérité, the "others" became the cinematic weavers of their own stories. Nonfiction films have documented the experiences of women, ethnic minorities, blacks, Native Americans, the youth counterculture—all those who ordinarily have had little voice in making history or news. In this sense, documentary filmmakers have provided insight into America's social and cultural history. Just as oral histories, county records, and diaries have proved useful sources to the folklorist in documenting the traditions as well as the popular attitudes and beliefs of the people (Dorson 1972d), the documentary film has provided an aural-visual record of the words and actions of various segments of the population.

The differences between documentary films and official news reports is analogous to the differences between folk and elite history. The history of the elite is that of the national government: the major figures (such as generals and presidents), the wars in which a country has been engaged, the treaties signed between various governments, the major legislation enacted, and the machinations of large political parties. These matters are also examined by film teams of television news programs and most network or government-sponsored documentary reports. *Years of Lightning, Day of Drums* (1966), produced by the U.S. Information Agency, concentrated on the programs established by Kennedy intercut with shots of him and his funeral. *The Kennedys* (1992) placed a mythological framework around the Kennedy family, reflecting the more intimate style that had developed since 1966. *The Children Were Watching* (1960) traced the school integration issue. *Point of Order!* (1963) consisted of television footage from the Army-McCarthy hearings, and numerous films made about the Persian Gulf War with Iraq in 1991 were based on network footage and the corporate sponsorship of such giants as Time-Warner. Such films are all meaningful documents, but those films which treated the events and experiences of the "common person" are much more vital to the folklorist, for they represent a type of visual folk history. Richard M. Dorson, in "History of the Elite and History of the Folk," stressed the importance of studying the traditions that derive from the folk, "a people united with common traditions" (1972b:240). He emphasized the need felt by radical historians and by folklorists to study the "anonymous inarticulate millions" (1972b:246). This history is the one which many documentary filmmakers have recorded. Dorson states that folk history is made up of "the remembered experiences of the regional, occupational, and ethnic groups into which we all fall. This folk history is an extension of our personal history, and it belongs to us as elite history never can. . . . By history of the folk I have in mind the history of the structures in which individuals play active roles, of what psychologists call 'vital circuits'" (1972b:241).

Of these social networks which involve the individual, Dorson lists schools and colleges, sports, factories, shops, neighborhoods, family units, business offices, and ethnic, racial, and regional affiliations. All of these structures—from Flaherty's reconstructions of the traditions of the Aran Islanders and the Samoans, to Grierson and the British film unit's portrayal of various occupational groups, Wiseman's filmed views of those who work in institutions and those who must cope within such systems, the festivals of the 1960s youth culture captured in such films as *Woodstock*, Victor Masayesva Jr.'s ethnic portrait of the Hopi, female union organizers in Chicago, and the miners' struggles in Appalachia—have been examined by the documentary filmmaker and have served as models for folklorists.

## Defining the Ethnodocumentary: Documenting the Other

Recognizing the factions, class stratifications, and variations within a society, some documentary films have celebrated difference while others objectify the people being documented as the Other—usually on the basis of ethnicity or gender. The ethnographic film takes the notion of the Other to its common extreme: exoticizing the "primitive" members of cultures outside one's own borders (but including the "savage" aboriginal peoples of one's own land).[13]

Because of the affinities between folklore and anthropology, ethnographic films have been of particular interest to folklorists and have often influenced the style of those in folklore who make films. Such documentaries purport to reveal something about culture to the viewer or to present a visual ethnography. Unlike the documentaries made by Grierson, Vertov, Wiseman, and others that were produced and directed by filmmakers, films called "ethnographic" documentaries have often been produced by or in collaboration with anthropologists. Assuming that the primary purpose of the ethnographic film is to show patterns of cultures, then any film about people may be classified as "ethnographic" and the term is unnecessary, marking a distinction that does not, in fact, exist. Any film focusing on the actions of people can teach the viewer about human interaction or behavior in relation to culture and society and, hence, will have ethnographic content. Whether such films are documentaries or fictionalized portrayals does not matter.[14]

The documentary film, unlike the film of fictionalized events, focuses on the interactions of human beings in actual situations. Because such films examine and document unrehearsed events as they unfold, their ethnographic content is more useful as a source of data to those who study expressive manifestations of culture than are fictionalized films. Documentary filmmakers who make films classified as "ethnographic" also document unstaged human behavior.

Many scholars have grappled with the problem of defining ethnographic film, both descriptively and prescriptively. For anthropological filmmaker David MacDougall, ethnographic filmmakers examine societies other than their own (1969). For anthropologist Walter Goldschmidt, former head of the University of California at Los Angeles Ethnographic Film Program, "Ethnographic film is film which endeavors to interpret the behavior of people of one culture to persons of another culture" (1972:1). MacDougall's initial stress is on "primitive" societies: "The most easily identifiable ethnographic films are those which deal with primitive societies" (1969:16). MacDougall further emphasizes "the intercultural aspect," which he believes distinguishes this type of film from documentary film. For MacDougall and Goldschmidt, ethnographic films focus on societies differing from those of the filmmaker or the viewers.

From these definitions, one must assume, then, that only films that treat "primitive" or "exotic" cultures are truly ethnographic. This assumption is obviously based on cultural evolutionary thinking which presupposes that the "civilized" filmmaker will be able to interpret the interactions of the "primitives" for a sophisticated audience made up of members of the filmmaker's own society. Visual anthropologist Jay Ruby has commented that "in the popular mind, anthropologists study exotic, primitive people; therefore, any film about these people, including *Mondo Cane,* is thought to be anthropological" (1971:36). Yet if such an idea exists in the popular mind, it does so because anthropologists have, in fact, made those they conceptualize as more "primitive" the focal point of their studies and films. Some anthropologists have based their definition of ethnographic film on this point. MacDougall no longer "primitivizes" the Other but again addresses the "portrayal of experience across cultural boundaries" (1995:222-23). Even those scholars who do not define ethnographic film on the basis of subject matter have repeatedly filmed non-western societies and, with the exception of Jean Rouch, rarely point the eye of the camera at members of their own societies. Marcus Banks notes that "the more exotic and non-Western a group of people are, the more anthropologists can claim them as their own" (1992:121).

Consequently, ethnographic film either documents the traditions and behaviors of exotic or primitive peoples (those who are not members of the filmmaker's society) or includes documents made or used by anthropologists to study peoples or illustrate anthropological principles and theoretical concerns. Whether modern conceptions held about other cultures as primitive persist or not (as for most scholars they do not), the emphasis of ethnographic filmmakers has been and is to record different cultures in an attempt to discover something about their own. This consideration does, indeed, differ from the documentary tradition of Grierson, who sought to analyze behavior in his own society.

The difficulties of definition are most evident in *Ethnographic Film*, wherein author Karl Heider defines his subject as "film which reflects ethnographic understanding" (1976:8). He comments that the definition can be summed up in one sentence, but a whole book is needed to exemplify what that sentence means. For Jay Ruby, "ethnographic film has always been a field dominated by documentary filmmakers who fancy themselves amateur anthropologists" (1991:4). He does not underscore a focus on other societies, and he tends to use *ethnographic* and *anthropological* somewhat interchangeably (cf. Ruby 1971; 1991). Ruby comments that "anthropological film" has usually been defined by subject matter or by having an anthropologist involved in the production. Ruby asserts, "For purposes of discussion, anthropological film can be divided into two categories, primarily upon the basis of intent and the corresponding techniques employed: research film, which is a part of the general body of scientific films common to many disciplines, and interpretive film, which is really a special kind of documentary" (1971:36). Focusing on those films which are intentionally interpretive and which range from "general cultural overviews . . . to the accounting of a specific event," Ruby uses the term *anthropological documentaries* (1971:36). Such films are a part of documentary films in general, but they meet the needs of anthropologists. In recent work, Ruby has chosen the more inclusive term *documentary* to refer to both documentary and ethnographic films (1992:43). Nonetheless, his criteria for judging the success of a film described as "ethnographic" are whether a film successfully addresses anthropological issues, results from ethnographic research, and has the fieldworker involved in the decision-making process of creating the film (1991:4).

Obviously, both ethnographic and documentary filmmakers record human behavior. Those films whose makers intend to use them either to portray the customs and traditions of the cultural Other for the purpose of elucidating anthropological research or to construct visual ethnographies may therefore be regarded simply as that type of documentary film that I call "ethnodocumentary."

The ethnodocumentary follows the same conventions as the documentary film. It uses narration, sync-sound, montage, and such techniques as cinéma vérité. The filmmaker often expresses many of the same suppositions about culture as the documentary filmmakers, for example, romantic notions about the people being filmed, such as Flaherty espoused. The filmmaker may use a biographical model, such as Nanook, or he may reconstruct history as Flaherty did in *Man of Aran*. Or the filmmaker may place an emphasis on form or structure akin to Vertov; blend the rhythms of work with the thoughts of the people as did the British school; concentrate on single events in a culture as is done in *Woodstock;* present cinéma vérité situations; or use a reflexive, intersubjective mode in which the filmmaker is an integral part of the action.

Just as researchers making ethnodocumentary films have developed their styles and approaches from the documentary tradition, those folklorists who engage in filmmaking have derived many of their techniques and areas of concentration from the ethnodocumentary film movement. Ethnodocumentaries provide a foundation from which the form and direction taken by scholars working in folklore film can be understood.

## Ethnographies on Celluloid: Event Films

As a filmmaker, Flaherty was an innovator and a master, but he was not an ethnographer. Flaherty's main preoccupation was with one individual's struggle and his relation to his environment untempered by any scholarly attempt to be objective. Margaret Mead and Gregory Bateson, both trained ethnographers, examined events with the use of film to elucidate scholarly inquiry. Flaherty's film work preceded that of Bateson and Mead by more than a decade, but whether he had any influence on them is not clear. In her autobiography, *Blackberry Winter* (1972), Mead mentions that she used magazine photos of Flaherty's *Moana* sent to her by a friend for a picture-naming experiment in Samoa, but she says nothing about actually seeing Flaherty's films. If Bateson and Mead had seen his work, they were not affected by his methodology, but rather were compelled to initiate a new approach to meet their research demands. Observing events occurring within a culture to generate hypotheses concerning the culture as a whole was a means of conducting research that Mead had developed with Reo Fortune in their 1929 study of the Manus people of the Admiralty Islands (Mead 1972:174). This event observation technique, one which is most fruitful for today's folklorists who are making films, would later prove to be the organizing principle of Bateson and Mead's films.

Beginning their photographic investigations with stills, Bateson and Mead used visuals both to generate hypotheses about the human behavior and development they observed and to supplement their theories and research findings with visible verification. In addition, they hoped to provide a visual record of several societies for cross-cultural studies. By making such records, Bateson and Mead also anticipated that later scholars could examine their visual documentation to answer as yet unformulated hypotheses. Moreover, they believed that a written description of a culture would be subject to cultural inferences or translations of the ethnographer and his reading audience. Written records alone would not adequately convey the meaning of what Bateson and Mead called "those intangible aspects of culture which had been vaguely referred to as its *ethos*" (1942: xi). Visuals could present tangible representations of abstract concepts and nonverbal behavior.

*Balinese Character* represents the hallmark and the prototypic scientific use of stills to demonstrate and generate theoretical statements with photographs (Bateson and Mead 1942). Focusing primarily on family organization, child rearing, and children's behavior and development (which Mead had concentrated on in her earlier fieldwork in Samoa and New Guinea), the ethnographers also shot 22,000 feet of 16mm film in Bali (mostly in the village of Bajoeng Gede). *Balinese Character,* using the still photographs, was published in 1942, but the motion photography was not released until 1952 (because of World War II). Six films resulted, each part of the Character Formation in Different Cultures series. Two of the films, *Childhood Rivalry in Bali and New Guinea* and *Trance and Dance in Bali*, are illustrative of Bateson and Mead's approaches.

*Childhood Rivalry* demonstrates differences in child rearing and the subsequent behavior of children by contrasting the footage shot in Bali with that shot in Iatmul. Because the fieldworkers wanted to use film for culture comparison, they decided to spend six months shooting in New Guinea (where Bateson had previously conducted research) upon their return journey from Bali. *Childhood Rivalry* intercuts scenes from the two cultures for contrasting behavior as Mead narrates. Another film in the series, *Bathing Babies in Three Cultures*, and a later film, *Four Families* (1960), also emphasize Mead's stress on cross-cultural analyses.

For *Trance and Dance*, Bateson and Mead favored the analysis of a unique holistic event rather than culture comparison. One of the most interesting features of Balinese life is the enactment of a drama, the *Tjalonarang* (witch play). Although the play is performed with slight variation in different villages, Mead notes in *Balinese Character* that the plot is "essentially uniform" (Bateson and Mead 1942:34). Thus, one enactment of the performance is representative of the ritualistic drama as it occurs in Balinese life in general. The film, shot by Bateson with Jane Belo, communicates the essence of the plot visually while Mead narrates to explain the action. The witch, whose daughter has been rejected by the king, instructs a group of small girls in witchcraft. They then spread plague throughout the country. The king sends an aide to war against the witch, but she has now transformed herself into an ugly creature. The king's ambassador cannot fight against her, so he leaves the stage only to return in the guise of a dragon. The dragon's helpers, who carry krisses (double-edged daggers), try to attack the witch, who magically subdues them time and again. They are finally successful, but then they fall into a trance. The dragon revives them with holy water. Still entranced, they turn their krisses upon themselves in a state of ecstasy. Priests take away their krisses and lead the trancers into the temple to recover with the aid of holy water and incense. Mead concludes her narration by stating that the witch play represents "fear of death on one hand, and life protecting ritual on the other."

Without supplementary ethnographic data, *Trance and Dance in Bali* raises questions regarding the meaning and function that the drama has for those who perform it. In *Balinese Character,* Mead stresses that the trance state allows the trancers to express emotional behavior, such as grief and fear of witchcraft, that would be inappropriate and unacceptable in daily situations. In addition, the witch represents the mother who teases the child, a common occurrence in mother-child relationships among the Balinese.

With supplemental written data, Bateson and Mead's work demonstrates a unique advance in the use of film as a documentation tool. The witch play and its functions can be explained with the written work, but only film could capture the movements, such as the entranced state of the dancers, the theatrical gesturing of the performers, and their interactions as aspects of a complex holistic event.

Despite the scientific recognition of the validity and usefulness of Bateson and Mead's film research in recent years, attempts to analyze movement photographically did not occur again with any impact until the work of Birdwhistell and Lomax in the 1950s and 1960s. Although ethnodocumentary filming has been continuously conducted since the Bateson and Mead films were made, John Marshall's *The Hunters* (1958) marks the next major film of note. Rather than continue the model of following an unfolding event (which would become most popular with folklore filmmakers for theoretical reasons), *The Hunters* constructs an event through editing and narration.

## The Narrated "Story": Ethnographic Romanticism

Released twenty years after the Balinese expedition, *The Hunters* indicated that the romantic struggle of man's survival established as a film topic by Flaherty still held more appeal for filmmakers than the scientific approach of Bateson and Mead. Marshall had been a member of a family team that conducted research on the !Kung Bushmen of the Kalahari Desert in Africa. After amassing a considerable amount of footage on Bushman activities during the 1950s, Marshall collaborated with Robert Gardner, the director of the Film Study Center at Harvard. Gardner had completed graduate work in anthropology (unlike Marshall) and had worked with film. He edited Marshall's footage into the first of the !Kung Bushmen films, *The Hunters.* In this film, four hunters embark on a two-week search for food that culminates in the killing of a giraffe with a poison arrow. The story, compiled entirely in the editing room, has numerous drawbacks in terms of ethnographic "truth." The footage was shot on different hunting forays and does not represent one single expedition. By skillfully editing these various trips together, Gardner created the illusion that one hunt was being detailed. From the onset of his career,

Gardner stated that he wished to select "the major emphasis and outline for any culture" in his films, including the fact that "men are hunters" (1957:351). In actuality, the Bushmen did not depend predominantly on hunting for their subsistence, which the narration stresses, but rather on gathering. Because *The Hunters* was shot without synchronous sound, it relies on an annoying narration that overemphasizes the obvious. Statements such as "they ate and ate and ate" over visuals of the men eating insult the viewers' intelligence.

Although Flaherty romanticized his subjects, Nanook's search for food was a struggle that ultimately resulted in his death. For the Kalahari Bushmen, no such danger existed. The story *The Hunters* portrays is a pure fabrication. Karl Heider notes that "although the film is ethnographically faulty on the role of hunting in Bushman life, its portrayal of the hunting itself remains unimpeached" (1976:32). In this respect, the visuals are an accurate representation of an activity, but the editing process and narration created a distortion that served Gardner's purpose of capturing what he surmised was a disappearing culture. Marshall, whose father had begun documenting the !Kung in the 1950s, ended his collaboration with Gardner.

## Sequence Filming of Events

Following the production of *The Hunters*, Marshall worked as Frederick Wiseman's photographer on *Titicut Follies* (1967) and then developed his own series of films on the Pittsburgh police department. Marshall's long takes, which follow the drama as it evolves, and his use of synchronous sound without narration dominate the style of his police films, as well as the style that Wiseman continued to use in his series on American institutions. After working with synchronous sound (which was unavailable in portable form for his original location shooting in the Kalahari Desert), Marshall returned to the existing Bushman footage, cut it into short events and hand synched wild sound with his visuals to produce a new series of films on the !Kung Bushmen.

Emphasizing the complexities of human interaction as opposed to the earlier stress on plot coherence evidenced in *The Hunters,* Marshall developed the concept of "sequence filming" (Asch 1972; Marshall and de Brigard 1975). Abandoning the artificial constraint of constructing a plot made up of events that may not have occurred in the proper time perspective, Marshall cut his footage into naturally occurring interactions between people that could be analyzed to indicate the importance of their behavior within their own culture or society. This method marked a radical departure from interpretative films and filmed overviews in which small details and the statements of individuals in group situations were either not readily perceived by the viewer or else were not provided by the filmmaker.

In 1968, Marshall joined Asch, a filmmaker who had completed graduate work in anthropology, to form Documentary Educational Resources (DER). Recutting the Kalahari Bushmen footage into sequences, they released several films on Bushman life. For example, *N/um Tchai: The Ceremonial Dance of the !Kung Bushmen* (1968) is a film about a trance curing ceremony. To make the visuals comprehensible to the viewer, Marshall often first presents a series of stills with a narration explaining their significance. This portion of the film is then followed by the footage without commentary. Consequently, viewers see the "action" twice, once in stills and once in actual time sequence. Study guides further clarify the significance of the interactions within Bushman culture. Of special interest to folklorists, *Bitter Melons* (1971), one of the earliest !Kung films shot with sync-sound, focuses on one traditional musician and his songs. Marshall intercuts the visuals of the musician playing a one-string bow with shots illustrating the cultural aspects of the themes of the songs.

The Bushmen are perhaps best known by their representation in *The Gods Must Be Crazy* (1984). In *N!ai: Story of a !Kung Woman* (1980), Marshall includes a segment on a feature film crew working with the !Kung on how to act like themselves for *The Gods Must Be Crazy* (cf. Nichols 1991: 259). Because of their extensive expeditions in the Kalahari Desert, the Marshall family had accumulated footage over a long period. Combining this earlier footage with contemporary scenes of !Kung life and interviews with N!ai, Marshall documents one woman, from childhood to the present, following the Flaherty biographical approach of having one person represent a culture. Selecting a woman as the protagonist, including evidence of the value of the !Kung as a tourist attraction, and incorporating shots of the fiction film in production, Marshall intentionally breaks with the practice of depicting the members of another culture as the Other, mocking the practice and revealing it as a constructed deception.

After working with Marshall on the !Kung Bushmen footage, Asch adhered to Marshall's emphasis on complex events and created a film series on the Yanomamö of southern Venezuela with Napoleon Chagnon, an anthropologist. Chagnon had already conducted extensive fieldwork with the Yanomamö and wanted to make a film that would illustrate how the feast functions as a means of forming political alliances. This type of event had been detailed in Chagnon's monograph, *Yanomamö: The Fierce People* (1968:97-117), and it became the topic of *The Feast*, which Asch shot in 1968. Using the same technique that Marshall had established, Asch divided the film into two segments: stills accompanied by a narration explaining the event, and then the feast itself in sync-sound with English subtitles. Once *The Feast* had been completed, Asch and Chagnon began working on a series of films that could be used to compare the Yanomamö with the Bushmen (as the Bushmen had been the most thoroughly documented). In order to facilitate the cross-cultural comparisons, Asch used sequence filming, like Marshall, as a technique, and shot over 80,000 feet of film that covered sixty different events in one Yanomamö village (Asch 1975:398).

Many of the films in the Yanomamö series are short, being organized around one event. Because the films are presented with sync-sound, the dignity of the individuals is not reduced by the voice of an omniscient narrator providing an interpretation that is culturally biased. Many of the films, however, do have subtitles for English-speaking audiences. Such titles are direct translations rather than subjective analyses.

*The Yanomamö Myth of Naro as told by Kaobawa* (1971) and *The Yanomamö Myth of Naro as told by Dedeheiwa* (1971) have English voice-over translations and are effective for comparative analyses of myths told in two different villages. Performance, including kinesics and voice intonations, may also be compared as can the actual wording. In the second film, the tale teller assumes the roles of the characters as he discusses them. These two films demonstrate the function of myth in society, the performative nature of storytelling, and the competent use of film for folklore research.

## Gardner's Interpretative Montage as Ethnographic Romanticism

The idea of sequence filming developed at Documentary Educational Resources by Marshall and Asch grew in part from Marshall's dissatisfaction with *The Hunters.* After working with Frederick Wiseman and using portable sync-sound equipment, Marshall reorganized his footage and created a new filmmaking style, as evidenced in *N!ai.* Robert Gardner, following his editing work on *The Hunters,* also changed his style because of technological developments. Gardner's *Dead Birds* (1963), shot over five months in 1961, was one of the last ethnodocumentaries made without synchronous sound. Like *The Hunters,* exegesis conveys information about the visuals from the point of view of the filmmaker. Eleven years later, Gardner released *Rivers of Sand,* a wholly synchronous sound film in which a member of the group being filmed conveys her attitudes to the audience. Thus, by changing his methodological procedure from a nonsync style to one using sync-sound, Gardner made a radical stylistic shift in his manner of presenting cinematic data. All of his subsequent films are in sync, but the romanticism and salvage ethnography approach of *The Hunters* has continued to inform Gardner's work.

Following a pattern he had started with *The Hunters,* Gardner hoped to document three human types of ecological adaptation: hunting, agriculture, and pastoralism (Gardner 1979:430). He had completed the film on hunting and was ready to document an agricultural society. The Dani society of *Dead*

*Birds* was initially chosen for that purpose. Fascinated by the violence of Dani life and barred from agriculture as a major topic because it was conducted by women outside the presence of men, Gardner switched topics. *Dead Birds* remains compelling because of its unusual subject matter: the ritual warfare engaged in by the Dani tribesmen of the Grand Valley of the Balim River in West Irian, Indonesia.[15] A statement about man's method of dealing with violence in terms of cultural expectations and religious beliefs, *Dead Birds* emphasizes Gardner's vision of "the essential quality of Dani life" (Gardner 1979:435). Recognizing that he would be ignoring many aspects of Dani life in favor of focusing on violence, Gardner believed his approach was justifiable: "I was convinced that the topic I had chosen was of such central importance to the whole nature and significance of the Dani world that by treating it exhaustively I had my best chance to illuminate the culture as a whole" (1979:435). Warfare, in fact, is what makes the film memorable. Audiences are led to believe they are seeing a cultural overview, because *Dead Birds* also portrays many other details of Dani life, including gardening, food preparation, salt gathering, pig tending, and ceremonial occasions, such as a pig feast and a funeral. But the film does not stress these activities.[16]

In many respects, Gardner followed in the Flaherty tradition in making *Dead Birds*. Romantic notions of investigating a people that represented "a pure society" not yet westernized or acculturated to a larger outside group dominated Gardner's choice of the Dani tribe, dubbed the Dugum Dani by his associate, Karl Heider. Gardner has commented on his reasons for selecting a group known to be using Stone Age technology: "I was looking above all for as indigenously pure a society as possible. This meant finding a group sufficiently remote from governmental and missionary activities to have escaped the kinds of influence which lead to significant social or technological change" (1979:431). In part, this decision was also influenced by the Dutch government, which had been criticized for its colonization of the area. Gardner was told that "the Dutch government wanted an ethnographic study made in West New Guinea before their own development and pacification programs had irretrievably altered traditional culture in the remote and still uncontacted areas" (Gardner 1972:31).

Like Flaherty, Gardner used a biographical model to inform his film document. The film revolves around Wejak, a Dani warrior, and Pua, a young swineherd. By focusing on these two individuals and the events in which they engage, Gardner hoped to make a statement about the group as a whole (1979:431). In actuality, Gardner artfully chose his images to fit his own conceptions about Dani society. Both the Dani of *Dead Birds* and the Yanomamö of *The Feast* are cultures in which warfare plays an important role. For Asch and Chagnon, this aspect of cultural hostility and aggression is balanced within

1.5 Two small Dani armies fight a ritual battle in *Dead Birds*. Photo by Karl Heider. The Film Study Center, Harvard University

the framework of other facets of Yanomamö life. Using sync-sound and sequence filming, Asch and Chagnon present the Yanomamö as unique individuals and allow the viewer to hear and see them without the interference of a narrator. The editing structure of *The Feast* and other films in the Yanomamö series is dependent on the actions of such individuals, not on an imposed conception of the filmmaker regarding major "themes" in the lives of "exotic" or "unusual" peoples.

The structure of *Dead Birds* unveils Gardner's preoccupation with violence in Dani life—at the expense of other notable events. His opening shots establish the motif of the bird as a symbol in Dani life: a hawk is followed over the village in a long shot as the narrator relates a fable of a contest between a snake and a bird. Unlike snakes, which can shed their skins and live forever, birds must die. Because the bird won the contest to determine whether men should be like birds or like snakes, men too must die. Thus, the metaphoric relationship between men and birds is established at the outset. Shots of a funeral fill the screen and then fade in and out to reveal Wejak, who is making a thread shell band. The narrator states that he is a warrior and a leader of men who must be constantly vigilant of the frontier over which the enemy might cross. Pua is then introduced. Although his name is taken from the yellow clay that the Dani often place on their bodies, the narrator stresses that this is done when a relative or an enemy has been killed, but it is also done "sometimes for no reason at all." Thus, an act that does not always have significance is made symbolic of the results of warfare.

Establishing shots are presented of the Grand Valley and of "no man's land" between the frontiers separating Dugum Dani lands from the enemy. The narrator points out the location of the major battleground. Six shots of the watchtowers that are used to guard the frontier appear on the screen in a montage. Birds perch on or near the towers, and Gardner's connection of men, birds, and warfare is once again evident.

Throughout the film, the narrator stresses the importance of being prepared for a raid. The first skirmish, which the audience has anticipated, is finally seen on the screen. Gardner creates the battle out of numerous battles and presents them as one continuous event.

In his narration, Gardner often presumes to tell us what Wejak and Pua are *thinking*. The visuals are edited to prove Gardner's thesis about warfare. For example, a shot of Pua drinking at a stream is intercut with a bird watching, which acts as a foreshadowing of a later episode in which a boy goes to the river to drink and is ambushed by the enemy. When the narrator announces the death, a freeze-frame indicates fear, and shots of empty watchtowers flash across in the screen in rapid succession, suggesting that the men had been careless.

Gardner's extensive use of montage to build emotion is reminiscent of Vertov's shot arrangements. The shots, taken together, provide a message to the viewer of the importance of the relationships between the images. Yet it is Gardner's message, not the message of the Dani themselves. *Dead Birds* leaves the viewer with the lasting image of men killing other men. And, because a small group of "exotic" people are shown, the starkness of the human desire to conduct warfare or kill members of one's species is made more vivid to us than seeing the warfare of large nations. As "outsiders" to the Dani culture, we are forced to recognize that we behave in a similar fashion and hence we are not "different" from the Dani. To make this point, however, Gardner exploits the Dani by not treating the finer aspects of their lives.

Believing his responsibility was to reveal his own interpretation, Gardner viewed the Dani as vehicles for his own philosophical interests and thus violated one of the major ethical concerns of fieldworkers—that of treating others as unique and valuable human beings. In the module that accompanies the film, Gardner clearly acknowledges that his concern with "issues" took precedence over a concern for the people:

> I did not set out in 1961 to make a film excluding my own feelings and judgments; the opposite is more nearly true. I seized the opportunity of speaking to certain fundamental issues in human life. *The Dani were then*

*less important to me than those issues.* In fact, the Dani, except for a few individuals such as Pua, Wejak, and Walé, were important to me only because they provided such clear evidence upon which a judgment about, or at least certain reflections on, matters of some human urgency could arise. My responsibility was as much to my own situation as a thinking person as to the Dani as also thinking and behaving people. I never thought this reflective or value-oriented approach was inconsistent with my training as a social scientist or my goals as the author of a film. I felt this was especially true as long as I was diligent in gathering the evidence. That is, my first responsibility, both to my own purposes and to the Dani, was to document with as much discernment as possible the most telling and important aspects of their life. Only when this had been done was I free to try and determine the significance of their behavior for the audience which might see my work. [Gardner 1972:34, italics mine]

In determining what he believed was significant for an audience to see, Gardner structured and edited his footage to make a statement that was not necessarily the same statement that the Dani might have made about their own culture. Because, like *The Hunters, Dead Birds* was created in the editing room, an audience is swayed by the emotional impact of the montage sequences, the use of freeze-framing, and the narration. For a viewer to observe the data and openly interpret the action is difficult because the structure and narration are persuasive in their power to force us to reach the same conclusions Gardner makes.

Had the overwhelming "essential quality" of Dani life been warfare, one might conclude that the Dani would deteriorate as a culture were warfare to cease. In fact, after the Dutch government completed its frontier pacification program, the Dani adjusted to peace without difficulty. Gardner's film thus "salvages" an event that will not recur, but it does not sufficiently capture other events that were of importance in the lives of the Dani people.[17]

As director of the Film Study Center at Harvard, Gardner aided in the production of other films after he had completed *Dead Birds,* but *Rivers of Sand* was the next film for which he was wholly responsible. The film concentrates on the Hamar, a group of people located approximately 150 miles northeast of Lake Rudolph by the mouth of the Omar River where Sudan and Ethiopia come together. Gardner conducted his fieldwork with the Hamar in two four-month periods in separate years. In between his two visits, a husband and wife anthropological team, selected by Gardner, lived with the Hamar, learning the language and working on an ethnography.

In a discussion session that accompanied the screening of *Rivers of Sand* at Indiana University in 1975, Gardner stated that this film was very different from *Dead Birds.* Rather than concentrating primarily on men and their activities as he did in *Dead Birds,* Gardner selects a woman as his star informant. In

1.6 Hamar women dancing in *Rivers of Sand*. Photo by Jon Mitchell. Film Study Center, Harvard

addition, because of the notable cinéma vérité work done by Jean Rouch in France and by Richard Leacock and Drew Associates in the United States, ethnodocumentary filmmakers were no longer using spring-wound cameras and wild sound tape recordings. The development of portable synchronous sound film equipment caused most filmmakers to abandon the restriction of having a narrator explain the action. Filmmakers relished the ability to have the people in the film tell their own stories and convey their own attitudes. *Rivers of Sand* ostensibly makes use of sync-sound for this purpose. A Hamar woman sits before the camera and comments on her life and the activities of her people. Subtitles translate her words. The omniscient voice of the narrator heard in *Dead Birds* gives way to a more direct means of communication with the audience, and the film is structured around one woman's monologue.

Despite these differences, *Rivers of Sand* has certain marked similarities to *Dead Birds*. Once again, no overview of life appears. Gardner saw a central theme, which he believed was the most controlling force in the society, and he used a metaphoric symbol and the compression of time to convey his own vision of the society. In *Dead Birds*, warfare was central and birds became a symbol for men. In *Rivers of Sand*, Gardner examines the role of pain in the relationships between men and women, and the metaphor is a set of grinding stones:

> The metaphor is of two stones which rub against each other. They rub against each other because this is the way food is made. The sorghum grain is ground by a woman between an upper and lower stone. Now she [the woman addressing the camera] explains that the lower stone is a woman and that the upper stone is a man and that, at the end of a long series of episodes of rubbing, the upper stone fits the lower stone and vice versa. And this is a metaphor for marriage or for a relationship between a man and a woman. . . . I found, personally, that the way they worked out their relationship, the men and women in their society, was one which caused pain for both men and women. [1975]

Believing that pain is very important to the Hamar, Gardner chooses pain as the most important theme for the film. Scarification rituals, whippings, and the binding of iron neck, arm, and leg bands are interspersed with other visuals and build to overpower and obscure other aspects of the functioning of Hamar society.

Gardner uses the Hamar to make a statement about human beings in general. In response to a question regarding his moral responsibility to portray the Hamar in an objective manner, especially because this film would be most viewers' only exposure to the Hamar, Gardner replied, "Of course, it's an act of faith that you can take what I say to be reasonably accurate. . . . That the film is absolutely true to life as far as the Hamar life is concerned, you may never know, and I may never know. And I, perfectly honestly, don't care so much. And that's a big admission for me to make. But I don't care so much whether I am representing the Hamar totally accurately as I care that I am representing what theme and what emphasis I've selected to portray in a way which is a revelation to you about a general condition of humanity" (1975).

Both warfare and the giving and receiving of pain hold a certain fascination for us because we can identify with these themes in our own lives. Thus, Gardner does make his point. He shows us that such acts shape our lives as well as those of the Dani and the Hamar. Yet his statement is not a pleasant one. Had Gardner used film to compress time and rearrange events in our culture, he could have shown us to be very similar to the Dani or Hamar, and we might have been outraged that he had not shown other features of our lives to balance the picture.[18] We wonder why Gardner didn't choose the qualities of gentleness and love and the common need for food, shelter, and family to make a statement about the similarities between peoples. The Hamar might ask the same question.

Gardner's subsequent films (*Altar of Fire* [1976], *Deep Hearts* [1981], *Forest of Bliss* [1985], and *Ika Hands* [1988]) have followed the pattern he established with *Dead Birds*. Despite Gardner's acceptance by some anthropologists and filmmakers, most critics and film analysts would agree with Ruby: "Rather than regard his films as anthropology, I believe it is more productive to critique them as the work of a Romantic artist who believes that the exotic Other provides him with a unique chance to explore his personal responses to humanistic questions such as death (*Forest of Bliss*), the role of women (*Rivers of Sand*), and gender identity (*Deep Hearts*)" (1991:15).

The mixed reception Gardner has received is somewhat ironic in terms of newer attitudes about subjectivity and reflexivity. Gardner is easy to critique, but in some ways he is a predecessor of a newer, more subjective ethnodocumentary. He realized the impossibility of an objective portrayal and focused on issues of ultimate concern rather than rosy depictions of a "family of man." The major difference between his work and that of later reflective filmmakers is that Gardner does not explain how subjective the films are in the films themselves. One must look elsewhere to find the references he makes to his own subjectivity.

When the audience for *Rivers of Sand* asked Gardner if the Hamar had seen the film, he replied that he had no way to show it to them because the Hamar did not have electricity. "It rather frightens me—the idea of showing them the film. I don't think they'll like it. But I don't think that matters. I didn't make it for them" (Gardner 1975). Gardner's approach starkly contrasts with that of Flaherty, who projected his footage to those he filmed, and of Jorge Preloran, who makes films to provide those being filmed with a means for conveying their lives to others.

## Shared Anthropology: The Work of Jean Rouch

For filmmaker Jean Rouch, unlike Gardner, feedback has been a primary concern. Calling Flaherty and Vertov "the first geniuses" of ethnographic and documentary filmmakers, Rouch has utilized their concepts in his own work (Rouch 1974:41). Rouch shows his rushes to the individuals in the footage and then expands on this device of Flaherty's to have the people comment on the visuals. Their remarks are then incorporated into the final film document. Like Vertov, Rouch has used the camera as a "living" entity that moves with the action to become a "cine-eye." By abandoning the use of a fixed camera, which is zoomed in and out to detail movement, Rouch, in what he calls the "cine-trance," coordinates his camera with the movement as if he were in a dance. Portable equipment made this technique possible, although it is based in principle on Vertov's philosophy of the cine-eye. The term *cinéma vérité* is directly derived from the Russian *kino-pravda*. Combining this idea of film truth with the viewing of the footage in a participant observation manner by the filmmaker and his subjects (called the "participatory camera"), Rouch pays homage to the ideals of both Flaherty and Vertov.[19]

Rouch began making films during World War II at a time when 16mm became an acceptable professional medium. On a camera foray in Nigeria, he lost his tripod and was forced to develop a handheld shooting style. Skilled as both a filmmaker and an ethnographer, Rouch has created films that range from ethnographic "re-creations" of possible "realities" to the documentation of unstaged events.

In *Jaguar* (1954/67), Rouch depicts a journey made by three migrant workers to the coast of Ghana. Fictional in the sense that the actors made the trip for the camera and improvised as the shooting progressed, *Jaguar* nevertheless depicts the kinds of behavior that would be exhibited in the migrant situation. Rouch uses plausible characters in plausible situations to record a subjective truth: "I've made many films, fiction films, in fact, on real subjects, and which are much more real than I myself would have been able to make. I did a film called *Jaguar* about migrant laborers who work in West Africa, in Ghana, and at the same time I did a sociological, ethnographic investigation. Well, the only objective document is the film, which is, however, a fiction film, acted by people playing plausible roles. Why? Because they show what an investigation would never show, that is, the context: how it happened, where it happened, the relationships between people, their gestures, their behavior, their speech, etc." (Levin 1971:136). Perhaps *Jaguar* reveals aspects of human behavior less subjectively than would a monograph on the same subject. The camera documents actual human behavior despite the fact that such actions have been extemporized. Following the filming, the actors commented on their behavior and their dialogue was then put into the final film.

For *Les Maîtres Fous* (*Mad Masters*, 1955), Rouch edits skillfully to make a statement about life in a colonial situation. Shot in the Accra capital of Ghana in 1954, *Les Maîtres Fous* treats a religious cult, the Haukas, who go into a trance on Sundays and act out the roles of those in the British colonial government, such as generals, truck drivers, and governors. After killing a dog and drinking its blood, the adepts become entranced and hold roundtable conferences. The following day, they behave normally and perform their jobs. *Les Maîtres Fous* points out how people cope with the problems of living within conflicting worlds. In contrast to *Jaguar, Les Maîtres Fous* was entirely unstaged.[20]

With *Chronique d'un été* (*Chronicle of a Summer,* 1960), Rouch brought Flaherty's "participatory camera" and Vertov's *kino-pravda* together to create *cinéma vérité.* Rouch's cameraman, Michel Brault, had used portable sync equipment in filming for the National Film Board of Canada in 1958 and, to Rouch, Brault's use of the traveling camera was revelatory (Rouch 1974:40). Rouch used this technique to make the cameraman become part of what he is focusing upon. With Edgar Morin, Rouch walked about Paris in the summer of 1960 to document the attitudes of "this strange tribe living in Paris" at a time when the Algerian conflict was in its last throes (Freyer 1979:437). Using sync-sound, the filmmakers ask several people about their lives. Rouch and Morin follow them about in their interactions, interview them, and even listen to one woman talking to herself as she walks along, using the camera as a device to relay her inner feelings. While viewing the footage, the people in the film comment on their actions and the film includes these remarks and visual reactions. In a final sequence, Rouch and Morin discuss their attitudes about using cinéma vérité as they walk in the Musée de l'Homme. Thus, just as Flaherty and Nanook determined which scenes needed to be shot while viewing the day's footage, Rouch and Morin integrate the ideas of their film subjects to create a document synthesized by the filmmaker and the actors. Instead of imposing his own preconceptions about behavior on his filmic data, Rouch uses film as a tool to evoke responses and shape the final message. Rouch calls this technique "shared anthropology": "The anthropologist has ceased to be a sort of entomologist observing others as if they were insects (thus putting them down) and has become a stimulator of mutual awareness (hence dignity)" (Rouch 1974:43).

Rouch's approach has seldom been followed by other ethnodocumentary filmmakers. His habit of allowing those filmed to explain their perceptions of the action is relatively unusual, although it is now acquiring popularity as we recognize that fieldwork and filmmaking are negotiated acts. One need only contrast an interactive technique with Gardner's manipulation of images to convey his own attitude about people. Gardner feared projecting his film to those he had portrayed; for Rouch, the act brought greater understanding.

Rouch's use of making the camera an essential actor in the drama has also had little effect. The cinéma vérité style of Leacock, Pennebaker, and the Maysles brothers has been more influential. The camera stands outside the action to record it objectively; it does not become a participant. Perhaps Rouch's style has not been adaptable to filmmakers whose theoretical bias causes them to conceptualize those being filmed as different from the camera crews themselves. Today, questions of authorship and representation challenge filmmakers to build upon the principles Rouch established.

## Reconstruction: The Netsilik Eskimo Series

Rouch's use of reenactment in *Jaguar*, in which actors assumed roles they identify with and act out a psychodrama of a possible situation in which they might be engaged, has certain parallels in the reconstruction efforts of Asen Balikci and Quentin Brown. For Balikci and Brown, the reconstruction focuses on what might have happened in the past, as opposed to viewing how people might react now in a given situation. In *Jaguar*, a fictional plot is acted out to portray Rouch's ethnographic "reality." Balikci, an anthropologist under the aegis of Brown, the film producer, worked with a camera team to re-create the cultural "reality" of the Netsilik Eskimos before the process of acculturation had made an impact on traditional life.

In 1959-60, Balikci conducted research with the Netsilik Eskimos who were living near Pelly Bay in the Northwest Territories of Canada. In 1962, the Educational Development Corporation (then called Education Services, Incorporated), with a grant from the National Science Foundation, asked Balikci (in cooperation with anthropologist Guy Mary-Rousseliére) to create a series of films on Netsilik Eskimo life for educational uses in social science classes. The films, however, were to depict life before the advent of urbanization and industrialization. Unlike Rouch's interest in present-day problems and his focus on the analytical use of the film situation, Balikci conducted a "salvage ethnography" on film by asking people to replicate what their migratory subsistence cycle was like before the rifle facilitated hunting and before missionary camps created new settlement patterns.

In the Flaherty tradition, Balikci chose hunting and fishing as his main topics, and primarily filmed one man, Itimanguerk, and his family as they moved from one locale to another with the change of seasons. Flaherty and Nanook worked together to determine what should be included, and Balikci and Itimanguerk also engaged in a joint project. Balikci chose the year 1919 as his ethnographic present (the last year before rifles were adopted) and told Itimanguerk which tools and items of clothing were not to be included. Other than these restrictions, he did not tell the Eskimos how to act.

Each film in the series focuses on the subsistence activities at a campsite used in what had been the annual migration pattern. The titles point to this emphasis: *Fishing at the Stone Weir* (1967), *At the Autumn River Camp* (1967), *At the Caribou Crossing Place* (1967), and *At the Winter Sea Ice Camp* (1967), among others. Shown on educational television and used in the classroom, these films (nine in all) have had tremendous educational value. No narrator intrudes on the action, so the viewer may contemplate the significance of the events. To aid in understanding the activities, a packet of materials has been designed to accompany the films. Balikci's book, *The Netsilik Eskimo* (1970), further explores Netsilik life.

Despite the apparent value of filmic reconstruction, one might analyze the underlying assumptions of conducting such research. The project team members obviously believed (as was the case) that the traditional ways of Netsilik life were preserved only in the memories of a few older individuals. By reconstructing this lifestyle for the camera, Balikci echoes the romantic picture of a Flaherty who believes that people who are unhampered by technology, and who live close to nature, are inherently better film topics than those who struggle with the problems of the present. The series evoked varied reactions. Balikci commented that Eskimos in northern Canada reacted unfavorably: "We don't live like those Eskimos in the films; they are savages, we are civilized people." In Alaska, however, the series has been lauded as "an invaluable record of the people's own history" (Balikci 1975:199).

Fortunately, the National Film Board of Canada chose the same family as a film topic in 1970. Depicting the present-day life of Itimanguerk, the film shows the changes that have transpired since the period seen in Balikci's portrayal. Curiously, Balikci did not arrange to include such a film in his own series. Other changes in Alaskan native life are evident in such films as *Tununeremiut* (1972), *At the Time of Whaling* (1974), *On the Spring Ice* (1975), *From the First People* (1977), and *The Drums of Winter* [*Uksuum Cauyai*] (1988). Produced by filmmakers Sarah Elder and Lenny Kamerling, the films are a collaborative effort made with the Alaska Native Heritage Project with which these filmmakers share royalties and copyrights. A truly indigenous film series in Canada emerges with the work of Inuit producer Zacharias Kunuk, whose films include *From Inuit Point of View* (1987), *Qaggiq* (1989), and *Nunaqpa* [*Going Inland*] (1991).

## Observational Cinema

Recognizing that such features of society as kinship systems and the distribution of goods, with which most social scientists are concerned, could not be easily demonstrated using film, Mark McCarty and Paul Hockings decided to make a film that would not be a mere "window" into a culture. *The Village* (1967) treats a group of townspeople in Ireland in a locale where Gaelic is being revived. A project of the UCLA Ethnographic Film Program, *The Village*, as well as many of the later films made under the auspices of UCLA, reflects the stance of Colin Young (then director of the Motion Picture Division) to create films that use the style of "observational cinema." Observational cinema is opposed to reconstruction films such as those done by Balikci. It does not stage events or fictionalize them as Rouch did in *Jaguar*. An observational film, for Young (1975), is one that shows the intimate relationship existing between the filmmaker and those being filmed. Although observational cinema does not employ the interview technique that cinéma vérité cameramen initially used to allow subjects to reveal their ideas, it is related to cinéma vérité and is preferred by anthropologists because it is similar to anthropological discourse and is mimetic of their methodology.[21]

To pretend that the camera is somehow invisible and detached from the situation implies that the filmmaker's presence doesn't become part of the event and that the film records the action from the outside with an objective and omniscient eye. But objectivity is a fabrication. In *The Village*, the filmmakers make their presence known in the total filmic experience. We see the cameramen in the pubs, in the fishermen's hut, and in people's homes. The film crew is addressed, and these interactions are a part of the film. The film is structured to portray the emphases of those filmed rather than the emphases imposed on the events by the filmmakers.

This observational approach informed many of the films once produced at UCLA, such as *To Live with Herds* (1972) by David and Judith Mac-Dougall; and *Naim and Jabar* (1973), *An Afghan Village* (1974), and *Afghan Nomads* (1974) by David Hancock and Herb DiGioia—all made when the Ethnographic Film Program was well funded. Jorge Preloran of UCLA also adopted this style for *Zulay, Facing the Twenty-first Century*. The MacDougalls have expanded on the observational style in their Turkana Conversations series (*The Wedding Camels* [1977/1973-74], *Lorang's Way* [1979/1973-74], and *A Wife among Wives* [1982]) by using intertitles (a screen with text that appears between the active visuals) to represent the filmmakers and draw our attention to the relationship existing between filmmakers and subject. The intertitle may be created long after the actual encounter, but it does acknowledge the filmmakers' presence, breaking down what has been called "the fourth wall." Tim Asch and John Cohen, among others, have adopted the intertitle for some of their work.

## Conveying the Cultural Point of View

In order to circumvent the problem of imposing the filmmaker's perceptions regarding the importance of the events being observed, "observational cinematographers," in the tradition of Rouch, became part of the action and tried to present a portrait of those actions from the inside. Yet, because the focus was still on the culture of the Other, the filmmaker could neither perceive nor present events the same way that a member of that culture might. Recognizing that films depict one's own vision of "reality," and that notions of continuity and structure in a film are based on cultural worldview, communications specialist Sol Worth and anthropologist John Adair chose to conduct an unusual experiment in which the Navajo would film themselves.

Worth and Adair drew upon the demand of Malinowski that ethnographers must attempt to convey the native point of view. Although researchers ethically were bound to communicate such points of view in their scholarly work, they reduced native structuring and perceptions to what they imagined were equivalent or parallel structures, terms, and processes in their own culture. Malinowski, for example, tried to use the terminology of the Trobriand Islanders to describe their verbal folklore and their magical systems, but he then translated those terms into his own categories (1961 [1922]; cf. Georges 1968). Rather than film an overview portrait of the Navajo and their lives in the general technique of the ethnodocumentary filmmaker, Worth and Adair sought to compare their impressions of the people with the Navajos' self-perceptions to determine whether or not film, like language, was culture specific. In the written results of their project, *Through Navajo Eyes: An Exploration in Film Communication and Anthropology,* Worth and Adair explain that their approach was twofold: "to present a method of teaching people to make films showing us how *they* see *their* world, and to present a way of analyzing these films in their cultural context as a communicative code" (1972:141).

The first objective was met in the summer of 1966 in Pine Springs, Arizona, where Adair had previously conducted research with Navajo silversmiths. Within two days a group of Navajos learned the basic aspects of film loading, camera winding, exposure reading, and focusing with spring-wound Bell and Howell triple lens turret cameras, and they shot their first footage. In the following weeks, they learned how to use editing equipment, such as splicers, viewers, and rewinds. Throughout the training sessions, Worth was careful to communicate how the equipment worked but not what he might choose to shoot or his own sense of editing sequencing. He wanted to discover the Navajo system for selecting shots and organizing the footage within frames of reference that the Navajo found meaningful.

Comparing the means of structuring verbal utterances with that of structuring visual film images, Worth and Adair analyzed film as a type of language to further test the Whorfian-Sapir hypothesis that language structures the way one perceives the world. To determine what the codes and patterns of such film language were, they studied the semiotics of film (cf. Worth 1972). Once they discerned the codes and patterns, Worth and Adair could compare the film language with other aspects of patterning expressed within cultural codes, such as folk narratives.

Eight Navajo filmmakers made twenty silent films, seven of which Worth and Adair classify as "full-length" films (ten to twenty minutes long). An analysis of the films clearly demonstrates that they are structured in terms of motions, primarily the act of walking. What is important is the motion itself, not arrival at a particular place. When the students told Worth and Adair that they had, for instance, filmed someone approaching a fence, the researchers assumed that the fence would have primary importance. When the footage was developed and shown, Worth and Adair realized they had misinterpreted what the students had said. The approach itself was the central concern.

For the folklorist studying the narrative style of Navajo myths, Worth and Adair's analysis is illuminating. To tell a story about Navajos, the filmmakers thought it was essential to include scenes of walking. In presenting their structural analysis of the films, Worth and Adair used myth and folktale as verbal communications having sequences that could be compared with visual sequences in films. Worth and Adair built upon Lévi-Strauss's 1964 examination of the series of events in myths and applied it to image events. *A Navajo Weaver* (1966), for example, depicts a series of walking events in which vegetables are gathered to make dye, wool is sheared, and other materials are collected to prepare for the actual weaving. A twenty-minute film, *A Navajo Weaver* has fifteen minutes of walking and gathering and less than five minutes of weaving. Such coming and going scenes are similar to the walking images in Navajo folktales and myths, especially the chantway myths in which the culture hero often takes a journey: "It has frequently been noted that Navajo myths tell of the culture hero who 'travels freely among the gods collecting ritual information as he goes.' From this series of supernatural contacts the hero's own fund of power is collected and increased. The structure and narrative style of the films, *Navajo Silversmith, Antelope Lake, Intrepid Shadows,* and *Navajo Weaver,* resemble one of the chantway myths. Johnny Nelson, for example, shows the craftsman at work but has his craftsman set out on a journey for an ancient silver mine. The fact that silver was never mined on the reservation is inconsequential; the origin of silver and the travel to the origin, like the origin of the horse (depicted in the origin myth as emerging with man), must be accounted for in the Navajo universe and is depicted in his film." Worth and Adair further observe that the importance of showing "the beginning" or origin of an item in the films "is basic to Navajo cognition and is manifested in their mythology and their ritual and visual arts" (1972:205).

Two films made by Johnny Nelson provide insight into the various ways in which the rules of communication differ according to the context in which the communication occurs. *Navajo Silversmith* (1966) has frequent walking scenes, although walking is not a necessary act in creating silver jewelry. *The Shallow Well* (1966), on the other hand, does not depict walking, despite the fact that building a well requires a great amount of walking. Worth and Adair explain this incongruity by pointing out that silversmithing is a traditional Navajo activity and must be shown using the rules of communication for Navajo myth and storytelling, whereas building a well is not subject to traditional coding. In fact, one of the Navajo viewers stated that he did not understand the film about the well because it was "in English," although the film had no soundtrack (Worth and Adair 1972:151–52).

The use of facial close-ups is another structural difference between the films of the Navajo and those that Worth and Adair shot. For Worth and Adair, close-ups identify the actor and his emotions; for the Navajo, facial close-ups were avoided much like the Navajo avoid direct eye contact. Hence, the film is structured as a communication in keeping with other cultural coding.

In editing their shots together, the Navajo also used a unique system. Pieces of film generally are cut together in the Hollywood tradition of continuous action to provide for a smooth flow without any jumps in the action. This method requires marking with a grease pencil the frames that are to be joined, cutting them, splicing them, and viewing the completed result. The process is often repeated until the cut is precise. The Navajo, in contrast, seemed to cut frames at random. Upon closer examination, Worth and Adair discovered that the Navajo filmmakers could remember not only the location of various shots but the images of individual frames. The Navajo explained that they did not need to number shots or mark frames because film was "like weaving," in that the design was always present in one's mind.

Thus, the research of Worth and Adair has broad implications for the study of folklore. Using Boas's notion that folklore is a mirror of culture (1916, 1935, 1940) and extending it to examine film as a mirror of folkloric patterning may provide folklorists with a new means of analyzing structure from the informant's frame of reference. Of course, certain limitations are immediately evident. As Heider pointed out, if such films are not "in English," can an outsider understand them? (1976:43). A similar problem has long frustrated folklorists working with narrative. Barre Toelken, in analyzing the coyote tales of a Navajo informant, found that the meanings of tales were difficult to perceive because outsiders interpret them within the framework of their *own* categories of reference (1969, 1981). Films made by informants would be subjected to the same process of ethnocentric analysis that has hindered narrative scholars. Folklorists generally conduct research with groups whose filmic structure is influenced and shaped by western mass media, so teaching informants to film themselves might provide more information about the pervasiveness of the Hollywood approach than it would about folkloric behavior. Folklorists working outside of the United States, however, might discern different patterning systems just as Martha Wolfenstein and Nathan Leites discovered that films of different countries reflected national fantasies (1950).

Like folklorists using a comparative approach for the study of content elements in folk narrative, Worth and Adair extended their research on filmic coding to groups other than the Navajo for cross-cultural comparisons. One of Worth's students, Richard Chalfen, taught filmmaking to several groups of teenagers, some white and some black, in Philadelphia. He used the term *sociodocumentary* to describe his work, which focused on the group activity of filmmaking in contrast to Worth's focus on the structure of a film made by an individual, a process Worth labeled *biodocumentary*. The data obtained in conducting research with the Navajo and with Worth's white middle-class graduate film students were compared with Chalfen's research findings.

Chalfen and Worth discovered that whites chose to film activities occurring outside their own environment. Just as anthropologists sought unusual or exotic people to study or film, and folklorists analyzed their "different" rural neighbors before they began to analyze urban groups, the white film students made films about those whom they conceptualized as the Other. Black students, like the Navajo, tended to film themselves and their own activities. In addition, the white filmmakers wanted to be in control of using the equipment and had no desire to appear in the film itself, whereas blacks strove to be the actors. Worth and Chalfen attribute this difference to status orientation: the whites found status in manipulating equipment; the blacks in acting. Thus, Worth and Chalfen once again point to the problem of limited vision that exists when one tries to interpret the coding systems of other people: "We tend to undervalue the appropriateness of other motives for communication activity and hence to insist that members of other cultures see things (literally) our way" (Worth and Adair 1972:251).

## Blended Voices

Yet another means of conveying the cultural point of view is to establish, in the film record itself, the negotiation process between the filmmaker and those filmed and allow both the authority to speak about their interaction and the events depicted. Recognizing the subjective nature of the filmmaker and seeking feedback, Asch created a series of films that fuse the subject and object and overcome the self/Other division. In 1978, Asch began a collaborative project with Linda Connor, an anthropologist working in central Bali. Asch wanted to test a repaired camera and some old film stock while he was on his way to film in Indonesia. He had heard of Connor and proposed to shoot a short film on her research. They chose to document one event, a seance conducted by Connor's star informant, Jero Tapakan. To test the old film stock, they shot three rolls of Jero in her other occupation as a massage healer. Delays in his planned trip to Indonesia kept Asch in Bali, and he became interested in documenting a cremation ceremony that the village was preparing in order to partake in a centennial purification ritual that would be held by all Balinese Hindus on the island. Once new film arrived, Asch shot twenty-two rolls of film on this event. Upon learning that the film stock he had used for the test footage was bad, Asch reshot the massage session with fresh film. He also decided to record Jero Tapakan talking to Connor about her life. Connor recognized that they were acquiring not one film but a corpus (1988:101).

She narrates the first film completed, *A Balinese Trance Seance* (1980). Using an event to structure a film had been a successful approach for Asch, but in a trance seance, the medium could not comment on her own experience and clients did not wish to discuss why they had come for help. Connor believed this was a major problem, and she looked forward to returning to Bali with Tim and Patsy Asch (who had been editing the footage) to show the people the completed film and record their responses (Connor 1988:107). Jero looked at the seance film, and her reactions became *Jero on Jero: A Balinese Trance Seance Observed* (1981). For instance, her conversation about allowing the film to be released becomes part of the film, which successfully breaks down cultural barriers. Jero becomes another individual to whom we relate as an equal. Showing the seance film and the rough footage of the cremation ceremony in video to audiences in the village led to a "home movie response" of recognizing oneself and one's friends, but also provided some thoughtful feedback that would be incorporated in the cremation film. In addition, the participants were now much more aware of what the film team was doing. During this period, the team shot additional footage for *The Medium Is the Masseuse: A Balinese Massage* (1983), a film in which Jero Tapakan treats a client, the client and his wife talk about Balinese medicine in contrast to western methods, and Jero discusses her activities with Connor. Connor notes, "I was included in the images to show how I worked and the kind of rapport I had achieved with the participants in the event" (1988:103). *Jero Tapakan: Stories from the Life of a Balinese Healer* (1983) also benefited from additional shooting during the second trip to Bali. The film is made up of Jero's personal experience narratives as she tells how and why she became a healer. Folklorists will appreciate not only the tales but Connor's written discussion of the narratives as performances (Connor, Asch, and Asch 1986).

All of the films were to have study guides. Instead, the three collaborators wrote a monograph that would not only be more extensive but also would have the credential of publication that study guides lacked. The result is *Jero Tapakan: Balinese Healer* (1986), which discusses the data and the filmmaking process and includes transcriptions and shot-by-shot descriptions. With both the monograph and their use of video monitors to show the participants reacting to the film and the filmmakers at work, Linda Connor, Tim Asch, and Patsy Asch extended Rouch's shared anthropology, Young's observational cinema, and Asch's event approach to reveal the self of the subject and the filmmakers.

More than a decade after shooting the cremation footage, they completed the fifth film in the series. *Releasing the Spirits: A Village Cremation in Bali Eastern Indonesia* (1990) focuses on a rite of passage so elaborate that the dead are buried until relatives can afford to cremate them properly. In 1978, all Balinese Hindus prepared their dead for cremation to cleanse the island for *Eka Dasa Rudra,* a purification ceremony. When the film team returned in 1980, they recorded the comments of four participants as they watched the videotapes of the ceremonies. They become the film's narrators. Linda Connor's role as the anthropologist is clear. The film makes extensive use of intertitles, some of which reveal the decisionmaking process of the filmmakers. Tim and Patsy Asch argue about how to portray certain scenes, and the "curtain" shielding the filmmakers from the audience is raised on the subjective nature of film.

## Culture Clash: The Global Village

Indigenous people throughout the world are now seeing themselves in movie theaters and on TV. Edmund Carpenter has discussed some of the inherent dangers and ethical dilemmas: "By the time administrators, missionaries, social workers *and* anthropologists got through with indigenous peoples, most were eager to forget their pasts. When *Dead Birds* . . . was shown at the Administrative College, Baroko, one student angrily turned off the projector: 'What right does anyone have to record what we choose to forget?' His statement was applauded" (1972:190). Thus, within one decade, while Americans and the developed countries continued to believe that what they were seeing on the screen as they watched Wejak and Pua fight their ritual wars was a cultural truth, the Dani rejected Gardner's vision.

Three decades later, tourists visit Papua New Guinea to see "the primitives" who were once cannibals. Although many do not know that he was the sound recordist for *Dead Birds,* they do know the story of Michael Rockefeller's disappearance and his presumed demise at the hands of cannibals. Tourists base their notions of the people on the images they have seen. Dennis O'Rourke's *Cannibal Tours* (1987) highlights the problems of preconceived notions that members of one culture have about another and the cultural conflict and change that ensue. Tourists to New Guinea travel the Sepik River documenting people as if they were animals in the zoo. They glide by and snap photographs of men carving canoes or paddling, and they visit the villages to take photographs of the "cannibals." Often, they pay to pose with a native or take pictures inside the spirit house. While some remark that the natives are "indolent" and need to be taught how to live like the tourists (a mind-set much like that held by the missionaries whom some tourists blame for destroying the culture), others lament the passing of a simpler lifestyle. Some recognize that they have changed the culture by introducing a monetary economy and buying art objects, which are now made by artists competing to satisfy the tourists' demands. The villagers are baffled by the tourists' desire for photographs, and they wonder why the tourists do not pay for photographs taken in the village but will pay to enter the spirit house with their cameras. They know that a photo of their own spirit house is available on a postcard; a villager's daughter sent him one. The villagers look upon the tourists as strange beings. One remarks that they are wealthy and that if he had their money he would travel to their countries. No doubt, his children will.

*Cannibal Tours* demonstrates that the desire to document the Other with still photographs and camcorders and the ability to do so has created a tourist "culture." O'Rourke sees tourism as a western colonialistic phenomenon with the tourists collecting art and taking snapshots as a metaphor for colonialism.

Of course, O'Rourke is also "taking photos"; using his film camera, he makes everyone an object of his own manipulation. For O'Rourke, filming both the filmed and the camera wielders, the irony is obvious. Giving voice to both groups, O'Rourke provides a lens through which we see the absurdity of people reducing each other to stereotypes or to images in a frame.

## Ethnography as Folklore

Worth, Adair, and Chalfen called for a new means of investigating the visual medium of film as cultural data to draw conclusions about the cognitive processes of different peoples. This approach demonstrated that filmmaking is not difficult to teach and that groups and individuals will structure film according to their own cultural perceptions. The Asches and Connor created a multivocality in their films so that all voices and opinions would find expression. While their films demonstrate an often common pattern of collaborative effort among filmmakers and anthropologists, that collaboration is expanded to include the participants in the film (cf. Asch 1988; Connor 1988). Different worldviews are presented, but the worldview of the subject is still framed within the filmic formatting of the cameraperson and editor, which differs from the process of people filming themselves. What has actually happened since Worth and Adair's work is that those minority independent filmmakers who have succeeded in learning how to produce images effectively for their own communities often use their success to gain a foothold within the established media system. For most, their voices ultimately are subsumed as they emulate Hollywood and become part of the mainstream.

If the only people who should represent the community are insiders, as many now insist, then Rouch's shared anthropology approach can help the filmmaker determine the accuracy of the image by collaboration within the community.[22] In this case, the filmmaker is one of the people, not an authority figure asking if he or she presents the culture accurately. Rouch predicted that the camera would "pass automatically into the hands of those who were always in front of the lens. At this point, anthropologists will no longer control the monopoly on observation; their culture and they themselves will be observed and recorded" (1974:43-44). To a certain extent, Rouch's dream is now a reality. The Inuit have their own broadcasting satellite, and both the Kayapo in Brazil and the Walpiri of Australia have used video to document themselves and create their own media systems (see Ruby 1992; Moore 1994).

Indigenous peoples, women, gays, lesbians, and others who have had little access to the media, unless they have joined the dominant culture, now have the power to document themselves with camcorders, although their access to distribution is limited. For folklorists, the problem of the Other and the self is

1.7 *Woodstock.* MOMA/FSA

mediated in folklore films and videos because the producers are part of the community, documenting their own societies and often documenting an auto-biographical self as close to home as their own families.

The contestable process of cross-cultural representation discussed in *Writing Culture: The Poetics and Politics of Ethnography* (Clifford and Marcus 1986) has caused the neocolonialist position of anthropological filmmakers to crumble.[23] The indigenous media, which are lauded by Faye Ginsburg (1991), and the new distribution methods of people who shoot films about themselves will eliminate the authority/subordinate positions of filmmaker and subject, or self and Other. In documenting the self, folklorists have avoided constructing overviews of a cultural Other. Films about occupation, region, gender, and eth-nicity, when they are made by or in collaboration with the people being represented, approximate indigenous media. A fundamental difference be-tween folklore films and indigenous media is that the folk often need no authority figures to teach them the means of production and distribution. They develop alternative means of educating themselves and release their narratives on cable access channels and in film and video festivals. The folklore film, while overlooked by film scholars, may be truly reflexive, openly revealing the self.

# 2

# The Folkloric Film
## Definition and Methodology, Texts and Contexts

*No longer . . . can the folklore collector stroll into the field with pad and pencil. Now the fieldworker calls on an arsenal of technological aids: still camera, tape recorder, videorecorder, motion picture camera. These resources provide much fuller context, aurally and visually, for the folkloric event than a written ethnography can convey.*
*—Richard Dorson*

*The film movement* in folklore begins much later than that of other fields, but it reflects all of the techniques and preoccupations of earlier documentary film-makers.[1] Like the "films of fact" shot in the early 1900s, folklore films are often made up of short clips of interesting phenomena captured for posterity. Certain folklore films have a heavily narrated and expository style similar to those doc-umentaries made before World War II and lasting through the 1960s. Other folklore films utilize either a cinéma vérité or postvérité approach or one that combines sync-sound or voice-over with linear depictions for the recording of complex expressive events, including interactions, performances, and the many facets of creative processes in their entirety. Yet others are reflexive and inter-subjective. In the realm of nonfiction film, certain trends have become firmly established. Stylistically, then, the folklore film does not differ from documen-tary and ethnodocumentary film.

On a theoretical level, many folklorists who use film are tied both to the models used by their documentary film forerunners and to the conceptual premises of early folklore scholars. Like Flaherty, some folkloristic filmmakers tend to focus on romantic visions of the noble savage or preindustrial folk. Just as this bias on the part of folklorists gave way to more enlightened notions of the folk as being *a* folk, not *the* folk (Dorson 1952:6) or "any group of people whatsoever who share at least one common factor" (Dundes 1965:2), film-makers also shifted their attention from Flaherty-like romanticism to examine present-day issues involving diverse groups of people. This idea informed the films of Grierson as well as those of Rouch, Asch, and Marshall, among others. Yet in folklore films, both attitudes can be found, existing side by side.

2.1 Filmmaker William Ferris. Photo by Hester Magnuson. University of Mississippi Archives

The use of montage developed by Vertov, the reconstruction of history found in *Man of Aran* and the Netsilik Eskimo series, the biographical emphases of Flaherty and Gardner, and the central concern of Bateson and Mead, Asch, and Marshall on holistic events are all seen in folklore films as well. Indeed, as ethnographers have become less concerned with cultural overviews and more interested in events (e.g., a feast, a funeral, a carnival), their films have become more like folklore films. Folklore films combine the goal of the documentary to record unstaged events with the goal of the ethnodocumentary to provide information about culture. The folklore film focuses primarily on traditions, those expressive forms of human behavior which are communicated by interactions and whose formal features mark them as traditional. The folklore film covers a wide range of traditional behavior, from rituals, ceremonies, folk art and material culture to games, sayings, and songs and to the lore of various peoples bonded by ethnicity, age, gender, family, occupation, recreation, religion, and region.[2]

The folkloristic filmmaker does not *limit* himself or herself to so-called exotic or primitive cultures. Despite recent urban anthropological research, few ethnodocumentary filmmakers record their own "modern" or "industrialized" cultures. The reconceptualization of the "primitive" has led anthropological filmmakers to seek out Third World and aboriginal peoples. As Dorson pointed out in his list of the "skills, perspectives and methods that set folklorists apart from other scholars," folklorists need not travel far to discover folklore being generated (1972a:6). The most successful folkloristic filmmakers have, in fact, examined traditions in their own locales.

These differences of major focus and locale set the folklore film apart from other documentary film traditions. Both documentary and ethnodocumentary filmmakers have included footage whose content is of interest to folklorists: for example, a Wolof woman making pottery, two Yanomamö narrators telling a myth, Haanstra's segments of hand glass blowing in *Glass,* and Vertov's use of folksong in *Three Songs of Lenin.* Such films represent the precursors of the folkloric film, for they include folkloric material and predate the use of film by folklorists per se. *Any* film having folklore content that can be used for the purposes of folklore research and teaching might aptly be called a "folkloric" or "folkloristic" film. Such films include ones created about folklore by folklorists themselves or by non-folklorists who are filmmakers or videographers recording folklore. Put simply, the point of these films is to document folklore.

## The Early Film Movement and Folklore

Most initial folklore films reflect a preoccupation with texts to which visuals have been added. The earliest such documentation of folklore on celluloid is a March of Time series film made in 1935. This film depicts John Lomax interviewing Leadbelly (Huddie Ledbetter) and recording his songs for the folksong archive of the Library of Congress. Lomax and other folksong specialists of the 1930s were most interested in obtaining and preserving the texts and tunes of folksongs for posterity. Although a visual medium is used, it provides little more than a text or recording with the addition of the visual mode and reflects the fascination that must have been felt by researchers who could now add cameras to their text-gathering procedural tools. Despite the text-oriented approach, the film adds the extra dimension of seeing the songs performed.

A second film, *Three Songs of Leadbelly*, shot in 1945 by Blanding Sloan and Wah Mong Chang and edited by Pete Seeger, shows Leadbelly singing "Pick a Bale of Cotton," "Grey Goose," and "Take This Hammer," with twelve-string guitar accompaniment.[3] The film provides close-ups of finger picking and of Leadbelly's facial expressions and body movements. Yet this eight-minute film does not show him singing before an audience; the performances are staged for the camera. The viewer wishes for a more complete picture, such as the meaning of the songs and the performances in relation to Leadbelly's life and to the tradition of which this music is a part, as well as audience reactions and feedback. In the historical development of folkloric filmmaking, this film exemplifies the concentration on texts translated into a moving image.

Other than the two Leadbelly films, American folklore films were not produced again until the late 1950s (coinciding with the folksong revival). In Europe, short, straightforward camera shots of folkloric subjects were taken for documentation purposes by the Institut für den Wissenschaftlichen Film. After World War II, the institute sponsored a program in fieldwork to train ethnologists in the use of film equipment. In 1959, the institute published its own "rules for the documentation of ethnology and folklore" based on its training program, which demanded that fieldworkers be adequately trained, that they keep precise logs, and that they document only authentic events "filmed without dramatic camera angles or movement, and edited for representativeness" (de Brigard 1975:29). The institute organized a film archive in 1952 and began editing the *Encyclopaedia Cinematographia*. The ethnological films, which are categorized first by world region, then by country, and finally by region, are of great value for comparative folklore research. They are short, unnarrated, and deal with only one subject, such as a children's game from West Africa, a festival dance in South Africa, or the performance of an epic heroic song in Romania.

In the United States, Pete and Toshi Seeger produced the Folklore Research Films series from 1956 to 1966 to "celebrate musical expression around the world."[4] The films are both personal and familial. Of the fourteen films in the series, six show Pete Seeger either interviewing the film participants or listening to their music.

*The Country Fiddle* (1959) details Seeger at the 1957 National Folk Festival in Oklahoma City. *Music from Oil Drums* (1956) shows Seeger interacting with those who make and play the oil drums in the steel drum bands of Trinidad, followed by Seeger playing some of these drums in his own backyard with his neighbors. *The Talking Drums of Nigeria* (1964), *Imrat Khan Demonstrates the Sitar* (1963), and *Duke Tritton, Australian Sheep-Shearer* (1963) seem to be home movies of Seeger's travels, coupled with his observations of musical styles. These films portray Seeger gathering visual, verbal, and musical data. The clips of interesting folk performers do, however, provide us with useful information on various musical styles and are the forerunners of interactive films in which the presence of the researcher is fully acknowledged.

Three other films in the series are visual presentations obviously intended to teach the viewer "how to" master a technique: in *Finger Games* (1957) the Seeger family plays several finger games; in *The Many Colored Paper* (1959) they create designs on newspaper with various dyes; and in *The Five-String Banjo* (1958) Seeger demonstrates such techniques as frailing, hammering on, and double-strumming.

Some films in the series portray music in different locales. The relationship between music and work is apparent in *The Singing Fishermen of Ghana* (1964). *Italian Folk Songs* (1964), filmed in the Abruzzi region of Italy, is event oriented and shows folksongs being sung during a family gathering. *The McPeake Family of Ireland* (1964), shot in Belfast, also depicts a family singing. The films that focus on family singing events are useful for contrasting various family traditions. As folklorist James Porter has pointed out, the technical quality of these films "seems to suggest that they were made more as personal records than as professional films for pedagogical or scholastic purposes" (1976:519-20). This statement could easily be applied to most of the films in the series. Yet these films focus on the family and the self, establishing them as central subjects for the content of folklore films.

*Afro-American Worksongs in a Texas Prison* (1966) departs somewhat from the other Seeger films, since it provides more information about the social and cultural circumstances of the music it presents. Narrated by Bruce Jackson and shot at the Ellis Unit of the Texas Department of Corrections near Huntsville, the film covers black prisoners chopping and felling trees while singing in a call-and-response pattern. A group of men hoe to "Move Along 'Gator" and "Down by the Riverside." Both close-ups and wide-angle shots give a sense of the daily work activities of the men, although no shots of their lives inside the prison are included. Jackson's useful narration discusses the function of the worksongs. This film is an excellent visual companion to Jackson's book, *Wake Up Dead Man: Afro-American Worksongs from Texas Prisons* (1972).

As research footage, the Seeger series provides raw data for comparative analysis. All of the films require supplemental information. *Afro-American Worksongs* comes closest to being a presentation with an analysis, but as its title implies, the songs themselves are of primary importance, rather than the singers or the events. Hence, the musical textual bias is obvious.

During this same period, folk music films that emphasize the performers rather than their songs were also produced. For example, "Masters of American Traditional Music," a series of five films produced between 1967 and 1969 include *Fred McDowell, Reverend Gary Davis, Jesse "Lone Cat" Fuller, Doc Watson with Clint Howard and Fred Price*, and *Buell Kazee.*[5] The films open with printed biographical statements about the performers and then show the men performing onstage. Although the performers occasionally introduce their pieces with comments, the films, similar to the Seeger series, capture situations staged expressly for the camera. Like those films that concentrate on textual data, these films treat the people as objects because they do not show the processes of communication and interaction between performer and audience. Adherence to this approach has continued, especially for films about folk musicians. Released in 1995, *Doc Watson: Rare Performances 1963-1981, Doc Watson: Rare Performances 1982-93*, and *Legends of Old Time Music* (which features Clarence Ashley, Roscoe Holcomb, Tommy Jarrell, Doc Watson, Sam McGee, Pete Seeger, and Jean Ritchie) join a growing inventory of performances on videos that list the tunes each performer plays in much the same manner as a compact disc or tape recording might.

Preservationism and romantic survivalism underscore *The Georgia Sea Island Singers* (filmed in 1963, released in 1974), made by Edmund Carpenter, Bess Lomax Hawes, Alan Lomax, and others. The film focuses on a staged performance. Against a dark backdrop, John Davis sings lead with four other performers from St. Simon's Island, Georgia. They present four songs: a spiritual, two ring shouts in call-and-response style, and a buzzard lope dance song that is acted out. A caption states that on St. Simon's Island "spirituals can be heard as they were sung perhaps a century or more ago." In fact, Lydia Parrish's preservation work with the singers, who performed this style for white tourists visiting the island, is the only reason for their performance during the 1960s.

*Buck Dancer* (1966, released in 1974) was also produced by Carpenter, Hawes, and Lomax. Ed Young, a fife player from northern Mississippi, discusses the making and playing of fifes. With vocals and clapping by the Georgia Sea Island Singers, Young blows a fife and performs a buck dance. The romanticized narration and the advertisement description of the film compare Young to a "dark Pan" who steps "in an ancestral dance." According to a Film Images ad, this dance is a "traditional dance of male country Blacks of days past" which "may be the only living reminder of the glories of Southern Black music in the days before the minstrel shows." The film thus superficially treats the historical connections of fife and drum traditions with Africa and is an attempt to preserve a tradition that the filmmakers thought of as "dying out." Like other folklore films of the 1960s, *Buck Dancer* is filmed as a stage situation. We see the performers on a front porch, but are shown nothing of the significance of this musical style within the community.

Hawes told me that Carpenter, who chaired the anthropology department at what was then called San Fernando Valley State (now California State Northridge), "had set up a subsidiary anthropological film unit at the college. We had a lot of equipment—not very many people, but a lot of equipment. So he was intrigued by the notion of doing filming on this kind of level." *Buck Dancer* and *The Georgia Sea Island Singers* would be "an experiment on how to make films out of context," since the Sea Island Singers were passing through Los Angeles. "The Sea Islanders shouldn't have been there. I mean we should have gone to them. On the other hand, I'm glad we did the films because I've talked to a number of filmmakers since then about making films in the Sea Islands, and no film as yet ever emerged except ours. So I was glad we grabbed it while we could."[6]

Survivalism is also the apparent intent behind the making of *'Oss 'Oss Wee 'Oss* (1971), which was scripted and directed by Alan Lomax. Unlike the initial folklore films, which tended to focus on folk music, *'Oss 'Oss Wee 'Oss,* shot in Padstow in Cornwall, deals with folk belief and custom. Basically, the viewer sees the preparation for and celebration of May Day. At midnight, gatherers sing a night song. Children run through the streets singing as the film shifts from black-and-white to color. Celebrants cut sycamore branches in the woods and decorate the Maypole. A greengrocer makes a speech about the tradition of the hobby horse, revealed as an elaborate costume worn by one man. A young man dances with the horse at several houses and they return to the marketplace where a girl goes under the horse and dances. The script, narrated by Charlie Bate of Padstow and Charlie Chilton of London, indicates that the May Day dance is ancient. The narrators tell us that "according to scholars," this dance relates to "the time when we lived in caves." The purpose of the horse's dance, which includes feigning death and leaping to life again, is compared to grain jumping up. Lomax apparently filmed this event to preserve a survival from ancient times; unfortunately, by writing a script to be read over the action, Lomax did not allow the people to express their own attitudes about their May Day customs. However, such an approach was not common when the film was made; these first films reflect the theoretical concerns of their times and thus should not be overly criticized.

## Re-creating Previous Models

Although I could certainly unearth other such films for inclusion in the early history of filmed folklore topics, those I have discussed above are representative. In terms of style and theoretical approach, such films share much in common with documentary and ethnodocumentary films. Makers of folkloric films initially sought to add the magical dimension of movement and apply it to those traditional processes and interactions which they had theretofore reduced to texts and tape recordings. The Seeger series is indicative of this approach. *Three Songs of Leadbelly* has similar implications as it emphasizes the death of Leadbelly (by framing the film with shots of the churchyard where he is buried) and captures his performance style on film.

Seeger's Music around the World films are akin to the city symphonies produced by the continental realists, such as Ruttmann, for they are montages that give the viewer a feeling of musical expression. Like the films of Bateson and Mead, Marshall, and Asch, who endeavored to document events for eventual cross-cultural comparisons, the Seeger series has the same implicit purpose when taken as a whole. As with the work of Flaherty, romanticization and preservation of unusual peoples or activities also became a major theme. Produced forty years after *Nanook of the North*, the Carpenter, Hawes, and Lomax films have affinities in viewpoint.

Because of changing research models, which examine documentation of interactions and processes within their social and cultural milieux and which ask questions about people as communicators rather than about texts as communications reduced to print or film, film is a logical tool for meeting the demands of folklore inquiry. Despite the burgeoning numbers of folklore films, most folklore filmmakers tend to reinvent the filmic styles of their ethnodocumentary precursors. Many folklore filmmakers today still emphasize context and that which is produced (a song, a story, an art object) as opposed to exploring expressive events.

## A Methodology for Analyzing Intent, Content, and the Self

What is required for a successful folkloric film is not the mere visual recording of the context, but a more encompassing endeavor that provides a glimpse into the processes of traditional human behavior. Using film, we have the ability to study these processes and how they operate. Since the camera as an observational tool is limited to the portrayal of the reality of the filmmaker, most filmmakers strive to present the data to an audience in as unbiased a fashion as possible (cf. Collier 1986:10). Yet all films are personal documents that reflect the self. How open we are about that subjectivity becomes the greater issue.

Upon examining the similarities and differences of filmic technique used by present-day filmmakers as it relates to the treatment of the film subject, the viewer can analyze individual styles and theoretical approaches. Although I am concerned with folklore film in general, I have focused most of my discussion on the films of Les Blank, John Cohen, Tom Davenport, Bill Ferris, Pat Ferrero, Carl Fleischhauer, Bess Lomax Hawes, Judy Peiser, Jorge and Mabel Preloran, Ken Thigpen, and Paul Wagner, in addition to my own films. Obviously, I could add numerous other filmmakers, but I have narrowed the discussion to filmmakers who have concentrated on folkloric subjects and restricted the analysis to a representative group.[7]

Blank, Cohen, Davenport, Ferrero, Fleischhauer, Jorge Preloran, and Wagner are primarily filmmakers, whereas Ferris, Hawes, Thigpen, and I have all received academic training in folklore. Judy Peiser, who was educated in broadcasting and film, now considers herself a folklorist as well as a filmmaker, and Mabel Preloran is an anthropologist with a keen interest in folk traditions. Many of these filmmakers have collaborated with folklorists. (For example, Davenport has worked closely with folklorist Dan Patterson.) These filmmaker-folklorists have structured their films around the events in which the film subjects participate, or they have designed their films to portray their own ideas about folklore, or both. Film critic James Arnold has asked, "Does the filmmaker simply record reality, and let the structure of that reality control his editing and selection of shots? Or is he an interpretive expert or artist, who imposes his own reactions and vision, and shapes his film to produce a specific emotional or intellectual effect?" (1979:485). The larger question is how does the filmmaker's view of that reality determine his or her filmic presentation, and how does the filmmaker's conceptual framework influence the reporting of folkloric events?

As noted in chapter 1, in addition to the overt reasons for a film's existence, such as the filmmaker's intent to document quiltmaking or a curing ceremony, film can also be used to analyze gestures, facial expressions, proxemics, and interactions, while theoretical biases may be communicated through the filmmaker's editing style and sound devices.[8] The filmmaker's theoretical assumptions about folklore are disclosed by and determine the techniques used. Films that purport to deal with folklore (in the broadest sense of creative expression) generally focus on either (1) the individual performer or artists; (2) interactional events and processes (singing, narrating, playing, building); (3) the community (region, family, occupational group) or the "culture"; or (4) texts, technological processes, or artifacts. Furthermore, notions of folklore as having a space-time continuum often generate films having a historical or typological focus.

Films that profile individuals or groups of individuals tend to demonstrate creative interactional processes and events (like the films of Bateson and Mead, and the sequence filming of Marshall, and Asch and Chagnon). Such films are most often not narrated and are shot and presented in a vérité or observational style with sync-sound or the sound-over voices of the participants. On the other hand, films that attempt to demonstrate technological processes, examine texts and artifacts, and set up typologies or (as did Balikci and Brown) reconstruct the historicity of folklore productions generally make use of narration and a montage of images that are unrelated in filmic time to actual events. This style also predominates in interpretative films (like *Dead Birds*) in which a narrator explains either the action on the screen or the thoughts of the filmmaker (or the people in the film). For historic reconstruction, the narration may be assembled from the words of journal, diary, and letter writers. Such films are edited to overtly convey the filmmaker's ideas about the subject, similar to the interpretative editing style of Gardner and Wiseman.

The reasons for these methodologies are readily apparent. If the filmmaker concentrates on people and their creative output and interactional processes, then these people will be allowed to convey their own tastes and aesthetics to the audience. Narration may be used as a complement to add information lacking on the soundtrack, but it cannot be allowed to dominate the film, for if the filmmaker focuses on individuals, they will speak for themselves. In this way, the feelings of the individual shape the work of the filmmaker and he or she must structure the film around a sequence of linear events in which the individual is engaged. Occasionally, that structure is determined openly by both the filmmaker and the persons being filmed, and the process of the negotiation becomes part of the completed film.

My analyses of the intent of representative films most often used and discussed by folklorists not only reveal the inherent assumptions of the filmmakers as reflected in their stylistic treatments but also indirectly offer a history of recent folklore films. By comparing the content focus of these films with the film techniques used, I suggest a model for studying folkloric films in general and illustrate why certain approaches to filming are particularly successful.

## Films Documenting Texts and Artifacts

Films that look at folklore as items replicate a model established by scholars interested in content and form. Lynwood Montell's *Folk Housing in Kentucky* (1969-70), Jim Young and John Burrison's *Echoes from the Hills* (1970), and Bill Ferris's *Made in Mississippi: Black Folk Art and Crafts* (1975) are examples of films that study objects. Henry Glassie has aptly pointed out that "the student of material folk culture must be concerned with both the form and material of construction, observable from the finished product, and the process of construction which may be inferred from the object and can be understood through description, but which is best learned through a close observation of the process in progress" (1968:11). This process in progress is usually ignored in films about artifacts. They provide little feeling for the significance of the creative process.

*Made in Mississippi* was produced by the Yale University Media Design Studio in cooperation with the Center for Southern Folklore. Ferris begins with tracking shots and the vocals and harmonica playing of Napoleon Strickland as sound-over. Ferris uses a bricolage technique of filmmaking by including basketmaking, quilting, sculpting, house construction, pottery, and the manufacture of walking sticks interspersed with cane blowing, harmonica playing, and blues singing with guitar. Sync-sound conveys the ideas of the craftsmen and subtitles provide their names, but a somewhat intrusive narrator also comments on the significance of the crafts. The narrator, however, does not romanticize the art-making process, but stresses the function of the products in three short comments that add to those made by the individuals appearing in the film. *Made in Mississippi* uses rural folk art as an organizing principle, but it does not glorify country over urban lifestyles.

Rather than emphasize the form of house types, Ferris includes a sync-sequence of Richard Foster, a house builder, discussing how the houses were built, what materials were used, and how the design functions. The narrator notes, "The folk builder learns his trade from older craftsmen who cut and trim local wood for homes in their community. They build the dogtrot home with its central breezeway to survive the hot Mississippi summer." This narrative serves as the transition from one craft to another.

Because Ferris is primarily concerned with the products made, the filmic technique consists of a sequence of vignettes of individual artists with or at their work, accompanied by brief statements about how or when they learned their crafts. No one individual is detailed at length, although Othar Turner and James Thomas are familiar to viewers of Ferris's earlier films from which some of the footage in this film is duplicated. *Made in Mississippi* is an overview of traditional art forms locally produced by black Mississippians, which might serve as an introduction to the topic of material culture for some viewers.

Other films that represent a vignette style or a spliced together series of scenes on a single topic are Ferris's *Mississippi Delta Blues* (1974/1968-70) and *I Ain't Lying: Folktales from Mississippi* (1975). The former consists of footage from Ferris's field research in the Delta from 1968 to 1970 and focuses more on musical styles than on the musicians or the pieces played. Originally filmed and edited in Super 8mm, *Mississippi Delta Blues* was later blown up to 16mm. To Ferris's great credit, he was one of a very small number of folklorists who ventured out into the field with film equipment at a time when fieldworkers were untrained and generally not encouraged to make films.

*I Ain't Lying*, another Yale Media Design Studio production, includes footage from *Mississippi Delta Blues* and other Ferris films with only a few new scenes added. Using a combination of sync-sound, sound-over, and narration with a series of vignettes, Ferris begins with his star informant, James Thomas,

2.2 Earl Collins at the Berkeley Folk Festival (1970), used for the end title sequence in *Say, Old Man, Can You Play the Fiddle?* Photo by John Bishop. Media Generation

telling a tale about a woman and a preacher. Included are various tales, such as one about John and Ole Miss (a variation on the John and Old Marster tales), religious tales, toasts, and the dozens. Ferris shifts from James Thomas to Shelby Brown, back to Thomas in a graveyard in Leland, and then to Mary Gordon on her porch. Scenes follow of the Rose Hill congregation with Reverend Isaac Thomas, and of Brown and James Thomas and a group of men in a bar. A harmonica instrumental provides space for Ferris to act as narrator and to comment on the folktales. These narrative portions are not intrusive because Ferris does not have the typical newscaster's voice, and he does not romanticize the visuals. The narration indicates the presence of the folklorist rather than an anonymous interpreter and serves only as a means of identifying informants and linking diverse scenes shot in Leland and Rose Hill, Mississippi. Although the tales are told "in context," the film emphasizes types of tales, and because the scenes do not portray the sessions as events, no real sense of the function of storytelling in rural Mississippi is provided.

In her film *Say, Old Man, Can You Play the Fiddle?* (1971), Bess Lomax Hawes focuses on the repertoire and fiddling technique of the late Earl Collins, but pays little attention to his personality and interactions with other musicians. Akin to a taped interview or a series of cuts on a record, the film dissolves from one straightforward shot of Collins sitting on a couch playing a tune to a similar shot. In voice-over, Collins explains when he learned to play, when he likes to fiddle, and how his fiddle was made; conversations between Collins and Hawes, whose voice is heard off-camera, are interspersed with the tune performances. At one point Collins's son, a guitarist, magically "jumps" into the scene at Earl's side, a surprise that results because all the interactions and intervening comments between shots have been deleted. *Say, Old Man* concludes with a printed roll-up of the tunes played. The filmic technique—a series of dissolves—indicates that the film's primary purpose is to present fiddle tunes as visual "texts."[9]

Although films that examine texts, artifacts, or the historicity of folk traditions and practices are valuable as visual records, they may leave unanswered questions about how and why folkloric traditions are generated. By not fully presenting step-by-step construction of creative-interactional processes in progress, filmmakers often structure their films with narrations and interviews or with vignettes or montages. These films reveal more about the filmmaker's assumptions than they do about the folkloric communications of those being filmed. By contrast, filmmakers who focus on process and event also reveal themselves and simultaneously enable viewers to perceive folklore as human behavior.

## Historic Reconstruction

The reconstruction of the past was one of the prime motivators for studying folklore at the inception of the discipline. Scholars believed that they had arrived just in time to catch, in Edgar Allan Poe's words, some "quaint and curious" pieces of "forgotten lore." Filmmakers have followed suit by emphasizing texts as a form of preservation "for the record" or by reconstructing the past out of memories.

The way in which the reconstruction is presented is essential. For Asen Balikci, reconstruction is achieved by acting out a time gone by. Flaherty employed the same artifice for *Man of Aran.* Some filmmakers try to incorporate "texts," the processes or events, and the dynamism of folklore into one film. Sometimes this approach works. These filmmakers use a variety of techniques to achieve such disparate ends and rely on montage, both visually and aurally, liberally sprinkled with live action and interview, and reconstructed action or historical footage to create the effect of documenting folklore thoroughly.

*"We Shall Overcome"* (1988), by Jim Brown, Ginger Brown, Harold Leventhal, and George Stoney (well-known documentarian and pioneer of community-based public access media), glorifies a song text, discusses the process of variation, and explores the function that a text has for those who sing it. Ultimately, it addresses a single song, singing events, and historicity. This film creates a bridge between films that look at texts and those that present events and communities. The song "We Shall Overcome" has an interesting textual history. Its origins and the origins of the social movement for which it became a symbol are intertwined by the filmmakers. Harry Belafonte, who brought famous entertainers together to appear at the 1963 March on Washington, served as the film's narrator, and the 1988 twenty-fifth anniversary was the catalyst for the film. "We Shall Overcome" became the anthem of the civil rights movement in the United States, and the film demonstrates its power as a symbol of freedom and activism.

The film opens with Pete Seeger singing "We Shall Overcome." As the song continues, Seeger, Noel Paul Stookey, Bernice Reagon, and Joan Baez all talk about the song and its impact. Audio of the song itself ties the interviews together as a filmic segment. The concern with function blends with questions of origins as the filmmakers cut to a church on John's Island, South Carolina, where the Moving Star Hall Singers perform "I Shall Overcome" in a "shout" pattern of singing similar to the way slaves sang the song. Belafonte notes that by the end of the nineteenth century the song was well known in black churches. Taj Mahal plays "I'll Be Alright," another early variant.

The film raises the issue of multiple authorship for folksongs by including that portion of the Seeger interview in which he remarks that people ask him who made up the song. He replies that the song is a product of Africans, Europeans, and Americans and is the result of interaction between blacks and whites. The exact historic or geographic origin of the song may not be found, but the film captures the variation process, continuing with black-and-white footage from 1945, when strikers from the Negro Textile Union used the song for social protest in Charleston, South Carolina. At a strikers' reunion, people remember how they added "We Will Win Our Rights" to make their version, "I Will Overcome," fit the occasion.

In 1946, activists introduced the song to the Highlander Folk School located in Montego, Tennessee. The film depicts this school for labor organizers in old footage. Participants at the school taught the song to Sophia Horton, and she taught it to Seeger, who changed the timing and sang it at a hootenanny. Martin Luther King was at the twenty-fifth anniversary of the Highlander School and heard the song there. Guy Carawan, who became the director of Highlander in 1959, made both "Eyes on the Prize" and "We Shall Overcome" popular songs. Seeger comments that Carawan was more important than he. Indeed, Carawan, who was a white Californian, taught the song to people throughout the South and introduced it to the civil rights movement at Nashville sit-ins. The song gave civil rights workers "confidence and a framework for nonviolence."

This confidence is underscored by Jamila Jones, who describes how deputies came to a meeting at Highlander one night and turned off the power to intimidate those present. Fifty people sat and sang "We Shall Overcome" while the deputies with their billy clubs and guns walked among them ransacking "luggage." Jones, then a teenager, began singing a new verse, "We Are Not Afraid," and kept everyone's spirits up. The deputies were unnerved. She comments that the song told the men they were not afraid and gave the singers assurance. The song made their fear disappear: "And everybody—just seemed like nature came into that room: the water on the outside and even the trees just picked up and we were a part of that nature, in tune to what was happening." Finally, the deputies left. The song functioned to produce a sense of unity and an emotion that was felt by both the singers and those who would terrorize them.

The Student Nonviolating Coordinating Committee spread the song through a college tour booked for the Freedom Singers. Today, as the film shows the group singing "This Little Light of Mine," the visuals shift and voices and photos relate the tale of the singers spreading "We Shall Overcome" to the North. Charles Neblett observes, "Music was a stabilizing force. . . . The music was a glue; it gave us power . . . strength." They sing "O, Freedom," and the audio advances the viewer to the 1963 Newport Folk Festival to which the Freedom Singers were invited. There they met Bob Dylan and Joan Baez. In this

scene, the connection between the civil rights movement and the folksong revival is again emphasized. Mary Travers of Peter, Paul, and Mary notes that the
festival was a moment you knew would always be a memory marker and remarks how important having a drummer boy is, as the film shows her group
performing "Blowin' in the Wind," an antiwar song written by Bob Dylan.
Andrew Young says the counter culture was an added component of the movement. "Blowin' in the Wind" expressed the same feelings as "We Shall
Overcome."

These connections made by film editing allow viewers to make strong
inferences about multiple contexts and the function of folk music to effect
change and create emotion. As a viewer, I recall my own reaction to the Newport Folk Festivals of the 1960s with tremendous nostalgia and recognize the
importance of the folksong revival to my own career as a folklorist. I wondered
about the impact of the scene on those of my undergraduate students who
were not alive when these events occurred. The impact was startling. Students
recognize the singers who are now legends and are able to see clearly the alliance of the folksong revival, the counterculture, and the civil rights movement.
By moving back and forth between them, the film shows the threads that tie
them together, conveying the relationship in a way other visual materials (such
as *Making Sense of the Sixties* [1991]) or printed historical documents do not,
because they tend to present each aspect separately. Televised events, like the
March on Washington, brought the message of the movement to the rest of
the country. Joan Baez recalls the honor of singing "We Shall Overcome" on
the Mall during the March on Washington. She remembers the heat, the crowd,
and the emotion. As we see that moment on this film—the moment before
Martin Luther King Jr.'s "I Have a Dream" speech—we recognize the scene as
one we have seen on film many times. The song, Baez notes, made people "feel
connected."

A different song, "Another Man Done Gone," moves the film to a black-
and-white funeral scene and introduces stories and visuals of the Ku Klux Klan
and other racist killings of blacks in the South. By 1965, twenty families had
lost loved ones. Black-and-white footage of a funeral at which the family sings
"We Shall Overcome" has a haunting shot of a young boy singing as tears roll
down his cheeks. This segment serves as a brutal transition to the Selma marches
and Leroy Moton's tale of the murder of Viola Liuzzo, a white civil rights
worker. As Moton and Liuzzo drove together singing the song, Russo was
shot and killed. Still photos help to tell the grisly story. The song became so
powerful that President Lyndon Johnson used the phrase "we shall overcome"
in a speech following the Selma marches when he passed the Civil Rights Act.

The filmmakers connect this event with the Poor People's Campaign and
Martin Luther King Jr., who sang "We Shall Overcome" the night before he

died. As the film cuts to the twenty-fifth anniversary of the March on Washington, the Freedom Singers and the whole audience join hands and sing.

The film comes full circle back to Pete Seeger, who explains that the song could be personalized for many different situations, from Selma to any event in the world. He has come to think of "We" as the main word. "We're either going to make it together or we're not going to make it at all," Seeger observes. Seeger himself and the media introduced the song in other countries. He notes that it only needs one person to teach it to thousands or millions. Shots of Russians, Koreans, and other peoples, singing the song in their own languages, fill the screen.

Belafonte concludes with how the song belongs to causes and people in trouble. The women's movement has adapted it for its theme song, and it has spread globally from the time of the anti–Vietnam War protests to become an antinuclear message. It is a song for struggle, Baez asserts. For Bishop Desmond Tutu of South Africa, where the song is also sung, it is about overcoming the policy of uprooting people and starvation. The song says what we "long for with every fiber of our being." The film ends as it began, with Seeger addressing the camera: "There are probably millions of people who could say, 'This song changed my life.'"

Montage, vignettes, and narration are the keys that indicate a concentration on folklore as text in this film. This film about one song uses all the techniques of films that document texts, and indicates that this approach can be extremely effective. A film that places a text within multiple contexts displays the mutability of folklore. The interviews and historical footage point to the myriad functions this folksong serves for individuals and groups, and inverts the idea of textuality by expanding the song beyond the boundaries of an entity. In painting a very broad picture, *"We Shall Overcome"* demonstrates folklore's complexities.

Multiple contexts are also explored by Pat Ferrero in *Hearts and Hands* (1987), in which the quilt as artifact is the central focus. Again, a montage of images reveals the underlying message of folklore as object, but the filmmaker uses that object to recount a social history of women. Woven together with musical pieces, journal entries, still photographs, and shot after shot of the quilts of both anonymous and famous women, *Hearts and Hands* unfolds the great events of the nineteenth century and the powerful role that women and their textiles played in the drama. Few images are of movement, which is normally emphasized by the film medium, but the placement of the photographic stills of daily life against the voices of many women generates its own rhythm.

Backed with music of the era, a close-up of a woman's hands working at a spinning wheel and skeins of yarn hung on a wall take us to another time. A superimposed title states the film's topic: "In the nineteenth century women

2.3 A nineteenth-century ambrotype of women with sewing goods in *Hearts and Hands*. Hearts and Hands Media Arts

made quilts: to cover their beds, to create artistic visions, and to express polit-ical sentiments." The functions, both practical and aesthetic, of quilts are well known. The political aspect is a departure from our usual conception of quilts as utilitarian objects.

The film moves from the textile mills of the North to the issue of slavery in the South, explains the importance of quilts and fabrics in the Civil War, sweeps through the settlement of the Midwest, rolls over the prairies to the western frontier, and reconstructs the temperance and suffragist movements. The story of Lucy Larkham traces her growth in a small Massachusetts whal-ing village. Quilt patterns appear of ships, whales, and waves in appliqué and patchwork designs familiar to quilters: Mariner's Compass, Ocean Waves, World without End, Ship of Life. Lucy became a bobbin girl at age eleven. Songs reflect the joy many girls felt at receiving cash wages, aiding their fam-ilies, and becoming independent. Their excited voices detail how hard they worked. In contrast, Ferrero indicates the drudgery of this life by presenting the stark noise and looming movements of the machinery. The voices grow weary describing the workers' toil, fourteen hours a day, six days a week. The mill girls, who made both fine calico and rough slave cloth, signed a petition to abolish slavery; Lucy wrote of her sorrow for her black sisters who toiled in the South. Her story, captured from archival research, helps illuminate feminist history.

With Lucy's words about slavery, Ferrero moves to the South and acquaints us with Elizabeth Keckley, a house slave whose master was also her father. Southern white women's quilts, with extensive time-consuming appliqué, indicated their leisure; the quilts of the slaves in the field displayed African patterns and designs.

The visionary quilt of Harriet Powers boasts a West African design. Powers dictated the stories of each block when she sold her quilt: Jonah swallowed by a whale; the falling of the stars on November 13, 1883; a woman frozen at prayer; the independent hog (a symbol for an escaped slave). Quilts hung on lines indicated safety for runaway slaves and such patterns as the "Underground Railroad" began appearing on the quilts of abolitionists, visually linking women to the antislavery cause. "Quilts were now a form of nonviolent protest."

The film weaves in the story of Harriet Tubman, who escaped from a plantation and brought others out to freedom. Women raised money with quilts and wrote on their needle cases, "May the use of our needles prick the conscience of the slave holder." Individual quilts highlight the poignancy of the "great war": a "Rally Round the Flag" design, another inscribed with the forty-seven battles the quilter's husband fought in and survived. Photos of the handwritten count of the dead and wounded dissolve into each other on screen. Ferrero tells us that Confederate uniforms hung in rags at the end of the war. One woman made a quilt of such materials; others made quilts showing coffins. Photos and words from Keckley's autobiography detail Lincoln's death, and quilts patterned after flowers slowly bloom, evoking a new hope for tranquillity following the war's turmoil.

As the midwestern prairies began to fill, quilts became road maps, showing the counties and states of the settlers. Photographs of log cabins, which highlight their structural components as they are erected, shift back and forth dramatically with shots of numerous variations that the log cabin quilt pattern assumed: Barn Raising, Courthouse Steps, Light and Dark, Streak of Lightning. By 1876, the Midwest was settled and, in celebration of the nation's centennial, red, white, and blue quilts explode on screen in dazzling designs of eagles, stars, and stripes, with fireworks and patriotic music used for background sound.

The third major segment, "Crossing the Plains, 1850-1880," portrays the saga of Abigail Scott Duniway, who set out for Oregon's free land as a child. Women journeying on the trail began to incorporate the geometric shapes in Native American women's baskets as well as the sights along the way: Indian

Tepee, Prairie Sun, Cactus Basket, Feathered Star, Rocky Mountain Road, a saw-toothed edge mirroring the trail of feet leaving the road to look at graves, crosses stitched with names of those (like Abigail's mother) who died before reaching their destination. Put in charge of keeping the family's journal, Abigail would later write a novel about the overland trail. Pine Tree, Dove at the Window, Log Cabin—all suggest the lushness of the Willamette Valley in Oregon where Abigail settled. Duniway put out *The New Northwest,* a newspaper in which her editorials raised the issue of the double-edged power of needlework. On the one hand, it kept women overworked and in their place; on the other, it freed their creativity and often allowed them to make political statements. Duniway herself used the money from a quilt sale to support the suffragist movement.

*Hearts and Hands* closes with the story told by the Women's Christian Temperance Union (WCTU) quilts. Women who bore the brunt of men's overindulgence of alcohol joined together to close down taverns. For thousands of housewives, the WCTU became a network for social reform. Frances Willard worked tirelessly on a petition for temperance and dreamed of one day running the country as its first female president. Women in the WCTU, using blue and white as their colors, crafted quilts with *T*'s, created the Temperance Goblet pattern, and stitched Drunkard's Path. Two hundred thousand women from fifty countries created a crusade quilt. The power of women's needles brought the women's movement to a crescendo as the nineteenth century ended. And in 1914, Duniway had the suffrage amendment passed into legislation in Oregon. At age seventy-nine, she became Oregon's first female voter.

Each quilt becomes a story. For Ferrero, these quilts are texts, and needles are the pens that create a pattern of historical fragments carefully gathered and arranged to reveal an aesthetic picture of women's power in the nineteenth century.[10] By scrutinizing the visual images created by women, *Hearts and Hands* chronicles society and history through the artifacts that gave voice to domination and freedom.

With a total of 986 cuts, *Hearts and Hands* employs montage to tell a story of the ultimate triumph of women during a century from which we usually hear few female voices. Reconstructing the era with those voices and placing the quilt into a historical perspective differs from films that only look at the patterns of quilts (or songs or tales). For Ferrero, the quilts are the outward expressions of women's experiences.

Films that examine the struggles of different labor unions almost by necessity fall into the category of oral history, because they often educate the viewer about the events that led up to the formation of the union and the workers' perceptions of those events as they affect the present. Such films have certain common touches: they invariably contain interviews with workers who

2.4 Shooting *Miles of Smiles*. Jack Santino works with equipment in the lower left corner.

enumerate the conditions of their employment, and they blend sound-over and personal experience narratives with historical still photos, old motion footage, and the contemporary attitudes of laborers. Although many oral history films attempt to evoke nostalgia for "the good old days," those films which specifically look into union history demonstrate that life in the past was a heroic struggle. Unionization alleviated some distress, but for many the fight continues, albeit in different arenas.

*Miles of Smiles, Years of Struggle: The Untold Story of the Black Pullman Porter* (1982), by Jack Santino and Paul Wagner, documents an era that has come to a close. As part of the oral history film genre, it uses interviews and montages of old photos as recurring images and topical songs to create soundtracks that stir memories of past eras.

The film is about storytelling and presents many narratives describing experiences of black porters. Taken together, these stories tell the porters' story. The "untold" story is the one not found in history books about Pullman or the railroads because most historians, unlike folklorists, would not have asked porters to tell tales that construct *their* story.

*Miles of Smiles* documents the rise and fall of the Brotherhood of Sleeping Car Porters, which should interest labor union and minority history enthusiasts. It also places great weight on occupational folklore, addressing traditional expressive behavior of the black porters who served the nation's railroad passengers.

Folklorist Jack Santino, then at the Smithsonian Institution's Office of Folklife Programs, began the project that resulted in *Miles of Smiles* as a series of oral history interviews with porters at the Smithsonian in 1978. When the Brotherhood of Sleeping Car Porters merged with the Brotherhood of Railway and Airline Clerks in that same year, Santino told me, he decided to make a film that would note the passing of the union. In a sense, the film begins at the end. A scene of the annual reunion of retired porters shot in Washington, D.C., is used to both open and close the film and sets the stage for the reminiscent interviews with men who have gathered from all over the United States.

The narrator is Mrs. Rosina Tucker, the eloquent 100-year-old widow of a Pullman porter. She recounts how George Pullman built his railroad empire, and black-and-white still photographs effectively take us back to the turn of the century. By the 1920s, Pullman employed more blacks than any other company in the country.

The film shifts to the retired porters of today walking through the now quiet and abandoned cars. Old footage depicts the trains moving down the rails, and honky-tonk music helps capture the excitement of the age of steam. Former porter Ernest Ford stands in the kitchen and dining cars and describes how the food was prepared and served, as stills document the dining car in operation. A similar technique is used to show the activities in the lounge and parlor cars. To demonstrate one type of occupational folklore, Santino has two porters make a bed, and they jokingly discuss the "proper way" to make it fancy. Signs about cardsharks and confidence men remind the porters about their own card games and the in-group experiences of helping each other as they rode the rails and lived in the company's facilities.

One particularly striking scene uses footage from the 1933 film *The Emperor Jones,* starring Paul Robeson. As we see Robeson catch his train amid a crowd of well-wishers, Tucker points out that being a porter gave one status within the black community. A scene from *The Girl in the Pullman* (1927) demonstrates a demeaning white attitude about black porters as the bearers of inside confidences. A white actor in blackface advises a male passenger in a sleeping car to tip him well or he will divulge the man's adventures with his previous female companion to his present one. The image of the porter as an Uncle Tom figure appears in *The Holdup of the Rocky Mountain Express* (1906). Such film clips reinforce the visibility of porters as a group in the popular culture of yesterday to today's audiences, most of whom have never traveled by train, let alone one with porter services.

On the train, the porter played host to famous white people, and children were entrusted to his care. When the train pulled in, the porter again became a black man—a second-class citizen. Every porter was called "George," Tucker says dryly, "as if he were George Pullman's boy." Customers expected a constant smile, so porters called the job "miles of smiles." Reactions to stereotyping, in the form of folkloric jargon, indicate the use of folklore as a device for strengthening one's sense of identity within the group and as a mechanism for expressing one's true feelings about the work.

Much of this film concentrates on tales that demonstrate what those who study ethnicity refer to as the "lore of accommodation."[11] The narratives of the porters often revolve around how they could be servants and still maintain self-respect without "Uncle Tomming." In relating their experiences with customers who insulted them, the men explain how the porter was able to "put on" the customer, manipulate him into making a fool of himself, and cause him to realize that the porter had power although he played a subservient role. African American scholar Edwin Coleman notes, "In porter lore, we can see this balance of submission and aggression dramatized" (1982). Contact with whites is a large part of this lore, and the ability to deal with the customer is underscored in the film interviews.

The film shifts to the story of how Ashley L. Totten, the leader of a group of porters, came to A. Philip Randolph, a socialist who agreed to help blacks organize. No white union allowed black members. Randolph said the porter was the perfect man to represent the struggle of black workers because his home was everywhere. Included in the segment on Randolph is E.D. Nixon's account of the now traditional story of how the Pullman Company tried to convince Randolph to abandon the Brotherhood by offering him a blank check, payable in six figures. The details of what Randolph did with the check—he framed it, tore it up, sent it back, even cashed it—vary with storytellers, but Nixon recounts the most inclusive version. Randolph photocopies it, frames the copy, returns the original check, and lets Pullman know the black man cannot be bought.

The story of the unionization of Pullman porters has been well documented in Brailsford Brazeal's *Brotherhood of Sleeping Car Porters* (1946). Jervis Anderson's book, *A. Philip Randolph* (1972), covers the rise of the now famous civil rights and labor champion, and volumes containing the Proceedings of the Biennial Conventions of the Brotherhood are available for readers who wish to delve further into background materials. Santino and Wagner, however, make the fight to unionize vivid, combining still photos of Randolph with his voice addressing the Brotherhood. The film takes us up to the beginning of the civil rights movement, Randolph's work to make Franklin D. Roosevelt grant equal employment, and the key role of the Brotherhood in the 1963 March on Washington. We learn from Nixon, a porter from Montgomery, Alabama, how he organized the Montgomery bus boycott and was successful in recruiting a reluctant Martin Luther King. Rosina emphatically states, "I want it to be known that the humble Pullman porter, the man who had been kicked around and shoved around . . . fought for this boycott."

The humble Pullman porter is, indeed, the star of this film, which goes beyond the stock oral history documentary to impress us with the pride, humor, and style of men who gather to tell a dramatic tale. Rosina Tucker also shines, not only as a narrator but as a major character in her accounts of leading the powerful Ladies' Auxiliary of the Brotherhood, holding secret meetings, and surreptitiously collecting dues. Tucker further delights us by playing on the piano a song she wrote in 1939 about the Ladies' Auxiliary.

In 1969 the Pullman Company went out of business, in 1978 the Brotherhood merged with the Brotherhood of Railway and Airline Clerks, and in 1979 Randolph died. As the porters file out of a derailed Pullman, the annual reunion comes to an end. Obviously, nostalgia for a time when they had a noble cause to uphold permeates many of the tales told in this film, but the film primarily serves as an unbiased document of a now historical union and an occupation that few of us have seen in operation and even fewer of us from the insiders' point of view.

By looking at historical factors, *"We Shall Overcome," Hearts and Hands,* and *Miles of Smiles* demonstrate a reverence for the past and indicate the filmmakers' interest in folklore as things that have survived through time. But survival is less important than the dynamism of the past, the rediscovery of the suppressed stories of oppressed people, and the recognition that folklore is a constantly evolving process.

## Cultural Contexts: Films Emphasizing Communities and Regions

Using film as a means of depicting traditional activities enables us to analyze folklore dynamically and to conceptualize folklore as dynamic. Many folklore filmmakers have examined the various events of individuals in communities. For some, the focus is a regional one; for others, it is a specific community. The community may be as large as the Hopi nation or as small as a family. For these filmmakers, social and cultural environments—contexts—serve as the impetus for the generation of folklore. Their films convey the ways that folklore functions as facets of culture.[12] All of these films, much like that of their ethnodocumentary forerunners, bring culture to the screen. One major variation is the link that the filmmaker has with the studied society.

Bill Ferris, for example, is a white scholar who has spent much of his life successfully documenting the folklore of black Mississippians. His intent in *Give My Poor Heart Ease* (1975) was to present the musical vision of Mississippi bluesmen. To do so, he contrasts the blues styles of rural black musicians

2.5 Joe "Poppa Rock" Louis, disc jockey a WOKJ/WJMI radio station in Jackson, Mississippi, spins platters at the beginning of *Give My Poor Heart Ease*. Photo by William Ferris. University of Mississippi Archive

with urban performers who came from the Delta region. The opening shot of Joe "Poppa Rock" Louis, a radio disc jockey, talking to his listening audience about the blues implies that the blues are prevalent in urban centers. "Why I Sing the Blues," by B.B. King, plays, and over a King instrumental Ferris cuts to King himself discussing his memories of hearing blues in the cotton fields. Ferris thus connects King, who hailed from the Delta, with rural blues performers. The soundtrack moves to James Thomas playing "61 Highway" over tracking shots of the countryside (presumably while on Highway 61 in the Delta). Barber Wade Walton sings "Rock Me, Momma" while playing guitar, and artfully composed shots capture his reflection in a mirror. Another barber rhythmically sharpens his razor. Over an outdoor shot of marching prisoners, B.B. King states, "The blues did have its roots and it still does in prison. To me, I think this is how the blues actually started."

A prisoner in the state penitentiary at Parchman recalls how tough it was when he arrived. Work gangs chop logs as they sing a worksong, and another prisoner says that singing eases the mind while one is working. From Parchman, the film moves to Shelby Brown in Leland. Brown discusses the relationship between plowing, cotton chopping, woman trouble, and the blues. Scenes of James Thomas performing "I Wanta Ramble" and "Rock Me Baby" in a juke joint, talking about women giving men the blues, and playing "61

Highway" with Cleveland "Broom Man" Jones, who scrapes a broom against the floor, are effective in showing various blues performance contexts. Tracking shots along the boarded up storefronts of Memphis's Beale Street and the sound of Muddy Waters singing "Hoochie Koochie Man" lead to a salesman in a clothing store who says that some of the causes of the blues are being poor and losing a girlfriend. In the last scene, B.B. King sits on a couch singing "The Thrill Is Gone."

With the available transcript provided by Ferris, one can identify the participants and their precise locations in *Give My Poor Heart Ease*. The reasons for showing worksongs in a film about the blues indicates Ferris's emphasis on the Delta region, but he also implies that worksongs are blues. The purpose of interviewing a salesman is also unclear. Although technically good, the film is too loosely structured to actually present the role that music plays for more than a few selected members of the Delta. His style of including too much material without detailing each event from beginning to end reveals Ferris's preoccupation with context rather than event in this film. A narration to clarify the purpose behind stringing these scenes together might have strengthened his implicit hypotheses about the roots of the blues without impairing his technique of having bluesmen present their ideas.

Ferris's *Gravel Springs Fife and Drum* (1971) also would benefit from a narration. Othar Turner, a cane fife player from Gravel Springs, Mississippi, explains how he began making and blowing a cane at the age of thirteen. By means of sound-over, he presents his views on living on a farm and growing up the hard way. Turner's statements about his life are interesting, but he says little about the music. That African American fife and drum band musical styles are related to traditional West African ones might have been noted in a sub-title or short narration.

This film was the first that Bill Ferris and Judy Peiser produced together. The footage had been shot when Peiser, who was then a freelance filmmaker, joined Ferris's team as the editor. The film begins with Ferris's usual tracking shots of the countryside, which serve to identify the setting as rural. These shots dissolve to a kitchen scene and then to Turner saddling his horse and riding off to cut cane in the woods. The processes of making the cane fife and playing it follow. With their instruments, a group of men take off down the road in a truck and arrive at a country picnic where they perform. Unrelated shots of animals, knife sharpening, cow milking, clothes washing, and butter churning are used as cutaways. Ferris then cuts back and forth between the musicians and a woman preparing fried chicken. These scenes never seem to connect, unless the viewer assumes that the chicken is for the picnic. After an incongruous shot of the fife maker riding his horse, the film cuts to him playing and then freeze-frames for the end titles.

2.6 Othar Turner plays his completed cane fife in *Gravel Springs Fife and Drum.*
Photo by William Ferris. University of Mississippi Archive

Either Ferris did not know what questions to ask or Turner did not volunteer enough information to indicate that this music is not widely popular throughout the South but is confined to a few communities. As he did in the bluesmen film, Ferris documents social contexts. *Gravel Springs* is more valuable in restricting its coverage to one individual within one community. The film's short running time of ten minutes does not allow for an in-depth portrait of either Turner or the residents of Gravel Springs. Instead the film accentuates the rhythmic patterns of work and music. Longer shots and more coverage would present the factors that make fife and drum music viable. Peiser was working with existing footage; thus, the film is a compromise of the visions of two imaginative people. In 1972, Ferris and Peiser launched the Center for Southern Folklore and continued to collaborate on films.

Film can be used to convey the function of folkloric expressions within communities. John Cohen's *The High Lonesome Sound* (1963) details the frustrations of a community that depends on industrialization. Cohen shows a fairly clear overview of life in Hazard, Kentucky, through scenes of workers on their way to the mines, men in the streets discussing hard times, and personal accounts of the economic picture in the mountains. Instead of showing the viewer a small slice of life in the mountains, Cohen's camera picks up housing

2.7 In a frame from *The High Lonesome Sound,* Bill Monroe and the Bluegrass Boys play on the courthouse steps in downtown Hazard, Kentucky. Copyright John Cohen

and working conditions and social interactions. Within this context, he allows the audience to infer the function that music has for the people who play the instruments and sing the songs.

Cohen does not isolate the viewer from seeing the use of songbooks and the influence that hearing rock 'n' roll on the radio has had in shaping the musical tradition. He obviously does not feel that this contemporary music causes a degeneration of the old music but that it can exist with traditional music, each influencing the other. He documents singing in church, on the street, and in the home. Cohen asserts that in a state of economic depression, music is a way of holding on to the old dignity. It is a means of celebrating and serves to express religious feeling. In the film, Roscoe Holcomb relates his personal experiences regarding music. Being out of work, he says, he needed something to do. Cohen tells the audience that for Roscoe Holcomb, music is a gift from God. Yet the viewer tends to believe that music may provide an escape or a mode of adjustment for Holcomb in a time of economic instability. An excellent film for examining the entire cultural context in which artistic expressions are produced, *The High Lonesome Sound* explores the meaning of music for the group and for the individual. The narrator makes few remarks and serves only

2.8 John Cohen filming a Huayno singer in Lima. Photo by Alicia Benevites

as an unbiased guide, allowing the audience to see an honest, thorough film. This film contrasts well with *Harlan County, U.S.A.* In one, the music predominates and the work in the coal mines heightens some of the reasons for the music's persistence. In the other, the mines take center stage as a strike erupts, and the music illustrates the miners' struggles.

Cohen has always been interested in folk music. He was a member of the New Lost City Ramblers, a folksong revival group during the 1960s. His films have all dealt with music as a means of getting inside a culture. Since 1962, Cohen has made more than fifteen films. Their topics range from traditional American music to ballads in Scotland and England; the music and weaving of native peoples in Peru; a performance by the legendary Sara and Maybelle Carter, whose music helped found the country music industry; and a portrait of a Greek American clarinetist.

In 1979, Cohen released the first of many films on the Q'eros Indians of Peru. For *Dancing with the Incas: Huayno Music of Peru* (1991), Cohen looks at a form of popular Andean music that differs from the panpipe music most outsiders associate with the Andes. What the Andean people enjoy is Huayno. Throughout Peru, Bolivia, Ecuador, Columbia, and northern Chile, the radio plays Huaynos, uniting its listeners. Based on Inca melodies, using saxophone,

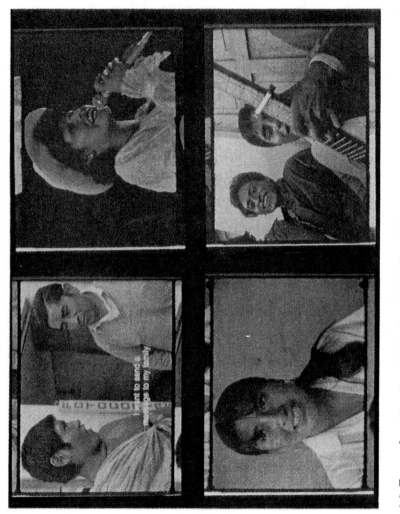

2.9 Frames from *Dancing with the Incas*. Mari Elena Ochoa, lower left. Copyright John Cohen

fiddle, harp, and traditional flute, Huaynos were once limited to small indigenous communities. The native peoples who move into the cities for work have no access to the media and no power in the communities in which they live. But every night from four to six in the morning the radio plays their music, sung in both Quechua and Spanish. In the film, Cohen avers that while the city is sleeping, it is dreaming to Huaynos. "What I'm really saying is that those people who think they own the city—who are the wealthy—while they're asleep during that night air, there's forty radio stations transmitting Huayno music" (Cohen 1992). At 6 A.M., the stations end their broadcasts.

Cohen details the complexities of this phenomenon by showing the function of Huayno music for three female singers in Lima, Peru. One of the singers featured, Julia Illanes (known as the flower of Huancayo), is part of the commercial music scene in Lima; another, Gomersinda Cortabrazo, must work at additional jobs to make a living. Like Illanes, she believes her record company is exploiting her. For Cohen, the music is a political tool, bringing together those with little means of transmitting their ideals to each other except through the Huayno music of the night. Unbeknownst to the elite who hire native Peruvians to work as domestic labor in their homes, the performance of Huayno music at dance clubs and on phonograph records and radio binds together a group of people who are almost invisible outside their social class. Cohen makes this point by accenting the lack of knowledge that an employer and her daughter have about the music and life of their maid, Andean dancer and singer Maria Elena Ochoa, who lives in their home and is close in age to the daughter. Cohen asks the daughter about her life as compared to Mari's. The visual contrast is striking.

An evocative scene depicts Ochoa in her room preparing for the day and singing for the camera. She discusses her life with Cohen, whose voice is heard on the soundtrack. The scene, with the camera moving around Ochoa as she sings a traditional song in the privacy of her room, achieves a great intimacy. Cohen quickly cuts to Mari dancing and singing a Huayno in public performance. As he did in *The High Lonesome Sound*, Cohen highlights the relationship between popular and traditional music. A closing segment briefly touches upon *chicha*, which incorporates rock, *cumbia*, and Huayno to form the music of a new generation. The function of music as life-affirming is the central theme. For Cohen, the film is a message about the music of an oppressed people, a message he presents from the point of view of those tyrannized by the Shining Path guerillas from whom they have fled and by the record companies who use these musicians as a bonanza to create their own recording empires.

Music is also the focus of the films made by the Center for Southern Folklore. The Ferris/Peiser film team dissolved in 1982. Ferris became more and more involved with the responsibilities of running the Center for the Study of Southern Culture, which he established at the University of Mississippi in 1979; Peiser assumed responsibility for the activities of the Center for Southern Folklore and began working on multimedia events in Memphis. Located on historic Beale Street in Memphis, the center houses archives with over 30,000 slides and historic photographs; produces exhibits; distributes films, books, and records about the South; and markets a Slice of the South gift box filled with southern foods, recipes, music, and other delights for tourists and homesick southerners. Each year, the center presents the Memphis Music and Heritage Festival (formerly the Mid-South Music and Heritage Festival), a weekend of blues, jazz, rock, soul music, and ethnic bands from Jewish klezmer to Cajun zydeco on three stages; food demonstrations; ethnic and southern concession stands; and crafts and heritage pavilions. For executive director Peiser, the festival shares the diversity of the community with the community itself. The center's film, *All Day and All Night: Memories from Beale Street Musicians* (1990), directed by Robert Gordon and Louis Guida, with Judy Peiser as executive producer, is a portrait of Beale Street in its heyday.

Because Peiser hosts a local television show on which she interviews musicians and craftspersons, she is a celebrity in Memphis. Through her work at the center, which has included an eighteen-projector multimedia show and the installation of permanent public outdoor exhibits that interpret Beale Street, Peiser has come to know some of the former Beale Street musicians well. The film is a personal look at Beale. From the 1920s to the 1950s, Beale Street was a neighborhood "where the lights never went out" and "the music lasted all day and all night." Black-and-white photos introduce the neighborhood and give way to B.B. King telling the camera, "I thought of Beale Street as Memphis." The film cuts to him in a club singing and establishes him as a performer. Rufus Thomas quips, "If you were black for one Saturday night, and on Beale Street, you would never want to be white again."

The film returns to old black-and-white footage and stills and then moves to Evelyn Young, a saxophone player. Peiser cuts back and forth between interviews and performances to provide a feel for the era. Sunbeam Mitchell always helped out those in need at his restaurant. In one scene, the performers eat Ernestine Mitchell's famous chili and talk about how the musicians learned from each other. For Rufus Thomas, Beale Street was like a college. At Pee Wee's Pool Hall, men played pool as a front for the gambling that went on in the back room. Others talk about the Palace Theater: "If you had talent, it was the place to be." At that time, the management gave out prizes for the talent show winners, and a dollar would carry a person through the week. Rufus Thomas ran the stage show and often made certain that the struggling young B. B. King would receive a dollar prize. After the show, everyone went to Mitchell's place to eat chili and to jam.

Rufus Thomas, sitting at the control board of radio station WDIA, where he still hosts a Saturday morning show, reminisces about the days when he and B.B. King worked together as disc jockeys. WDIA was the first station to have an all-black disc jockey roster and an all-black programming format. Once other station managers heard the music, they would often add the recordings to their playlists, and the music would be heard around the country. In this way, some Memphis performers acquired national recognition.

One sequence consists of old footage of the Brown-Skinned Models in performance. A voice observes that if you were in that show you were a success. Musicians report that success did not mean acceptance for those traveling on the road. Few hotels would house them, so arrangements had to be made to sleep at private homes.

B.B. King compares the experience of those days to one of dropping a pebble in water. The music spread out from Beale Street and across the country. In a closing scene, B.B. King, Rufus Thomas, Evelyn Young, and others play in a club, recapturing the live performances that were the hallmark of Beale Street. For Peiser, the film is a tribute to a lifestyle and a locale. Examining the importance of the past in shaping musical traditions, the film allows the people themselves to speak about the function of music. Here, similar to scholars who study region, such as Richard M. Dorson in *Buying the Wind* (1964) and *Land of the Millrats* (1981) and Suzi Jones in *Oregon Folklore* (1977), the filmmakers add the important element of a sense of place.

Like the work of Peiser, Cohen, and Ferris, many of Jorge Preloran's films deal with the processes of creativity, specifically in the area of folk art. Preloran told me in July 1973 that his work in the 1960s was an attempt to "document some aspects of the folkloric realities of Argentina." His early films often look at rituals and folk art. *Quilino* (1969), for example, documents the straw and feather craftsmanship of a small village in the province of Cordoba. Shot in five days, it is one of a series of twenty-two short folklore films made by Preloran through grants from the Fondo Nacional de las Artes for the Universidad Nacional de Tucuman. *Valle Fertil* (1972), which is ninety minutes long, represents a different style of filmmaking that Preloran developed to portray what he called "the dramatic flow of life." Shot between 1965 and 1970, *Valle Fertil* touches not just on crafts and industrialization or modernization but on all aspects of community life. A similar format was used by Preloran for *Araucanians of Ruca Choroy* (1971). Using one seasonal cycle as an organizing principle, Preloran examines the crafts, religious rituals, and traditions of the tribe living at Ruca Choroy, a reservation in a small valley of the southern Andes.

2.10 Damacio Caitruz declares, "I am Mapuche," in *Araucanians of Ruca Choroy.*

*Araucanians* opens with two brief titles that identify the people and land-scape shots that depict the environment. The sound-over voice of Damacio Caitruz, who serves as the primary narrator, declares that the Indians fled the Spaniard conquerors before finally setting at Ruca Choroy. This vision of history, though incorrect, is not commented on or censored by Preloran. In a January 1976 interview for *El Cronista*, in Buenos Aires, Preloran explains:

> I prefer a more humanistic vision in which one protagonist gives me his view of the world. For instance, in *Araucanians*, Damacio starts out saying: "That's where the Spaniards came from, killing and taking captives." They are actually Argentine soldiers, but he believes they were Spaniards. I don't correct him. An Argentine audience will say, "My God! What's this man talking about?" Well, that's the way he sees it, because he can't believe that the Argentines could have done such a thing to [the Indians].
>
> That's my stand. I don't want to know too much so as not to influence what is happening with the characters that I am shooting, who are not in-tellectuals; they *live* their lives personally, not through the experiences of others.

These experiences include the daily round of activities of Damacio, his two wives, and his children during the summer. As Damacio discusses the weaving patterns employed by the women who make bedspreads and trade them for food, he notes that they frequently are cheated by their customers. Araucanian children often die young or are born deaf and dumb. Damacio remarks that he doesn't "know what that comes from." Once again, Preloran does not intrude to reveal that syphilis and inbreeding are factors. He chooses to let the viewers feel Damacio's bewilderment and draw their own conclusions.

A midwife's burial procession is shown in great detail. Mourners carry a cross decorated with flowers. At each rest stop, they light a small candle. The dead woman's daughter expels smoke from a cigarette that sends her words to Heaven. Meats and sweets are placed in the casket so that the body will not suffer. Damacio speaks of the woman's importance in the community, explains the rituals and their functions, and discusses belief in the separable soul. Preloran also shows food preparation and house building. Piñones (pine cones) are gathered, buried in running streams, peeled and dried on strings, and then ground into flour.

Damacio participates in a ritualistic dance, the *Nguillatun* ceremony, in which men imitate ostriches to bring rain. Rather than dwell on this ceremony at length for its unusual features, Preloran told *El Cronista*, he elects to treat it as one facet of Araucanian life: "In my film on Ruca Choroy, that is fifty-two minutes long, I only dedicate four minutes to the *Nguillatun*. That's the importance that I give it in the whole, within a year's cycle. [I do] not blow it up out of proportion, because it's the one 'exotic' feature of their culture." Preloran's approach is thus quite unlike that used by some ethnodocumentary filmmakers who make films that emphasize behaviors that appear primitive or exotic to western audiences.

Preloran does share much in common with Flaherty in his stress on the relationships between humans and their environments. He focuses on what he calls "folk pockets," areas in which Indian culture blended with the Spanish colonizers and became Creole. Preloran sees these cultures as ones that have often been cut off from urban areas and therefore have maintained their traditions. Although *Quilino* and *Valle Fertil* show the effects of increased communication between areas in Argentina, Preloran does not lament the changes; he serves to document their effects as felt by the people experiencing them. Likewise, the problems of living in seemingly hostile regions, such as the cold and harsh Andes and the windswept pampas, are presented as factors to be reckoned with by rural communities.

In *Araucanians,* Preloran brings the summer season and its beauty to the screen with his excellent camera work. Looming over the mountain dwellers are the prospects of winter and the need to prepare for the snowfalls of April. Preloran, like Flaherty, depicts the struggle for survival against the forces of nature. Despite this reliance on an environmental theme, Preloran structures his sequences to communicate events of significance to the individuals in the communities depicted.

> I'm more than aware of my responsibility. First of all, I believe that I make films for the people that I shoot. For *them,* to help them better their plight and those in their situation. To give them a means to communicate their truths to us. So I must be very careful that I don't give an erroneous image. . . .
>
> I consider the greatest problem in this type of film to be the transition of the sequences, to achieve a good continuity with such diverse footage one comes back with. That within all this variety we can have a perfect fitting and a logical development. These transitions can be through visuals, or sounds, or through what is said on the track.

Preloran uses transitions to convey the spirit of the community. Likewise, in *Hopi: Songs of the Fourth World* (1983), filmmaker Pat Ferrero uses images of corn as transitions and symbols of the spirit of the Hopi. The film opens and closes with a tale spun by Spider Grandmother, who speaks of the emergence of the people into the fourth world. The first three were destroyed because the people became corrupt and greedy. (Viewers familiar with the ancient myths of the Sumerians, Babylonians, Israelites, and Greeks will most likely think of a similar tale of the destruction and rebirth of the earth after the Flood.) Today, for the Hopi, myth has prophesied the events of the fourth world, a world they must keep in balance for us all. Ferrero inserts NASA footage of

2.11 Howard and Zelma Honyuma bring roasting ears home to shuck. Location photo taken while filming *Hopi: Songs of the Fourth World*. Ferrero Films

the manned lunar module with its report, "The eagle has landed." The Hopi, who have a myth about the eagle in their own belief system, have expected this event or, at least, are not surprised by it.

Ferrero has singer Ronnie Gilbert (of the Weavers) narrate the film. Her voice works well. The Hopi are matrilineal and matrilocal, and Ferrero places an emphasis on women in all her films. The corn is a metaphor for the female and fertility. Like the people, corn has emerged from the earth. Ferrero follows the planting, nurturing, harvesting, and storing of the corn and shows the empty lifeless stalks left at the end of the season. The corn will be planted again from its seeds and the process will be repeated like the seasons of the earth and the human cycle of birth, death, and renewal. The Hopi say, "We are the corn." Ferrero uses the growing of the corn to structure the film. The Hopi sing to the corn and have songs and chants that relate stories, and the soundtrack is a beautiful blend of the wind and song. Like all the visuals, the colors of the corn, which represent the cardinal directions and the races of the peoples of the earth, stand out with startling clarity.

The film presents both Hopi daily life and art. A farmer, a religious elder, and a grandmother talk about the Hopi way of life, as do a painter, a potter, and a weaver. World-renowned potter Nampeyo has introduced ancient designs unknown to contemporary Hopi until they were unearthed during an archaeological excavation. She imparted these designs to her daughter and grand-daughters, reviving pottery as an art form. Women are known for their pottery and their basketry; men are the weavers and carvers of katchina dolls. Ferrero paints a broad picture by covering such topics as the piki grinding stones (a foodways item considered heirlooms for the next generation), contact with Euro-Americans, the use of clowns, the ceremonies and songs for rain in this dry land, and the meaning of women's hairstyles presented in a series of stills. Although Ferrero documents the katchina dolls, she does not include coverage of the ceremonies in which katchina spirits arrive and give blessings to the people because she did not want to destroy the relationship she had with the people by showing that which they did not wish to share with outsiders (Ferrero 1993).

Ferrero has created an extensive guide, *Hopi: Songs of the Fourth World, a Resource Handbook* (1986), which contains scholarly articles on Hopi society, corn, linguistics, songs, and the environmental ethos of the Hopi, as well as essays about the film itself. Capturing the essence of another culture on film is a difficult task. Ferrero made extensive use of Hopi consultants and experts. Her key collaborator was the film's Hopi narrator, Emory Sekaquaptewa, and the film has been extremely well received by Hopi (Ferrero 1993). The visual brilliancy of the images of Hopi life in this region sparkle on film. Ferrero matches the pacing of the film with the growing of the corn, leaving viewers with an image of the corn whose leaves wave slowly in the wind that blows across the arid Southwest.

Far from the leisurely pace in *Hopi*, the films of Les Blank often have a kaleidoscopic feel. In his community-oriented films, Blank sometimes bombards the viewer with an abundance of scenes. Whereas Preloran prefers to document craftsmen, Blank often explores the lives of regional musicians. Both filmmakers are also concerned with folklife in general, and neither man uses narration. Unlike Preloran's use of nonsync for many of his films, Blank uses sync-sound in addition to sound-over and his films thus have a *vérité* quality that the majority of Preloran's films lack.

*Spend It All* (1970), Blank's first film on the Cajuns of the Louisiana Bayou, features the Balfa Brothers, Nathan Abshire, and Marc Savoy, well-known white Cajun musicians. The film opens with titles that detail how the English moved into Nova Scotia and forced the Acadians to leave. The Acadians then settled in the bayou country where, Blank tells us, they remained isolated for two hundred years. Despite the recent influx of radio, television, and oil companies, Blank notes the people have retained their Cajun lifestyle. This Flaherty-like romanticism permeates the film, which intercuts idyllic shots of wildlife and watery reflections of the bayou with scenes of Cajun life.

At a horse race, Blank asks a spectator if Cajun life is all about having fun. The reply to this leading question is affirmative; they work to make money to

2.12 Alphonse "Bois Sec" Ardoin converses with his family in *Dry Wood*. Les Blank, Flower Films

spend it all having fun. Blank shows the Cajuns clam fishing, making shingles, preparing tobacco, and slaughtering a hog. In one sequence, as Savoy makes an accordion in his shop, he comments that living in New York would be like prison. Blank's romanticization of the virtues of rural living continues as another laments how today the dollar is too important. Blank deals mostly with familiar traditional activities, giving us shots of gravestone art, dancing, musical performances, picnics, and food preparation. We see a man "treating by hand"—holding his finger in a woman's mouth—and in another scene, a man extracts his own tooth with pliers while the band plays in the background. Dewey Balfa, shown driving a school bus, explains in voice-over that he also sells insurance and plays music on the weekends. The extremely well recorded soundtrack holds the film together, but the individual scenes, though professional in quality, are only superficially connected.

Blank used the same approach for his companion films, *Dry Wood* (1973) and *Hot Pepper* (1973), both about black Cajuns. *Dry Wood* features accordion music by "Bois Sec" (Dry Wood) Ardoin, his sons, and fiddler Canray Fontenot. The film begins with costumed dancers and a chicken slaughtered at a Mardi Gras celebration. Children observe the adults. Using the sound advance of a bell ringing as a transition, the visuals cut to a church service on Ash Wednesday, the day following the carnival, and "Kumbaya" is sung. Men then irrigate a field. At this point, the film fragments into seemingly unrelated sequences. Blank asks Fontenot how he made his first fiddle, and Fontenot

2.13  Clifton Chenier, *Hot Pepper*. Photo by Edmund Shea

responds that he made it from a cigar box. Shots follow of log preparation, a man operating a tractor, children walking, and a group playing baseball. The musical soundtrack emphasizes the rhythms of these activities. A woman describes her home life and the chores of working the garden, feeding the hogs, and tending children. Youngsters catch crayfish and play basketball, men seed the fields, and the sprouts come up.

In a long sequence, men eat a chicken (presumably the one being prepared earlier), dance to fiddle music, get drunk, and have a mock battle. Blank allows the scene to continue past the point of interest in the camaraderie into the base aspects of a party of sloppily drunk men. The film depicts the slaughter and dressing of a hog, including making cracklings and hogshead cheese by the women. In the final sequence, a woman chastises a man: "Every time we slaughter a hog, you get drunk and I work, you bastard." One woman says that life is now too fast; records and television are partially to blame. She also notes that women and children are placed together on holidays while the men drink and that "there's no jobs; nothing to do. They're leaving one by one."

Blank never shows the reasons for his inclusion of the final comment. Unlike Preloran and Cohen, who visually portray the causes of unemployment within the communities they film, Blank allows one woman's statement to convey this message. Whereas Preloran prefers to show any ceremonial behavior, such as the *Nguillatun,* within the framework of everyday activities, Blank focuses on the spectacular—treating the Mardi Gras with its capture and slaughter of a chicken, the drinking party, and hog butchering at length. Daily activities appear, but only briefly and in random order. In both *Spend It All* and *Dry Wood,* Blank is enthralled by blood, food, drink, and rowdy behavior, and he implies that these are at the center of Cajun culture.

*Hot Pepper,* which Blank considers the companion film to *Dry Wood,* portrays Clifton Chenier, the "zydeco accordion king," performing in various settings with his brother Cleveland on rub-board and with his blues band. Filmed mainly in Lafayette, Louisiana, *Hot Pepper* opens with street scenes and cuts to Chenier performing for dancers in a bar. After shots of people on the railroad tracks, men hoeing, and other work activities, we see men lining track. Tracking shots follow Chenier and his band traveling on the road, and the band plays at a club. Blank makes apparent Chenier's family connections with accordion music as Chenier visits with his cousin, who also plays accordion. Their instruments differ: Chenier's is amplified for zydeco, a form of music evolved from Cajun styles to one with a heavy African beat also heard in the Caribbean Islands; Carleton King, Chenier's cousin, plays a push button accordion. Chenier and King sit on a porch playing music and drinking.

The film shifts to an interview with a woman who addresses the camera about racially mixed marriages. Blank cuts back and forth from the jam session to discussions with a barber and other townspeople on the lessening of tension between the races. A scene of Chenier prompting his 108-year-old grandmother to agree that life was different when she was a girl is tedious. After much badgering, the partially deaf woman says yes, things have changed. This sequence and shots of the countryside, sunsets, geese flying, and a piece of wood floating in the water to the sound-over track of Chenier's music serve no apparent purpose other than to romanticize a rural lifestyle.

Chenier sings a song about his mother, who died before she heard it, which provides additional insight into Chenier's family relationships. Blank visually illustrates some of Chenier's songs; that is, while Chenier plays "I'm a Hog for You, Baby" in a club, Blank intercuts shots of hogs being chased and slaughtered. A female faith healer discusses conjuring and reads a letter from the mother of a cured boy. Blank emphasizes the words of the letter by titling them in capitals that are zoomed out to fill the screen. This technique once again demonstrates Blank's focus on the unusual.

*Hot Pepper* is basically a document about Clifton Chenier and the people of Lafayette. Both *Dry Wood* and *Hot Pepper* show differences in rural and urban traditions of black Cajuns, as well as differences in musical styles, but each film could easily be viewed independently. They are not sequential. *Hot*

*Pepper,* despite its focus on one musician, lacks information about Chenier's offstage life, other than the visits with his cousin and grandmother. Where Chenier lives, what his house is like, whether or not he has a wife or girlfriend, and how his home life influences his professional life—such questions are left unanswered. Hence, *Hot Pepper* is more about the community than it is about Chenier, although his music links the action together. *Spend It All, Dry Wood,* and *Hot Pepper* would be visually disconnected without the music tracks. Blank uses both sync-sound and montage. His style lacks the long dramatic linear buildup seen in the cinéma vérité films of Pennebaker, Leacock, and the Maysles brothers, and instead becomes a documentary forerunner of a postvérité mode that mixes a number of styles.

In *Chulas Fronteras* (1976) Blank once again investigates regional music. As with the Cajun film series, he uses subtitles to translate conversations and song titles. *Dry Wood* and *Hot Pepper* were partially funded by Chris Strachwitz of Arhoolie Records and John A. Lomax Jr., but were projects initiated by Blank. *Chulas Fronteras* was conceived and produced by Strachwitz, well known for his recordings of folk music. He became fascinated with *Norteña* musical traditions of *Tecano* (Texas-Mexican) performers and issued recordings of some of the better-known musicians in the border region. Strachwitz then teamed with Blank to make the film.

The film opens with a *corrido* on the soundtrack, a map of the Rio Grande and Bravo River, and a float with an automobile and group of men being manually pulled over the river. Using music as his primary cohesive force, Blank introduces José Morante, who discusses how German polkas and *Norteña* music both draw heavily on push button accordion. The film features Los Alegres de Teran, Rumel Fuentes with Los Pinguinos del Norte, Santiago Jimenez, Flaco Jimenez, Narciso Martinez, and Lydia Mendoza. Blank lingers on a wedding and an anniversary celebration to reveal aspects of community life.

The film devotes a long sequence to Lydia Mendoza. Photos of her as a girl playing mandolin with her parents in 1927 give way to a scene in which she prepares tamales at home. Stills depict her in different performance situations. A live performance in a club follows, intercut with her telling the camera how she feels about the songs she sings. Obviously, Mendoza has acquired a large following over the years, and Blank's use of old photographs indicates her importance.

Willie Lopez, a local disc jockey, plays a *corrido* about the melon strike of 1967. The lyrics lead to scenes of farmworkers in the fields and packing houses. We hear songs about Connelly, César Chavez, and the Texas Rangers, and Lopez discusses discrimination against Mexicans. A car blessing segment and old photos of men leaving to work in Louisiana, Indiana, and Chicago visually express the content of the songs. At one point, Rumel Fuentes considers why

2.14  Lydia Mendoza, *Chulas Fronteras*

children leave school to work in the fields and learn to drive trucks. We then see him playing "Chicano" with his band and the visuals shift to a cockfight.

The owner of the Del Bravo record shop, who is also a songwriter and recording artist, tapes a record in his studio and makes the actual pressings and labels. A band at a dance plays a song about not having the proper licenses to cross the border or drive a car. The film also emphasizes the continuity of musical traditions. Eugenio Abrego explains that he learned to play from his father, and Blank shows him playing with his band, Los Alegres de Teran.

Strachwitz's insistence on featuring certain musicians obviously determined what Blank would shoot, but the cockfight, a barbecue, and the preparation of hogshead tamales display Blank's usual style of combining blood, food, and music and presenting them as outstanding community features. Few interactions occur. Despite the use of sync-sound for certain portions of the film, most of the long segments have sound-over music. No one is fully characterized, and thus Blank structures the film as an overview of border life. Without the music, the film might not hold an audience for the entire sixty minutes. The soundtrack is available from Arhoolie (LP 3005), and with liner notes the record may be more informative than the film. A brochure that discusses the performers is most helpful for determining their importance, but for those viewers with a limited background in *Norteña* music and border life, the film does not offer enough information to create a sufficient understanding of the material. Local record manufacture, the fieldworkers' situation

2.15 Lloyd John Harris at the Gilroy Garlic Festival in *Garlic Is as Good as Ten Mothers.* Photo by Ann Ashley. Les Blank, Flower Films

conveyed in regional music, and the importance of song lyrics as a reflection of regional concerns are subjects Blank presents well in *Chulas Fronteras.*

Mexican music as well as Cajun, French, Flamenco, Italian, and Moroccan fill the soundtrack of Les Blank's *Garlic Is as Good as Ten Mothers* (1980). Blank tours a community bound together by its love of garlic—from harvesting and processing it to preparing, serving, eating, and ultimately celebrating it. Various people introduce this foodways subject by addressing the camera about how they use garlic for taste and health. Blank begins in his own backyard[13] at Flint's Bar-B-Que, a restaurant in Berkeley, California, where meat is prepared as a song about barbecue is heard. A man tells a story about eating garlic and tomato sandwiches after the Spanish Civil War. Lloyd John Harris, founder of Lovers of the Stinking Rose (a fan club for garlic lovers) and author of *The Book of Garlic*, explains the appeal of garlic as Americans look for their "folk roots."

A scene in which piglets suckle from a sow who has eaten garlic has the subtitle "These little piggies say, 'Oink, Oink, Oink' (pure garlic milk)!" Following a segment on the restaurant Chez Panisse, dead pigs appear with the subtitle, "These little piggies say, 'When you're dead, you're done. Long live the living!'" For me, these scenes are awkward at best. They are similar to Blank's early films, where the ordinary has a bizarre twist placed upon it. Imposing his own humor on the film, Blank's Gardner-like presupposition results in a pat cuteness.

A potpourri of garlic-oriented topics parade across the screen. Blank cuts to the Balfa Brothers, well-known Cajun musicians seen in his other films, playing at a garlic festival while garlic is chopped and the pigs are stuffed with garlic mixture. At Chez Panisse, cook Alice Waters says she made all the dishes with garlic one day a year and it became a tradition. People wanted more and more garlic. Lloyd Harris discusses California as a garlic growing center. Many elements combined in Berkeley: health food, herbalism, folk medicine, organic growing, and gourmet cooking. He found himself "in the middle of it." Les travels in a car with filmmaker Werner Herzog and asks him about his film *Nosferatu* and the use of garlic for warding off vampires, which leads to an insiders' discussion about the trick eye movement created by rapidly cutting a film. Andalusian Gypsy Anzonini del Puerto sings about bulls, and the visuals of his performance are intercut with him mashing garlic and making sausage. At a Hunan restaurant, Blank presents the entire process of stirfrying a meal. Pesto making at an Italian restaurant follows. By now, viewers who like garlic will be salivating and all vampires will have left the theater.

A somewhat awkward scene has an interviewer at a park asking children if they like garlic. Do they like its smell? They respond negatively. Blank cuts to reveal the true purpose of the segment—a spoof on a Signal mouthwash commercial advertising a way to fight the smell of garlic. A reverse message on a sign behind La Vieille Maison in Truckee, California, reads "Fight mouthwash, eat garlic." Robert Charles declares that women who rubbed garlic on their bodies had beautiful suntans and mosquitoes didn't bite them. "Italian marijuana," a cook says as he adds garlic to squid at the Gilroy Garlic Festival, where people wear T-shirts about garlic and belly dancers wear garlic chains.

A historical film spoof segment proclaims that garlic is ancient; it was mentioned in Genesis and eaten during the building of the Great Pyramids of Egypt. A mock scholarly narrator's voice accompanies a map with garlic appearing, tracing its route much like a World War II film map would do. Here the humor works well, and Blank's use of visuals and knowledge of film styles

2.16 Les Blank filming Dick Pilar during the Polkabration at Ocean Beach in New London, Connecticut, for *In Heaven There Is No Beer?* Maureen Gosling, wearing headphones, records the sound, and Chris Simon sits on the curb interviewing.

adds to his upbeat approach. The narrator includes such fascinating trivia as the fact that Eleanor Roosevelt daily ate three cloves of garlic dipped in chocolate.

The medicinal and beauty uses of garlic are touted and the fear that processing will increase is expressed as Blank turns to a scene of harvesting the garlic in the fields. He follows the workers rapidly cutting the cloves from the plant, chucking them into a bucket and then into sacks—showing the entire process all the way to the processing plant where the garlic is sorted and trimmed. A freeze-frame allows Blank to insert his own message directly via a subtitle inside an outlined eagle symbolizing the workers' union: "Support the people who grow the food we eat."

Various shots of garlic being drawn, mixed, and cooked are intercut with the end titles. Basically a tribute to garlic, the film covers every imaginable use. The focus on one food item gives the film its vignette and spliced-together quality; when it presents the garlic lovers as communities of food aficionados, it lingers in a linear style. Grower Warren Weber, chef Alice Waters, author Lloyd John Harris, Chez Panisse, and the Gilroy Garlic Festival enjoy ample coverage. As is true for all of Les Blank's films, the music carries the viewer easily from one scene to the next—a reminder of the importance of audio transitions.

Musical transitions and food also play a role in Blank's tribute to the polka, *In Heaven There Is No Beer?* (1984). The title is taken from a scene in which a man comments that one should drink beer while one can. Behind him a sign reads, "In Heaven there is no beer, so we better drink it here." Blank follows polka celebrations across the country. He begins with the Polkabration. What began in 1964 as one day of polka bands later became a weekend and then a whole vacation, a musician explains. Since then, polka festivals have sprung up across America. A montage of festival announcements underscores this statement. The film moves from the Polka Fireworks at Seven Springs Resort in Champion, Pennsylvania, where huge crowds eat, drink, and dance, to the International Polka Association banquet, and to a polka Mass at which a band plays while the priest gives communion. Obviously, "polka power," as orchestra leader Jimmy Stuhr calls it, is everywhere. People laud the polka as healthy exercise. One man reports that people can use music instead of drugs. As he did in *Garlic Is as Good as Ten Mothers*, Blank addresses the issues of function and provides a historical framework for the viewer, smoothly moving from one scene to the next by association. A musicologist notes the development of polka in southern Poland and Czechoslovakia. Today, he states, the polka is an American phenomenon identified with Polish Americans; it doesn't really exist in Europe anymore.

A segment follows that emphasizes the Catholicism of the Polish Americans and depicts decorated Easter eggs, stained glass, and Polish sheet music. The sheet music serves as the next transition to music store owners who recall Polish immigrants coming in to listen to the music and meeting each other. This account leads to a wedding in Stevens Point, Wisconsin. Thus, Blank manages to take us along scene by scene from dances and fund-raisers and band after band. In his Hitchcock-like manner, Blank appears to throw a ball at a dunk-the-girl-in-the-water game at the fund-raiser. The Polka Star Dancers of Staten Island explain how important it is to belong to an ethnic group. Their words are contrasted with a remark made in Connecticut that people of any ethnic background may dance the polka.

The acting out of music, evident in many of Blank's films, appears here as the film covers the popularity of Walt Solek's hit, "Who Stole the Kiszka?" Another popular song, "The Beer Barrel Polka," is presented, and album covers show the popularity of polka recordings. A man comments in sound-over that today young musicians have taken up the tradition, and we see a young female band whose leader wins an award at the International Polka Association annual banquet.

In one scene the camera tilts up a young woman's body at a swimming pool polka party, revealing the sexism that plagues some of Blank's early work. Later, the camera watches the buttocks of the girl in the staged kiszka segment as she runs off with the kiszka. Although the editor and the collaborating folk-lorist on this and other productions are female, such sexist shots detract from the films.

The following shot is an example of what Blank does best. He places us at the scene with a good overview shot of the whole party, the pool, and people dancing. A woman notes that polka fills a need; it gives one a sense of identity. Others contrast polka with rock and wish polka could be everywhere. Blank's film convinces viewers that polka *is* everywhere.

Despite its drawbacks, *In Heaven There Is No Beer?* provides a functional analysis of polka as celebration and develops the role of polka in building a sense of community. Obviously, polka dancers are a folk group as are Polish Americans. But the film shows so many bands and dances that connecting emotionally with any of them is difficult (unless, perhaps, the viewers are polka dancers or musicians). Maybe such is always the case. The perspective of the viewer will determine his or her connection with the topic (for example, I have folklorist friends who adore this film and who are polka enthusiasts). Never-theless, many films whose topics are not a part of our experience enlighten and provoke us. Certainly Blank's *Yum, Yum, Yum!* (1990) makes me feel like a Cajun (which I am not), and *Marc and Ann* (1991) places me in their family. Here Blank is carried away by the proliferation of polka music in America, but, like any other folklore activity, how many examples of traditional behaviors do you need to prove they exist?

Blank keeps the focus on music, but returns to Louisiana for *J'ai Été au Bal (I Went to the Dance): The Cajun and Zydeco Music of Louisiana* (1989). Nar-rated by folklorist Barry Jean Ancelet and Michael Doucet, the film includes such musical greats as accordion players Bois Sec Ardoin, Marc Savoy, and Nathan Abshire, as well as the Balfa Brothers, Paul Daigle, and Clifton Che-nier. The film follows the evolution of musical styles and instrument use and covers both black and white musical developments. The differences in how Cajun music is played on fiddle and accordian are explained by Marc Savoy, who notes that the accordion is indestructible and loud enough for parties where a fiddle would not be heard. As Marc and Ann Savoy play together in a scene intercut with farm animals (most likely on their own farm), Blank shifts to the first couple to record a Cajun song in Lafayette, Louisiana, in 1928. The historical roots of the music and major musical events are well cov-ered with Ancelet talking to the camera about the influence of country music on Cajun music and the return to the Cajun style after World War II by sol-diers who wanted to hear this music in the dance halls.

Zydeco music parallels Cajun in its blend of French and African music, but with a heavier emphasis on African blues and French musical styles. Clifton Chenier revived the old styles and made the innovations that created zydeco.

2.17  Vintage photo of Joe and Cleoma Falcon, the first Cajun recording artists, from *J'ai Été Au Bal.*

After the mid-1950s and 1960s, Cajun music rose in popularity as the sons of Cajun musicians were influenced by rock 'n' roll and created swamp rock. Folk festivals added to the notoriety of the musicians who were encouraged by scholars Ralph Rinzler and Harry Oster to come to Newport where they played to standing ovations next to Joan Baez and Bob Dylan and other national folksong revival figures. Blank skillfully blends the tale with archival footage and stills, and the heirs to the music speak of the inspiration they gained from the festivals and the previous generation. Paul Daigle, for example, recounts his uncle's influence. Many talk of how they learned by watching others. Rare recordings and live performances make this film a treat for lovers of Cajun music. Blank artfully emphasizes the role of folk music in strengthening ethnic identity, and vice versa. The film was inspired by Ann Savoy's book, *Cajun Music: A Reflection of a People* (1988), and the film demonstrates that reflection by blending the music with the dances, history, and visions of Louisiana.

Les Blank's later work, *Yum, Yum, Yum! A Taste of the Cajun and Creole Cooking of Louisiana*, is an overview of the gastronomical delights of the Cajun and Creole communities in Louisiana. Les Blank went to school at Tulane in

New Orleans, and Louisiana culture has figured prominently in his work. Although he usually deals with music as his primary topic (with food seen enticingly in the background), Blank reverses the emphasis for *Yum, Yum, Yum*. In this film, Blank shares equal billing as producer with editor Maureen Gosling. The film covers the actual process of making a number of dishes. It opens with Marc Savoy, who has served as Blank's star informant in several films. Marc prepares goo courtbouillon and the film documents the process, beginning with purchasing a fifteen-pound fish and preparing kindling. He and his friends talk about how they learned to cook by watching, and the idea of traditional foodways is highlighted.

An off-camera voice asks if they have heard of Paul Prudhomme. When they reply that they have not, the film shifts to Prudhomme signing a copy of *Chef Paul Prudhomme's Louisiana Cookbook* at his restaurant in New Orleans. Prudhomme says he learned to cook from his family. "Everybody approaches their cooking with a lot of passion." This passion is demonstrated in the kitchen where food is tossed in frying pans, shaken, flipped, and poured to a musical accompaniment.

The idea of tradition is again reinforced by Savoy, who talks about cooking and playing the accordion. Savoy states that he is not opposed to changing recipes or songs, but he adds, "If you really love it, you're going to try to do it just like the person you heard it or tasted it. You'll do it, just like it. To me, when you really love something for what it is, you leave it alone." Savoy is more than aware of his role as a "tradition bearer," having appeared in so many of Blank's films and played at folk festivals, and he has become known outside his small town of Eunice, Louisiana, as a result of such exposure.

Margaret Chenier, widow of musician Clifton Chenier, talks about using real ingredients. She prepares "dirty rice," and describes the recipes she learned from her mother. A song in sound-over about biscuits leads to Chenier's narrative about making small biscuits. Queen Ida, a San Francisco zydeco musician from a Louisiana family, prepares okra étoufée with shrimp and responds to a question about why French people never cook in small quantities: "In case you have company." Back in Louisiana, Ann Savoy discusses the making of roux, the seasonings, and the number of pots needed—one for the main dish and one for rice. Cooking roux "is elusive"; "it's a feel." Marc prepares crawfish étoufée and other delicacies, and he presents a number of recipes.

For Blank, what ties these people together is food and culture. Where the food is caught is important, as are the narratives and recipes. At Holly Beach—the "Cajun Riviera" in Hackberry, Louisiana—Marc and Ann Savoy and their children sing about crabbing, catch crabs, and cook them. Les asks, off-camera, "What do you think about the popularity of Cajun music and food all over the world these days?" Marc says it is about time for this global recog-

2.18 Queen Ida, *Yum, Yum, Yum!* Photo by Irene Young

nition, but also laments that most people think it "has to do with a lot of pepper." Other scenes include the making of hot boudin (a sausage with rice in it) as a song about it plays. The preparation of tongue and a meal eaten by the crew with the Savoys at Marc's home emphasizes the freshness of the food.

This film has a number of interactive moments. Although Blank is only seen briefly on-camera, those interviewed address him and the crew directly and we hear the questions. Sometimes the interviewed and interviewer switch roles, indicating the camaraderie established by fieldwork situations. Marc: "Les, know what's better than a bowl of gumbo?" Les: "What?" Marc: "Two bowls." Blank is good at breaking down the "fourth wall" between the film and the audience. He shows us Marc Savoy's humor and gives the viewer a genuine feel for Savoy's life as a cook. Blank covers the foodways of Cajun and Creole Louisiana, including the music it inspires and the function such food has for those who cook it and find it to be a source of identity.

Blank continues his emphasis on music in *Živeli: Medicine for the Heart* (1987), a collaborative film made with anthropologist Andrei Simic in association with the Center for Visual Arts at the University of Southern California. Like Jill Godmilow's film *The Popovich Brothers of South Chicago* (1978), Blank and Simic examine the importance of music and ethnic traditions for the Serbian American community. Godmilow limits her coverage to Chicago; Blank and Simic cover northern California and Chicago. Godmilow begins with a fiftieth anniversary party held for the Popovich Brothers. She intersperses formal concerts with local Serbian gatherings to demonstrate the significance of the brothers' music. Newspaper clippings and interviews with Serbian Americans point out how individuals maintain cultural identity within a multicultural milieu. In *Živeli,* Simic accomplishes this point by noting in his narration that one could be Serbian and American at the same time.

The immigration experience and the role of music and the church are underscored by Simic's narration, combined with the comments of the people; Godmilow allows them to talk about their history, the church, and the changes in the music and culture. Interviews with the Popovich Brothers, who are in both films, figure prominently. Godmilow uses still photos and conversations with family members to characterize the link felt by the third and fourth generations. While she was shooting, one of the brothers died, as did the father, and a brother indicates that the Popovich Brothers may not continue to perform. The close-knit relationships and the strength of music as an expression of ethnicity demonstrate that the music will endure. Likewise, in Blank and Simic's film, various tamburitza groups demonstrate the continuous force of the music. These two films contain much of the same material, although Godmilow moves out from one family to describe the culture, and Simic looks at the culture as a whole. After seeing these films, one would certainly agree with

2.19 *Živeli: Medicine for the Heart.* Photo by Chris Simon

Teddy Popovich's comment, "That's what it's all about—tradition." Comparatively, *Živeli* lacks the emotional quality Godmilow achieves. She includes the same data—the religion, the occupational experience of the first generation that worked in the mines, the immigration process, songs, and urban lifestyle—but does so without a scholar-narrator. She also focuses squarely on one family, which allows viewers to identify as insiders.

Many scenes are extremely similar, which shows how accurate both films are. Music carries each. Blank's film is certainly more ambitious about the icons, slava, food, and how exactly the music has changed. These details make the film rich but cause the viewer to relate to the people as an outsider. By combining music, religion, and food with ethnicity to portray the Serbian Americans, Blank and Simic look at culture in a large frame.

Like Blank and Simic, filmmaker Paul Wagner and folklorist Marjorie Hunt also look at a community for *The Stone Carvers* (1985), but restrict their portrayal to a small group, the carvers of the National Cathedral in Washington, D.C.[14] In this film, which won the 1985 Academy Award for Outstanding Short Documentary, Wagner and Hunt demonstrate the importance of the connection between ethnicity, folk art, occupation, and family. As is true for much of Wagner's film work, the fieldwork of a folklorist generated the idea for the film. Marjorie Hunt brought the carvers to the 1978 Festival of American Folklife and later worked with Wagner to obtain funding for a film.

Although the film tends to focus in great depth on master carver Vincent Palumbo, it includes the reminiscences of other carvers gathered for a reunion, an event focal point Wagner also used for *Miles of Smiles* and *Free Show Tonite* (1983). Here, however, the reunion is a meeting for lunch rather than a formal event.

The film opens with Palumbo breaking open an apple with his hands: "You can do this if you have the carver's hands." Immediately, viewers know that this carver is a different breed of worker, one with a sense of humor who draws us into the film effortlessly through Wagner's placement of this shot as the introduction. Palumbo's life story is told in both sound-over and sync-sound as he carves an arm for Frederick Hart's sculpture *Creation*. Palumbo was born in Italy, a fifth-generation stone carver since the age of nine. He describes the learning process and how he improved his skills through competition with the other carvers. The film stresses how traditional art is learned informally through imitation within a known community's sense of values; such art reinforces and validates cultural and familial norms. Today, Palumbo notes, few apprentices join the trade: "I'm one of the last traditional stone carvers left."

The filmmakers demonstrate the difference between "free hand" and "working the model." To work the model, the carver must reverse the sculptor's process of adding clay by subtracting stone. The carver creates the figure by reproducing another's work exactly. In free hand, he may do as he pleases, and the gargoyles and grotesques surrounding the towers of the cathedral are often renditions that the carvers have made of each other. "In a building like this, you have so much freedom," Palumbo remarks. As Palumbo talks about the men who worked on the cathedral and the songs that they sang to "make more production," stills detail the building of the cathedral, beginning in 1907. "It was not work . . . just everyday living."

A cut to the lunchtime reunion with a small group of men joking and telling tales (as Italian music plays on the audio track) is intercut with Palumbo carving an arm, a process shown from beginning to end. He points out the ways one learns to recognize the cracks and veins of the stone from their sounds. Retired carver Roger Morigi recounts starting to carve at the age of eleven, when the cathedral was full of workers. One time, he broke a lily he was carving. His boss told him to take the lily home and "smell it good" every morning. Another talks about how carvers "steal" from each other by watching their techniques to develop their own personal styles. Morigi tells a tale of master carver Scafaro, who had broken-up tools but always had the right one for particular jobs. Morigi borrowed a tool and forgot to return it. Scafaro was not angry: "It makes my heart feel so good . . . to see you make good work, [to be] so interested." These tales reveal much about the methods of acquiring occupational skills.

Another segment reviews the antiquity of carving as one man notes that it is the second oldest profession after prostitution and that the Ten Commandments illustrate carving's great significance. Stills trace carving through the ages and then detail the great buildings in the nation's capital. The men lament that modern buildings have little carving and that "carving is going to be like the carrier pigeon." In fact, the film proves just the opposite. The Italian carvers are using a form popular in Italy since before the time of Leonardo da Vinci. Although it may not endure in America, it may do so in Europe and other forms will emerge to take its place. One need only think of something as different and yet as similar as chainsaw carving where a form is released from the wood much like Palumbo releases the arm from the stone. The film demonstrates folklore as a process that is ongoing. The cathedral will be completed (it was finished in 1990), but other work will take its place. The scale of the work and numbers of workers may never be quite the same. That is true of all occupational and folk art; it changes because people change and new forms of creativity emerge from those that preceded them.

The grotesques and gargoyles guarantee a kind of immortality. As Morigi and Palumbo walk around the cathedral, they discuss the significance of their work. Even after they grow old, they can look at the cathedral as their monument. "It was my life," Morigi concludes.

*The Stone Carvers* has an intimacy because it documents not just an end product but a process. It presents personalities, ideas about individual creativity, the importance of ethnicity, and the notion of how folklore changes through time to meet new demands. One need only compare it with *Washington National Cathedral* (1993), a piece produced on the cathedral after its completion that focuses on the building's history and architectural style. Like *The Stone Carvers*, it uses stills and music, but its interviews with architects and those who served as head of the cathedral, as well as its use of a narrator (George Page), lack the lively quality achieved in Hunt and Wagner's work. It does look at the carvers, but only briefly. When it does so, the film takes on a sparkle that it otherwise lacks. *The Stone Carvers* is a remarkable film that blends folk art and narrative within the framework of family and ethnic occupational folklore. In presenting one small group of artists, it speaks to the artistic process on a grand scale.

With no reference to occupation, religion, ethnicity—all the usual folk identifiers—in *Gap-Toothed Women* (1987), Les Blank, Maureen Gosling, folklorist Chris Simon, and Susan Kell take on the folklore of gendered beauty. The filmmakers interviewed one hundred gap-toothed women who ranged in age from eighteen months to eighty-eight years to ask them if having a space between their front teeth made a difference in their lives. Those viewers without a gap will be surprised to discover its significance. The filmmakers open

2.20 Master stone carver Roger Morigi discusses the gargoyle that represents him on the Washington National Cathedral in *The Stone Carvers*. Photo by Larry Albee

2.21 Carrie Lauer in *Gap-Toothed Women*. Photo by Chris Simon

with close-ups of mouths and comments about dentists wanting to close the gap, the beliefs many cultures have about such gaps, and a scholarly analysis of Chaucer's Wife of Bath as both lecherous and amorous. Cleopatra and Saskia (Rembrandt's wife and favorite model) are other famous women known to have had gapped teeth.

Women's beauty standards, the filmmakers demonstrate, are based on magazines and popular culture. In an interview, Lauren Hutton indicates how she made the image of the gap-toothed woman acceptable by becoming a successful model. Cartoonist Dori Seda says that straight-teethed women let life happen to them. Those with gaps have to *do* something: "If I had nice straight teeth, I might never have done anything." Stories follow of women who do things, such as drive a truck. One is making a Super 8mm film of women waxing off their body hair. At first, viewers might wonder if the film is moving away from the topic, but a quick second thought makes them realize that this issue also addresses what beauty is. Supreme Court Justice Sandra Day O'Connor, another gap-toothed woman, appears in a clip from her address to the Salvation Army. Belly dancer Sharlyn Sawyer, who had leukemia, says a gap is not important in the grand scheme of things. The forty women who appear in this film do comprise a "community" that scholars don't often study. These women talked about acknowledging their gaps when they would meet other gap-toothed women. Narrated entirely by the women themselves, the film explores the feminist issue of beauty and reminds viewers that the "folk," in Alan Dundes's terms, need only share one common factor (1965:2). These women share two: their gender and the pattern of their teeth.

*Quilts in Women's Lives* (1980) comprises six portraits of female quilters. Pat Ferrero draws on the quilt as a feminist metaphor for the artistry of women's lives. As Blank did for *Gap-Toothed Women*, Ferrero uses the voices of women and concentrates on gender. That the quilts themselves are not Ferrero's main interest is evident in the way that she constructs the film. Rather than concentrate on quilts and their designs as artifacts by showing the myriad patterns of quilts, Ferrero lingers with each woman to uncover the meaning that quilting has for her.

The portraits indicate how quilts function as a form of self-expression. A needlework pattern appears on the screen to introduce each woman and acts as a transitional device to tie the vignettes together. Susanna Calderon of Sonoma County connects her country appliqué quilt with her rural life. Her "back to nature" discussion in a studio in which she speaks of her art indicates that she represents the "new" quilter who has learned to quilt in a formal way, relies on books, and uses fabric less as a tradition than as a different medium to create art. Grace Earl, a retired Chicago Art Institute teacher, sees the pieces she places on a felt board "shimmering." A fine artist, she has returned to that which she was taught as a child, but like Calderon she takes a fine art approach. A Bulgarian immigrant who learned quilting to deal with family problems now is commissioned to create quilts for others who use them to deal with personal problems. She pieces together a quilt out of a dead child's clothing for the mother.

These three women are using fabric, but do not seem to meet the folklorist's criterion of traditionality for folk art. Thus, the contrast with the other three portraits has great impact. For example, quilting expresses Lucy Hilty's Mennonite background. Ferrero presents her at a Mennonite quilting bee and auction in California. Yet Hilty is a transitional figure between tradition and innovation; her segment concludes with her saying that she is not interested in traditional designs anymore. For Nora Lee Condra, a black Mississippian, quilts are the heirlooms of generations of work in her family. She discusses each quilt and the special significance of the design and the relative who made it. This very traditional quilter represents the women who learned within their own families and used whatever material was available, in this case, flour sacks. The last vignette is of the Miller sisters, who quilt together and fuss over who has quilted the most and which one is a better quilter. The pile of quilts made for the weddings of their nineteen nephews and nieces is imposing. The sisters echo each other's remarks in a delightful way and play a duet on the piano that serves as the musical link for the vignettes. Each segment has still photos and voice-overs describing the woman's life, followed by a scene of her working on a quilt, talking about why she quilts, and what quilts mean in the context of her life. Individual creativity is a central issue here, as evidenced by the use of portraits that focus on individuals. The vignette style, though, demonstrates that these are not in-depth portraits. Instead, Ferrero is looking at women and quilters who provide a functional analysis of the quilting process and its significance for women's identity.

Like gender, age is a unifying factor. In *The Grand Generation* (1993), Paul Wagner and folklorists Marjorie Hunt and Steve Zeitlin team up again. Related to the 1981 White House Conference on Aging and The Grand Generation: Folklore and Aging program held at the 1984 Festival of American Folklife, the film also serves as a companion to the catalog *The Grand Generation: Memory, Mastery, Legacy,* by Mary Hufford, Marjorie Hunt, and Steve Zeitlin (1987). Because we all experience the aging process, it is powerful subject matter. This film presents six elders who tell their life stories to the camera. The film was shot during the Smithsonian exhibition. All the interviewees are framed from midchest against a well-lit dark background in the type of shot and nonlocation we have come to expect for interviews that lift people out of context. Items near the interviewees are mostly out of frame and are not focused on. In fact, Wagner told me such objects were not intended to appear in the frame (Wagner 1993).

The film is highly structured by the filmmakers and the people in the film. How do people construct their lives for the camera and for themselves? Most recall their occupations, locales, the historical changes they have experienced, and their major accomplishments. Life history has certain phases. How to delineate them is an issue that the making of a film raises. For Rosina Tucker, who had appeared in Wagner's earlier film, *Miles of Smiles,* working as a union officer and in the civil rights movement was crucial to her identity; for Nimrod Workman, folksinger and coal miner, it was the ability to effect change and use folksongs to relate that change; for Hispanic farmer Cleofes Vigil of New Mexico, being an oral historian was the key; for Chesapeake Bay waterman Alex Kellam and baker Moishe Sacks of the Bronx, occupational accomplishments and experience were determinants; and for Ethel Mohamed, storekeeper and embroiderer from Belzoni, Mississippi, her family, her art, and her sense of historical change became paramount.

The film opens with head shots of people telling their ages, number of children, and recollections from the past. Intertitles identify the individuals. Following the opening, each segment addresses an issue presented in an intertitle. For example, "Experience is what the old have to teach us—Barbara Myerhoff," followed by Alex Kellam describing how experience teaches one where the crabs are; or "A sense of continuity with generations gone before can stretch like a lifeline across the scary present—John Dos Passos," which dissolves to Cleofes Vigil playing music he learned from his grandmother when he was five or six years old. Thus, the lives of these individuals serve as exemplars of Experience, Work, History, Memory, and Continuity. Although Nimrod Workman believes one's days are numbered, Moishe Sacks says he will not die. Rosina Tucker sums up the perspective achieved by age. She was once asked what it was like "in your day." "Each day is my day. . . . If tomorrow comes, it'll be my day," she replied.

The last intertitle sums up the film's purpose: "Miss not the discourse of the elders—Ecclesiasticus." Totally unrelated, these people must be brought together for the film in vignettes, with the intertitles, rather than a narrator, acting as the thread connecting them. The intertitles are structural devices that point out the topics and move from such questions as "What do you remember that was different in your youth?" and "What does it feel like to be old?" The questions are not heard, but the answers indicate that they were voiced by the fieldworkers. No one tells a whole story. What is cut out and how directed were the interviews are questions that this film style intentionally clouds. Nevertheless, a quotation from Barbara Kirshenblatt-Gimblett, used as an intertitle, demonstrates the value of the film: "Older people are empowered by their history." As human beings who age each day, we are gratified to know this truth.

Wagner's films all catch the present just as it slips into becoming the past: the Pullman porter is now a memory, the stone carvers and the medicine show entertainers compare themselves to passenger pigeons, and the elders fade into death. Most of the people who have appeared in Wagner's films are gone (Wagner 1993). His films serve as a nostalgic re-creation in the reunions of the porters, the carvers, and the medicine show performers or as a vestigial capturing of a bygone occupation or lifestyle. Such work has great value in documenting traditional expressions, and Wagner is a master of this perspective.

The community most overlooked by professional filmmakers and most cherished by the amateur filmmaker is the family. In *A Singing Stream: A Black Family Chronicle* (1986), filmmaker Tom Davenport, folklorist Dan Patterson,

2.22 Top: Bertha Landis. Bottom left: John Landis. Bottom right: the Landis family portrait in *A Singing Stream*

and American studies scholar Allen Tullos examine family, gospel singing, and a reunion as the key features of the Landis family of Granville County, North Carolina. Davenport and Patterson established a working relationship with Davenport's film *The Shakers* (1970), which documented the rise and fall of Shakerism through stills, songs, and the narratives and oral history of the few Shakers who remain. The film garnered national recognition in the *New Yorker* and *Newsweek*. The Shakers are fascinating, not only because of the simple furniture for which they became well known but also for their persistence as a "family" despite their vows of celibacy.[15] (Members called each other "brother" and "sister"; the spiritual founder of Shakerism was Mother Ann.) The last of the Sisters were interviewed just as the community was coming to a close.

*A Singing Stream* depicts a family of a different sort and one whose vitality emanates from the screen.

This film is the fourth in the American Traditional Culture series, produced in collaboration with Dan Patterson and the Curriculum in Folklore at the University of North Carolina at Chapel Hill.[16] Bertha Landis, the eighty-six-year-old matriarch of the Landis family, introduces the family by discussing her children, shown in a family portrait. Her eight boys and three girls had a "singing stream," which they inherited from both sides of her family. Her father taught shape note singing, and she recounts how she sang with him as a child and then encouraged her own children to sing as they were growing up.

The music, history, narratives, and reunion of the Landis family are centered around three events that occur each August: a picnic at the family homeplace; a church service memorial reunion with four other families, and an anniversary concert by the Golden Echoes, led by John Landis (Patterson 1988). Although some family members have bought homes close to Bertha Landis, descendants who have moved away (most to the North) return for the reunion.

Woven throughout the reunion events are the family's religious musical traditions. The repertoire includes nineteenth-century spirituals, shape note singing, jubilee style singing, and contemporary gospel, some of which relies heavily on call and response. We see rehearsals for the concert, a duet between Bertha and son Claude singing a shape note song on the front porch, an informal jubilee quartet performance, and the gospel rehearsal of granddaughter Karen Landis Stallings's group, the Echoes of Heaven, from Akron, Ohio. Karen's father, Fleming Landis, leads them in rehearsing "Trouble in My Way" at the home of their cousin.

A scene in which the daughters reminisce over photos demonstrates the family humor and unity and leads to narratives about black segregation in the South and how Bertha Landis bought a farm through the Farm Security Administration in the 1930s. The children recall their life on the farm and their rise out of poverty into the middle class. Some discuss why they had to leave; others talk about the jobs and businesses they've built despite racial discrimination. Black-and-white photos help tell the political story of segregation and the fight for voting privileges. Bertha's grandson remembers his white schoolmates shunning him—with no regard to their friendship before he began attending their previously all-white school.

Clothing is symbolic of the family's struggle. A daughter tells of receiving a uniform as a "gift." Two brothers disclose how they had to share shoes and clothes. Today, John Landis discusses which clothes match appropriately as he shops for his concert clothing. "Fifty percent of your singing or how far you will ever get in singing is the way you dress. . . . They're curious of what you have on when you come through the door." Obviously, the Golden Echoes represent success for their audiences, and part of that success is measured by clothing. Dan Patterson has remarked that the Echoes "guard the secret of the handsome new uniform until the actual moment of their entry for their section of the program. They will not have revealed the secret even to their wives" (1988:98).

The rural character of the family is reinforced when the Echoes of Heaven arrive from Akron and some members are teased about how skittish they are around the animals. Davenport also intersperses young children listening to rock 'n' roll and other signs of modernity into this rural picture to make certain that the viewer will recognize how the past and present blend. Family members talk about returning to the country where they were reared. One brother returned after twenty-five years; a sister is moving back. The filmmakers use these comments to show the strength and pull of the family's ties. As the end of the film, the entire family poses for a photo at the Landis homestead.

The most moving scene is undoubtedly the anniversary concert. The Golden Echoes sing "Going Up to Meet Him" in a call-and-response pattern. Karen Landis Stallings spontaneously jumps up and joins her uncle John, and Claude Landis signals her group, Echoes of Heaven, to join her onstage and sing backup. By the time the film turns to the church service, where the family sings a number of songs, including "Union in Heaven" and "Mighty Close to Heaven," viewers have experienced the affirmative power of this remarkable family.

Film demonstates the importance of folklore in the lives of individuals. Ethnicity, region, religion, occupation, age, gender, and family are all identity markers that have become subjects for such folklore filmmakers as Blank, Cohen, Davenport, Ferrero, Ferris, Peiser, Preloran, and Wagner. All have tended to concentrate on key individuals within the larger framework of a community. They are primarily viewing either rural/urban changes, ethnic musical differences, traditional versus modern lifestyles, or the relationships between environment, community influence, and individual creativity. Those filmmakers who do not detail the community or region in depth are using film as a device for recording performance in context. Many of the performances are not seen from beginning to end or are not allowed to be heard in full. The situations in which such performances normally occur are shown, but the films in which social interactions and the function of music or craftsmanship in relation to the community at large are also presented provide the greatest insight.

# 3

# Documentation
## Interactional Events and Individual Portraits

*They're gonna put me in the movies*
*They're gonna make a big star out of me. . . .*
*I'll play the part but I won't need rehearsin'*
*And all I have to do is act naturally.*
— Vonie Morrison and Johnny Russell,
"Act Naturally"

*The event film* has been a necessary outgrowth of shifting theoretical models in folkloristics. Scholars made observations about the social or cultural setting to expedite cross-cultural, cross-regional studies or in-depth cultural analyses. Like anthropologists, folklorists might analyze the content and context to demonstrate possible functions of folksongs, narratives, and other folk expressions; filmmakers explored the cultural milieu in which folklore was generated. In their published work, folklorists described situations in general terms; that is, tales are usually told at a feast, or a wedding, or at the storyteller's home, or among certain ethnic groups. Films facilitating this stance resulted in such cultural overviews as *Araucanians* or *Spend It All.*

Few folklorists actually discussed specific events or particular performances. But slowly the focus of folkloristic inquiry began to change, placing greater importance on specific "contexts" (Bauman 1977, 1986; Crowley 1966; Dégh 1969; Toelken 1969). Since the reification of context, performance, and event, folklorists have greatly broadened their fields of inquiry to see the story, song, or art object as part of an all-encompassing communicative event. The focus is on the ever varying flow of traditional human behavior. Yet folklorists often use the terms *context, event,* and *performance* interchangeably. For example, Richard Bauman uses all three terms in *Story, Performance, and Event: Contextual Studies of Oral Narrative* and refers to "performance events" as a means of including both the artistic expression and "culturally defined scenes" (1986:3). Barbara Kirshenblatt-Gimblett studies "A Parable in Context" (1975), but she actually describes an interactive event generated by a parable. David Buchan uses the idea of "performance contexts" (1985). Regardless of the term used, many folklorists are concerned with folklore as *communication*—aesthetic, rhetorical, poetic, and interactional. For these folklorists, film offers a fitting methodological tool.

Just as performance studies grew out of Dell Hymes's work with the ethnography of speaking (1962), so too did the idea of communicative events, variations of which surfaced in the work of Dan Ben-Amos (1975, 1993) and Robert A. Georges (1969, 1976). Ben-Amos places the emphasis for folkloristic research on process and interaction, calling folklore "artistic communication in small groups" (1971:13). Although the group concept presents its own difficulties by implying that all participants in a folkloric communication have a common referent (cf. Blumenreich and Polansky 1974), Ben-Amos's contribution is his vision of folklore as dynamic and his insistence that folklorists engage in process studies rather than textual analyses: "The telling is the tale; therefore, the narrator, his story, and his audience are all related to each other as components of a single continuum which is the communicative event" (1971:10).

Most of the new theorists or "contextualists" (see Abrahams 1968, 1969; Ben-Amos 1969, 1971; Dundes 1964; Georges 1969; Goldstein 1967) borrowed their terminology from and blended the approaches of linguistics, social anthropology, and communication studies in developing their ideas. Georges, however, unlike the other so-called contextualists (Dorson 1972c:45-47), provided folklorists with a succinct set of postulates and a graphic model for viewing folklore as process and event as early as 1969 in "Toward an Understanding of Storytelling Events." His work provides a methodological and theoretical basis for using film or video for certain kinds of fieldwork and research studies.

Textually oriented folklorists, because of their literary bias, often focused on the words of an activity, such as narrating, which they reduced to a text. Generally ignored were the nonverbal aspects of the communication, including not only the gestures, voice intonations, and proxemics of the storyteller but also the role of the audience (akin to the role of the reader in literary studies) in shaping the message. For Georges, the message has multiple codes; the verbal aspect is only part of the event, and its isolation for analysis gives it an unjustified uniqueness and a primacy it simply does not have (1969:316-17). Folkloric communications, Georges asserts, must be studied holistically.

Although Georges's model is directed at storytelling events, it may be applied to any folkloric event, such as the process of creating folk objects.[1] One of the major concerns with "performance" theories is that they focus almost entirely on the verbal arts and exclude material culture studies. At a certain point in the continuum of ongoing communication between any two interacting individuals (including folk artists and their consumers), the communicative event becomes a narrating, singing, riddling, playing, or object-creating event that participants recognize on the basis of certain contextual markers, such as "Did I tell you the story about . . . " For ethnodocumentary filmmakers, the event film concept developed by Bateson and Mead became the construct for sequence filming (such as the Yanomamö and the !Kung Bushmen series). Folklore filmmakers followed who reconceptualized folklore from "text in context" to folklore as performance and behavior.

Events are never identical. They are dynamic, not fixed. Because the message is actually a process of communication, it is particular to the situation and to the relationships of the participants. However, singing and narrating events, for example, do bear similarities to other singing and narrative events because they represent social experiences common to all. A film on one illuminates others. A great benefit of film and video is that we can view the event many times (as we cannot with our notes and tapes) to analyze it and to see facets of the situation that were not readily apparent while the event was transpiring; humans get tired, but machines remember (Collier 1986:9; Jackson 1987:123). We need texts to talk about communication in our analytic conversations *on paper,* but to gain a sense of the *experience* of the communication we need film and video. As Leslie Devereaux remarks, "Sticking close to experience is, if anything, more possible in anthropological film than in writing" (1995:72). The same applies to folklore film.

## Process and Event Films

Research concerned with the processes of folk art and folk technology, narrating, singing, dancing, or playing benefits from film's capability to demonstrate those processes. Carl Fleischhauer's *How to Make Sorghum Molasses* (1971) illustrates this style by showing step-by-step technological production. The verbal interactions of the people preparing the molasses provide the soundtrack, while the event itself structures the film. The dialect of the speakers is somewhat difficult to understand and, for those unacquainted with the process of preparing sorghum molasses, many questions arise.

Although the event structures *How to Make Sorghum Molasses,* the individuals involved in the technological process are not the focus. We know nothing of the significance of the process, or the product in use, or the reasons for production. What relation does the making of the product have to the lives of the people producing it? What happens to the product once it is made? How is it distributed and to whom? Are the reasons for producing the product economic or personal? Although photographing the entire process so that steps can be viewed is important, Patrick Gainer, the folklorist on this project, neglected to address these other issues.

3.1 At the sorghum mill on molasses-making day at the Weaver brothers' farm near Tanner in Gilmore County, West Virginia, in 1970. Left to right: an unidentified neighbor, Herbert Shaver, sound recordist George Mayle, and filmmaker Carl Fleischhauer. Photo by William Smock

Fleischhauer was acutely aware of the film's limitations. To compensate for the omission of the history of molasses making by the participants, their attitudes toward it, and the uses of the product, he prepared an essay that also includes transcripts of the soundtrack and a selected bibliography. He believed this procedure would be more useful and less intrusive than using narration: "I am presenting this information here instead of in a condensed (and possibly oversimplified) soundtrack commentary so viewers may concentrate on the film's picture and natural sound" (1974a:1).

Fleischhauer allows the event to occur from beginning to end without interruption or staging. The men had considerable difficulty erecting their molasses-making contraption, hooking up the horse, and grinding the cane. To his credit, Fleischhauer leaves these actions in the film. In his focus on the event without any narration, he presents the molasses-making process without romanticizing it or glorifying its rural connections. He notes, "This is not a re-created event but an activity filmed in 1970, bearing all the inescapable signs of the contemporary world. Still, what emerges from this sweaty communal endeavor is a complex of values and personalities suggestive of an older way of life. The jokes, conversations, and work are shown in such an insistently specific way, however, that any hackneyed nostalgia about a pastoral way of life is avoided."

3.2 Brother and sister Sylvie O'Brien and Jenes Cottrell of *All Hand Work* at a folk festival in Cloe, West Virginia, in 1973. Photo by Carl Fleischhauer

Whereas Fleischhauer focuses on process as opposed to those engaged in it in *How to Make Sorghum Molasses*, in a later film, *All Hand Work* (1974), he juxtaposes the content focus to an individual and omits portions of the processes. While working as a cinematographer for West Virginia University's Office of Radio, Television and Motion Pictures, Fleischhauer and Patrick Gainer (a self-trained folklorist at West Virginia University) produced television programs on traditional life in West Virginia that document Gainer's visits with people in the community. Gainer's ideas about appearing as a central character who was saving folklore from oblivion clashed with Fleischhauer's straightforward vérité approach to film and his view of folklore as a dynamic process. Hence, the collaboration was not an easy one.

Gainer's presence in the molasses film is not evident without the supplemental essay, but in *All Hand Work* Gainer meets with Jenes Cottrell, a craftsman and musician. The film provides a glimpse into the character of the craftsman, the folklorist, and the filmmaker. Gainer insists on depicting Cottrell as a traditional man. For example, he asks Cottrell to sharpen his axes on a grindstone. Cottrell remarks, "Well, I use a file now to sharpen my ax and I don't use this [grindstone] at all." While filming nonfunctional or survivalistic aspects of Cottrell's work for Gainer, Fleischhauer allows the viewer to subtly note that Cottrell and his crafts are quite contemporary.

Shot in sync-sound, the film includes Cottrell making a rolling pin out of a piece of sassafras wood and then making a whistle. Neither process is shown

3.3 Hand-painted altar sign in the Church of God in Christ, Clarksdale, Mississippi, in *Black Delta Religion.* Photo by William Ferris. University of Mississippi Archive

from beginning to end. At the same time, Cottrell's sister prepares dinner in the kitchen and the film cuts back and forth between food preparation and Gainer and Cottrell in the workshop discussing Cottrell's life. Cottrell also sings and plays his banjo. Seemingly concerned with craft process, Fleischhauer actually has shifted his emphasis to focus on a most engaging individual in *All Hand Work,* but he does not allow the viewer to see both the man and his craft. *How to Make Sorghum Molasses* and *All Hand Work* are strong films, but each lacks the very element that makes the other film strong.

Contrasts in a filmmaker's corpus are common. Religious events form the content focus of Ferris's *Black Delta Religion* and *Two Black Churches. Black Delta Religion* depicts four events. Shot in 1968 with wild sound and Super 8mm film, *Black Delta Religion,* like *Mississippi Delta Blues,* reflects Ferris's early inexperience with the camera. The work is limited by too much cutting, the lack of sync, and minimal coverage of each event without showing how, why, or where such events occurred.

Seven years later, Ferris used his event approach for religious services and demonstrated his improved film technique in *Two Black Churches* (1975). Opening with baptismal clips from the previous film, followed by tracking shots of the countryside taken from *Gravel Springs Fife and Drum, Two Black Churches* then cuts to Greenwood Baptist Church. The first half of the film includes a sermon by Reverend Isaac Thomas, church members Mary Gordon and Amanda Gordon quilting (a shot also used in *Made in Mississippi*) and singing a gospel song, and the McGowan Gospel Singers performing "We Are Marching." These introductory sequences do not work well together because no connective shots clarify relationships between the scenes. But once Ferris shifts to a service at St. James Church in New Haven, Connecticut (identified by a title), their purpose is understood: they represent southern rural religious practices in contrast to northern urban ones. Using a voice-over technique during visuals of Reverend Coward delivering his sermon, Ferris presents Coward discussing how he was called to preach. As the service continues, Mrs. Coward "gets the spirit." Reverend Coward heals by laying on hands, the congregation sings, and church members embrace. This second half of the film is powerful: by focusing on all aspects of one church service, the film provides insight into the meaning and variety of religious experiences of a specific gathering of people. The first segment with its superficial overview of rural forms of black religious expression does not accomplish the contrast that Ferris obviously sought, whereas the remarkable and moving scenes in the second portion of *Two Black Churches* indicate the effectiveness of studying events through film.

One of the best-known event-oriented films is *Pizza Pizza Daddy-O* (1968), by Bess Lomax Hawes. Like Fleischhauer's sorghum molasses film, its success is based on effectively portraying an event from start to finish. It shows eight singing games played by twelve girls in a Los Angeles schoolyard. Hawes begins with random playground activities, then focuses on two girls playing and singing a hand-clapping game, "Oh Susianna," as more girls join in. The film freeze-frames while the narrator states that games brought over from the British Isles were blended with the African American heritage of the participants. The narrator has, as Hawes herself described it, an "up-town, high-toney" voice. After a comment that "each child can dance out her own fantasy," the freeze-frame ends and the next game sequence begins.

Zooms and wild panning indicate the camera's presence; however, the close-ups of the girls are quite effective. Obviously all taken from one session, the scenes in the film detail the interactions, gesturing and posturing, and dance patterns of the players, as well as the words of the games. One particularly interesting sequence begins with a girl leading the group in performing "Who Do They Talk About? The Mighty, Mighty Devil." Another girl complains that the leader doesn't know how to lead properly, an argument develops, and the game resumes with a new leader. In this segment, certain individuals stand out from the group, and we learn something about their personalities and interactions by watching for them in later games. The girls sing most of the games in a circle or in two face-to-face lines. Some games begin with pairs and expand to include new players. The narrator concludes that these games "live on" and that they link "the children's lives with those of their parents." The games reflect "the future in which each girl will dance her own game with her family in her own way." Hawes told me that she turns the sound down and talks over the overly intrusive narrator when she uses the film. She could easily discard the narration because the points made on the sound-track are available in the study guide.

The superorganic notion of folklore implied by the narrator's comments that the games were "brought over" is quite common among textually oriented folklorists and seems out of place. The use of sync-sound and the focus on a single situation implies an event and performance emphasis, yet both the narrator's commentary and the technique of cutting or dissolving from one game to the next without showing all of the interactions occurring between games point toward textual analysis. The accompanying study guide provides comparative notes, describes the performance, lists bibliographic sources, and includes transcriptions of the songs. Hence, for folklorists interested in texts or performances or both, the film has much to offer.

My own film, *Tales of the Supernatural* (1970), has certain content and structural similarities to *Pizza Pizza Daddy-O*. It focuses on a group of children engaged in one event and uses both sync-sound and narration. Yet rather than emphasizing the textual features, *Tales* tests hypotheses about the functions of ghost or horror tales (generally classified as legends) and notes the relationship between function and tale transmission.[2] In addition, the film serves as visual documentation of Georges's (1969) hypotheses raised in "Toward an Understanding of Storytelling Events."

The film begins and ends with short narrated segments. Empty candlelit interiors follow exterior shots of a mysterious castle with a strange being running past. A male narrator with an eerie voice asks questions that set the mood. This segment, though not scholarly, serves as a "hook" (in Hollywood terms) to pique interest and frame the event. Similar shots create closure as the film concludes.

In the film, I am seated in front of a fireplace with seven teenagers who tell eleven tales, including the "Vanishing Hitchhiker" (E 332.3.3.1); "The Hook," about a maniacal killer with a hook arm who has escaped from an insane asylum; and "The Boyfriend's Death," a tale in which a scratching noise frightens a girl awaiting her boyfriend's return. The filmed storytelling event is intercut with stills of other storytelling situations, famous art works on supernatural themes, and a series of photos from famous horror films. Over these stills, I comment about when and where ghost stories are usually told, the pseudoscientific "proofs" offered by narrators, and the influence of mass media. In a short staged scene, someone listens to the voice of "The Shadow" on the radio. Shifts from my interactions with the group to my narration serve to identify the folklorist's presence and imply that both the research and the analysis will be presented simultaneously.

Through an event approach, *Tales of the Supernatural* examines the storytelling situation, focusing on the roles, kinesics, proxemics, and remarks, reactions, and tensions of the participants, and demonstrates its major hypothesis—that the telling of such tales is a socially approved means of expressing a belief in the supernatural. The film explores how the social relationships of the participants determine who will be the listeners and the tellers and how these roles fluctuate. It also suggests that each tale is a re-creation, the quality of which depends on the skill and style of the individual narrator. On another level, the film discusses the process of localizing the setting of the tales and the use of asides that "document" the specific time, place, and participants to reinforce belief and form the nucleus of the story. Thus, *Tales* allows us to see the importance of these remarks, which were ignored by folklorists who collected texts isolated from the comments of the storytellers, and tests assumptions made by some folklorists that belief in the supernatural diminishes as a culture becomes more rational, demonstrating that these beliefs continue to be expressed via ghost stories or legends.

*Tales of the Supernatural* has obvious flaws. The contrast is low and the darkness of the film restricts its showing to very dark rooms. Because I kept the light levels low for a "natural" context, I had the film "pushed" in the laboratory and portions are consequently grainy. I have never shot another film in the dark, and I know that I would now use lights. The soundtrack for some stories is not clear because the hiss of the fire is picked up by the microphones. In addition, my narration occasionally seems to cut into the middle of a story in a distracting fashion. Although such intrusions are edited into the film in a manner that keeps the plot of the stories intact (the sync voice track picking up at the point where it was interrupted), some viewers find the narrator annoying unless they are warned of the filmmaker's structure in advance. A narration and eleven stories represent a large amount of material, and the film often is more effective when viewed twice. I once was opposed to reducing the event to the verbal code; many years after the film was finished, I made a transcript to accompany the film because I recognized that viewers would recall the event as they read it and the transcript would serve as an aid.

Whereas *Pizza Pizza Daddy-O* uses dissolves and freeze-frames to cut from one game to another, revealing a performance as text approach (akin to Hawes's other films, *Georgia Sea Island Singers, Buck Dancer,* and *Say, Old Man, Can You Play the Fiddle?*), in *Tales* my emphasis is on the event itself. Both films use a narrator to comment on the function of the activity. Hawes is interested in the function and historical connections of the games in general, and I state the functions I inferred from my analysis of specific aspects of the event depicted in my film.

Just as the cinéma vérité documentarians had turned their cameras on the rock festivals of the late 1960s and early 1970s, folklore filmmakers also used the festival as an organizing principle for documenting one event. Tom Davenport's first folklore film, *It Ain't City Music* (1973), uses a handheld vérité style to document the National Country Music Contest at Warrenton, Virginia. Before the titles even appear, a man announces, "Country music is everybody's music." Now, he comments, it has been taken "uptown." He recalls an earlier time when folks would play on the back porch, a time before big cities existed except "maybe New York." Davenport's choice of this interview as an opener indicates his own nostalgic notions about country music as old, as well as his recognition that country music is now a national phenomenon. Whatever country music is, the title tells us what it is not. As music fills the soundtrack, people arrive at the site and make comments about where country music comes from. They share a notion of rural antiquity, noting, "That's how the people lived," or that the music "started in a barn." The participants are obviously responding to questions asked by the filmmaker, and Davenport infuses the film with a functional dimension, as people discuss what country music means to them.

Shots of women with elaborate hairdos, boots, and shorts—a typical costume of female country music fans of the 1970s—place the audience on the scene and underscore, once more, the often inadvertent power that film has to

3.4 A fiddler practices on the grounds of the National Country Music Festival in *It Ain't City Music.*

recall an earlier time with accuracy. Davenport constructs the film with this pre–contest arrival segment, then he moves from one group of musicians to another performing on the vast festival grounds, and ends with the contest itself. Interspersed with the contestants, who are filmed from the side of the stage, are participants who tell the camera who they are, what they do for a living, and why they perform. They range from secretaries to car salesmen, all here to play out their other personas as country musicians. Davenport does not linger on the stage performances, although the presentations and shots of the audience provide a strong sense of the contest. Rather, he moves about the entire festival, demonstrating the drama of the small events occurring within and as part of the larger one. Some of the footage of performances of musicians and singers practicing far from the main event are evocative; viewers may find themselves "scoring" the performances they like best as Davenport draws them into the festival scene.

Davenport creates miniportraits of some of the participants. The camera lingers on a banjo player who hopes to win something. In a joking tone, he explains that he traveled here on a shoestring. Within fifteen minutes, Davenport reveals where the musicians believe the music originated, who the festival

3.5 Shooting *Free Show Tonite*. Steve Zeitlin sits on a chair and interviews; Paul Wagner stands next to the cameraman and directs.

participants are, and what the songs are about from their own perspectives. Despite a shaky camera and some mismatched editing, the film works because of the music and the filmmaker's recognition that the event is much more than the contest itself.

The function of a different performance event is taken up by Paul Wagner, who has often turned to the reunion as a central organizing motif in his films. For *Free Show Tonite* (1983), Wagner worked with folklorist Steve Zeitlin to film the re-creation of a medicine show. As was the case for *Miles of Smiles*, the folklorist collaborator conducted the fieldwork and the interviews for the production, and folklorist and filmmaker share the major credits as directors and producers. Narrator Roy Acuff explains that when a call was put out to stage this show, many former performers responded. This show would be the last one "before memory dies out completely." The nostalgia for the past is evident throughout the film. Organizers chose Bailey, North Carolina, as a suitable location for a two-day show because they wanted a place "where things hadn't changed much for fifty years."

As he did for *Miles of Smiles*, Wagner includes a history sequence. After the Civil War, the sellers hired entertainers to create the modern American medicine show. Wagner takes us to the present with performers arriving at the site and old coworkers happily reuniting. Although the film treats a re-created event, it documents the *process* of re-creation; it does not pretend that this event is ongoing, in contrast to the approach taken by Flaherty and Balikci. From the performers gathering to the show itself, we see the event unfold. The film clearly states that this show is a model, "one medicine show that would represent them all."

The show, of course, is a model of a time gone by. Fred Bloodgood, writing to say he will join the show, notes that the medicine show has "gone the way of the dodo, the dinosaur, and the passenger pigeon." For many, this last medicine show was "what heaven is." "Doc" Bloodgood, pitching "Hospital Tonic" with the audience buying, commented that to see all those hands holding up dollar bills again was a medicine man's dream. Certainly, the film captures an event for posterity. Soon after the film was shot, performer Greasy Medlin died. Today, like the porters Wagner and Santino documented in *Miles of Smiles,* most of the performers in *Free Show Tonite* are gone, including Roy Acuff. Wagner has told me he is very much aware of his work having often caught the end of an era. This film's nostalgic bent seems to keep the viewer at a distance, and the film lacks the emotional quality of Wagner's other work. This reaction may be based on my own position in history; older viewers who remember the medicine show may have a different sentiment, and many younger ones will, no doubt, find the re-creation to be a valuable document. With its combination of stills, old footage, and live action, *Free Show Tonite* balances the process of a real event with the data needed to place it in historical perspective.

People do not need to be stage performers to engage in folkloric events. For most, everyday life provides contests and rituals in which persons may "star." For example, the folklore of academe is rife with ceremony, competition, and ritual. In *Salamanders: A Night at the Phi Delt House* (1982), folklorist Ken Thigpen and filmmaker George Hornbein team up to watch college students eat live salamanders. Shot at Penn State, the film follows the contest in its entirety with a cinéma vérité quality. The first shot of fraternity members catching salamanders in a pond makes little sense until the film cuts to a fraternity party at which girls swallow salamanders taken from their beer glasses. The film moves from this scene, with a grainy quality that illustrates the use of available light, to the outdoors. The "Bowery Ball" sign on the fraternity house introduces the preparations for the party. Echoing another girl's on-camera statement, a female guest talks about how different this fraternity is. She, too, speaks directly to the camera: "I think that you should just interview people and ask them why they think Beta is our rival." The connection between filmmaker and filmed is immediate. We feel as if we are there waiting for the party to get under way. This fraternity serves beer and burgers on the lawn, whereas the other is concerned "with image," she remarks as a couple in formal dress walk by. Wheelbarrow races occur on the lawn as the camera rolls.

Students talk about how their traditions have changed. Beer races at night appear in collapsed filmic time as individuals disappear down long dark hallways and return, becoming more inebriated with each race. At this party (in an apparent change from previous years), the dates begin swallowing the salamanders and the boys follow. One man tells a "legend" of a frat member who had his stomach pumped but had it X-rayed first to prove he "ate eighty of 'em." A contest ensues as women try to outdo each other with the consecutive number of salamanders swallowed. The camera keeps returning to one girl who tongues the live salamanders at length before swallowing them. (Observers tend to make Freudian analyses at this point in the film.) Soon female participants begin swallowing more than one salamander at a time, competing with each other. The film ends as drunken students remark, "If you can eat it, go ahead."

Reactions to the film are strong. Student viewers are both appalled and fascinated. They find the activity in the film repulsive, but recognize immediately why it is similar to other ritual behavior and quickly make a connection with rites of passage and their own college and family rituals. Viewers also find the film refreshing in its coverage of an event without interference and without a narrator. One senses a strong alliance between filmmaker and participants that gives the film an "insider" value.

Despite vast differences in subject matter and secular versus sacred practices, I have shown *Salamanders* in class with my own video *Passover, a Celebration* (1983). Both productions examine rituals, use the unnarrated event as an organizing principle, and were made by insiders. Those who know Ken Thigpen also know that he teaches at Penn State and, in that regard, is an insider. *Passover* is a document of my own family's observance of Passover in Toronto.

Passover is a spring festival of freedom that commemorates the Exodus of the Jewish people from bondage in Egypt. A weeklong holiday, Passover begins with a ritual family meal called a Seder. The video opens with stills. Newspaper advertisements from banks, flower shops, and establishments such as McDonald's print "Happy Passover" greetings, and Kosher butchers and grocers advertise Passover foods. In cities with large Jewish populations, such recognition of a Jewish holiday is common. But for many viewers, the attention paid to Passover is a surprise; the segment is designed to inform them about the prominence of Passover in other locales. Music blends with a voice explaining the essence of Passover. To educate the uninitiated about the historical background of Passover, I insert a printed roll-up or crawl (a series of words that move up and off the screen for continuous reading). Although this video does not reconstruct history, stills and texts are common devices to explain a historical dimension. From this montage, the video then introduces us to one of the people in whose home the Seder will be held. She discusses the connection between Jewish food, Jewish identity, and neighborhood, and her remarks about the availability of Jewish food connect the two portions of the video.

3.6  The filmmaker's family at the Seder in *Passover: A Celebration* shot in
Toronto in 1983. Trudy Sherman, Brenda Kates, Stan Kates. Photo by Sharon
Sherman

The video follows the structure of the celebration as an event. It includes
shopping for and preparing the foods and the process of the Seder. By documenting the interactions and attitudes of one extended family, the videotape
reveals how Passover blends religious custom with sacred belief, myth, and
ritual. The voices of the participants are heard in sound-over during certain
parts of the Seder discussing the Seder food, the worth of family, the feelings
evoked by the singing, and the value of tradition.

The editing interweaves the sync-sound of the Seder itself with the
sound-over voices, which sometimes begin with a talking head interview and
which are intentionally inserted to communicate the functions of the seder for
the participants. For most, the Seder is not only a religious event; it also serves
as an expression of family folklore, as well as an affirmation of ethnicity in
modern society. Purposely tackling the question of change and variation in
folklore and myth, I return throughout the video to the family members' comments about how the Seder represents continuity and change. Although the
video documents one family's celebration, it relates this Seder to those celebrated by Jews throughout the world, implying that a recognizable core binds
Jews together in this event and that such events are also dynamic.

I was trained as a filmmaker while studying folklore at UCLA, and I had
never worked with video until *Passover*. Shot in three-quarter-inch video, the
production has some technical problems caused by low light levels (which the
proper film stock would have dealt with in 16mm). The sound for the Seder
itself uses the built-in microphone on the camera because the family did not
want a microphone on the table. Thinking I could easily shoot in video without a sound person, I proceeded, and the sound of those portions is hollow and

lacking in presence. Documenting one's own family also presents a host of problems, which I have detailed elsewhere (Sherman 1986).

Ken Thigpen documented his own family and members of his community for *Halloween '85*. Like many of the Indiana University folklore graduate students in the 1970s, Thigpen was encouraged by Linda Dégh to study Halloween as an important nonreligious American holiday. When he went to State College, he found Halloween was celebrated on a grand scale. In an interview with me, he remarked on this phenomenon. "People would come by in costumes on the main street. I'm not talking about ten people. I'm talking about hundreds and hundreds of people who would dress up and walk around town." Having shot *Salamanders* in 16mm, he decided to use video to cut expenses and have the freedom to shoot over a longer period of time than the cost of 16mm would permit. He began by documenting a number of events occurring in the weeks leading up to Halloween and interviewing people preparing for the holiday.

The video begins with children seated in a classroom. The camera moves from child to child as each recites what he or she will be for Halloween. "I'm gonna be a vampire"; "I'm gonna be a soldier"; "a punk rocker"; "a witch"; "a punk rocker"; "a pilot"; "a spaceman"; "a punk rocker." Obviously, being a "punk rocker" in 1985 was a Halloween craze. Audiences recognize immediately how transitory some costumes are and the great influence that popular culture has on desirable Halloween wear. Characteristic of Thigpen and Hornbein's approach, the camera has become an active participant and the audience is an involved voyeur.

*Halloween '85* is structured, as one might expect from a folklorist, into three parts. The film leaves the classroom by cutting to black. The following words each appear, one at a time, on the screen: IN OUR TOWN HALLOWEEN IS TAKEN SERIOUSLY. A woman decorates her porch with cobwebs and skeletons, and a man threads a skull onto the twig of a tree leading to the house. We understand that Halloween must be a serious event. With a black screen, the letters PART 1 appear, followed by a separate succession of words: ON YOUR MARK. A studio camera appears: SET. A short television segment begins with Thigpen and Bob Lima, an expert on the occult, talking about the origins of Halloween in Celtic times. The use of the "expert" to interprete calendrical customs is an inside joke to folklorists, who are invariably called upon by the media to do so. To students, the segment provides the background many folklorists otherwise would have to explain in class. Students unfortunately find its serious tone so different from the rest of the film that the experts seem out of place. The film shifts to people picking out pumpkins, a family carving a jack-o'-lantern, customers shopping for costumes, and a couple making their own costumes at home. The off-camera voice asks, "Where are you going?" "Just next door to our neighbors," they tell us. They plan to dress as Maid Marian and Robin Hood. In contrast to the felt hat being designed by "Robin Hood," the cash register at the store rings up a total of $36.56 for someone's costume purchase. With a quick switch to the studio scene, the experts comment on how people wear what they fear, and the film cuts to people transforming themselves in a store full of masks.

The next scene takes us back to the family carving its jack-o'-lantern. "What are you going to be?" someone asks a teenager. "Madonna." Her mother quickly says the weather will be too cold to dress as Madonna (the pop star singer known for appearing in lingerie). The girl also doesn't have a blonde wig, the mother remarks. The film further explores costuming as Thigpen talks about survivals in the "expert" studio segment, and "Robin Hood" says dressing up is an "excuse to get wild."

"PART 2, GET SET" appears in the pattern established earlier, and we return to the family carving scene. The jack-o'-lantern is lit, and the children place it outside. At a "haunted house," preparations are under way. A man building the sets demonstrates the electrocution room and a head drilling setup. The camera tapes people in various occupations in their costumes. Bank teller nuns, zany orthodontists, and card shop clerks with wigs appear. Adolescent girls prepare their makeup, a woman wearing a pumpkin costume sprays her hair orange, and everyone gets ready for Halloween night.

Adhering to the structure of the event, the film advances to "PART 3, GO." People parade through town, costume contests for children and seniors are juxtaposed, and kids walk from house to house through the neighborhood. A party scene includes "Robin Hood" singing a song about his costume character and a Nazi coaxing others to sing "Deutschland über Alles." The party is intercut with shots of clouds passing the moon to indicate time passing. We recognize the woman dressed as a pumpkin as the party continues with Palestinian terrorists, crossdressers, and other costumed revelers. The trick-or-treaters have come home and are trading their candy, which is spread out on the table.

On the street, some teenage girls who say they're "new wave" tell the camera they find people who dress up like them insulting; they're "distorting the idea." A young woman rants to passersby to "Turn to Jesus. You can dress up all you want. You have the mask of Satan on." Here the filmmakers present another facet of Halloween—those who fear it as paganistic—and then use the audio to cut to a man with a horrific beast mask entering a college diner. The unselfconscious cameraman catches himself in the mirror as the man walks by. "We're weird other days. Why not Halloween?" says the counterman, and the film moves to the haunted house where people wait in line to enter. Torture scenes, blood, and strobe lights provide a sense of the experience as we weave through the house with a group.

The film returns to the classroom to reveal what the children who were first interviewed actually have worn as costumes. The camera pans them as we hear the audio taken from the opening shot. Some are dressed as they predicted they would be; a few appear in different costumes. With this lighthearted scene, the film ends.

Thigpen and Hornbein transport the viewers through the multiple features of this celebration, bringing them from preparation to activity to closure of the holiday. Observing both adults and children, the filmmakers give us a rich representation of the collective experiences of this event. Following the family from carving to costuming to negotiating over candy undoubtedly reminds many viewers of their own childhood experiences. This family is Thigpen's own, and his personal connections make the film a document of himself as an insider. Thigpen also reveals himself in his role as a scholar. He participates on both sides of the camera, fusing his roles as filmmaker, folklorist, and family member.

Thigpen's other video work makes him an insider only in the sense of gender and region (as a Pennsylvanian); thus, the films are less intimate. *Buck Season at Bear Meadow Sunset* (1984) documents the gathering of men at a lodge to hunt, play cards, eat, drink, and tell stories. Using an unnarrated cinéma vérité style, the filmmakers trace the activities of the weekend as an event. Although still photos and stories testify to the bucks the hunters shot in the past, no one shoots a buck this season. The men hunt in a traditional way: they "drive the deer" to a point where the others can shoot them. That no one has bagged a deer in seven years seems unimportant; the issue here is spending the weekend with other men. Nothing seems to happen in this film; the cinéma vérité shots are dissolved to collapse time. Of course, my own gender may interfere with my appreciation of the film as a document of a mystifying male ritual. Perhaps a man would find the video stimulating. The camp gathering is certainly an event that creates male bonding, and the film makes that function clear without any editorializing in its straightforward cutting style.

For *Rattlesnakes: A Festival at Cross Fork, PA* (1992), Thigpen and Hornbein return to the male domain. But, as they did in *Salamanders,* they also demonstrate the adoption of men's rituals by women. In 1970, some members of the Keystone Reptile Club suggested that Cross Fork would be an ideal spot for a snake hunt. The store owners agreed, "It's a dead weekend. Let's do something." A marching band, shining fire trucks passing by, and all the usual sights of a fair appear. In this way, the filmmakers tell us that the festival is a gala event.

The video itself is crystal clear; one has a sense of almost being there at the festival. The filmmakers detail all of the festival's activities: numerous timed snake bagging contests in which men, women, and children participate, a greased pig chase, a pig roast, and the volunteer fire department's tug-of-war. Panning shots give a sense of the huge crowd attending the event. Intercut with the contest and game scenes are shots of people who relate narratives, jokes, and attitudes about snakes. One woman proudly tells her story of exchanging wedding vows in the snake pit.

As is often true of event films, the filmmakers follow the event to its natural conclusion. A man seen catching the snakes at the beginning of the film remarks that if no one was bitten and the weather wasn't too bad, then "it was a great weekend." The focus on snakes is unusual, but the festival meets expectations of what such an occasion should include—parades, contests, food, and prizes. By the time the video comes to a close, viewers have visited a festival whose coverage is so complete that they will now know much about snakes and perhaps even more about the similarities that exist among many festivals. It also indicates how folk events may be generated out of a meeting of disparate elements: a slow weekend, a suggestion, and willing participants.

The event film takes one activity and documents it in detail. Those films that deviate from the event to fill in background usually must use a narrator and stills or freeze-frame devices to bring the viewer away from and back to the event. Hawes uses an expository narrator; Wagner has Rosina Tucker speak for the porters and Roy Acuff present the medicine show. In *Tales*, the filmmaker narrates. In *Halloween '85*, intertitles mimic the setting-up process of a studio camera, but follow the event's progression. Fleischhauer, Ferris, Davenport, Thigpen, and I (for *Passover*) do not use narrations to identify or remark on the processes of the events in our films. For most filmmakers who document events, the participants tend to serve as the interpreters, and the filmmakers follow the unfolding of the events to construct the films.

## Portraits of Artists and Performers

Many of the problems of conveying folklore as a process of individual creativity are solved when filmmakers narrow their content focus and follow one artist or performer through a series of interactional events that structure their films. Such efforts are generally more successful in organization and overall comprehensiveness than single-event or community-oriented films (even of the same filmmakers) because viewers have a stronger sense of the significance of a tradition when they can identify with those who generate it.

Les Blank's early work includes two films centered on blues singer Sam "Lightnin'" Hopkins, *The Blues Accordin' to Lightnin' Hopkins* (1969), and *The Sun's Gonna Shine* (1969). Neither of these is as effective as his later films, *A Well-Spent Life* (1971), on blues singer Mance Lipscomb, and *Marc and Ann* (1991), on Cajun musicians Marc and Ann Savoy, but all four touch on the relationship between environment, personality, and style. In *The Blues Accordin'* *to Lightnin' Hopkins,* Blank's first folklore film, the stress is on Hopkins's rural roots, but the opening scenes establish an urban locale. In a living room, Hopkins sings, drinks, and plays the guitar with Bill Bizor on harmonica. The songs include "I'm Walking," "Good Morning, Little Schoolgirl," and "Meet Me in the Bottom." The visuals cut back and forth to enactments of the songs (e.g., a boy meeting a girl on the street is intercut with the performance to characterize "Good Morning, Little Schoolgirl"). Ruth "Blues" Ames sings a song with Hopkins and he chides her for singing like a man. With Hopkins playing guitar, Bizor hugs and kisses a pillow on the floor, and Hopkins adapts this action to his song. During this sequence, Hopkins also indicates some of the reasons one can get the blues: "You can have the blues about you're broke, or your girl done gone."

The film shifts to narratives as men discuss snakes at a railroad track, and Hopkins, in an insert, tells how he killed a snake. While fishing with a friend, he narrates another tale. Girls seen dancing in earlier shots are now identified as being at a rodeo, for the camera opens up to reveal the scene more fully, but the significance of the rodeo is unclear. At this point, the visuals cut to Centerville, Texas, Hopkins's home town. Close-ups of people on the street and shots of a rundown store and old houses give way to a church steeple as Hopkins stresses the importance of attending church services. From the exterior of a church we hear gospel singing and the preacher lining out, and see close-ups of well-dressed people (presumably churchgoers), but we do not enter the church. Obviously Blank is making a statement either about Hopkins's religious upbringing or about the significance of religion in the development of blues music, but the church scene seems ill-placed and the shots have no order.

As Hopkins plays "How Long Has It Been Since You Been Home?" Blank reveals a woman sitting on a porch and continues his technique of picturing the verses being sung, before cutting back to Hopkins singing in sync. Hopkins performs, two girls dance, and a man plays washboard plate at a barbecue. Blank also includes a buck dance. For the film's final scene, Hopkins sings a blues song about a girl named Mary. Close-ups of Hopkins's face and teeth are vexing. The visuals show little guitar fingering and do not indicate if anyone else is in the room or why Hopkins is singing this song. As the music fades, the film closes with flowers in a field and barbed wire.

The shots of women walking in town focus on their buttocks swaying and reveal more about Blank's interest in female anatomy than about the townspeople. Scenes of flowers and the countryside, the quaint rural church, the shabby condition of Centerville, and the depiction of Hopkins in a rural atmosphere signify Blank's romanticism. The filmic structure he employs is a montage of rural scenes that feature Hopkins and his music but are otherwise disconnected and choppy. Blank's romantic preoccupation overrides a structure that he might have organized more logically around events important to Hopkins (e.g., one day, week, or month in the performer's life).

*The Sun's Gonna Shine* was made from outtakes of the first film. According to Blank, this footage was not incorporated "mainly because it was too flowery and didn't fit the toughness of the main film on Lightnin'."[3] The advertisement for *The Sun's Gonna Shine* states, "A lyrical companion piece to *The Blues*. . . . this film re-creates Lightnin' Hopkins's decision at the age of eight to stop choppin' cotton and sing for his living." Structured into three major segments, the film begins with tracking shots of houses that dissolve to black people in different locations and then to shots of daisies and barbed wire, a recurring motif in this and other Les Blank films. In Centerville, Hopkins discusses his early education. In a field near a railroad track, a small boy with his guitar acts out the lyrics to the Hopkins song on the soundtrack. A train rolls past, and the boy steps onto the tracks and watches it fade into the distance as the film concludes. This film adds little to our understanding of why Hopkins decided to sing for a living, and a single scene does not constitute an adequate re-creation of Hopkins's childhood. Outtakes are usually stored for possible use as cutaways; they are rarely used to construct new films. Like *The Blues Accordin' to Lightnin' Hopkins, The Sun's Gonna Shine* represents the filmmaker's personality more than that of its subject.

Shot on the same trip as *Spend It All, A Well-Spent Life* (1971) was filmed in only one week, and it stands as a superior example of Blank's developing expertise as a folklore filmmaker. In sharp contrast with his other early work, the film allows the events and experiences of the subject to determine its structure. Although the visuals of daisies and acted-out verses depicted in some of Les Blank's first films do appear, *A Well-Spent Life* is primarily an in-depth portrait of Mance Lipscomb. Mance tells his own story, in sync-sound. Born in 1875 near Navasoto, Texas, he spent his early days as a sharecropper. "We were bound down. We couldn't do anything but take it." Mance plays guitar and sings "Big Boss Man," and then talks about dogs, the land, and black-white relationships. Landscape shots are intercut with close-ups of Mance singing. We see Elnora Lipscomb frying a chicken and hear "She's Your Chicken, Save Me the Wing," and then see Mance eating at a table. Mance and his wife explain the success of their marriage through anecdotes. A record player with one of Mance's albums as well as a shot of a University of Chicago Folklore Society poster featuring Mance and Buell Kazee signify Mance's fame as a performer.

Street scenes, a poker game, and Mance playing "Rock Me, Mama" in a local club indicate his relationship to the community. An effective segment depicts children playing in the yard while Mance explains that he raised twenty-three children in all—his brothers and sisters, his own children, and his grandchildren. He is then shown singing "Motherless Children" and playing bottleneck guitar with a penknife. After a baptismal ceremony and a church service in which Mance assists the preacher, Mance expresses his thoughts about religion. "Religion is a feeling; religion ain't nothing but love." The film concludes with Mance playing "St. James Infirmary." By integrating visuals of Mance Lipscomb's musical, personal, community, and professional life with his own statements, Blank succeeds in conveying the creative expressions and personality of an artist.

In a similar vein, my film *Kathleen Ware, Quiltmaker* (1979) examines the process of folk creativity and the individual artist. Mrs. Ware lives on a busy stretch of highway that leads to the Oregon coast. A handmade sign advertises her profession, and curious quilt enthusiasts stream through her living room as she goes about her daily activities. Sync-sound scenes of her interactions with customers and family members capture Mrs. Ware's humor and her role as quiltmaker, wife, mother, and grandmother.

The film opens as a prospective purchaser arrives. She looks at various quilt tops, chooses a lone star pattern, and places an order. The rationale for the selection of materials and colors indicates Mrs. Ware's own unique artistic sensibilities within the traditional structure of a folk craft. Sound-over comments by Mrs. Ware and her husband relate the Wares' outlook on life and the importance of quiltmaking for the family. Scenes of customers coming in and out, John Ware and the Ware children making a comforter, the family eating dinner, and John working in his vegetable garden are surrounded by the making of the lone star quilt. Thus, personality and process, as well as aesthetic and economic functions for the artist, rather than folk objects are the central concerns of the film.

I return to these issues in *Spirits in the Wood: The Chainsaw Art of Skip Armstrong* (1991). Armstrong is a chainsaw carver in Sisters, Oregon. The video intentionally asks theoretical questions about the differences between folk and fine art by exploring Armstrong's work in a variety of contexts. In *Kathleen Ware*, I was so focused on making certain I covered the entire quiltmaking process that I neglected to shoot any scenes of Mrs. Ware interacting outside her home (shots of fabric shopping, for example, are missing). *Spirits* is structured much like *Kathleen Ware*, but it is a further development of my own thinking about filmmaking and folk art. The soundtrack again allows the artist to express his own attitudes about his work and life. It opens amid scenes of central Oregon with Skip talking about the connection he feels with his environment. Oregon represents "the last of the pioneer spirit. . . . We have a wood culture here," he remarks.

The video follows the process of Armstrong making a coyote, from selecting a log to oiling the completed sculpture. Woven in are Skip's interactions

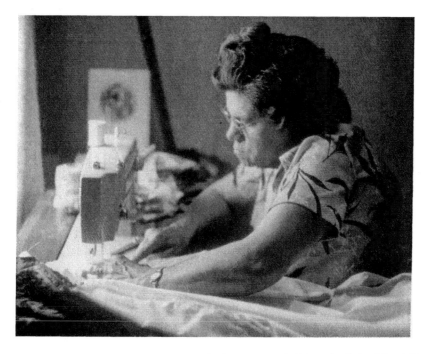

3.7 *Kathleen Ware, Quiltmaker,* creates the lone star quilt. Photo by Steve Mandell

with customers at local crafts shows and gallery exhibits. Two weekend market fairs in the park illustrate Skip's connection with his clientele. His wife declares that these interactions are "the fuel that keeps him going." Skip's relationship to the community is underscored in a series of scenes in which he visits customers at their homes and they talk about the sculptures they've bought. One man built his house with ceilings high enough to accommodate a mobile; another asked Skip to create dragon doors for the entrance to his house. The friendship that exists between consumers and artist is further established during a Christmas party where Skip carves a giant block of ice into a horse. Skip's bond with his family is briefly touched on with a birthday party scene and an interview with Skip's wife, but it is his work that dominates his life and the video.

Skip works in a shop separated from the house, and he likes being "man, the tool user." He has adapted all of his tools. The process is that of moving from a big chainsaw to a smaller one and then to smaller and smaller tools. What emerges is an art form that is startlingly polished. A montage of pieces that turn to music and gleam in the lights show the artistry and range of Skip's work. Skip recognizes that his work is difficult to categorize within the

3.8 Skip Armstrong "dances inside the log" during a chainsaw demonstration, *Spirits in the Wood.* Photo by Melinda Hoder

common stereotypes of what chainsaw art should be. He notes that he is part of a tradition of Oregon and northern Californian regional chainsaw art but that he is branching out from that. A scene of Skip in a fine arts gallery confirms his growing reputation in the West. For Skip, "If you put it in a gallery and call it fine art, then it becomes fine art; if you put the same piece in a local crafts show, then it becomes more folk." Viewers will undoubtedly argue about this definition; I place the gallery scene and the discussion into the video for that very reason. How one defines folk art is an issue in folkloristics, and the video is meant to grapple with the definition's elusiveness.

*Spirits in the Wood* includes a scene of Armstrong demonstrating his techniques with the chainsaw in the park. He says the chainsaw allows him to speed up the transmission of an idea from his head to the piece. Armstrong wants to be able to "dance inside the log." The video dances to a rhythmic editing pattern that visualizes his words. The advantage of video, including the accompanying chainsaw noise, over text is obvious when comparing this scene (and others) to an exploration of the same events in written form (Sherman 1995).

Throughout the video, Armstrong discusses his choice of materials and his methods of creating sculpture. Like narrative and folksong, the process is similar but the result varies: "Every piece is a unique piece; it's not just the same repetitive process." The video explores variation and creativity, and folk and fine art, from the perspective of the artist and the filmmaker.

Bill Ferris has also featured portraits of folk artists and has related them to his interest in black folklore from the Mississippi Delta. For his early field-work in the Delta he used Super 8mm film as a data-gathering tool. For *Delta Blues Singer: James "Sonny Ford" Thomas* (1970) he used 16mm. Shown at the American Folklore Society meeting in 1970, *Delta Blues Singer* was the first film Ferris released for distribution. As such, it is technically rough. Many of the visuals are improperly exposed, and the sound quality is poor. In addition, attempts to synchronize the wild sound with the footage point to the fact that the film was an amateur production.

The film is primarily about Thomas's music, but the lack of sync prevents an analysis or understanding of his guitar technique. Despite this drawback, the film does relate the significance of Thomas's music to his family activities and community life. Thomas plays "gutbucket" blues in bottleneck style in juke joints in Leland and with friends at home. The lyrics of gutbucket blues concern sex and suffering, and the dances depicted during the music sessions are imitative of sexual acts. Thomas discusses his childhood, lack of education, and the meaning of the blues.

Thomas sculpts skulls and faces out of clay and works as a gravedigger; he relates the clay to both activities. In a supplement to the film and a later published work (Ferris 1983), Ferris connects the clay art of James Thomas to West African sculpture. He shows the contexts in which Thomas lives and performs, although the soundtrack connecting these events is often unclear. Nevertheless, Ferris realized the potential of devoting a film to one artist, and he later polished his approach with professional sync-sound equipment and increased camera experience.

After Peiser had edited Ferris's *Gravel Springs*, the two collaborated on their first sync-sound venture, *Ray Lum: Mule Trader* (1973); it was also Ferris's first film concerning a white Mississippian. Lum appears at his home, his saddle shop, and his family auction house in Vicksburg. This film was made soon after such folklorists as Robert A. Georges (1969), Barre Toelken (1969), and Roger Abrahams (1971) published articles on narrating as performance, event, and audience feedback. By trying to show audience response, the film-makers cut off Lum's narration at points, but they don't quite picture all of the audience reaction either.

The film combines the sound-over voice of Lum describing his experiences as a trader with sync-sound scenes of Lum's daily interactions and storytelling abilities. Most of the stories Lum tells are personal narratives, but two contain common motifs. The first involves treacherous Gypsies (K 2261.1) who tried to trick Ray Lum in a horse trade but were outsmarted. The second is about a horse that drops dead shortly after a man trades for it (J 1455a). A man tells "Mr. Ray" and other listeners that someone who had

3.9 James "Sonny Ford" Thomas with one of his clay skulls in *James "Sonny Ford" Thomas: Delta Blues Singer*. Photo by William Ferris. University of Mississippi Archive

purchased a mule from Lum called and told him it had died. According to the teller, Lum replied, "Well now, you know, he never did do that while I owned him." Lum corrects the teller by retelling the tale: "I always tell them when they tell me about one that died, I said, 'Well, he never did play that trick on nobody before.'" Lum's version indicates his excellence as a storyteller and the process of maintaining narrative traditions. Other stories include the purchase of eight thousand horses at once and a tale about a horse so tall that no river was deep enough to drown him. Old photos depict the shift from horses to automobiles while Ray describes changes he has seen in his eighty-one years. As the yard fills with cars, Ray talks about why he became an auctioneer, and the film cuts to the arena where Ray conducts the auction, as people talk and bid on livestock. The film ends with Ray in his store, swapping stories. By following Ray Lum through one day, the filmmakers capture the essence of Lum as a narrator and the occupational events that shape his stories.[4]

The observational technique of focusing on events and using the voices of those filmed was also employed by Ferris and Peiser for their portrait of a black performer, *Fannie Bell Chapman: Gospel Singer* (1975). Chapman, from Centerville, Mississippi, discusses her faith healing powers and how songs come to her from God through a "pillar of cloud." We view her at her home with her husband and daughters, at a gospel gathering, and going from house to house on healing trips. Her daughters, who sing with her in several scenes, also discuss their mother's power, and her husband states that she is able to heal him when he's sick.

Shots of Fannie Bell in a chair addressing the camera directly are occasionally dissolved into each other and show her wearing different dresses. This technique and a cut from a medium to a close-up shot of the same chair scene are awkwardly done. Otherwise, the film is technically very polished. The home life and healing segments indicate the importance of faith healing and gospel singing for Chapman and her family, and the documentation of interactional events is thorough and revealing.

For *Marc and Ann,* Les Blank continues his Louisiana series by examining the lives of Marc and Ann Savoy. Subtitles explain who the Savoys are, but fans of Les Blank will recognize them immediately from *Yum, Yum, Yum!* and other films. Marc talks about his life, and black-and-white photos detail his career as an accordion maker and player. The film then cuts back and forth between Marc and Ann telling the story of how they met at a folk festival where Marc was performing. "You meet the nicest people at folk festivals," says Marc. Stills recall their wedding and then their children as the years go by.

In a scene familiar to fieldworkers everywhere, Ann conducts a tape-recorded interview with Octa Clark. We see the small cassette recorder in her hand, and the film dissolves to a large one playing back the interview as Ann transcribes her notes. Her book, *Cajun Music* (1988), began as a songbook. She wanted to depict the stories of the people as well, and as a photographer she began studying old photographs. This remark moves the topic to Marc's discussion of learning music from his elders when he was a child. Several scenes show Marc and Ann playing music at festivals. At one site, Ann sells her book. The importance of tradition is evident. Although not originally from Louisiana, Ann has become a member of the folk group she is studying. As Les Blank studies her, she documents herself.

Marc talks about how overwhelmed he is by the fast pace of the world outside his own domain. He believes in a need to make life simpler. Marc romanticizes tradition, perhaps because he has played this role so often in films or perhaps because he sees life in these terms. Certainly, he now is aware of the attitudes that folklorists, filmmakers, and others have about Cajun life.

Ann remarks that she is always busy. An off-camera voice suddenly asks if she does more with the kids, and Ann discusses her daily activities. Marc concludes that he is living as he always has. The filmmakers and the filmed are obviously at ease with each other, and this peek into the lives of Marc and Ann has a strong presence.

*Ray Lum, Fannie Bell Chapman, A Well-Spent Life,* and *Marc and Ann* represent what folkloric filmmakers can accomplish by detailing how the networks of performers' personal interactions and past experiences combine to produce creativity within a tradition. Ferris's work with the Yale Media Design Studio and his fieldwork films from 1968 to 1970 were overly concerned with texts and contexts. With Judy Peiser, Ferris shifted to an approach (which he had used for his first film) that documents the events of individual performers. These films clearly demonstrate the validity of such film use and, by contrast, point out the limitations of Ferris's previous work. With his expansion of the Center for the Study of Southern Culture, Ferris has since extended his representations of the culture of the South to other forms. Les Blank has moved from romantic overviews and mountains of irresistible filmic data that can sometimes overwhelm the viewer to relaxed, almost interactive films that show the joys of everyday life. His skill as an ever-evolving independent filmmaker continues to grow as does his reputation as a maker of films that fascinate.

Preloran has also changed his filmmaking style. After many years of shooting films on crafts and special festivities, Preloran decided to create an in-depth portrait of an individual. In an interview, Preloran explained to me how and why he changed his approach:

> While traveling so many times up to the high plateau I met a man, Hermogenes Cayo, who was an image maker. And little by little I started

shooting film on him, but not in the sense of the others. It was more as if I were shooting little things every time I went; but not something I thought in my mind I would make totally, like the other films. And this happened during two years. And at the end of the two years he died, so I started to put the film together. I did so using only his voice, which had been recorded before I filmed. So I started really without realizing a different type of film, a different style. This to me is what I want to do from now on, and all my films since then have been in that sense. It's to record somehow on film the life problems and everything that goes into living in a certain area through one character—except for *Valle Fertil,* which has fifteen characters.

So what I do is, generally, I take over a year to make the films. Although I may not live with the person or with a family, I travel many times, maybe once a month. And I know when something is going to happen. So I'm there and I go back to catch, if I can, the different things that happen in a cycle of one year, which in rural communities is very important. And these films are becoming longer each time. They started out being one hour, and now they are one hour and a half. And I guess I'm getting a little closer to the social problems around the people, to find out who they are. Perhaps I know now better how to ask the questions.[5]

*Imaginero* (1969), perhaps the best known of Jorge Preloran's films, was the result of his experiences with Hermogenes Cayo, a folk artist. Living on the high plateau in northwestern Argentina, Cayo carves images of the crucified Christ, paints church scenes, and lives far from the nearest village. The visuals include a trip Cayo and his son take to Abra Pampa, a small town thirty miles away, where the child first sees water running out of a faucet and a train. Preloran shows the influence of this journey on the work of Cayo in close-ups of his paintings, which illustrate the highlights of his trip. After visiting Buenos Aires in 1946, a feat accomplished by walking for two and a half months, Cayo built a shrine with colored bottle glass similar in style to a cathedral in Buenos Aires, and he expresses his thoughts about the experience. In speaking about the making of *Imaginero* in an interview with Howard Suber, Preloran states: "I feel that it's much more rewarding and fascinating to follow a member of a particular culture and to learn *through him* the mores and customs of that culture, watching him interact with his family and his society, than to take the easier way of documenting the overview of a culture and never quite getting to know the characters except in a superficial and stereotyped way" (Suber 1971:48).

By examining the major influences in Cayo's life, Preloran makes a powerful statement about the forces that shape creative processes. By becoming acquainted with Cayo we learn what generates emotion and creativity in artists. Adrian Gerbrands has suggested that "there is every reason to suppose that the aesthetic process of creation takes place fundamentally the same way in EVERY artist" (1957:123).

Like Flaherty, Preloran has used a biographical model, but Preloran makes no judgments about Cayo as an "isolated" man living in a desolate area. Further, no narrator editorializes the content. Preloran comments on this style in his interview with Suber: "If I went into the home of Hermogenes to film about a poverty-stricken old man who has to make images to survive, I'd be distorting the real truth in favor of making my point, and in the act, I'd be using Hermogenes as an *object* rather than as a *person*" (Suber 1971:49).

Some critics have stated that Preloran is a romanticist, choosing isolated men and doomed communities, often focusing on little-known celebrative rites and customs in his earlier films. Of Cayo, one can only note that if he appears as a romantic figure, that romanticism is because of the reality of his situation. The filmmaker does not impose romanticized notions on the film; rather, it is a feeling brought to the visuals by the audience's own interpretation.

*Cochengo Miranda* (1975) marks another step in Preloran's development of the biographical film. As was the case with *Imaginero,* the film is a composite sketch of one man and his family and their lifestyle. *Cochengo Miranda* documents a man who had been a active folksinger in his youth. In addition, he also wrote many *décimas* (songs). Preloran catches one of these songs being performed, and we recognize how popular Miranda's compositions are in this region. Many of the songs urge the listeners to maintain their traditions and to learn how to sing native songs and acquire knowledge of the roundup, branding, and work on the range. This work now occupies Cochengo rather than music.

Cochengo's music and sonnets are threaded throughout the film, but his daily activities and the customs of the area predominate. The film opens with one of Cochengo's poems printed on the screen over a clear, starry winter night. As Cochengo sits beside the fire, we see the sun slowly rise, and Cochengo saddles his horse and rides off. In sound-over, Cochengo talks about this arid region in western Argentina and how the customs of the last century are still maintained here. The horsehoof boot, spurs, boleadoras, and lassos are all used for work. Because the land is sandy, growing crops is difficult, and most people raise livestock. The lands are claimed by homesteading; a settler usually has two square leagues because grass for the animals is scarce. Each family establishes an "outpost" with its own well for water five to ten kilometers from the nearest neighbors.

For Cochengo, Preloran translates on the soundtrack as he did with Hermogenes. Preloran translates the Spanish of Maruca, Cochengo's wife, with the use of English subtitles. Maruca introduces us to their five children. Cochengo insists that one should help children get ahead, and education is an important theme in the film. In several scenes, we see the school-age children in their classrooms.

Cattle branding, a rodeo, horse racing, and a cattle auction are seen, and courtship customs of the region are discussed, but a journey taken by Cochengo serves to indicate the difficulties of living in a remote region. The radio, which is the tie to a larger world beyond the outpost, brings news from Chile, Uruguay, even North America. It also provides announcements and broadcasts a message that Cochengo must present himself as soon as possible in the provincial capital city of Santa Rosa to transact the adjudication of his land at the Office of the County Estate.

The trip to Santa Rosa involves riding thirty-five miles on horseback to the road. Cochengo sends his horse back but keeps his saddle to drop off at the next outpost. He then sits at the roadside until a vehicle comes along— sometimes waiting a day or two. When he returns, he will ask those at the outpost where he left his saddle to lend him a horse that belongs to a herd, so it will go home once Cochengo releases it. We watch the sun set and rise before Cochengo gets a ride. Aerial shots of the land fill the screen as he muses on the years when it used to rain more. He comments that they have no medical assistance or mobility: "We're out here in the middle of nowhere."

Cochengo finds himself offended by the government because it has forgotten these people. Rather than send an official to the outposts, the government requires that transactions take place in the capital. After Cochengo arrives at the nearest town, a hundred miles away, he must wait for the bus (which only runs twice a week) that will take him to Telen, where he visits his daughter at a boarding school. In Santa Rosa, at last, he sees his son at his school and then goes to get the title to his land. Cochengo is thrilled with a gift of three little pine trees, which he will plant at home. After thirty years of homesteading, he will now be eligible for bank loans because he has ownership. And the journey home begins. Cochengo's trip is intercut with the family's activities at the outpost, and Preloran makes us aware of the journey's length as family members wonder how far Cochengo has traveled each day.

Although *Cochengo Miranda* documents the seasonal cycles of this cattle rancher and former folksinger, it also shows the slow transculturation that is occurring. Cochengo laments the changing customs and festivities, but at the same time he wants his children to enjoy a more prosperous life.

*Cochengo Miranda* stresses the importance of documenting change and illustrating that folklore is not static but is constantly varying to meet new situations. Preloran, like early folklorists, had initially concentrated on survivals, or "relics from the past," but slowly recognized, as did folklorists, that what was fascinating about folklore was its dynamism. To document a point in time when change is occurring can teach us more about the significance of folklore than reconstructive, romantic portraits.

One of Preloran's major desires has been to better the lives of the people he films by making their needs known. When *Cochengo Miranda* was completed, Preloran arranged a premiere showing at the outpost. Because the film had been produced by grant funds from the province, a large celebration was prepared and the governor was invited. Having authorities see such films is a type of applied folklore that creates a dialogue between the community and the government. Preloran also believes that film has the power to make the members of that community and other viewers, such as ourselves, aware of how important traditional lifestyles and customs are.

Preloran turns to a traditional occupation for his next film on an individual. Sixto Roman Zerda stands out as a powerful representative of a life common to the woodcutters who chop down trees to clear pastures for their landowners' cattle. Living in the forests of central Argentina with his wife and ten children, Zerda spent thirty years endlessly cutting and chopping to earn three hundred dollars per year. *Zerda's Children* (1978) is a study of the Zerdas' plight.[6]

In his development of what he calls the "ethnobiography," Preloran has always chosen a spirited protagonist who exemplifies the folkways of occupational or rural communities or the traditional outlook and behavior of individual craftsmen and artists. *Luther Metke at 94* (1979) continues this emphasis. Like Zerda, Luther Metke uses an ax to cut wood, but he does so to create log cabins.

*Luther Metke at 94* differs from Preloran's other films because the central figure is American and the film was produced, but not shot or edited, by Preloran. Steve Raymen had been Preloran's student at UCLA in 1969-70. After completing his film degree, Raymen moved to Oregon where he later met and developed a rapport with Luther Metke, who was busily constructing log cabins in Camp Sherman, Oregon. In 1978, Raymen worked with Preloran to obtain funds for a film. Preloran would be the overall project director, and Raymen would shoot and later edit the film at UCLA in conjunction with Preloran, who was by then permanently on the UCLA faculty. Raymen shot the film but was unable to finish it, so it was completed under Preloran's direction. Thus, the result is a complex blend of Raymen's initial vision and Preloran's approach. Raymen shot much of the film with a sync-sound tape recorder, but he had mechanical problems, so Preloran used sound-over for many of the scenes. As a result, *Luther Metke* does have certain technical flaws. Several shots at the beginning are jump cut (spliced together without matching the action), and a birthday scene has a glaring white area that appears at the top of the frameline. Some scenes not shot in sync are unsuccessfully made to appear as if they were. A few shots are in soft focus. These flaws are minor, but omissions in the content are not. One of the primary concerns of folklorists in the area of folk architecture is the act of construction. Jump cutting prevents the viewer from seeing the process of creation in its entirety. Although we do see various stages of the work, placing them in perspective is difficult.[7] Moreover, we never see the cabin Metke is building completed. The problems are undoubtedly attributable to the interrupted shooting schedule and changes in personnel.

Despite the diffuse production and postproduction crew that Preloran used, the film bears the Preloran stamp. The process itself is not as fully documented as it is, for example, in *Imaginero,* but the importance of the process of folk architecture in the life of Luther Metke is. To understand folk processes, we must begin with the behavior and insights of individuals involved in these processes. *Luther Metke at 94* aptly demonstrates this relationship.

Luther has lived in the Cascade Mountains of Oregon since 1907 when he took up a homestead claim. Since then, he has built forty cabins. In addition to his creativity with wood, he has written numerous poems that embody his ideas about God and nature. The film opens with the sound-over voice of Luther reciting a poem as winter scenes and a cabin in the snowy woods give way to Luther speaking in sync to the camera. "I'm a wood butcher," he comments while trimming off the bark of a tree with his chainsaw.

Still photos of Luther's earlier years accompany his discussion of how he began building cabins at the age of fifteen in Minnesota and later came to Oregon, married, and raised children. The transmission of folk knowledge is stressed as we are introduced to Gussy and Taylor, a young couple interested in learning to build cabins. The film shows them setting the logs of Luther's current project, a hexagonal cabin. After his wife died, Luther's family wanted him to retire, and he did briefly, but found that he began to hate himself. When his daughter said she wanted a house, he decided to build another one.

A television crew from Baker, Oregon, arrives to shoot a human interest story. Luther is amused that they find a man in his nineties building a log cabin unusual when he doesn't think of himself as unique. He attributes his health to his parents. As for building the cabin, he believes, "You don't have to have much intelligence. . . . It's just work. A strong in the back, weak in the head proposition." We later see Luther and the entire Metke clan settle down to watch the television program. Thus we see not only the television crew in the process of shooting but also the finished program and its reception by Luther and his family.

Throughout the film Luther builds the new cabin, discusses the importance of preserving the timber forests, and impresses us with his independence and sense of humor. The film ends with a large family party held for Luther's ninety-fourth birthday. It then cuts to Luther, in sync, sitting in his cabin declaring, "I don't worry about death. . . . It's a condition we've got to go through, so what's the use of worrying about it?" As snow falls in front of his cabin,

3.10 Luther Metke in one of the cabins he built in Camp Sherman, Oregon. Photo by Einar Moos

Luther sits outside and smiles at the camera, and we are smitten with the personality of this vibrant woodsman who refuses to be conquered by age. In 1980, *Luther Metke* was nominated for an Oscar by the Motion Picture Academy of Arts and Sciences in the category of best short subject documentary.[8]

## Films of Negotiation

One method of revealing the process by which the filmmaker decided to interpret the events shot is to do so openly on film, with freeze-frames, asides, and acknowledgment that the filmmakers were on the scene by showing them in the film. Another is not only to show the filmmaker's presence but also to address the negotiation process between filmmaker and subject on film, thus fusing the two. Although more common in anthropological film than in folklore film, reflexive or negotiated film represents a very small portion of film work. It develops from the work of Jean Rouch on the participatory camera and Mark McCarty and David and Judith MacDougall on observational cinema. It reaches a somewhat reflexive extreme in Lynne Littman's film *In Her Own Time* (1985), in which anthropologist Barbara Myerhoff documents her search for the meaning of her own life as she approaches death.

As video becomes more and more popular with fieldworkers or researchers who pick up a camera to document a family activity and then think about that activity in terms of folklore and openly recognize their own participatory roles, the corpus of reflexive folklore films and videos will no doubt grow (see chapter 7 for the video revolution in folkloristics). Two films illustrate the issues of negotiated folklore filmmaking: John Cohen's *Carnival in Q'eros: Where the Mountains Meet the Jungle* (1990), and *Zulay, Facing the Twenty-first Century* (1993), by Jorge and Mabel Preloran and Zulay Saravino.

Cohen has been making films in Peru since 1956. He is well known to the Andean people and has shot four films in Q'eros. However, while shooting at carnival time in 1983, Cohen was attacked by Q'eros. A Japanese film team had worked in the region since Cohen's previous visit and reportedly had paid individuals to appear on film. On an earlier trip, Cohen had brought axes for the people; this time he brought sickles. But the other camera team had learned about Cohen's planned payment in sickles from an anthropologist in whom Cohen had confided. As a result, the other filmmakers chose to pay in sickles as well as in cash (Cohen 1992). Apparently those Q'eros not paid by the Japanese film crew had now come to carnival and displayed their resentment against both film teams (Cohen 1987).

On a subsequent trip to Q'eros, Cohen resolved the issue of paying those who serve as subjects in a film. The problems of a member of one culture filming another without exploitation are openly addressed and become a central theme in *Carnival.* As Cohen states,

In doing the right thing, they [the Japanese film crew] did sort of the wrong thing. Now the way I dealt with that when I went back and made *Carnival in Q'eros,* the way I rectified it, was I refused to pay money. I just wouldn't, and I set up a dilemma which is the heart of the film. I was working with Juan Nuñez del Prado, who's a good anthropologist down there. He knew the Q'eros. I purchased a thousand dollars worth of alpacas . . . because that's the local currency really. That's where the wealth is, in alpacas. And that's what I gave them, and they said, "Just give money," and I said, "No, I won't." The last part of the film is very much about the issue of how to distribute these alpacas across the whole community. [Cohen 1992]

Cohen begins *Carnival in Q'eros* with a romanticized statement: "High in the Andes in the isolated Peruvian community of Q'eros, one senses that time has stopped and that people are living in the past." Then a comment about bank loans strikes a wrong note. Could such isolated people have bank loans? Cohen then focuses on carnival as a series of rituals. He shows the offerings to the gods and to Mother Earth, the fertility rituals for the alpacas, and the Palcha songs of the women who sing about their troubles, and he incorporates a remark about the bankers who "are coming for our food." The men sing their own songs as Cohen shows the animals mating in the fields and states that the season celebrates fertility. At Hauton Q'eros, the ceremonial center where the mountains meet the jungle, Q'eros groups (ayllus) from throughout the mountains meet. In this powerful place, the men arrive on horseback to display their own power to each other. All night long, the groups visit, sing, and musically blow through shells. The next day, the carnival dance takes place. The clothing, woven for the carnival, has designs particular to the Q'eros. Chicha and coca leaves are distributed, and the carnival song for this year is selected. The carnival is an event highly structured by ritual, music, religion, and fertility rites. While the rain falls, the Q'eros sing. As he has done in many of his films, Cohen displays his absorption with traditional music. An intertitle explains: "The musical heterophony of the carnival resembles the sound of celebrations in the jungle. This musical structure exemplifies a connection between the Andes and the Amazon."

The carnival comes to a close, and one anticipates that the film will end by following the natural flow of an event to its conclusion. But a new event begins. The Q'eros men call a meeting with the film crew and anthropologist Juan Nuñez del Prado from Cuzco. Men from all five mountain villages attend, and the guide who brought the horses translates. The Q'eros are in trouble with the banks, they explain. They borrowed money to buy alpacas, but the alpacas were too old to reproduce. Now they owe the money plus interest and have no way to pay. Cohen says he will reciprocate their help in making the film. With some money he has made on the last film he shot in Q'eros, he will purchase alpacas. As the film makes more money, more alpacas will be purchased. The men

3.11 From *Carnival in Q'eros.* Photo by John Cohen

discuss all the problems. Will everyone share? Will some live long enough to see any reward? Although one remarks that he just wants the money now, another points out that Peruvian money goes down [the inflation rate was 2,000 percent per year] and the American dollar goes up and will be worth more as time passes, and thus the plan will work. They decide to agree and begin to spell out the details. At Ocongate, a few days later, young alpacas arrive that were purchased with the cooperation of the University of Cuzco. Cohen asks how the men like the animals, and they reply that they are fine, no problem. Seeing the Q'eros in town without their native clothing, Cohen inquires about this. The Q'eros are ridiculed in this place, they tell him. Cohen takes the opportunity to shoot the culture clash, showing the Q'eros amid an array of goods in the market. They sign a document agreeing to Cohen's gift of sixty-one alpacas. The alpacas trot down the road in beautiful sunlight (a sharp contrast to the dark, misty, and dreary mountain footage with which Cohen began the film). All the people hug del Prado and the film crew before they take off down the road. In Spanish, Cohen bids them good luck with the alpacas. A title tells viewers where to send contributions if they wish to help with the purchase of more alpacas for the Q'eros.

*Carnival in Q'eros* does document the carnival, but it becomes a film about collaboration and negotiation, authority and power. A hint of the problems that will later surface in the film are given in the opening when the Q'eros, in a seemingly incongruous statement, mention their bank loan. Obviously, Cohen places the remark (or allows it to remain) there as foreshadowing. One thinks the film will be about survival in the face of the modern world on a ritual level. Instead, the film is about survival on an economic level. When the Q'eros sing, "You must help us. You are like our father, our mother," they are beseeching Cohen as well as the gods. As viewers, we don't realize until later that some songs are directed at him. The fertility rites for the animals are also laden with ritual and practical meaning; the infertility of the alpacas is directly related to the Q'eros's problems.

By placing himself in the film, Cohen and the Q'eros share the project. They become the equals they should be in a transaction in which everyone gains something. In the process, each reaffirms the other's common humanity. As viewers, we glimpse something of a lifestyle unlike our own. Yet we recognize a commonality in the celebration of ritual. We see the Q'eros not as stereotypes of the mountain people of Peru, but as individuals who celebrate and have to cope with life in pragmatic terms as do people everywhere. Cohen's presence as an interactive force in the film gives us that window through which we see ourselves and through which the individuals in the film present themselves to us.

Interaction and negotiation are also the keys to the effectiveness of *Zulay, Facing the Twenty-first Century,* by Jorge and Mabel Preloran and Zulay Saravino. What began as a folkloric film on weavers in the Otavalo region in the Andean highlands of northern Ecuador becomes instead a dialogue. Preloran begins the film with a letter from Zulay's mother presented to her through the screen of the Moviola on which the film is being cut. Much of the first part exists as a flashback, with the conversations of Zulay and Mabel providing information about the images that represent the Otavaleños. All the usual material is presented: spectacular shots of the country where Zulay lives, the process of carding and spinning wool, weaving, and the needle embroidery done on a machine with designs said to be from the times of the Inca. Zulay discusses legends, food, ancestral ceremonies with bread effigies for the day of the dead, child-rearing practices, Catholicism, schooling, and ethnic differences in the region. Preloran documents a healing session, creates a montage of Inca masks that stress the antiquity of this civilization, portrays the lifestyle of members of Zulay's family, and demonstrates the importance of the marketplace and tourism. Zulay's family weaves, but she explains that the weavings are now made for tourists.

This first half of the two-hour film seems much like any film about another culture. At the end of the flashback, however, Zulay asks if she may accompany the filmmakers to Los Angeles to seek out new markets for the family's weavings. Still shots of Jorge shooting and Mabel operating the tape recorder allow us to see the film production situation for the first time. As Zulay's plane takes off from Quito, a long suspended shot marks the liminal world Zulay has entered. The filmmakers use an intertitle to suggest that we take our energy and talent with us when we emigrate and leave behind our roots and traditions—a puzzle the Prelorans have dealt with themselves as Argentines who live in the United States, yet travel back and forth.

After shooting the film on and off for eight years, Preloran suddenly saw the new direction it had to take. "It was going to be an ethnographic film, and then, eventually, with Zulay coming to visit so many times, we thought, well, *that* was the story" (Preloran 1992). In Los Angeles, Preloran films Mabel and Zulay as tourists visiting Disneyland and Marineland. Zulay poses with a man in a Fred Flintstone costume. Zulay always wears her traditional dress as a symbol of her identity, and she no doubt seems to be as strange and as much in costume to those who see her as the cartoon characters seem to her. The film contrasts these scenes with carnival in Otavalo.

The film now moves between Otavalo and Los Angeles with the filmed images presented through the Moviola and with Zulay's return trip to Otavalo. She sees Otavalo with different eyes and doesn't feel that she fits in as well as she did in the past. Once more, she departs for Los Angeles.

The relationship between Zulay and the Prelorans deepens. Mabel begins discussing her own anxieties about leaving her culture behind and traveling between worlds. Finally, the two women take over the film and Zulay begins to edit the film about herself and her family. The film closes as it began, showing the letter from Zulay's mother, who tells her that, if she is doing well, she should not return. In Otavalo, unmarried women who travel become the subject of gossip. Even more important, Zulay is no longer the person she once was. Mabel asks her pointedly whether she will stay or return. Zulay, in tears, responds, "I don't know."

Any line that ever existed between the filmmaker and the filmed is erased in *Zulay*. The film deals with the problems of what the filmmakers call "transculturation." It also creates a complex picture of the filmmakers—all three of them—who operate before and behind the camera. *Zulay* offers us the process of negotiation and interaction that is usually hidden from view and makes it a central issue. What begins as a project about the Other ends as a film about the self.

## Focus and Technique in Folklore Films

The focus on primitive societies, evidenced by ethnodocumentary filmmakers, has shifted to a focus on rural folk. Blank, Hawes, Peiser, Thigpen, and I have shot films on urban activities, and Ferris has included some urban locales in his work, but for others the folk are generally thought of as those who live in small towns or regions or those who are in some way isolated from mainstream society. With the exception of the event-oriented films and the films about individual artists or performers made by Blank, Ferris and Peiser, Preloran, and the author, most of the films discussed concentrate on communities, cultures, or regions. For Fleischhauer, the region is West Virginia; Cohen pictures Hazard, Kentucky, and the mountains of Peru; Ferris is filming the Mississippi Delta; and Blank looks at musical cultures from Louisiana Cajuns and *Tecanos* to polka dancers from coast to coast. In *Quilino, Araucanians,* and *Valle Fertil,* Preloran documents small villages and an Indian tribe. Wagner and Ferrero recall occupational communities, the elderly, and women. Yet the focal point of each film can either intensify the sense of community portrayed in the film or it can detract from it. Fleischhauer, in his presentation of technological processes, and Hawes, in her delineation of fiddle texts for *Say, Old Man,* acknowledge the dimension of the human creative process, but their filmic approach slights it. Films by Blank, Cohen, Davenport, Ferrero, Preloran, Thigpen, and the author that focus on a community place technological and expressive processes in the perspective of creative and emotional reasons for production. If the filmmaker wishes to focus on isolated items and their manufacture, as folktale and ballad scholars examined texts and their transmission, which is the organizing principle of films on texts and artifacts, the filmmaker artificially separates the expressive outward manifestations of human behavior from the people themselves.

The event as a major focus, seen in the work of World War II documentarians and films such as *Woodstock,* as well as in the film work of Bateson and Mead, Marshall, and Asch, has served as the organizing principle for Cohen, Davenport, Fleischhauer, Hawes, and Thigpen. The biographical model of Flaherty, Drew Associates, and Gardner has been used by Blank, Ferrero, Ferris, Peiser, Preloran, and the author. Films about specific individuals demonstrate the capability of folkloric filmmakers to capture the multifaceted processes of creativity as a cohesive whole by structuring their films around life's events, which for Preloran is where the emphasis must be placed. He asks, "Where should the stress of the film dwell? In material culture and details that show differences between one culture and another—leaving us unsatisfied and bored—or should the stress be on the dramatic flow of events, where the *ways* of doing things are brought in—rather unheralded, in the context of the normal routine" (Suber 1971:48).

By analyzing the techniques of these films, what conclusions can be reached regarding the interplay between content focus and filmic style and technique? Films that make statements about the historicity of tradition, that attempt to reconstruct history, or that focus on the outward expressive manifestations or artifacts of a people are generally narrated and are structured as a montage of subjective impressions. Films that follow step-by-step processes of technology are usually edited in proper time sequence. If the people involved in this process are secondary to the intent of the film, the film may be narrated for descriptive purposes.

The most engaging films illustrate contemporary theoretical issues by documenting events and processes in their entirety. Such films depict a narrative event from beginning to end and so include the interactions of participants as they unfold. Craft production films begin with the gathering of the materials, show the processes of creation, demonstrate the product's use, and concentrate on individual folk artists, to place folk traditions in the full scope of their lives. Films that focus on individuals allow the people to express themselves with sync-sound or sound-over and force the filmmaker to structure his or her editing around the events that give meaning to the creative acts of human beings.

Individuals who tell their own stories are memorable. Once we learn about their lives through film, we can no longer regard them as strangers. They are, in a sense, another reflection of ourselves. Negotiated and interactive films often achieve a dialogue that reveals the construct of film and a shared humanity. Film is a unique way of "meeting" individuals whose lifestyles may differ but who are nevertheless similar to us in their concerns and traditions, whatever they may be.[9] Sometimes, when such films are successful, we meet ourselves.

# 4

# A Search for Self
## *Filmmakers Reflect on Their Work*

*Filmmaking has become the recipient of all my creative energies. It
receives the same concern that painting, photographing, recording and
performing music would get from me. All these eggs are in one basket.*
— *John Cohen*

*Folklorists often privilege* the voices of their informants, allowing their words to
eclipse those of the folklorist. Of course, folklorists, like filmmakers, then edit
the material to construct their own notion of what is significant.[1] Cutting and
splicing the interviews, they impart the answers to those questions that interest them. An interactive discussion in film addresses the subjects both the
folklorist and the interviewee find significant, just as it does in the field. The
folklorist's job is much like that of the quiltmaker or the filmmaker: to cut up
all the pieces and put them back together again to create a new design. Thus,
much like editing a film or making a quilt, I have cut and pieced together a
new whole. Seeking to present my own concerns and those communicated
through the common voice of a group of folklore filmmakers, I deliberately
have grouped together their responses, rather than holistically printing my
transcriptions of each interview. In their remarks about general issues and
those pertinent to their own situations, the filmmakers' personalities surface.

Few folklore filmmakers have created reflexive films that call attention to
the film as a constructed reality of their own making, depict the negotiation
with those in the films on the film record itself, or reveal their thoughts directly
to the audience. Yet they have certainly reflected on their own creative
processes of making films. Their ruminations about what worked and why, and
how their attitudes were shaped, rarely appear in print (Cohen 1987, 1990;
Lux 1989; March 1978; Preloran 1975; Sherman 1986). Nevertheless, their
choices of subject matter, their techniques, the compromises they made, and
the processes of collaboration and negotiation reveal much about the filmmakers' conceptions of themselves as both self and Other.

Although reflexivity has been the subject of much interest in the humanities and social sciences (Babcock 1980; Clifford and Marcus 1986; Geertz
1988; Georges and Jones 1980; Rabinow 1977; Ruby 1982a), in-depth studies of the effects of specific film projects on the researcher as well as the subject
have been limited (Ruby 1988; Sherman 1986). As video use grows, and consumers and scholars discover that they are using folklore to document their
own lives, the demand for conceptual frameworks grows.

Current theoretical models question what behavior might be documented
and how, and filmmakers have contemplated the influence of their own craft.
To discover their approaches, I interviewed Carl Fleischhauer, Bill Ferris, and
Bess Hawes in 1974, and Les Blank, John Cohen, Judy Peiser, and Jorge
Preloran in both 1975-76 and 1992-93. I also met with Tom Davenport, Pat
Ferrero, Ken Thigpen, and Paul Wagner (all folklore filmmakers who have
emerged in recent years) in 1992-93. My questions and our conversations addressed both the technical and theoretical reasons filmmakers have or have not
changed subjects or techniques. What is involved in the creation of folkloric
films? What do folkloric filmmakers see as their objectives and how do they
perceive the role of filmmaking? What are their attitudes about the films they
have completed and how have these attitudes informed their film documents?
Have their productions and their subjects influenced them and, if so, how?
Their answers reveal much about the conventions of their films and the hidden
self behind the camera.

## Choice of Subject

In choosing folklore as their subject matter, these filmmakers reinforced their
own notions about the folk and often reflected their own concerns with a personal past being "worked out" through film. In a 1975 letter, Cohen noted that
his films, most of which document traditional musicians, "fall into the categories which folklorists study," although he asserted that he had never used the
word *folk* or the term *folklore* in any of his films. In 1992, he was still avoiding
such terms: "Fifteen films now and never used the word *folk* in them. At first
I didn't want to because I was in argument with the word. Now I'm in total argument with the word because it means so many different things to so many
people that it's not at all clear."[2] Cohen remarked that he had been called an
"'ist'—a folklorist, an anthropologist, an ethnomusicologist."[3]

In 1975, when I asked Peiser about her choice of subject, she said, "People
don't want to look at their own culture. . . . People would like to look at something 'exotic,' something 'foreign.'" As an example, she cited the work of
Timothy Asch (discussed in chapter 1). "I think it's a shame. . . . They should
be more aware of what's happening today in their own neighborhoods." Peiser

documented the people of the Mississippi Delta with Bill Ferris and wanted folkloric films to document local, not foreign, peoples, unlike the Yanomamö films of Asch. In 1992, we discussed these films again. Judy looked back at her corpus of films and commented on the changes in her emphasis: "All these were films that were kind of like little postage stamps. You know, *Gravel Springs Fife and Drum, Gospel Singer,* and a lot of it was just about rural life. . . . They were all good films, but in a way they didn't really relate to today. . . . They're almost like cultural artifacts now."[4]

When I asked how the films were like postage stamps, she replied: "They took small communities or a craft or a family and documented their lives and documented their community. When you put all those films together, they really do describe the rural South. But I was always interested in what the other part of the stamp would look like. I was really interested because I lived in Memphis. I was interested in the urban area, and much more interested in ethnic cultures and more contemporary communities."

Comparing ethnodocumentaries and folklore films, Ferris pointed out that subject matter, not technique, is a determining factor for his work. He remarked: "The anthropologist looks at aboriginal, what has been called 'primitive' behavior. The folklorist is looking at folk culture, which is culture within the boundary of literate society, in which oral tradition is a primary force. So I would draw a line between a film on the Navajo Indians and a film on the Cajun culture: one is anthropological, the second is folkloric. . . . But I think that film techniques are going to be essentially the same."[5]

After Bill Ferris went to the University of Mississippi, Ferris and Peiser began producing films individually. Bill had been interested in the rural; Judy now shifted her attention to her own backyard and undertook urban fieldwork. In the early eighties she started raising funds for what would become a huge multimedia project in Memphis. Les Blank's notion of folklore films also has changed. In 1975, Blank told me, "I'm interested in peoples, especially seeing how people operate. I'm mainly interested in primitive peoples who haven't gotten bogged down with sophistication and neuroses and cheap or shoddy value systems. And folklore, I guess, is something that's vanishing, and I would like to help preserve it, or at least make a record of it."

Blank's focus on rural groups and his remarks about Cajuns as isolated peoples in *Spend It All* indicate that his initial work was romantic in orientation. His notions of the folk reinforced stereotypes about folklore as disappearing traditions. In 1993, we discussed this issue again and Blank was surprised at his earlier assumptions. "I said that?" he asked. Today, his ideas about folklore have broadened: "I think folklore is an expression of ways of seeing the world and ways of communicating attitudes and feelings. Some folk express it differently than other folk. And I think that all of the folk or folklore were just different aspects of it—that you probably have folklore in almost any kind of popular culture you can look at. Even the stuff that's handed to us."[6]

Once Blank shared a theoretical stance with early preservation-oriented folklorists. Having worked in the field for over twenty years, Blank now has a wider view of folklore, as evidenced in his work. "I shoot what interests me and I guess my interests change over the years." I asked him if his recent films were profiles. He replied, "Each one is about that person, yes. What they do and how they do it, who they do it with, who they do it for." As he has developed as a filmmaker, Blank has focused more on the individual.

For Hawes, context and focal points in the communicative process, as opposed to cultural overviews, are the aspects of behavior that she documents. "The folklorist has always, by virtue of his discipline, focused on particular points in the stream of behavior and, if he's been any good, he has gotten the tangential behavior around those crucial events. That's what we call context. I think it's the lead up and the go away period that most of us have paid some attention to."[7] Hawes believes context supersedes categorization.

Preloran has filmed individuals who have interested him, and he has not been overly concerned about the categories into which these individuals might fall. Preloran portrays their folklore as part of a tradition, but as a tradition affected by transculturation. Like many folklorists, he assumes that folklore is part of a cognitive process. Preloran has made only one film that might be classified as an ethnodocumentary: his 1975 film on the Warao Indians of Venezuela. Preloran finds the film insignificant because it deals with a culture foreign to his own. He is more interested, like Peiser, in looking at groups within his own country who are not isolated or exotic. He calls these groups "folk cultures." In "Documenting the Human Condition," Preloran emphasizes these differences: "When filming folk cultures as I've been doing—because in Argentina there are no truly isolated cultures left—there is no exotic or fascinating action that one can use to give a punchy ending to the film. And sometimes dramatic undercurrents can be found in the course of filming long months: the process of a drought, the slow transculturation patterns, the feeling that evil exists but can't be pinned down—and thus the need for atonement through religious beliefs—the friction between local authorities, and the staid ways of traditional behavior" (1975:106).

This process of filming traditional behavior differs from films that have been called ethnographic. As Preloran notes, "The majority of them create a gulf between us and the 'primitive' people they usually depict" (1975:105). In a classroom discussion at the University of Oregon in 1992, Preloran emphasized the political and personal significance of subject choice:

> "Everything's politics. And, of course, the choice of my subjects is political. I chose that character instead of this one, and that's my choice. And the

way I present my character is my choice. I love those characters. I love them, so that's a choice. You can go in there like *Dead Birds*. Gardner didn't like those people; you can tell in his narration. Listen, assume you were in Beruit, and you were at war for ten years—there must be something going on there. You just can't go in from outside and say, "These people are warring all the time." You have to have a view from inside. And if you don't do that, then what's the point, you know?"[8]

Preloran chooses his subjects because he has an affinity for them, and that choice is entirely his own. Similarly, folklorist Ken Thigpen teamed up with his neighbor, George Hornbein, a filmmaker, and together they chose their film topics.

We came up with an ambitious list of things that we wanted to do. George, I guess, latched on to folklore as this kind of preindustrial documentation project. . . . So we started with ideas of things that people did that continued the heritage of some tradition that in a way would not romanticize it, would not trivialize it, would not marginalize it but try to get it from within—to use the film as a way of getting people to speak about their own experiences, and to live their own experiences on the camera for us.

And so we came up with elaborate topics. Migrant workers were interesting to us for a while—and we never did this film. There's a skill of picking the fruit that's being lost. . . . There's a kind of a dignity to what they do that comes from knowing how to do something that's not as simple as it looks—for somebody to take fruit and put it in a bag and to not have it bruise and so on, and so it very quickly is interesting. Because I couldn't do it, you couldn't do it. You know, it takes practice, it's a tradition, it's learning, it's a folk occupation. So anyway, we wanted to show that, not from the point of view of pitying the poor migrant, but rather to show that it was a folk technological or pretechnological kind of activity that was dying out. But that wasn't the point. The point was that it's something people know how to do. So we came up with ideas like this.[9]

The idea of filming what was "dying out" soon changed to documenting the students on Thigpen's campus, and the shift from studying the folklore of the Other shifted to studying the folklore of academe by looking at the salamander-swallowing ritual of one fraternity at Penn State.

Tom Davenport remarked that it was the folklorist, rather than the filmmaker, who was focused on the past. He asserted that folklorists need to look at the self:

Most of the things that are folklore that are really alive folklorists never see because they are so much a part of their lives, like a fish not knowing what water is because it's so close. Usually, folklorists tend to, it seems to me, be interested in things that are already beginning to wane. For example, nobody would make a film about—maybe they would—mechanics in a garage that fix cars, but they'll make a film about basket makers or people who make rugs in a certain kind of way because there are only a few of

them left and yet there's just as much skill and probably just as much folklore in . . . the group of guys that fix your car and the way that kind of
occupational folklore would develop as there would be in a basket maker.
Maybe folklore has changed a little bit, but that's where your vitality would
be, with the mechanics. Generally they just sorta look back . . . not realizing
what is just around you.[10]

Paul Wagner and I talked about carver Vincent Palumbo's comment in
*The Stone Carvers* that stone carving was "going the way of the passenger
pigeon." A similar phrase appears in *Free Show Tonite*. We joked about whether
I should write that Wagner thought folklore was dying out. For Wagner, folklore is not dying out, but some traditional behaviors have disappeared, perhaps
forever. I noted that many of his films seemed to be catching people at an end
point. Wagner replied,

Right, on the cusp, the disappearance or whatever. What do I think? Do I
indeed think these things are dying out? To me it's pretty obvious that
given cultures are dying out or at least the lore is in many different areas. It
gets quickly into how you define folklore and everything, 'cause you'd say,
"Xerox art is alive and well," which is one they talk about as a contemporary thing. Well, that's fine, but in my mind there's a pretty clear distinction
between that and an Appalachian musical tradition or an Italian stone carving tradition. Yes, I do think those things are dying out. You can relate that
directly to the number of televisions manufactured in the U.S.[11]

I remarked, "Well, *Free Show Tonite* seems to me to be especially nostalgic. I
guess *Grand Generation* does, too, because it's catching people before they're
dying." He responded,

I think all these play on it. You were talking earlier about how some of the
films are about things happening and others are about things remembered.
I appreciate the dynamism you capture on film by filming something that's
happening. On the other hand, there's a lot to be said for the emotional
tone that can be captured and sort of the irony and more complex emotions
that can be captured by making films about things that happened in the
past and are filmed through people's memories and psychological life. And
I don't know if that's folklore or psychology or history or whatever, but
memory is sort of the ongoing thing I think my films are about, more than
folklore. It's just that folklore was a way into that in terms of leading to
subject matter and . . . to provide sort of a scholarly vocabulary and context
for dealing with it. But the Irish film [*Out of Ireland* (1994)] is really much
more of a film about history than it is folklore, if you want to talk about
academic division.

Many of Wagner's films were initiated by folklorists who wanted to see
their dissertation topics or fieldwork projects become films. Wagner's folklorist
partners worked for the Smithsonian, and he found his notions about folklore
often expanded to correlate with that of the folklorist with whom he was work-

ing: "You can do film forever. You know, there's an unlimited number of folk-lorists with an unlimited number of really pretty interesting subjects. They all virtually revolve around people or a community. And they're all amazingly filmic, whether it's a musician or craftsperson or some other more hybrid form of folklore study. They all make great films really. And you can just go on for-ever."

What made some films more significant than others Wagner attributed to style and the ability to capture folklore as well as transcend the boundaries of folklore film: "I think they all have their plusses and minuses. I think *The Stone Carvers* has become the thing I'm best known for principally because of the Academy Award. But also because compared to the others it's sort of the most polished in a way. And, certainly, for a broader audience outside the folklorist circle, it sort of works. Even though I think it's a solid film as folklore, it trans-lates well to a general audience." The more a film encompasses, the more people will like it because audiences can relate to it in multiple ways.

Carl Fleischhauer's considerations of who and what folklorists document is similar to my own. Subject matter becomes one determining factor. He re-marked:

> It's perfectly clear that if you have a film like Bess Lomax's film about the fiddle player playing six tunes, that you've got a film that's about folklore and ethnomusicology, and if you have film about circumcision rituals amongst the Gisu tribesmen of Uganda, that you've got an anthropological film. And that may be finally the answer. And that begs the question, of course. But the question that it begs isn't a question about film, but the question that it begs is what is the difference between anthropology and folklore. We often joke about the fact that if you collect oral histories from the Trobriand Islanders, you're an anthropologist. If you collect oral histo-ries from Czechs from South Side Chicago, you're a folklorist, and if you collect oral histories from Navajos, well, I don't know what to say. But it is very hard to distinguish the activities, at least the fieldwork side of it.[12]

How filmmakers perceive themselves as part of these activities becomes the vital question. Fleischhauer calls himself an artist: "It seems pompous to say this—I think finally I am an artist . . . in my function as a writer and a pho-tographer, still photographer, and sound recordist. I like to make things like that and they are generally called documentary, but a documentary in photog-raphy is an art category." Although subject matter may help to categorize film, the activity itself becomes paramount for most filmmakers.

The filmmaking process as an artistic endeavor ultimately blends with the categories imposed by content. Pat Ferrero has collected oral histories from Native Americans and from women in San Francisco. She is unconcerned with categorization and prefers to cut across these arbitrary divisions. Ferrero chose folklore as her subject by looking at women as folk artists. As an artist, Ferrero found herself thinking about how women's voices had been stilled by having their art labeled "domestic." An exhibit at the Whitney Museum framed quilts in a section separated from the work of well-known artists, thus emphasizing their dissimilarity. "And I responded with just a sense of frustration and outrage that the quilts were anonymous art. And I think it was realizing that they were made by women, that the formal qualities of Amish quilts—and it was the first time I'd seen Amish quilts—was so extraordinary and to my sensibility more interesting . . . and it brought home for me those questions of who's making the decisions and why is this work anonymous."[13]

Ferrero mounted an exhibit at the San Francisco Art Institute with three colleagues experienced in art and textiles. Her ideas about art and being a woman coalesced. As a rebuttal to art exhibits that valorized "high" art, Ferrero decided to stretch the boundaries with a show placing quilts in a social historical context. Ferrero displayed the quilts in terms of their function, which led to an examination of how art is classified: "It was organized around a woman's life cycle from birth to death. . . . Quilts were hung with excerpts from diaries and journals, with some photographs, and the exhibit became our first exploration around that issue of the definition of high versus folk art."

In the context of the show, Ferrero invited members of the community to bring in their own quilts and talk about their creation and meaning. Her colleagues then dated the quilts and discussed what they knew about them. This experience would eventually lead to Ferrero's first major film, *Quilts in Women's Lives*. A dozen Mennonite quilters from the central valley of California arrived wearing traditional dress. Learning that such a community existed, Ferrero began to visit the central valley and conducted over sixty interviews with quilters there. This research prompted her to think about a film that would look at contemporary traditional quilters from a variety of backgrounds: "That's how the film evolved. It really came out of, first, the exhibit, and then the public response to the exhibit, and the people who kind of surfaced out of nowhere and made me realize how lively an art it still was."

Ferrero knew she was working in a realm outside the interdisciplinary arts program in which she taught. "The experimental art world at that time I don't think was particularly interested in women, or women artists, and certainly not traditional artists. So in that sense I was on the fringe of what was considered "cutting edge." . . . And I was using my own interests in traditional and folk art to really question some of those definitions about art."

Ferrero's film looks at some quilters who might be considered traditional, hence folk artists, and others, artists working with fabric as their medium for innovation, who might be considered elite artists. Like Ferrero, I found myself at the crossroads of high versus folk art, a debate which most folklorists ignored but one with which I had long grappled.[14] In 1985, I met chainsaw

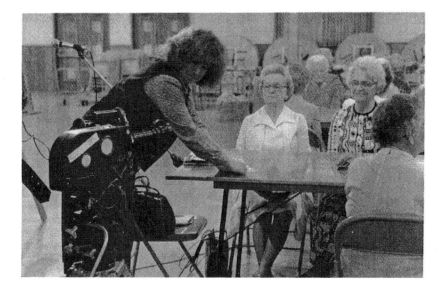

4.1  Pat Ferrero on location at a Mennonite quilting bee in Reedley, California, for *Quilts in Women's Lives*

sculptor Skip Armstrong. Because he defined his art in terms of context, Armstrong was the perfect figure to film, literally "in context," as a means of addressing questions about the effect of context on definition. Although his work did not reflect directly on me in the same manner that quilts spoke to Ferrero as a woman and to me for *Kathleen Ware, Quiltmaker,* Armstrong's work struck a regional chord in me. How did such art reflect the Oregon experience with wood and the environment? How might questions about definition affect the ways viewers, particularly folklorists, saw art?

Ferrero found that film offered a voice to women and their folklore, even though they had been largely ignored. Tom Davenport, working closely with folklorist Dan Patterson, found that studying "the folk" was another way of opening the window to an understanding of humanity. Stereotypes of the folk no longer held. Showing that change became a valuable endeavor, Davenport pointed out:

> What Dan was particularly able to do on those films, he was able to see and articulate the importance of the subject so that even though we'd get discouraged in the editing process, we felt, especially I felt, that I was doing something significant. That this wasn't just an obscure folkloric kind of, little aberrant bit of, American culture. That, in fact, the Joines and the Landis family were spokespeople for much larger trends in American society and they represented almost a seed bank of ideas and ways of thinking about things. A seed bank, you know, where they preserve these traditional

strains of seeds, and then they can make hybrids out of them later on. But if you don't have the traditional seeds, you can't make the hybrids.

Filmmakers select spokespeople who are not often considered exceptional, but who nonetheless become representatives or "stand in" for others. For *Tales of the Supernatural,* my emphasis was on storytelling. The children were not the focus. I met a number of teenagers who all knew each other, and I selected those with whom I felt a rapport. Drawing upon the teenagers telling ghost stories, I hypothesized about the function of legends for American teenagers at large.

Filmmakers determine the spokespeople for the group and choose the particular subject or subjects who will appear in the film to fit the intent of the project. For a film about an artist, the choice is already made; for films about communities, the choice often is made on the basis of filmic personality, narrative style, or finding and focusing on a central person. Wagner noted,

> Certainly the choice of particular stone carvers included was largely Marjorie's. I met them, liked 'em, and thought they'd be great and I certainly agreed with that, but those were the guys she'd principally worked with. So that was a given. In terms of actual carving? I think part of the feeling was, and I might be totally wrong on this, I imagine what we thought at the time was Roger was sort of the more domineering or prominent storyteller, which certainly proved to be true, and that therefore it made sense for Vincent to be the person who did the carving. Plus the fact he was the one who was actually there working, so it was an easier fit in terms of structuring the scenes and everything. His carving the arm we probably could have set that up, staged that in some way, but, in fact, he was carving the timpen, that semicircular piece over the front door, and so the timing worked out well for us to film him doing that and then we, in part, filmed real carving on that arm, but you realize a lot of that is set up.

In the case of *The Stone Carvers,* Wagner relied on Marjorie Hunt's well-established relationship with the carvers.

The choice of subject for some films grows out of a project already in progress. Blank, for example, was watching his film about garlic as it came out of the lab, and he noticed that two women had gaps between their two front teeth.

> And that set me off wondering what would happen if this film I'm watching was not my film about garlic, but was a film about nothing but gap-toothed women. . . . So I sent a grant application off to the American Film Institute, and they had turned down every one of my other films, and this one they liked and gave me the money. And even prior to that I had been made curious when I was attending a lecture at Tulane University, where I was majoring in English. And the professor was a very inspiring teacher and was reading to us from the Wife of Bath's tale, and he commented on the line that "Gat-toothed was she." And she had many lovers who were wandering along the way and he explained that gap-toothedness

in the Middle Ages implied that a woman was likely to be lusty and have a strong appetite for sexual activity, and that, to a young man, was very impressive. So, when I saw the gap-toothed woman in the film, who happened to be one of my employees—I just threw her in at the last minute to get an anti-garlic attitude into this film that was totally pro-garlic—I felt like making that film. And then later found out that the second woman did not have gap teeth. It was just a quirk of lighting on her teeth that made her look gap-toothed.

An interest Blank had since he was a Tulane student and a quick idea in a screening room presented a film topic. Serendipity is the mother of some film topics.

For other films, Les Blank sometimes chose people with whom he had become friends. He met Marc Savoy while working on *Spend It All*, and Savoy eventually played an important role in the film. Over the years, Blank and Savoy maintained a friendship and, while making *J'ai Été au Bal*, Blank stayed at Savoy's house. At the same time, Blank began a film in New Orleans about three gifted individuals, one of whom died before the film could be completed. Part of the film focused on chef Paul Prudhomme, who became famous as Les was starting to shoot. To salvage the footage, he decided to make a film on Cajun and Creole cooking. "And then I went to Marc to help me out and he became, more or less, the essential character in the film *Yum, Yum, Yum!* And after shooting *Yum, Yum, Yum!* and *J'ai Été au Bal*, I realized that there was a lot of material of Marc and Ann that didn't get used. And I thought that they should deserve a film of their own, so I shot more footage just to tell their story." In this way, more than the music or the unusual, Blank turned to the familiar. His friends thus became the subjects for *Marc and Ann*, one of Blank's best films because it displays Blank's warm relationship with the Savoys.

The major rationale for shooting tends to be an interest not only in the topic at large but in the uniqueness of the seemingly ordinary people who appear in the film. Davenport remarked that asking significant questions allowed him to discover what really concerned those he was filming: "Well, a lot of times when you're a filmmaker, you have to do things that you wouldn't normally do in polite society, but there are interesting things people do and you almost approach the subject like a child. . . . I mean that's the impulse—you have to have a certain kind of naïveté and a feeling when you're making the film that you're genuinely interested in the people. You like them, you're not trying to put them down, but you really think they're doing something odd, but it sure is interesting, and you have that kind of feeling."

Often the choice of subject is shaped by an event as much as or more than by the participants. For Thigpen, the idea for making a film about university students swallowing salamanders on his own campus was suggested inadvertently to him by his wife. Although he and Hornbein had been searching for a somewhat pre-industrial topic, events occurring in front of him led him to a very different idea:

> My wife, Ann Marie, was telling me about some of her students that year, and I had been teaching folklore classes where I had gotten student papers on, you know, the "folklore of academe" type of thing. And I was aware of a lot of the fraternity things that were going on at that time. And this one came up because one year, I think it was about '81, her students were real tied up in this Bowery Ball. She said, "What is the Bowery Ball?" They had to miss her class, so they started telling her in detail about this fraternity party they had had forever. Of course, it's kind of interesting that the depth of tradition might be four years or forty years or four hundred years. And actually, for them, the notion of it does go back several generations. But they had developed the salamander ritual, the brothers had done it for a number of years, maybe twenty-five years formally with salamanders. I found out later from a student that his grandfather had gone to Penn State and, as this young student was growing up, had always challenged the conventional wisdom that Harvard had invented goldfish swallowing, that actually the fraternities at Penn State had come up with this, and that this was a precursor of the salamander swallowing thing. . . . But anyway, the fraternity party turned into the first film, which was *Salamanders: A Night at the Phi Delt House.* And that's probably gotten the most publicity of anything we've ever done . . . partly because it was sensational. I was a little worried about that at the time, that here we're starting off the idea of doing folklore films and you come up with something like this, whose attraction to people, even folklorists, but especially nonfolklorists, is the very sensationalism of it.

*Salamanders* engendered multiple levels of analysis by audiences and caused Thigpen to reflect on the effects of his film. The sensationalistic appeal was unexpected. The fraternity members saw the film as a validation of their Bowery Ball rites; others were appalled by the fraternity's actions. A transspecies rights group asked if the filmmakers were promoting this behavior. The cinéma vérité style of the film allowed for a wide range of interpretations, and Thigpen began to see new aspects of the film through others' eyes.

For *Halloween '85,* Thigpen placed the analysis into the film, playing with the various ways academics and revelers explained the function of Halloween. Again, Thigpen's family was a factor, in this case appearing in the film. The event was once more the focal point. *Halloween '85* became a community portrait of that night.

Thigpen was fascinated with correlating his film to an earlier documentary on Halloween:

> I had been using in my class a film that Maurice Mook, the anthropologist, and Leslie Greenhill had done for the *Encyclopedia Cinematographica* that

Penn State had been involved in, in archiving these, this raw footage of things. The film that I'd use in the class was called *Central Pennsylvania Halloween Costumes*. And it was done in the mid-sixties, and so it was in black and white, no sound. It lasted about eleven minutes. I thought, "Gee, this would be an interesting parallel to the thing that we're going to do." George had never seen it, the cinematographer who collaborates with me on this. And it struck me that this would be really a neat kind of follow-up to do twenty years later. I said, "Well, why don't we call this *Halloween '85*," because it was also a playoff for some people. At the same time, the Hollywood films had *Halloween I, Halloween II, Halloween III*, and they were building up to a large number of Halloweens. So we said, "They'll never get to 85; we'll call this *Halloween '85* and people will make of it what they will." But, to me, part of the hidden thing that could come out for some people later on was the idea that there would be a follow-up of the earlier film.

The film operated on numerous levels, dependent on the surface to anyone with a knowledge of Halloween who could relate as a Halloween participant, but also communicating the "hidden thing" addressed both to folklorists and to film buffs albeit in different ways. Folklorists aware of the 1960s film who would eventually see a film Thigpen might make in 2005 might make a connection between the films in much the same way that others saw the link between the Hollywood Halloween films.

But Thigpen also used the film to reflect on his own relationship to Halloween. His children appear as they discuss costume possibilities with their parents, go out and "trick or treat," and then divvy up their candy; Thigpen appears as what he calls "the resident folklorist, court jester" expert asked by the media to comment on Halloween.

Several years I had gone on television to talk about these holidays, and they always call me up for Halloween. Radio stations from all over the country call, AP wire services call, wanting to know about Halloween. Well, I just was, you know, this was in '85, I was already getting tired of this and I'd started trying to deflect them to other folklorists around the state. . . . What they wanted to know was either if it was occult or if children were the only ones who did it and that sort of thing. But should we answer this in the video? I had been on this public television station for years and years discussing Halloween. So they called me up when we were doing the film, and I said, "Look, you can have me on, if we can film you having me on." So they said, "Fine," they would be happy to do that.

Although an analysis of a film may reveal how the self of the filmmaker behind the camera is manifested in the film, few folklorists include themselves on the film record. Thigpen's choice of subject includes his image of himself as a folklorist and, for those who know him, as a member of the family depicted. Thus, he reveals himself in a direct way.

## Revealing the Self

The choice of actual subject matter often is made merely by being receptive to the idea of folklore. Those interested in film and who saw folklore as meaningful in their own lives, professionally, politically, and/or personally, recognized when folklore might become a film topic. Folklore film can capture the metaphoric meanings of heightened moments in people's lives, the extraordinary experience of ordinary people. Looking for that heightened experience in everyday life, folklore filmmakers were attuned to all of the possibilities. The film topics touched a deep spot in their own psyches, allowing them to explore aspects of the self.

Preloran chose people who, like him, were solitary, and he moved away from the scrutiny of the Other, which was popular when he first began filmmaking. From his earliest films on rituals and celebrations to the portrait of the filmmaker seen in *Zulay*, Preloran was on a continuum from documenting the Other to documenting the self.

> We always went out to get the exotic. And I was always against that. However, I am Argentine, and I shot in Argentina, and I shot people that were not of my culture but they were Argentines. Well, you know, so what; I had the same language.
>
> Now I have been making films of rural people for thirty years. I think it was based on an inferiority complex I've had. I was always manic and I was always alone. I felt much more at ease with people in rural areas than in the city. So I just sat and listened, and I started making the type of film that I liked.

The reflection of one's own joy in that of others is the basic impulse for certain filmmakers. Blank remarked, "I enjoy seeing people enjoying being alive, and I enjoy listening to what humans enjoy doing." For *It Ain't City Music*, Davenport observed, "Now that film has a lot of joy in it, and when we were thinking about doing it, it was like those peasant festivals in the Bruegel paintings—that's what it reminded me of." He commented that the film was "trashed" in a review because the reviewers thought he was "looking down on" the people. Davenport was surprised. He pointed out, "It's been the most commercially popular; it was picked up by Home Box Office and so forth. . . . If you show that film to anyone who likes country music, they really like that film."

Davenport's film *The Upperville Show* (1970) is about the oldest horse show in the United States: "The cutting style on that was exactly, or similar to, the cutting style in *A Singing Stream*. Very funny, quick cutting, I did a lot of weird things in it. I would run my camera fast or slow and things like that. And that was the first one I did, and then I did *It Ain't City Music*. But the two of them are interesting because they're two looks at life in two different classes of people in this one Virginia county." From the rural Virginia country set to the wealthy upper crust of Virginia society, both *It Ain't City Music* and *The Upperville Show* document events in Davenport's own backyard.

Blank was also interested in his own setting. Rather than looking at those most like himself, he learned about himself from studying the differences. He recalled, "As a kid, I was always fascinated with different cultures. I grew up in Tampa, Florida, where there were Cubans and poor white people, also known as 'Florida crackers,' and African Americans. It always intrigued me to go into their neighborhoods and see what they're eating and how they're different, the music they made." The camera opened up that world for Blank. His interest in the various cultures in his own Floridian surroundings led him to see the richness of daily life.

> For *Always for Pleasure* [1978] I was in New Orleans at an AFS meeting, and they announced that there would be a jazz parade that people could follow if they wanted. And no one came except me and two or three others. And I found it curious that right here they had to walk three blocks to see one of the most genuine, rich, cultural traditions in New Orleans and no one bothered. But while watching this jazz parade as a second-liner and dancing along behind the band, I felt this would be a fun film to make. I kept seeing shots that I would shoot if I had a movie camera. And a friend offered to help set me up with people to include in the film, and he was familiar with the Mardi Gras Indians and the Jazz Theater and the Jazz Festival. So I applied, but also that year I got the Guggenheim grant, so I used that money and an NEA grant to shoot that one.

Blank then felt a need to concentrate on what he knew best—his friends and his own immediate area. He turned to the garlic eaters, growers, cooks, and diners of the Bay Area. "And the garlic film was totally self-motivated and out of my own pocket—*Garlic Is as Good as Ten Mothers.* Because I wanted to do something locally, just on people I was familiar with, friends of mine." Other films developed out of a wholly new experience. For *In Heaven There Is No Beer?* Blank was in Minneapolis showing films when he was invited to a polka bar. "And I found doing the polka so exhilarating—the wild whirling around—I had a glimpse of what they refer to as polka happiness. And while whirling, I decided, 'This has got to be a film.'"

*Burden of Dreams* (1982), perhaps Blank's best-known film, finds Blank documenting the making of Werner Herzog's film *Fitzcarraldo* (1982). Herzog becomes an obsessed filmmaker shooting the tale of an obsessed man attempting to drag a thirty-ton steamship over a mountain. Despite tropical weather changes and fights with the film crew and with actors Klaus Kinski and Claudia Cardinale, Herzog is as determined as the hero of his film. The film allows us to see what we normally do not see. It is essentially a film about a filmmaker. For *Sprout Wings and Fly* (1983), a film about fiddler Tommy Jarrell, Blank

4.2 Olympia jazz band returning from a New Orleans jazz funeral in *Always for Pleasure*. Photo by Michael P. Smith

draws attention to the film as a film as the credits roll. Jarrell is sitting with a young woman and saying, "Oh, yeah, that's Les Blank and he's making this movie. And that's [folklorist] Cece Conway." When the credits to the National Endowment appear, he says, "He got the money from the government somehow, it ain't none of my business where." Blank says he hates to be asked what grants he received. "They always assume that a film can't be made without a grant." This conclusion shows who is making the film and what the relationship is between the filmmakers and the filmed. At the same time as it shows film as a construct, it tells the audience something about Les Blank, something which Blank likes to do. In many of his films, Les Blank makes brief appearances in a Hitchcock-like manner.

That film reveals the self is evident in Blank's assessment that film must be analyzed. The self is uncovered: "If they want to know what I think, they can figure it out by watching the film and how it's edited or how it's shot. My decisions are there to be seen."

I asked, "So a lot of the films are, in a sense, about you?"

Blank replied, "I shoot generally what I'm interested in. And if I like someone I'll put them in a film; if I like what they're doing, I'll shoot them doing it. And sometimes people say things that I agree with, and I'm more inclined to put that in the film than people saying something that I don't agree with."

4.3 Les Blank filming Tommy Jarrell and friends at his home in the Blue Ridge Mountains of North Carolina for *Sprout Wings and Fly*. Photo by Cece Conway

The filmmaker brings his interpretation to the audience, and as Blank says, they can "figure it out." Yet the filmmaker's vision and the audience's interpretation do not always match. The self of the filmmaker is filtered through the self of the audience members.[15] For example, Cohen pointed out how astonished he was at reactions to *The High Lonesome Sound*. Because of his artistic background, Cohen inserted a number of shots to evoke a mood and an aesthetic tonality to the content. Viewers see such shots differently. Cohen explained,

And the great sadness is that the kids now are trained to say, "That's senti-mental," or they say "That's romantic." They've got their guard up. And I have received very funny flak for these shots. That film was shown in one of the early Flaherty festivals and I was just a young innocent. That was my first film. Some guy got up and said, "Who does this guy think he is, taking pictures of spider webs. Who does he think he is? Flaherty? He's not Fla-herty." And I didn't know what Flaherty's shots were like. I was just responding totally with my own personal history, my memories as a child, things that I like, things that I still like. I live out in the country. The shot where the two dogs were jumping in the fog, I got up early, early one morning just, as they say, "to dig the scene"—it was the days of the beat generation and I was part of that. I just wanted to enjoy the beauty of the early morning and there's these dogs doing their thing down the road.

Well, a man from a record company saw that—this was in the early sixties, just as the civil rights thing was starting—and said, "Don't you think your symbolism was rather heavy-handed there?" "Why?" "The black dog struggling with the white dog." I said, "My goodness, is that the way they're gonna read it?"

That film is a subjective experience is obvious. That you are filming yourself when you are filming someone else is not always so clearly seen. Cohen continued:

Somebody asked me about a shot at the end of *The End of an Old Song* [1970] where Dillard Chandler walks across the fields and there's all the tobacco piled up there, and he just walks between them. And he had told me that that's how he gets from one place to another, so I asked if I could film him walking there. Okay. But as I saw the shot, I remembered a childhood terror that I had. We used to go to the country in the summers, and there was some man who, around 11:30 every morning, would walk across the fields and we'd have to run in the house 'cause he was supposedly drunk and he might be dangerous. And that feeling of a man walking across the fields and how that existed in my mind all these years—I suddenly saw it coming through when Dillard walked across the field. I said, "I'm gonna film it like I feel it." There is no other objective point 'cause it's just somebody else's definition of objectivity anyhow. And this at least will be charged with my own (not "will be"—I wasn't calculating), this is charged with what I understand.

Just like I won't film music, I won't do a film about something on commission, I'll do it because I *feel* the music. When I did *Pericles in America* [1988], that was a huge commitment. I just thought the music was so interesting that it would be worth spending a bunch of years trying to understand that music and understand what was making me feel so strongly about it. *It's partly to understand the music and partly to understand myself.*

Film also provides a window through which the subjects of the film may see themselves. Both gender and art brought Ferrero into film. Her New Mexico background surfaces in her Hopi film and an early film on pottery and perception. Of the pottery film, she emphasized that, like her quilt films, it was about women's work. Ferrero talked about the insights the women in *Quilts in Women's Lives* gained through their participation and Ferrero's filmic ability to make connections such as that between one quilter and her textile background or between another quilter and the traditional roots she knew as a child. "If people are telling you something absolutely significant about their lives, they're getting clearer about it. And they can say it more precisely. They feel they're communicating clearly around their own intentions, of what they want to share with you. I think that's why they come across 'natural' because they really want to say what they're saying."

Just as film helps subjects gain insights, the audience is watching from another perspective. The Prelorans created *My Aunt Nora* (1982) with a script written by Mabel. Although it was a feature film, Mabel was constructing scenarios about the roles available to women in Argentina. By extension, it was about women throughout Latin America. Audience response was overwhelmingly positive. Jorge explained, "I showed it all over Europe. Everywhere they thought it could have happened there. In all the Latin countries, France, Spain, Italy, absolutely, and Scandinavia." Mabel interjected, "Somebody came to Jorge and said, 'Oh, I have an aunt, a cousin'—everybody has somebody in the family. In each audience somebody came and said something like that." Despite the limited positions for women portrayed in the film, the central character is a strong female who is the head of the household. Perhaps because she is a widow, she imposes her will on the family. That aspect of the film also touched audiences. Jorge said, "In a way what this tells you is that the matriarchy is a common occurrence. That the man is a patriarch outside the home, but inside the home matriarchy reigns."

On multiple levels and in numerous ways, film can act as a means of the filmmaker, the subjects, and the audience seeing themselves. Like the folk artist creating with a specific type of consumer in mind, the filmmaker is creating for an audience and anticipating its reactions. In some cases that audience is difficult to discern. Wagner remarked that distributing *Free Show Tonite* was a struggle because it didn't have an identifiable audience, unlike *Miles of Smiles* and *The Stone Carvers*. Those films presented "more accessible ideas, whereas somehow the medicine show film seems to be about a more arcane corner." Davenport had problems with audience reactions to *Being a Joines* (1980). As long as the viewers saw themselves reflected in the film, they liked it. When the subject of the film became the Other, they rejected it. Audiences identify with Joines until he tells a religious narrative about an out-of-body experience, "where he starts talking about flying out of his head and looking back on himself like a Kewpie doll. Well, at that point, they all think, 'Oh, this guy's crazy, or a fundamentalist.' They fall out of the film, because he's sort of like the 'good old country boy' up to that point. That's your average viewer's reaction." Davenport experienced problems having the film shown on North Carolina public television, and it was only shown once. In contrast, when *A Singing Stream* was nationally broadcast on PBS, letters came in from all over the country from audiences who saw themselves mirrored in the film and wanted to order the booklet made to accompany the film. Dan Patterson remarked, "As far as I know we did not get a single one from a scholar or an academician."[16] Scholars did not request it, perhaps because they did not see themselves. Patterson pointed out, "What the requests came from were little sheets of lined notebook paper, written in ink or ballpoint pen, saying, 'Dear folks that made this film,

This was about the best film I've seen on television. I want to show it at my family reunion and please send me the booklet. Does Echoes have a tape?' It's this kind of response—it's from the community itself." Local audiences are also eager to purchase video copies. Such audience response has reinforced the cohesion of the Golden Echoes with their community and with each other. Sales are a self-evident mark of their success. Patterson reported, "The chief sales have been made by John Landis. I don't know how many Tom has sold. . . . John Landis has sold probably three hundred at his concerts. We know it's been pirated in the community."

That the audience identified with the content of the film was evident from the first screening. The audience immediately comprehended that the film was about them. Patterson described that jubilation of recognition:

> The first showing of it was at a theater in their county and we did it
> through the local arts council, so all the arts council people had to come
> and all of the home folks came. And the arts council put on a cookies and
> malt cider reception, and we had only intended one—it was shown in an
> old events auditorium theater on the main street. And the black commu-
> nity came for it, and in such numbers that they had to do a back-to-back
> showing. So a lot of people didn't get their cookies and cider. But they
> wanted to see the film and they filled up the auditorium twice and we had
> thought it would be just half that number and even wondered whether any-
> body would come. . . . And they came there. . . . It was something that they
> were very proud of. There was one earlier showing, when it was still on two
> reels, to the Landis family alone in the home church. And it was just a tone
> of elation and hilarity almost.

At the other end of the spectrum, Cohen wanted to change the color of audience expectations, presenting his films so that viewers might learn the "truth" about those they thought of as the Other. I asked Cohen if he started out with a theoretical position that changed as he was in the process of creating each film. He gave *Dancing with the Incas* as an example of his position in relation to a westernized audience:

> I'm not sure which of the many layers of thought that I have is my theo-
> retical position because even in the film about the Huayno music, it's a
> theoretical position to make a film about Huayno music at all. An unspo-
> ken agenda for the film is that Americans and Europeans have a very clear
> understanding of what Andean music is based on—these bands with the
> panpipes and the ponchos and the drums that you see on the streets
> everywhere. And in the subways. And you hear them in film scores now.
> And the only place you can hear that kind of music in Peru is in restau-
> rants or where tourists go. The Andean people do not listen to that. It's a
> construction made by people who've migrated from the Andes or who've
> taken up that kind of music. But it is not what the Andean people play
> and listen to.

Now, I could make a film about the lies, but I'd rather just go to Peru and say, "This is what the people listen to; this is the way that music is organized. And this music here in Peru is music of an oppressed people which never gets out even though they sell millions of records there." It's never gotten out to the outside world, so that in itself is an agenda for the film, even though it's not spoken as part of the film. That's already at work. Maybe if this film is successful, that will seem very obvious to people. "Oh, this is what the Andean people listen to." But is that a theoretical position? I think it is, to serve as a corrective there.

Cohen wants film to make people think not only about film but about life. He pointed out that contemporary films made in "other" cultures were "partly an investigation of a slightly new world. There's no exotic world."

Some of Cohen's American films became a reflection not only of the subject in the film but of the audience seeing it. For *End of an Old Song*, Cohen feared he had revealed too much about ballad singer Dillard Chandler:

Dillard Chandler, when he talks about his love life, he talks about his very personal life of picking up women, bringing them out to his cabin, and he hasn't been in love for years. I went through a year of agonizing as to whether that should be in the film or shouldn't. And since my underlying motive in that film was to show that the ballads were personal and not this impersonal thing which the folklorists had described, that they're reflections of personal lives and that this man was preoccupied with love songs—and rather violent love sometimes, or not pleasant things, not romantic love, really. So that I thought it would be very important that you could hear his interior.

But then when I showed the film in his community, I'd forgotten that scene was in it. There were all his neighbors. They're going to hear him talking about his personal intimate love life. I started to perspire, but it was in the dark and nobody saw me. But as that came onto the screen and Dillard said those things, I started hearing the men in the audience saying, "You tell it, Dillard; tell it like it is." These are mountaineers saying that. It was wonderful, and from then on . . . the audience sang along with the ballads.

The self of the subject and the audience merged, and Cohen achieved his objectives. Perhaps because of the insider specificity of the viewers, however, *End of an Old Song* has not enjoyed the same success with general audiences as Cohen's *The High Lonesome Sound*, a film which Cohen says was "attacked by people in film," who saw it as a collection of stills.

Ferrero also talked about the appeal of her films to general audiences but not to filmmakers. Like Cohen, she sees her films as a theoretical vehicle:

I've always felt that I have used the kind of veneer of being accessible as a political tool to get much larger messages out and accessible to people. So it's been very important to me that my films get out to public libraries, get out on public television, get out on cable. I want them used in the university market, and I definitely want them to meet the kind of critical standards and criteria of folklorists or anthropologists or historians. I feel that I do my homework in those critical areas, so that they hold up formally for those people.

Because of the accessibility of her films for both academic and general audiences, Ferrero said that other than commentaries I had written for folklore journals about her work, the films were "essentially not ever critically reviewed" by academics. She lamented that her films were not screened in filmmakers' shows. Because of their mass appeal, most filmmakers did not see the films as political, nor were they able to see them as reflections of themselves as filmmakers. Nonetheless, some filmmakers altered their approaches after seeing the films, and an audience of feminists, historians, and folklorists embraced the films, in part because Ferrero's collaboration with the academic world ensured that the films would mirror its research questions.

> *Hearts and Hands* really affected the direction of how people did their work, how other scholars went on and did research projects, how other filmmakers worked. It brought together a lot of issues that a lot of people were thinking about at that time. It was just something at just the right moment. And there were so many aspects to the collaboration—you know, the exhibits, the book, the film—so many people worked on it. It really was based on a decade of many other scholars working, particularly women historians who were beginning to do primary work in all these facets that the film touched on. That film couldn't have been made a decade earlier, because the work hadn't been done.

Ferrero used the exhibit format, combined with film. The exhibit at the Oakland Museum broke all attendance records:

> The curators could not believe the level of interest in the project. One hundred and thirty thousand people saw the exhibit in a period of three months. And it was a great pleasure for me to have the film *Quilts in Women's Lives* in that exhibit.[17] And then we also showed those women's quilts in a small contemporary wing.
>
> I'm very interested in the way in which films can work in the context of the museum exhibits and the display of material culture. And that film really worked, both in terms of resonating with the historical material in an exhibit and showing the continuity. And we actually went out and raised the money to build a small theater that would hold fifty people in the exhibit and showed it as a film [rather than a walk-by video]. And it screened every day, seven times a day, for three months. And finally, the last month, there were so many hundreds of people going to the exhibit—I mean there were almost a thousand people a day going—that they had to open up the large auditorium and then screen it there.

Ferrero's use of folk art to make a political statement about women had vast appeal. Knowing that folklore is the product of a creative process and has had use and continuity through time and space, people commonly react positively to folklore—especially folk art, because of its tangibility. Folklore holds meaning for its creators and for subsequent narrators, riddlers, dancers, and quiltmakers, for example, and this establishment of tradition has a personalizing effect as each participant or viewer internalizes its customary significance. Attendance figures at quilt shows and exhibits are evidence of folk art's popularity and the public's interest in tradition, both their own traditions and those of others.

Like subjects and filmmakers, audiences relate best to films that ask them to explore the realm of the self. As a topic, folklore is a touchstone to the self. Folk art films, because they combine that emotional recognition with the power of the visual dimension, evoke meaning and have a tremendous allure. Ferrero accentuates the force of film to an audience. "Here it's been years, and people are still saying, 'That show changed my life.'"

## Training: A Process of Discovery

Each folklore filmmaker was trained either in folklore or in film and therefore sees through that filter, laid over individual life experiences, to create a project. Blank, Ferrero, Davenport, Wagner, Fleischhauer, Peiser, and Preloran are filmmakers whose interests led them to produce films on folklore topics. Cohen, Ferrero, and Davenport were led to film through an interest or background in art. Hawes, Ferris, Thigpen, and I received graduate training in folklore, but we had no expertise in filmmaking. Despite their lack of a formal film background, these scholars sought out film and video as useful tools for their own research. Hawes acted as folklore coordinator or adviser on her film projects; Dan Patterson advised Tom Davenport; Thigpen worked with filmmaker George Hornbein; Ferris taught himself basic film techniques; and I pursued standard academic training in film while working on a graduate degree in folklore.

For most, the interest in folklore film grew out of a background in a related field, but often it was attributable to a chance event as well. Cohen told me that he had never had a filmmaking course, but had "picked up filmmaking as an extension" of his interest in still photography.

> Actually I started as an artist who played music. I was an art student, got my degree in painting, but for the written part of my degree I wrote about weaving. . . . As an art student in graduate school, I was taking courses at Yale in anthropology and New World archaeology. Very prophetic—during a test there in that class in New World archaeology, suddenly there was a question: "You are given a grant to do work in the New World. What would you do?" And I'd never ever thought about it, and I said I would go down to the Maya who are living there now and look around and do ethno-

graphic work and photograph and look at their culture now, to see how well what they're doing now jibes with what you archaeologists tell us they were doing hundreds of years ago. Like a little bolt of an insight that I had. And that's what I've been doing ever since. I read what the archaeologists or historians say, or what the folklorists or the ethnomusicologists say, and then I go into the present and see if that's so or how it's changed or what are the presumptions there. And it's been very interesting.

Cohen's films became an extension and reflection of his musical self. He has referred to his films as "musical documents" (1990). Cohen had been a member of a popular folk singing group formed during the 1960s. His first films, *The High Lonesome Sound* and *End of an Old Song,* focused on questions about the traditional ballad in America:

Oh, way back in 1959, I had gone to eastern Kentucky to make a record of music. I thought I was gonna learn about the Depression. I was born during the 1930s Depression, and I'd never really consciously experienced one, and the New Lost City Ramblers, my band, was doing a record about the Depression and here I was a photographer interested in music. I said, "I'll take this opportunity to go to eastern Kentucky and try to make recordings and find out about the music and—there's a Depression goin' on—to get a sense of it." It was just, you know, a desire to know. Had nothing to do with making films or making money. And so I made that first record in '59 for Folkways, and during the making of that I met Roscoe Holcomb [a folk singer in Hazard, Kentucky], and then we became quite close. I think not all my films, but the majority of them, I've been very touched by the music first and have gotten to know the people through recordings and other efforts before filming.

This experience combined with his still photography led Cohen to his first film:

Part of me still thinks as a still photographer and some of my own history, why I started film in the first place, was to bring still images or visual images together with my feeling for music. That was my initial film, *The High Lonesome Sound,* because what I'd seen and what I'd experienced were not being duplicated properly or communicated properly on phonograph records, even though I had booklets of photographs and notes. . . . So this need to see these things in sequence made me use 16mm from the outset.

Cohen's desire to record more of the event caused him to leave still photography behind and leap into the motion of film.

Pat Ferrero also began her career as a filmmaker by first becoming an artist; she has had no formal education in film production. Experimental filmmaker Maya Deren was a major influence. One of the few female filmmakers working in the 1940s, Deren became well known for *Meshes of the Afternoon* (1943), a now famous surrealistic piece that affected the direction of the American avant-garde movement in film. A later film, *The Divine Horsemen* (1977), studied voodoo. Ferrero pointed out her sense of connection with Deren.

4.4  Roscoe Holcomb singing a ballad in *The High Lonesome Sound.* Photo by John Cohen

My training was in art . . . and I came to Deren's work as a filmmaker be-cause I'd been doing experimental filmmaking in the sixties, and I was very active in the independent film community in the Bay Area. And she was someone who was interested in a number of areas I was interested in. At that time I was running an international children's art school for a living, and I was interested in the question of symbolic thinking. And Deren was an artist-filmmaker asking the same questions I was. . . . I felt she preceded a lot of theoretical thinking both in anthropology and film around how she positioned herself with the work and research she was doing. So, to me, that was the inspiration for my own work.

And then I decided to do a film on children's art. And that sent me back to school, and I went to San Francisco State—actually took the degree in an interdisciplinary art program—but it put me in touch with John Collier and the whole field of visual anthropology. I studied with John and then he hired me to do some research . . . and then through that network I met John Adair. And then I actually went back to school in medical anthropology at UC Medical, so I felt the need to do more training in anthropology. I didn't make such a separation myself, and I was reading very broadly in all of the fields—in psychology, some in folklore, and certainly in anthropology.

Ferrero's movement into film was a natural outgrowth of her combined interests.

Like Cohen and Ferrero, Tom Davenport had no training in filmmaking, but he was led to it both by travel to another country and by the subsequent desire to document what he saw. His artistic use of still photography soon developed into filmmaking. In 1961, he graduated from Yale as an English major. During his senior year, he was given a two-year teaching assignment in Hong Kong. "And while I was in Hong Kong—I think it was kind of normal—I got a camera. I wanted to start taking pictures. It was different. I mean it was the complete opposite of the significant and everyday. It was the exotic and faraway that I wanted to photograph." Later, Davenport made albums with artistically arranged photographs and little Chinese stamps. He recalls that he enjoyed doing so, and when he returned he didn't want to go to law school "like everybody else in my class." Instead, he applied to the nascent East/West Center at the University of Hawaii. His scholarship paid for his expenses and his travel to China as a language student. He had asked to study filmmaking, but that was not an option. After he was in China, he met a Yale graphic arts professor who admired his photography. Davenport decided to continue: "And I got so engrossed in this stuff. It was the first time in my life where I didn't care whether I slept, I ate, or anything. . . . I'd go take pictures and I'd rush back to the darkroom. It was a passionate kind of discovery."

A series of opportunities led Davenport to Nepal and then to New York:

> So I bought a camera, an old Bell and Howell that I still have, and went to Nepal and shot this footage . . . and then I came back to New York and I decided that I was going into the filmmaking business. I found a job right away with a company called Leacock/Pennebaker [see chapter 1].
>
> And they were kind of a famous company, and I worked for them as a kind of janitorial assistant at fifty dollars a week. And had a little apartment in New York, and made some friends, people who were editors, and I learned just by talking to people about how films were put together. I'd take the cameras out and clean them and occasionally they'd let me shoot a pick-up shot. I met a whole lot of people who were all very interested in this vérité work.

Davenport returned to Taiwan to complete a still photography assignment for *National Geographic,* but the magazine took over the project. Left with nothing to do in Taiwan, Davenport began a film on T'ai Chi Ch'uan, the meditative martial art, which was relatively unknown in the United States at that time. "So I just bought some film in Hong Kong and came back and did this film, and then the Rockefeller Foundation gave me three thousand dollars to finish it when I got back to New York. And that was the first film that I actually made and sort of began the process gradually." Like other filmmakers, Davenport's early vocation served as a natural transition into filmmaking.

Art and still photography led Cohen, Ferrero, and Davenport to film, and anthropological approaches encouraged Cohen, Ferrero, and Wagner. Peiser,

Preloran, and Blank attended film school. All became independent filmmakers. Peiser, Preloran, and Blank returned to their communities to film. Blank's impetus was based on folklore in the form of narrative:

> I went into making films because I liked the whole medium of film and storytelling. . . . I was inspired by the films of people like Fellini and Vittorio De Sica and Luis Buñuel and Ingmar Bergman—films that had a rich spiritual exploration, and drama, and things that deal with the human spirit. And then when I went to film school, I got more interested in the aesthetic aspect of making films, and I was also introduced to documentary films. I saw Flaherty's films and saw *The Hunters,* the film made by John Marshall and Robert Gardner. I saw that film and I was real impressed with the idea of going into a strange land among strange people and making a record of it. . . . Then when I got out of film school I didn't get very far in the narrative world, and just to make a living I went out and did whatever work was available—as an assistant cameraman, or assistant electrician, or assistant editor—did training films for the air force and got sick of the content of those films. But I learned the basics of how to shoot a camera and how to edit quickly and how to read a scene and shoot it in such a way that the story of that scene was told.

Eventually Blank began to work for independent filmmakers in Los Angeles. These first films concerned motorcycle gangs, the early California Pleasure Fair in Los Angeles, and drag racing at Long Beach. "So these weren't your projects?" I asked. "No, but I related to them, and I realized I had a feeling for this type of material. And I found it rewarding to have a whole different experience of a whole different culture of people, and being a filmmaker gives me a reason to be there and to open my eyes and to shoot things."

Using a borrowed camera, Blank shot a piece on the first love-ins in Los Angeles. The local PBS station liked it and agreed to finance a longer film on the huge 1967 Easter Love-in, *God Respects Us When We Work, but Loves Us When We Dance* (1968). The station allowed Blank to keep the negative. One project led to another: "I got the negative and recut it and scored it with a psychedelic rock band in L.A., and it was fun and fulfilling and gratifying and it was placed in a lot of festivals. Almost at the same time, Lightnin' Hopkins came through Los Angeles." Blank was then working with a partner who had learned filmmaking from him. This partner was able to borrow funds, and he also knew John Lomax, who knew Hopkins. Hopkins agreed to do a film for a fee. "When the film finally got made, it was something of a new approach in filmmaking to do a film about a narration and structure it according to the emotions and feelings, almost like composing a piece of music." The film, *The Blues Accordin' to Lightnin' Hopkins,* opened up a new world. It prompted John Lomax to put up money for a film on Mance Lipscomb, a performer whom Lomax wanted "preserved for history." After Blank paid off his lab bills, he had funds to make another film: "I decided I'd like to do a film on Cajuns, and I had met the Balfa Brothers at a folk festival in Chicago, and I met a man in Texas who invited me home and cooked me a gumbo. He was a bandleader."

Blank soon left for Louisiana. With five thousand dollars, he bought a used camera and some film. To pay the lab bills for the Cajun film, he went to work making industrial films for two years. A grant from the National Endowment for the Arts launched *Dry Wood* and *Hot Pepper*. To finish that film project, Blank worked on a rock 'n' roll film. Shortly thereafter, record producer Chris Strachwitz asked Blank to make a film on Texas-Mexican border music. As is often the case for filmmakers, each film led to the next.

Preloran found himself drawn to film, although he was supposed to be studying architecture.

> I had a very bad childhood and a very possessive mother. I was always alone in my room with asthma, and I hated to go out, and I felt very awkward with people. And I became an intellectual—not really, but I went to college, I went to a university. I went to study architecture, and I was supposed to be an intellectual. But I'd hate to sit around talking about Sartre when I didn't like Sartre. I would bury myself in the movies, and I would just see movies from one o'clock in the afternoon to nine at night. Nobody knew. And every day I would go to the movies. And when it came time to actually start making movies at the age of thirty, I went into the boondocks of my country to find people where I felt very comfortable. So I did not carry with me this sense of superiority which, in a way, almost all filmmakers have because the fact that you're an expert in this incredible technology makes you feel you're better.

Preloran changed his major and pursued a film degree at UCLA. His preoccupation with structure had led him to architecture, and his foray into architecture translated well to film.

Wagner also was a student motivated by an academic course somewhat peripheral to his major field:

> I was in the process of leaving the University of Pennsylvania doctoral program in communications, and while I was there, I took a class in documentary film from a guy who was essentially an anthropologist. . . . His name was Sol Worth [see chapter 1]. But I didn't have any training in film other than what I got from him. But because he was coming from anthropology, that was the slant of the film study I took. . . . And then, actually I totally decided to leave Penn, but before I did I took the summer class that Worth offered, which was a course in visual anthropology, not a filmmaking course.

Wagner and I talked about his technical development. When asked if he had any training in film production, Wagner replied, "No, I hadn't, and even in that course with Sol Worth, I had very, very little, because it had a heavy theoretical interest. In fact, Worth wouldn't let us use the zoom lens, and we could not use sync-sound to make our films. It was a rigorous learning of film as language. Deemphasizing the technology and even the technique of good film versus bad film. It wasn't really about that so much as it was about communication issues."

I remarked that at some point Wagner had to learn how to work with a light meter, how to sync up the "dailies" [film processed by the lab on the same day it is shot, ready to look at by the next day], and other basics. He responded, "Yes, but barely, barely. Mostly I've learned the craft of filmmaking by doing it and reading. I did an incredible amount of 'woodshedding.' You just go to the library and read through the shelf of technique books and that sort of thing."

Wagner's first film idea would fix on his own region and the notion of family; it also demonstrates his basic conceptualization of the folk. Like Cohen, he began thinking about Kentucky:

> I think, like a lot of people my age, I grew up in a suburban setting and folklore has been a way for me to feel involved and kind of satisfy an interest in things that seem more substantial, in some ways, or more satisfying in terms of lifestyle, values, or whatever. I know that's hypothesizing about my generation, and particularly about my own place in it. But I think that's true for a lot. I would even extend it to folklorists. . . .They're not part of a folk community but are drawn to it. I think there's something going on there. I mean in Kentucky, for example, it's almost a geographic comparison. I grew up in Louisville, but was always sort of interested in people from other parts of the state, and the small towns, and rural areas, and the mountains. . . .
>
> I've never really thought about it, but my first idea for a film was to do something on the Combs family [a well-known folk music family] in eastern Kentucky and centering thematically around the idea of family and region and filming the family reunion they had every year. . . . I did have this one idea, which I never made, for a film. It wouldn't have occurred to me to call it at that time, but in retrospect, it was a folklore film.

Wagner also had a chance meeting that determined his direction.

> That film idea led me to talk to a woman I had met at Penn. I guess she had been in American studies and she had taken folklore courses and communication classes, so I met her. I was in the Annenberg School—and she helped me actually conceptualize that film idea. And I went down to one reunion and interviewed people and she listened to some of the tapes and helped me think about subject matter.

This friend, folklorist Amy Kotkin, introduced Wagner to folklorist Steve Zeitlin as a potential working buddy. Zeitlin was then embarking on the film project that became *Harmonize: Folklore in the Lives of Five Families* (1976).

4.5  Filmmaker Paul Wagner. Photo by Andrew Wyndham

I found the material interesting. I was going to say that it was just through
the contact with these people who became friends, of course, too, that I got
excited by the material. But I was sort of headed in that direction, certainly
in terms of the anthropological training, but also in terms of the specific
project that I was interested in doing. Obviously it didn't occur to me,
coming out of the Annenberg School and studying with Sol Worth, to
march off to Hollywood.

Thus, Wagner began a collaborative working relationship with Zeitlin and
with other folklorists at the Smithsonian Institution.

In every instance, these filmmakers combined their training with a curiosity about the aesthetics of everyday life. Approaching film through art or through folklore, each began by looking at one and then joining it to the other. As a result, the questions each poses through film make a personal statement and illustrate their sense of the value of marrying film and folklore.

## Collaboration and Compromise

If folklorists shoot and edit their own footage, the film ideally will represent their vision. Some folklorists must compromise with film crews who shoot and edit, and the end result may not resemble the initial concept. This collaboration may lead to new insights or may be frustrating both to the filmmakers and to the folklorists looking over their shoulders.[18] For example, Hawes had difficulty communicating her objectives to the film crew. Hence, the content of her films does not entirely portray her intent as a professional folklorist. Hawes became, in a sense, a member of the team, overseeing the location shooting and working closely with the editors. She commented at length on her role in productions and the need for film to be well shot so as not to produce distortions.

> I think it might be of use to point out that although people keep calling me a filmmaker and I keep calling myself a filmmaker—because I don't know what else to call it—I have never looked through the business end of a camera, nor have I ever done sound. . . . I've been involved in final editing because that is really where the action is, I think, from the point of view of folklore. . . . The big advantage that I've had is that I've worked with extremely artistic people and extremely technically competent people, and that my contribution has been knowing the area that was being explored well enough to work with them ahead of time and tell them what was going to happen before it happened. I was able to make predictions for them, and I was able to tell them what I thought was important. In *Pizza*, for instance, I was able to tell them that the beginnings and endings of games are probably the most important feature and that's a very hard thing to do—to get the beginning of something before you know it's started— and they were not able to do it all the time, but where they did, sort of by accident and sort of because I had really hollered about this ahead of time—I made a big point of it—we got a couple of sequences that I think are really remarkable in terms of the organization of game behavior and how games end, in a sense. I mean, that's easy, you can just keep it rolling. In the case of Earl [*Say, Old Man*], I was able to tell them that the action was in the bow arm beforehand so that, although we had to use a certain number of those dumb shots of the bow on the bridge simply because cameramen cannot resist taking it—we had to use it because we didn't have sufficient coverage—two-camera coverage with good enough shots—so we had to put it in there if the guy had zoomed in on that spot. There are a few places where I thought it was very effective.

Many academics who make their own films, according to Hawes, run the risk of creating documents that do not tell "anything like the truth" because of poor technique.

Paul Wagner pointed out that few filmmakers wanted the type of collaboration he enjoyed with folklorists. "For me, it makes an exciting collaboration. On other projects, I haven't had it that much because the world isn't set up that way. . . . Traditionally or habitually, filmmakers don't want the content person to be on an equal footing with them. They want them as consultants and not as coproducers." For the folklore films, Wagner said, "I was happy I was being considered a producer." Wagner works as a writer-producer-director-editor in collaboration with a cameraman.

Fleischhauer wanted the folklorist to take on a greater role. He faced the problem of not receiving enough fieldwork data from the folklorist to create a competent film. Working for a television station that wanted to produce programs for a general audience, Fleischhauer was the cinematographer. Patrick Gainer would be "the local go-between because he was the expert folklorist and knew West Virginia. Previous attempts to work with him had not resulted in good programs." Fleischhauer found himself in contention with Gainer's ideas about how the program should be structured and with Gainer's view of folklore as a relic from the past:

> We went out and filmed four or five different things. One of them was
> *How to Make Sorghum Molasses.* It was the title of the film, but actually it
> was for a thirty-minute television program called *Mountain Folk.* In its
> original presentation, there were some videotaped studio signals, and
> Gainer explained his views of oldtime life in West Virginia. He was prone
> to talk in what I consider a romanticized way about life in the past and,
> again, sorghum molasses is important to him as a sort of survival, if you
> will, of an older way of life. He has a vision of that older way of life. He
> used these things to illustrate his vision.
>
> I remember at the time I was unhappy with Gainer's insights as a folk-
> lorist into the event and what the event added up to. And in retrospect it is
> clear that there were certain kinds of information that any good fieldworker
> would probably have gathered. I think, in a way, the responsibility for gath-
> ering certain kinds of information on that scene would fall on the
> folklorist's shoulders, as supposedly the social scientist there, and not so
> much on mine. At least that was the way I excused myself for not doing
> things then. . . . Someplace in there, the missing aspects became more
> bothersome as I became more aware of what people making films in an-
> thropology were doing. . . . I went back. Only at that point, I tried to
> collect the information from the farmers about why they did it, what they
> did to the product, and how long they had done it, and so on. We simply
> didn't know up until that point. Gainer had never asked those questions.

Returning and interviewing the men, Fleischhauer gathered material for a brochure that could be distributed with the film—a task that he took up on his own initiative to round out information missing from the film.

Collaboration can be a blessing or a headache. Vikram Jayanti produced *Živeli: Medicine for the Heart*. Les Blank was pleased that Jayanti "handled all of the problematic areas like clearing and music rights, and paying whoever had to be paid, and lining up schedules for people to be filmed—a lot of the tedious work he took care of, and raising the money." "Sometimes," Blank remarked, "because producers are doing all of that, they have a lot of control and they end up doing things they want." Blank used the *Roots of Rhythm*, a film with Harry Belafonte, as an example of loss of control for the filmmaker.

> It's a three hour series that aired on PBS a couple of years ago. They were the producers, they raised the money, they picked the musicians to shoot, they made connections with Cuba to get permission to go down there, they got the NEH grant. I was the director, and after the film got shot, then they started running low on money. They stopped paying my salary to come down to oversee the editing. So they oversaw the editing themselves and did what they wanted to do. And they ended up doing it differently from what I was first led to believe I was doing. So, there, it got away from me because I gave up so much of being involved in the little details. Not to mention not getting a contract.

I asked if the film had any resemblance to the one Blank had imagined. He responded, "There are a lot of good sequences, a lot of great music scenes and dance sequences. But then to make it acceptable to PBS they had to tone it down to a typical educational TV kind of a production."

Cohen encountered similar problems working with NOVA, whose producers wished to recut Cohen's *Q'eros: The Shape of Survival* (1979) to fit its established format. When Cohen had first talked to people at NOVA about funding for the project, they wanted to make the film with their own cinematographer and have Cohen serve as the consultant. In "Musical Documents," Cohen discusses the problems he faced:

> They wouldn't consider that the cameraperson could also be the researcher or an expert on the subject. In their view, camera- and soundpeople are technicians who are experts within their technology but are not expected to contribute on any other level. They could not accept the possibility that a cameraperson and a soundperson could do the entire job without the presence of a director and consultant-anthropologist-specialist as well as assistant camera on the site. They didn't consider the disruptive effect such a large group of people might have on the tiny community of Q'eros. [Cohen 1990:465]

Cohen decided to make the film on his own, partly because NOVA would not consider Hilary Harris (who had shot *The Nuer*) as cinematographer. A year later, after the film was finished on a low budget with a two-person crew,

NOVA leased the film and recut it for broadcast. They placed wedding music over a funeral and intentionally moved the translation of one woman's voice to the image of another. Because the woman spoke Quechua, Cohen notes, "They felt free to translate her words any way they pleased," something they could not have done had the woman spoken Spanish, German, or French (1990:465). NOVA added a narration that placed Cohen in the position of anthropologist, implying that a woman was explaining to him rather than speaking openly to the audience. "I reveled in the possibility that a Q'eros woman sitting on the ground in her cold Stone Age house in the Andes would be communicating directly to the film viewers seated safely in their living room chairs. For NOVA it seemed more important to distance this possibility. NOVA changed traditional music to music with which viewers would be more familiar. "Their intent was to translate everything into the easiest recognizable symbols for the audience." Cohen sued NOVA for the errors and the loss of some of his negative film, and the film aired only once, according to the terms of the settlement, which required that the errors be corrected before any subsequent broadcasts. "They weren't," Cohen explains, "and I never worked again for NOVA" (1990:466). Here, a collaborative project led to distortion, a lawsuit, and a filmmaker's nightmare.

Generally, collaboration is a more intimate process of compromise between scholars and filmmakers. Perhaps the best-known example of such collaboration is the working relationship established between filmmaker Tom Davenport and folklorist Dan Patterson. Davenport's film on the Shakers brought them together. Davenport conversed with me about their meeting.

> The Shaker film started much before I met Dan. I worked with a fellow by the name of Frank DeCola on the film on New Orleans Jazz. . . . I'd gone to the Far East, come back. . . . In Japan I'd been visiting the Zen temples, and I liked the architectural style. I was very interested in that. I was very interested in Zen generally. And I was looking for some kind of, I guess, equivalent in my own culture that I could draw on, and I came across a book of Shaker photographs. And I said, "Gee, these things look like Zen temples. They're all so simple. They were these really great pictures." And so I was talking to my friend Frank, and he said, "Gee, I've been thinking about it. I really love the music." He was a composer and musician.
>
> Frank was an editor, and I was a photographer. He was going to have primary responsibility on the film. I'm sure that I basically felt that I'd better stay out of it because, you know, you can't go around telling an editor what to do if he's a cofilmmaker with you. If he's working for you that's another thing. But if he's not, it's very presumptuous to go on unless you have a very good working relationship, because it's usually during the editorial stages that you have your disagreements about where the film should go. So I felt that Frank was going to finish the film however he felt he wanted to. And I had moved down to Virginia at that time, and he got sick. He had a

brain tumor. And then he eventually died, and I essentially inherited the film. In 1970, when we moved down here, we began editing that film. And Frank had been in correspondence with Dan Patterson, and my sister was a student in Greensboro, North Carolina, and I was going down to visit her, and I called Dan. And we met for lunch in a town in between Greensboro and Chapel Hill. And I got very excited and I remember we drank a lot of coffee and got excited about the whole idea of working together, and liked each other, and Dan, I think, was seeing possibilities in which he could build up his curriculum and work in areas where film was a perfect way to deal with folklore. . . . So he basically cooperated as consultant.

And the fact is that Dan had such good relationships with the Sabbath Day Lake [Maine] Shakers—he absolutely kept his hands clean from this playing favorites—that his presence gave them a lot of confidence that the film would come out all right. He'd come up and we'd have these editing sessions together, two or three times, I guess, before the film was finished. And he didn't know much about films, so he was very tentative about giving advice. But essentially, in the beginning, he was taken on as an adviser I think. That's what his credit is in the film. But later, the roles are much more equal between him and me. I think that just grew. That was a very fortunate relationship. Dan's been very helpful in my career, and he's helped a lot of people, other younger people and folklorists. He's got a tremendously devoted following. He's a wonderful teacher.

Patterson remembers that he had heard from Frank DeCola but didn't know him, and he had never met Tom. Tom wanted the film to be accurate and sought Dan out.

When DeCola died, Tom felt like he didn't know a lot about Shakerism and didn't know quite what to do. And so he wanted to talk to some people that were working on Shakerism, and I was working on a book that eventually came out: *The Shaker Spiritual* [1979]. And so he invited me to come up. Called me on the phone first and told what his dilemma was and asked if I'd be interested in coming up and seeing the footage. And from my own vantage point I thought that was good because I thought of song types that they might not know about—the pantomine songs in particular of which there was no film record. There were only four of them remembered out of what had been a large repertoire in the olden days. And so I wanted to lobby some for that kind of documentation I couldn't myself do.

So I went up and looked at the footage and we talked about it and I made suggestions about things he should ask about the songs . . . and to get different eras of Shaker songs that I knew about, and the layers of it— genres and so on—that he might ask for. And then I talked about the communities and what I thought was significant in Shaker life and its history and so on with him. It ended up with his asking me if I'd be willing to be one of the consultants for the film. So I said yes, and we'd go back up and look periodically at his footage and then as he started the editing I got kind of pulled in a little bit more. I helped him draft those narrated sections in the film. There were problems in the film.

Patterson talked about the schism that had occurred in the Shaker community. Those who had left Sabbath Day Lake and had gone to Canterbury were considered to be out of union and thus no longer Shakers. Davenport was caught in the middle. He believed he was obligated to finish the film. Patterson recognized Davenport's predicament.

> Well, the problem that developed in the film that was a kind of an ethnographic nightmare was that the two communities split while he was in the editing process, and, well, I guess before all of the filming had been done, over the issue of admitting another member. . . . Now, how is Tom supposed to complete the film? The people at Sabbath Day Lake wanted the film to say their position. The people at Canterbury wanted their position. Canterbury didn't want the people who were now apostates of Sabbath Day Lake even in the film, and Sabbath Day Lake wanted to make this apostatizing vehicle, I think. And Tom was just in a terrible dilemma because he wanted to finish the film. So his decision was to cut, make it as though the film had ended at the point where he began work, when they began work with the film, and stop it before the controversy arose. Which was another dilemma, because the story was breaking in the press. . . . Of course, when it was over, both of us felt disappointed that the film couldn't please the Shakers.

Yet the two men had formed a partnership which would lead to making numerous films with Patterson's graduate folklore students at the University of North Carolina, Chapel Hill.

The film collaboration suggested a wholly different way of conducting fieldwork for Patterson. "It had been for me an interesting thing to work on because I'd never thought cinematographically before. I taught expository writing, and I never even dreamed there was a difference. I never even thought about it, you know, so it was an exciting and interesting thing for me to see another way of thinking and constructing."

Shortly after Davenport and Patterson completed the Shaker film, Patterson realized how many of his students were conducting research projects on subjects that would be well served by documentary film.

> So we said, "Well, we'll do another film, some film on southern material where we are." And Tom liked the idea, and we had a session at my house one Sunday morning where all the students and the faculty members who were involved came together, and then fought together about what the most important traditions were that we had kind of an entree into, that we felt needed to be documented because nobody had done this thing before. And so we decided that we'd apply for a grant and we'd do two films, two short fifteen-minute films, one on Peg Leg Sam and the medicine show and one on Mr. Joines, Frail Joines, and his tall tales.

Patterson and Davenport did not see the material similarly. Each used his perspective as folklorist or filmmaker when conceptualizing the projects. Patterson recognized the different ideas of the two collaborators and produced an academic solution that would satisfy the demands of folklorists.

> Tom, as a filmmaker, I think, found some of the folklorists' interests boring—we were too pedantic for him—and he wanted something that would reach a larger audience, that ordinary human beings would see and enjoy and be interested in, even if they were not folklorists. I thought that was a wonderful thing, too. I don't see any reason why we have to restrict ourselves to in-house academic discourse. I simply wanted to make sure that these films were as sound as we could make them from a folklorist's perspective and that they would be usable in the classroom, too. So kind of early on we began to say, "Well, okay, maybe there are two kinds of things we could do. We could do the film and also something ancillary to the film, and some of the material needs to go into the booklet and some in the film." And we tried to distinguish between what really belonged in the booklet as background and documentation of what we were doing and what for the aesthetic form of the film as a satisfying form for presenting the materials. And we wanted to do research.

Davenport welcomed this scholarly approach. The research of Patterson and the graduate students, combined with Patterson's expertise and thoroughness, pleased both filmmaker and scholar. Davenport talked about the working relationship.

> In *A Singing Stream*, because of the folklorist's presence in the movie, there was a really concerted effort to have examples of different singing styles, all the way from a cappella to early gospel, to singing in the church in different styles—where they have the church singing, and then modern hymns, and hymns that came from country western. . . . They did have this broad spectrum of religious musical styles that were from the beginning of the century. So that it was all scholarly worked out, but it wasn't explained. But in the booklet, it's quite well developed. The same thing was true in the Joines film—that we wanted a development—and I hung all these things on the story of Frail Joines's life, but the folklorists wanted the early hunting stories, they wanted the war stories, the conversion stories, genres.
>
> It's very helpful to me as a filmmaker to have all this information; they'll know right away where this song comes from or what kind of tradition this is. It's like having my research already done.

The Davenport/Patterson team created the American Traditional Culture series and produced four films related to folklore: *The Shakers* (1970), *Born for Hard Luck: The Life of Peg Leg Jackson* (1976), *Being a Joines: A Life in the Brushy Mountains* (1980), and *A Singing Stream: A Black Family Chronicle* (1986). Perhaps the most powerful and best-known film is *A Singing Stream*.

Not all collaborative partnerships are as successful as that of Patterson and Davenport. Often the folklorist does not have the control needed to serve both academic and aesthetic ends. And some folklorists prefer to work alone. For these scholars, such as Thigpen, Ferris, and me, the folklorist who wishes to use film should serve as either cameraperson, editor, or both, so that the results meet the folklorist's demands. Although he was collaborating with a professional cinematographer, Thigpen edited 95 percent of *Rattlesnakes* and 50 percent of *Salamanders*. Ferris noted the necessity of training folklorists to use film equipment:

> I really feel film is the only way to give a total sense of the drama of an event, a folklore event, which involves audience and facial expression and gestures, and that we really are working with only a small fraction of our resources if we don't use film. And we are really handicapping our students if we don't train them in the use of film and still camera and the tape recorder. And I had no training in any of that at Penn. . . . I don't think it's enough just to say, 'We have these cameras here. Take 'em out, see what you can get.'. . . It's like giving somebody a pencil and paper and expecting them to write without having been taught. We are really crippled by inadequate knowledge of the media and our inadequate knowledge of how to use it. Most teachers can't even run a slide projector, can't even run a tape recorder. How in the world are we going to do effective fieldwork unless we are trained in-depth in what a really good recording means and how it can be set up? And we should be technically trained as well as theoretically trained.

Ferris made this remark in 1974, but the situation has changed little. Most fieldwork courses today do not teach students how to use film equipment or explain the ethical and negotiational issues that medium raises.

All film projects are collaborative. The filmmaker has to work with the people he or she is documenting and often has a consultant or is the consultant who has hired a cinematographer. Even the labs, distributors, and audiences may be seen as collaborators. Training subjects as true collaborators is an idea still in its infancy. Although Worth and Adair taught the Navajo to film themselves, and filmmakers have been teaching indigenous and Third World people how to use the technology, these approaches are still uncommon. Shooting and editing a film with those in the film stepping back from the screen to become the film's creators on both content and technical levels is rare. Also unusual is Jorge Preloran's collaboration with Zulay Saravino, who offered to be the Prelorans' guide in her own Otavaleño region of Ecuador; *Zulay* started out as one of Preloran's films about a folk culture, but it turned into a collaboration between a filmmaker and a subject who evolves within the film as she manipulates the images. The processes of collaboration and compromise reached a zenith that led the collaborators to a new filmmaking design. The Prelorans were searching for a theme and a character who would serve as the biographical model and thus epitomize the culture at large, a pattern Preloran had established previously. After following Zulay from one event to another and filming dances, costumes, celebrations, foodways, and other features of folk-

4.6 Preloran and Saravino edit the film *Zulay* on the Movieola.

lore, the Prelorans returned to Los Angeles with the footage. "Zulay wasn't interesting enough, and she was part of society. She wasn't a loner. So what I was shooting was a lot of participatory events that she was in, and she was more or less lost in them because I didn't feature her in them. I'd feature her brother weaving and things like that but never intimately because they were very short scenes. So in a way what I had was a mess, and I didn't know how to glue it together, really." Building a film from the footage became burdensome for Preloran. He and Zulay did not think Zulay could speak authoritatively about her culture. She was too young to know all that one needed to describe the culture, and she feared making errors. Preloran had always worked with older, more experienced people. Zulay could not serve as the protagonist telling her own story, the technique Preloran frequently used, although she did attempt to work with Preloran on the film when she came to Los Angeles.

A chance incident transformed the direction of the film. Polish director Jerzy Antczak, a colleague of the Prelorans, saw the story that the Prelorans had overlooked. Jorge explained:

> He saw the film and he loved it, but he said, "You know, all the things you're telling me about her are not on the film."
> "What do you mean?"
> "Well, I mean, you say how she came, she's adapting, she's learned English and all this. That's where the film is supposed to go."
> And I thought, "Of course! Probably what I have to do is switch it totally around and make it a film about transculturation." I don't know if I did it consciously, but I think I gave it to both of them [Zulay and Mabel]. I just

said, "Look, why don't you just decide what you want to say in the film as to what happens when two people try to adjust to another culture." [Mabel had immigrated from Argentina.] And so they sat for hours deciding, and with me, because I more or less knew the footage. . . .

So I reconstructed the whole film and reedited it . . . and every so often I'd say, "Well, listen, why don't you look through the footage and get me that stuff." So she started to use the Moviola looking for the material, then I'd edit. But then as she got good, and she really got good, she started. I'd say, "Well, you know if you want to deal with that scene. What'd you do with it?" She didn't do too much, but she did have a sense of how to work with the scenes. I did most of the editing. I mean, it's not that she edited, but in a way she did make decisions with me also, and I wanted her to be involved.

Preloran notes that soon Zulay understood and participated in the entire process.

One thing is structure—she started to understand structure—and the other thing is timing, rhythm. She understood that she had to be very succinct, and she is very succinct. She is very to the point. She doesn't mess around. That was easy. And then it turned out that the three of us directed the film. That's the fact, no doubt about it.

Collaboration implies that a folklorist/filmmaker team constructs a film. Negotiation, on the other hand, involves the interaction of filmmakers and informants. When it merges with the negotiation process, collaboration becomes much more than the operations filmmakers engage in with folklorists or anthropologists. When that negotiation is portrayed on film, the subject is transformed into the filmmaker/collaborator and operates both in the known or everyday world and in the world of the camera.

The self peeks out from the frame on multiple levels. For example, Blank sees his Florida background and Peiser sees Memphis, whereas Preloran sees Argentina. Additionally, the filmmaker's academic background determines aesthetic style and content focus. When filmmakers compromise with collaborators, they create a product that reflects their possible divergent views. Subjects and audiences see themselves in films they admire. The choice of subject and the means of depicting it are revelatory. Both disclose the filmmaker's theoretical stance. Other than what is seen, the structure by which the filmmaker enables it to be seen is a key to understanding how the filmmaker discloses the self.

# 5

## Projecting the Self
### *Filmic Technique and Construction*

*When you know the structure, then you can construct.*
*—Jorge Preloran*

Film is always a construction. Film "truth," whether it be cinéma vérité, *kino-pravda,* or observational cinema, is a misnomer because film is never objective. Even the placing of the camera for a film consisting of a single "take" (uninterrupted shot) is a manipulation. The camera reflects the filmmaker's view.[1] Most filmmakers believe, however, that their manipulation creates a "greater truth," what Flaherty's wife, Frances, called "that high moment of seeing, that flash of penetration into the heart of the matter" (Jacobs 1979:8). The film's structure is the mark of the filmmaker's truth and the truth he or she discerns in the topic or persons being depicted.

Filmmakers speak to an audience, blending their sense of themselves with that of the subjects. Filmmakers cannot help but be bound by their cultural vision; only a naive filmmaker believes that a common reality empirically exists. Yet film and video prove that "something exists, or did exist, which is like what's in the picture" (Sontag 1979:5).

## Editing "Truths"

Film and television communicate to millions of people, and the filmmaker's presentation of ideas has the potential of being cultural dynamite. The danger is that the filmmaker might lose sight of the ideas of those she is depicting in favor of her own theories and espouse those theories above all else.

Preloran spoke to me about the power that film provides and the temptation to manipulate beyond the "reality" of the people in the film. Using the voices of the people he documents, he unfolds their "truth": "Let the people, from the inside, tell you what it's about. That's why my films have this appeal. They are nonpolitical, nonthreatening in a way, but they're the truth. At least, the truth of the characters that are living that truth. They're living their lives, and I am asking what it's all about." Preloran's films are, nevertheless, political in subtle ways, uncovering the lives of impoverished peoples to effect change (for example, showing *Cochingo Miranda* to the governor of the province). Preloran believes he has resisted deception by manipulating the image to match what informants tell him is significant.

Paul Wagner also talked with me about his notion of documentary as truth: "One of the crucial differences between dramatic and documentary films is that in dramatic films you know it's a lie, whereas in documentary films you're made to believe that it's the truth when, in fact, it's as much a lie in that sense as the other stuff. It's all controlled and manipulated and the danger is, in documentary, you somehow think this is the real thing or that it's reality that you're seeing. As viewers—in terms of visual literacy and how people approach film and video—they need to have a sense of that."

A knowledge of editing tricks sometimes angers viewers. For example, when Wagner discussed the making of *The Stone Carvers* at VITAS, a film festival organized by the UCLA Folklore and Mythology Program, he was criticized for his honesty about how he edited the film: "I showed *The Stone Carvers,* and I said, 'Now you see Vincent on-camera here, and there he goes off-camera. Well, there's a sound edit there, and a sound edit there.' In other words, making clear what he says was not what he actually said during the filming, that it was an edited version of what he said. I guess for some people who are of a more purist mind, this is just appalling—that you could do that." Some audience members were dismayed by his juxtaposition of nonsimultaneous film and sound to achieve an effect. The details unmasked the power of the illusion.

Wagner's first film idea was to document the Combs family reunion. Although he ended up not doing so, the reunion became one of his favorite themes. For *Free Show Tonite,* Wagner staged an entire event as a reunion. *The Stone Carvers* includes a reunion of the carvers. *Miles of Smiles* concerns the reunion of the Brotherhood of Sleeping Car Porters. Wagner noted that the difference between the Combs family reunion and these other reunions is that these "others are totally filmmaker manipulated."

The reunion of performers for *Free Show Tonite* was Steve Zeitlin's concept, and the film was based on Zeitlin's interviews.

> It was Steve's idea to do research on and to present a medicine show which would include medicine show performance material and narrative material at the [Smithsonian] folklife festival. In the wake of that and because we'd been working together, very early on we started talking about it as a possible film subject. The difference being that we would re-create, use the same formula, but actually re-create it out on a location to be chosen later, re-create a medicine show and bring together the people to do it and to interview for oral history narrative material.

Re-creation of individual actions is another issue about which Wagner talks freely. In the opening scene of *The Stone Carvers,* Vincent Palumbo manually halves an apple and nonchalantly remarks that one needs to have carver's hands to do that. This powerful scene, both artful and symbolic, displays Wagner's genius. In a sense, the action with the apple results from a collaboration between filmmaker and filmed.

> The apple's sort of an interesting topic. That was something Marjorie Hunt never mentioned or talked about when we talked about ideas for the shooting. But in the times that I had gone out with her—we'd go out at lunch time very often, during their lunch break, so that they could sit and talk to us—I had noticed that after his sandwich Vincent would take an apple, would actually do that, break it in half and then eat it. It sort of caught my eye. Of course, it has nothing really to do with stone carving, the traditional stone carving or anything really, but it sort of comes across as what I'd never done and don't regularly do, but maybe a guy who works with his hands might be able to do.
>
> So when we were actually out there doing the filming, at some point we just asked him to do that, got three or four apples and had him break a couple in close-up, break a couple in medium shot, and talk about it. These were all structured situations. Of course, when we got in the editing room, perhaps for that reason, it didn't really fit in with anything else. It doesn't have anything to do with the carving. . . . We could have done it around the table and used it in the montage.
>
> He just says, "Well, you know, stone carver, you gotta have pretty strong hands, you can break an apple open just like this." But that was in response to the filmmaker saying, "Vincent, could you show us how you break an apple and just say something about it being because you're a stone carver?" That was just sort of an ad lib thing. . . . It was in response to a question.
>
> Anything you say to a subject is a prompt. If you're trying to relay some sort of vérité standard, you know, if you sit him down for an interview, you're prompting him. You have expectations and they have expectations of what you want to hear.

The re-creation of an act appears on film as if it happened in the course of the action. Many scenes are re-created in documentary so that the camera can record them. Wagner mentioned this technique in relation to a scene of Vincent carving an arm. As depicted in the final film, the "setup" is fairly obvious in that Vincent addresses the camera.

> We re-created the carving of that arm because, yes, he does do that all the time but wasn't necessarily going to be doing it the day we were filming. And, indeed, that was a Saturday he was doing it and he would have been at home. That's what I'm saying. Everything's your own manipulation at some level and as long as you accept the responsibility for it. To me what was interesting was—because the apple was a little bit different in the source of the material—it didn't fit in with any of the other scenes. So the

logical thing to do with it became to use it at the very beginning where it doesn't have to relate to anything, but sort of works like a teaser.

Sometimes the material is so visually or theoretically exciting to the filmmaker or the folklorist that it cries out to be included by any means. Use of that material is deemed necessary, as is the repetition of an observed action not previously caught by the camera.

Missing sound presents another problem of re-creation. A crucial scene in Davenport's *A Singing Stream* had to be rerecorded in the studio. The climactic concert at which John Landis is joined on stage by his granddaughter was well shot, but the sound was not balanced correctly. Sound from the on-stage musicians' and singers' microphones was mixed on the spot into a single channel. Although well blended in the overall scene, the recording of the lead singers lacked the potent presence needed for use with close-ups. Karen Landis and the Golden Echoes sang with their own image to re-create and overdub the soundtrack. Like Wagner, Davenport addressed the issue of the filmmaker's authority:

> What happens is when you started off in folklore, it was "Well, you can't do that. That's not really true." But every film is totally arbitrary anyway. I mean, I think that filmmaking is so, so much construction. You can take a film like the Landis family film, *A Singing Stream,* and I go down there and I say, "Here's the house." And people walk in the house who have seen the film and say, "My god, I didn't realize it was so small." The spatial relationship has all been changed by the camera.
>
> And so there's a lot. And there's a tremendous amount of manipulation. You're manipulating everything in the film. You tell the story that you feel from the footage that somehow resonates in your heart. And so that aspect of the creating, you're creating. Again. I always felt that . . . we were choosing folklore subjects. But in a way what we were doing was—and I don't know if I can articulate this completely—we were able to unleash or portray or somehow express our idealism about people in general through these specific folklore things.

This idealism drives the folklore filmmaker. Issues of authority, construction, and manipulation are never absent in the filmmaker's mind, but they tend to be subsumed by the folklore filmmaker's desire to make a statement about the essentials of the human condition and the weight of tradition in our lives.

Morality and ethical standards determine the way in which the filmmaker selects what to shoot and how to include it, and these are influenced by the participants. Who is in *control* of the film often becomes an issue. If subjects have control, will the filmmaker adhere to an ethical standard, and will the results somehow be more true to life? Wagner noted that the filmmaker is inevitably in control; what he or she does with the data has ethical accountability:

You could let the subjects have 99 percent control of the film, but you could be totally unethical with your 1 percent and distort the whole picture as far as I'm concerned. It doesn't let you off the ethical or moral hook by virtue of turning over control to the people about whom it's being made. When I go out and talk about these issues, my big point is that in most cases the filmmaker is in control of the film and, for example, there are certain biases, particularly in anthropology, about how and when you edit things, how long a take is. You know, is it appropriate to have short takes and cut together a scene? Do you have to give a sense of the vérité moment out in the field and retain that in the editing room? Those kinds of issues. My thing is, on one level, I'm a total libertarian. Look, you're the filmmaker. Do anything you want to do; you are in control. Having said that, you're also totally responsible for the ethical and moral integrity of what you do. What bothers me is that there's somehow a sense—that may be coming more from the subject matter side, you know, the anthropologists or folklorists— that it's wrong somehow to too heavily manipulate the image of a community or whatever. But my feeling is that it's all a matter of degree, clearly, and that the instant you pick up the camera and turn it on you're manipulating. You've chosen who you're going to film, when, where, and how. And everything else you do . . . is a manipulation, but it's just more manipulation than the initial manipulation you made when you decided to make the film. So you can't insulate yourself from the moral responsibility of trying to be well informed and trying to perform in an ethical manner by not making an edit there or by underediting the film.

The filmmaker always acts as the bricoleur; her construction and manipulation convey, often subtly, what she saw as the primary message about the folklore behavior depicted.

Films made primarily out of stills are overtly the message of their creator. These films are wholly created in the editing room. For example, Ferrero juxtaposes the 986 still images of *Hearts and Hands* to construct her filmic vision. "I wasn't sure I could make a film out of it. I worried that I'd have the most expensive slide show in the world." Using quilt patterns, newspaper clippings, photographs, and other images, Ferrero was able to make a statement about the Civil War as a war of textiles, showing the economics of the war and its effect on women. Re-creation for Ferrero thus became a different issue than that faced by Davenport and Wagner. The re-created voices of women from diaries and letters serve Ferrero's political analysis. "The Civil War was essentially two economic systems vying for each other, and women were intimately involved in the story in both positions. Quilts can serve any ideology. They can be serving the abolitionists, or they can be serving the plantation mistress." For Ferrero, film tells a tale: "I'm not of the school that feels that documentary is capturing any absolute reality at all. I mean, I truly feel that it is storytelling that is collaboration and that someone with a point of view is making it."

Ferrero hoped "to demystify quilts" and uncover their function in a realm undiscovered by and created by film.

Editing decisions disclose that point of view; they make a statement about the filmed data and demonstrate the importance of that data to an audience. As Cohen commented, films "raise questions and challenges." Editing communicates the ideas of the filmmaker at the same time that it presents significant folkloric topics because the way filmmakers arrange their films indicates their biases. Films structured around events generally are closely related to actuality because the data imposes a structure on the film editor. The event model of folklorists is echoed by ethnodocumentary filmmaker David Mac-Dougall in his concentration on events. "Some films construct narratives out of other people's lives," MacDougall writes, "but many other films . . . take their structures from the events they record" (1994:29).

In either case, the film is a portrayal subject to various meanings. Thigpen remarked, "You bring to it an interpretation, or I bring to it an interpretation . . . whether or not we're ever asked to articulate it, it should be discernible by the clever people in the audience. . . . It's documenting other people through my eyes." The theoretical standpoint of the filmmaker always underlies the end result.

## Sound Devices: The Filmmaker's "Voice"

The editing selection process is often determined by the sound devices used when filming. Films that rely almost entirely on exegetic narration do so as a means of connecting diverse scenes to present the ideas of the filmmaker. Films that use the sound-over voices of those being filmed tend to be structured around the acts that are meaningful to those individuals. Sync-sound, which requires a more continuous shooting style, is usually employed for event-oriented films. Most creators of folkloric films find sync-sound to be the most valuable approach for the folkloric film, but many believe a combination of narration, voice-over, and sync-sound allows people to express themselves while the narrator-filmmaker observes or adds information lacking on the soundtrack.

Hawes, who used narration for *Pizza Pizza Daddy-O,* commented on the criticisms she had received regarding the narration and why she believed the narrator was needed:

> I made a very deliberate cultural decision on that [the use of a narrator]. I wrote the narration and I hired the guy that said it. . . . I was not making the film for folklorists. I was making it for the people of Watts so they would look at their children and see how beautiful they were and how nice they were. You know, how cooperative and pleasant and friendly they were.

And that's what hit me when I first looked at the raw footage. I'd rough-cut the film and . . . I showed it to black and white audiences in rough form. . . . The black audiences were looking at it and saying, "So what? That's typical Whitey stuff. Come in and take a picture. You know. Who cares? Who cares what kids do?" This is not a reaction that is confined to black parents. You'd have the same reaction from white parents if you took traditional games of kids and made a big to-do about it. From the black point of view—this was just very shortly after the riots—from the point of view of Watts, what those kids were doing on the playground had no interest whatever and damned little importance. They had an awful lot of very important bread-and-butter issues on their hands. White audiences looked at it and said to themselves, "Aren't they cute and haven't they got rhythm?" And I began to feel that the film was going to do tremendous amounts of social harm, and I deliberately went out and wrote an overblown beginning and ending and hired a gentleman, who happened to be, by the way, on the advisory committee of the Panthers, to narrate it in as "up-town, high-toney" a voice as he could, to in effect say, "This is an educational film. It is important. This is a dignified upper-class cultural presentation because we think it is important. We think you should look at it." The interesting thing is that it's had that effect and it worked exactly the way I intended it to. . . . But I got so much backchat from social scientists on the narration—that it wrecked the film and so on—that I got in touch with the media center [UCEMC] people who distribute the film and offered to redo it. I thought, well, maybe I'd gone too far. Maybe what I should do is just have a kind of ordinary voice—not this fancy voice. And the media center people . . . they kept saying, "Teachers love that. They think his voice is so beautiful, and he says such beautiful things." So apparently it worked the way I intended it to. It made a bridge between this trivial behavior, from the point of view of most people, and the social scientists looking at it and the fact that it's important to take a look.

Dialect differences and the possibility that certain people might not be able to verbalize their own behavior were additional reasons Hawes cited for narrating films:

When I put on *Pizza*, what everybody said to me at that point was, "Why didn't you let the children talk about it themselves?" Well, (a) these are totally nonverbal children—most children are pretty nonverbal anyway. . . . In the second place, no one would have understood them.

Earl Collins speaks with considerably refined diction. You notice the difference between Earl and the people talking in the sugar-making film [*How to Make Sorghum Molasses*]. He happens to speak extremely clearly so that we could assume that most people would understand most of what he said. So we could do it there. I've seen it done all kinds of ways. I think the *Imaginero* example [a sound-over translation of the speaker's exact words] is superb.

Hawes further commented that narration should not be used if the person in the film explained his or her own behavior, but that rules for filmmaking should be based on the needs of the individual film project:

> It's a problem that has to be considered in terms of each film that you produce. How is the audience going to tie in, interrelate with the film, and what are they going to get out of it? And that is the filmmaker's responsibility, to make very clear what he thinks should be got out of it, as far as he can. But I'm very much opposed to these "slice of life" films. I think they're very dangerous—without any attempt on the part of the filmmaker to do anything more than just show it. . . . And another thing that I feel very strongly about is that we have not reached the stage where we can afford to say that ethnographic film has to be "this" way. "It can't have a narrator, or it must have a narrator," or whatever.

Whereas some filmmakers have embraced narration, most have cursed it since documentary's early days. It is still frequently used, often in a popular manner in productions such as the geographical-cultural treatises shown on the Discovery Channel. Its very popularity in this venue and its use in films attempting to have mass appeal further torment the independent documentary filmmaker who suffers with the knowledge that documentary filmmakers created a product inextricably linked with narration.

Circumventing their own disdain for narration, folklorists who find narration necessary avoid a newscaster's style by narrating their own films. Ferris, who is generally opposed to the use of narration, has narrated some of the films produced with the Yale Media Design Studio. He notes, however, that these narratives serve to introduce the people, not to interpret their behavior:

> I'm strongly opposed to any narration which is not the voice of the people that you're working with. . . . I think one of the best examples of how that [type of narration] affects these is *Pizza Pizza Daddy-O*, which is a very fine film and the materials are really exciting, but when that narrative voice of the scholar comes in you really resent his presence. I've been working with some film . . . surveys of black folk traditions. . . . In place of the narrative there is simply going to be a very, very basic introduction of each performer—who are they, where are they, and nothing beyond that. . . . There's no attempt to analyze or to systematize the materials through the narrative.

Ferris remarked that narration imposes a theory on the film data. He believes that theories are tied to living scholars and hence any analysis of folkloric materials should be separated from the material itself to facilitate future research:

> It is important to keep a session intact for someone who comes along fifty or one hundred years later. I'm sure that all of our theories are going to pass in time. . . . I feel that as a folklorist my commitment is to the people who

are the folk and to transmit their materials and their culture in the most honest and authentic way to the viewer or the listener. Granted that we affect the situation by being there, but I try to work in a direction which moves away from theory and away from conceptual frames which might be imposed on the material and to let the material speak for itself. That's the sense in which I try to do all my work.

Thus, Ferris insists that narration should not be used for analysis.

Both Hawes and I use narration for analysis to, as Hawes says, make tie-ins for the viewer and point out important aspects of the visuals. One reason that the narration is intrusive in Hawes's *Pizza* is that she chose not to narrate the films herself or to indicate that these were her own conclusions or interpretations. Hawes remedies this problem for her own screenings by speaking over the narrator; I narrate *Tales of the Supernatural* to inform the audience that the hypotheses raised in the film are mine. Filmmakers recognize that not all film data can stand alone without additional information. Cohen noted that since the production of *The High Lonesome Sound*, he has used various means of deleting narration, for example, the use of captions, the cameraman's voice as interviewer, or an initial statement that introduces the film.

Like Ferris, Cohen believes that narration is sometimes needed but that its use may create additional problems. In 1975, Cohen wrote me:

> I have wrestled with the concept of narration in my films and tried several approaches to this problem. It seems unfair and unethical to have an interpretation given to raw material from another culture or subculture. Too often the narration sets both the mood and the direction of perception and gets in the way of communication between film and viewer. Narration makes it too easy for an audience and can remove the element of challenge from the viewing by offering easy explanations instead. The tone of voice which is connected to narrators often is in conflict with the spirit of the culture being presented. In my first film I was the narrator, but still feel discomfort at being the spokesman for people who don't need me as such. . . . I have increasing trust in the intelligence of the film audience and their ability to perceive things and draw conclusions for themselves.

In 1992, when we discussed the narration in Cohen's more recent films, shot in Peru, he mentioned the problem of communicating his work to a non–Spanish-speaking audience. He found that he would sometimes use titles and at other times use a voice.

An early Peruvian film, *Q'eros: The Shape of Survival* (1979), had quite a bit of narration by Robert Gardner, whose voice affected some viewers negatively. Cohen had admired Gardner's filming and voice from *The Nuer* (1970):

> A beautiful, beautiful film. I was very moved by the filming. A friend of mine knew Gardner, and I said, "Gee, who was the voice in that film?" It was beautiful, a great voice. This was in the days when narration was not a

no-no, or as much of a no-no. He said, "That guy's a friend of mine." I said, "Do you think you could ask him to record my narration? I'd like to have that voice," . . . and Gardner did it one afternoon in about two hours. He read my script. I wrote a narration. . . . He didn't change the content. And that's the narration for *Q'eros: The Shape of Survival.* Well, a friend of mine who's an anthropologist in New Zealand who had worked with the Q'eros, I sent him the film. And he said, "This is a good film and I really like it, John, but I have my arguments with Gardner and many of his positions. I disagree with him on this and I disagree with him on that." And so you suddenly realize that Gardner's voice and the associations with Gardner's voice were what colored his perception.

Cohen is inclined not to use a narrator, but narration nevertheless becomes imperative in certain instances:

> I think the guiding rule that we use is we get as much into the film without any narration at all. See how much is said in speaking, in the setting, in the images, in the ritual, and the situation—how much is there. And then say, "Well, what else isn't there? What might be needed?"
>
> Another factor is that sometimes for me the only place that my films can ever make any money is getting on television, and television prefers a voice-over to subtitles. My new film, I was fortunate that the BBC took it with the subtitles. They put the subtitles on, actually. In the States I can't get any response to that film at all.

Cohen wants to make the effect of the narration poetic. Thus, in *Dancing with the Incas* (1991), Cohen explains that Huayno music fills the airwaves at night so that "while the city is sleeping, it is dreaming to Huaynos." "That's not totally a clear statement, but I love that statement and it goes by in the film and I'm sure it will make some connection in somebody's brain that goes a little beyond logic, but may get to something—a poetic essence of what's going on. I'm not trying to be a poet as such, but I felt that, and I feel it, and I'm willing to include that in a film" (1992). In contrast to Ferris's fear that narration interferes with future analysis, Cohen sees "the danger that in years to come, some of today's meanings will be lost" (1975). For films without any narration, future audiences will be at a loss to interpret the actions of the people, for example, what certain ceremonies are and what they mean. Allowing the action to dominate the structure of the film will alleviate some problems with narration. Of course, film is a representation. The filmmaker uses narration to show openly what that representation is. In so doing, the narration represents the filmmaker as well.

Peiser, Blank, Preloran, and Fleischhauer are opposed to any form of narration. They believe that a narrator separates the audience from the viewing experience. Fleischhauer commented that study guides or brochures accompanying the films could provide information normally placed on a narrative track: "I'm perfectly content to distribute a brochure, or a paper, or an essay, or utilization guide or something with the film. This doesn't seem wrong to me. There was a point, I think, when I might have believed that a film ought to be a homogeneous unit and include everything, but I believe myself that narration spoils film and that voice-over spoils films because it inevitably distracts from the watching."

The problem of narrating a film for didactic purposes raises certain questions about whether the folklorist's remarks should be confined to a separate study guide or accompanying essay. A volume of *North Carolina Folklore* (Tullos, Patterson, and Davenport 1989) was devoted entirely to a discussion and transcription of *A Singing Stream*. Fleischhauer and Hawes have both integrated background materials for their films into study guides. Ferris and Peiser have issued study guides as well as transcriptions of their films and have been involved in producing records and slides for much of their material so that it will be useful for various scholarly needs. In 1993, Peiser reflected on remarks she made in 1975 about "just showing the personality of people." She laughed. "I was young then." I asked what she thought now, and Peiser replied, "Well, basically what I was saying is that you show people in their own context but you don't tell people what you should be thinking about those people. I've gotten a little bit more sophisticated and think that there are ways that you can interpret that so that you build a bridge to whatever community you're doing. And I think it's important to help people know about people. . . . You've got to think about ways to do that. But I still have only used a narrator once—in a slide show."

Blank has also experimented with ways to impart knowledge. He noted that he rarely used narration:

> *Burden of Dreams* has the most of any. And *J'ai Été au Bal* has narrative content, but it's not what you think of as a narrator. We were careful to interview Barry Ancelet, Marc Savoy, and Michael Doucet and use their answers as a narrative structure. So you get them telling about the history of Cajun music and the accordion and the development of the music during the changes in American history. But it's not written out and thought out. It's spoken spontaneously, and I like that way of conveying information. So you feel good. The audience participates in the learning experience. It's the pleasurable kind of learning. It's not information thrown at them like so many information films are.

This unrehearsed narration is similar to voice-over. The interviewees speak to the camera in a relaxed and casual manner, talking about what they know and doing so on their own terms and turf. For Blank, they are not alien voices but people involved in the action.

In my own films, I have employed both narration and voice-over. For *Tales of the Supernatural*, I wanted viewers to know what a folklorist thought about the storytelling behavior exhibited in the film, and so I provided additional background data on legends and their functions. Initially using a narrator to read my written script, I shifted to using my own voice, since these were my own remarks. In many respects, the narration holds the heavily edited film together. In subsequent work, I abandoned this exegetic approach entirely. Yet, in my other films, the participants, such as Skip Armstrong and Kathleen Ware, in a sense, become narrators. Although their interviews are edited and woven into the framework to match the visuals as seamlessly as possible, the words are their own.

So that Wagner can use his participants' voices in the film to tell their own stories, he "pre-interviews" the participants for every film. Sometimes he provides them with a written text, as he did for Roy Acuff in *Free Show Tonite* and Rosina Tucker for *Miles of Smiles*. In *Miles of Smiles,* for example, Wagner pointed out, "That is narration written by Jack Santino and me. It did not come out of Tucker's mind. It came out of ours." Because of the numerous sequences of events, performers, and speakers in some of his films, narration served as a connecting thread for Wagner.

Although Davenport emphasized that using narration was much easier, he abandoned this style after *The Shakers.*

> We embarked on these films where we weren't using narration any longer. . . . It's much easier to structure a film 'cause what you can do is use your narration to make bridges from one good scene to the next good scene, and your narration is your bridging mechanism. But in our case the subjects were speaking for themselves, so we had to find the narrative within their own statements, and sometimes they wouldn't flow in the right direction and would lead us off into some area where we wouldn't go. It's funny how you put these films together. You're gonna go edit and then, zoom, "You know, back here was a problem." "Okay, now we're going straight." Then, zoom, we go off again, and you back up a little and put it together and keep on going. . . . Say we want to go from here to here. Well, it doesn't work visually. We'll just put some narration in, and we'll be able to get from here to here.
>
> The trouble with narrative films, narrative films will typically—like National Geographic specials or NEH things—all look very dated to me after a while. The narrative style often reflects the peculiar aspects of the time in which the film was made. Of course, many things reflect that. I mean the film stock look, the colors, what people are wearing. It always seemed to me that those were particularly the things that make the film dated. Although there's a lot of filmmaking skill that goes into the whole thing, we tried to make it so our presence wasn't as obvious. But anyone who knows anything about filmmaking realizes that, of course. It takes more skill to make a film without a narration, I'll tell you that for sure.

I asked if the Shaker film now bothered him as a result of the narration. Davenport replied, "Well, it looks a little old-fashioned to me now. The style is very traditional. I did the narration myself on that film, because I felt it had to have sort of a personal quality, but part of it was to save money, too."

For many, the question of narration is tied up with the filmmakers' notions of themselves as ethical and unbiased. Both Preloran and Thigpen remarked, for example, that the subjects themselves determine what's important. Using their own voices, the subjects direct the filming.

Obviously the need for and use of narration depends on the content of the film, the language of the participants, and the purposes of the filmmaker. If the film seeks to show not only the research but also the analysis of the data, a narration or an accompanying essay telling the viewer how the research proved the filmmaker's hypotheses is useful. This practice also allows the viewer to review the data, evaluate the hypotheses raised, and concur or disagree with the filmmaker using the same data for analysis. The decision to use narration is based on the individual dictates of each film project.

Although narration may be used to complement or add information to the film, most filmmakers interviewed agreed that either the sound-over or sync-sound voices of those appearing in the film should dominate the soundtrack. For events, interactions, and performance, sync-sound equipment is generally used. The processes of craft production may, however, be fruitfully described by having the artists explain their actions in sound-over. Thus, in *Spirits in the Wood*, Skip Armstrong is heard speaking above the din of the chainsaw. Folk art tends to be a singular activity wherein an inner voice is not outwardly verbalized during the creative process. When Armstrong performs with his chainsaw and speaks to his audience, the video renders the scenes in sync-sound. Likewise, for Preloran, who has primarily documented craftsmen, sound-over is a means of glimpsing the protagonist's own philosophy and capturing the essence and significance of the events of those being filmed:

Well now, in my films after Hermogenes [*Imaginero*], I've developed a style which I think is very important to what I'm doing, no? And that is that only the people speak. . . . Now, the main problem is that if you put in a narrator, it's as if you were looking at something through a window, but you couldn't really be part of the thing. Because you always have a polished narration, spoken by a beautiful voice, and it's all very, very plastic. But life is really quite different. . . . The power of the sound of a film is *incredibly* important. I think it's the magic of the film. . . . Let's say that I'm speaking now to you, or writing, and the main thing is that it's the only way I can tell you what I'm thinking. And my thoughts are my soul. My philosophy is my soul. I can tell you how to do something, but what I am doing is now telling you my thoughts. So that's the soul of a man. And what he does externally would be his body, how he did things. In the film, if you don't have a soundtrack that has the soul of that person telling you what his thoughts are, his feelings, you won't see anything but the exterior, which is just the material part. And I think that is the secret. [1976]

By using sound-over as opposed to sync-sound, Preloran has been able to film with a very low shooting ratio. With sync, one must keep the camera on so that dialogue and action are perfectly matched.

Preloran was at UCLA when Colin Young's theory of "observational cinema," based on cinéma vérité, became popular. He discussed some of the advantages and disadvantages of this approach:

> Since the advent of sync-sound around 1960 . . . the whole concept of documentation of human experiences has changed. And new theories popped up right away. One of them was right here at UCLA, through Colin Young, in which the idea was to try to document what was happening at a medium distance, the camera would be at a medium distance, so that he could go in with the tele lens, a zoom, or he could pull out to a wide angle and try to capture what was going on—the reaction and the action. And the sound man would be picking up the sounds where they would be most telling. . . . So, synchronous sound brought in the need of a two-man production team in which the cameraman and the sound man had to be in such good rhythm—it was really a team—that they got to be very, very polished in this. It brings also an aloofness, perhaps; it makes them technicians making a film. I don't know if this is best, because if you film intently to bring out exactly what's happening, you're more interested in form than in content. . . . If you have only one camera and you're only in one position, and you don't want to turn off your camera, you can't run around, you can't look for things that are happening, which is what actually the anthropologists were always criticizing us filmmakers for—that we were cutting and editing in faces and reactions and things that weren't happening at the same time. Well, that doesn't bother me at all because the important thing is the truth, the real truth, not the apparent truth that is going on onscreen. So, for one thing sync is good as a scientific approach because you see exactly what is happening in the same time continuum. But, on the other hand, to make a film is different. Film to me has a different connotation. It's an art form. You have to try to synthesize what happened. And in so doing, you're creating a new object which is film. . . . I would rather use sync-sound—of course, you use it—but not as something that you are bound to by a technical possibility. But rather to record the sounds and the music and things that are going on, but then use it with, perhaps, voice-over to give you what I was talking about before, the soul of the people. [1976]

Preloran's style, resulting from equipment limitations, led him to shoot inexpensively and create his "ethnobiographies." His artistry helps inspire and form the postvérité film.

As Preloran indicated, certain folkloric subjects, notably narrating and musical performances, are most often shot with sync-sound. Peiser also mentioned that sync was essential for filming these activities, but it was not necessary for documenting material culture and crafts. For Cohen, the filming of music requires sync-sound, but like most of the filmmakers interviewed, Cohen uses sound-over as well. He observed, "Voice-over is occasionally a more effective way to present the images in conjunction with the statements. In this way, the voice can be contradicted by the image presented, showing both sides of a question simultaneously." Blank also uses a combination of sound-over and sync for his films, which generally focus on musicians. He noted that sync provides a sense of intimacy, "because it gives the people a chance to talk and it gives you a feeling of being there with the people" (1975).

## Tools of Choice

Folkloric films that document narrating, singing, play activities, musical performances, or any group event are most effective when the sound is synchronous with the visuals. These films rarely require narration. Dance, craft processes, and some ceremonies and folklife practices can be explained with voice-over. Like the use of narration, the decision to shoot with sync-sound will depend on the film's topic and the filmmaker's outlook. If the visual material can be effortlessly segmented into parts that do not demand the juxtaposition of motion or images or the demonstration of process and interaction accompanied by appropriate soundtracks, then texts, tapes, and slides may best suit the fieldworker's needs.

Cohen aptly commented, "Although film can be used as a tool in fieldwork, or can be equivalent to a written document, or equivalent to a phonograph or tape recording, for me its primary function is as film—and if that function becomes subservient to any of these other uses, the film loses its own value and potential." Photography, still or motion, cannot always record the nature of some events that depend on invisible tensions. A textual discussion can describe more easily and completely the unseen, but felt, forces operating in certain events.[2] Just as texts may explain aspects of events more fully than other representations, the value of film lies in its ability to convey behavior that is difficult to document in other dimensions.

Judy Peiser pointed out, "Certain things don't need to be filmed and work better as slide shows, especially when everyone's dead and all you've got is photographs." Peiser and Ferrero have exhibited materials about culture that did not require film. For instance, Ferrero has staged large quilt exhibits at museums. Likewise, Peiser's eighteen-projector multimedia Beale Street presentation—cultural "maps" of the South that combine slides, music, and audiotape—and her weekly radio show on a community station are other forceful forms of media. The fieldworker's focus will determine the most effective tool. These areas of focus and the tools of choice may be represented as follows:

| *Focus* | *Tool* |
|---|---|
| texts: content and structure | manuscripts, tape |
| artifacts: form and structure | stills |
| vocal and musical expression | tape |
| texts and artifacts in context | tape, written documents, stills |
| process, performance, inter-action, movement, holistic events, individual behavior | film |

Filmic structure combined with content focus tells the viewer as much about the filmmaker as the content does about the topic. It also allows the viewer to perceive how the filmmaker views folklore, whether as text or object or as behavior and process.

# 6

# Structure Shifts and Style
## *A Montage of Voices and Images*

*Kodachrome*
*They give us those nice bright colors*
*They give us the greens of summers*
*Makes you think all the world's a sunny day.*
—*Paul Simon, "Kodachrome"*

Effective folklore films provide a sense of involvement in the event for the audience by following the actual structure of the processes of narrating, singing, ceremony, dancing, playing, and similar events and conveying them as holistically as possible through myriad styles. How one chooses to present folklore shifts as a result of one's growth as a filmmaker at the same time as one's attitudes about film and technique shift. A look at my own work quickly reminds me how filmmakers change not only what they choose to shoot but how they do so. Filmmakers are not the only ones who determine the transformations, however. Like a puzzle, the film is made up of many pieces. Working without a fixed picture such as the storyboard common in fiction film, the documentary filmmaker views a constantly changing image, a new picture, with every piece of the puzzle that falls into place. Technological advances create new ways of seeing the picture. Negotiation with subjects transforms the image that the filmmaker envisions. Funding is often the key piece, the essential component that completes the puzzle.

All of the filmmakers interviewed here appraised the ways they put together these pieces of the filmic puzzle. Films that follow a folkloric event seem to have an intrinsic design, shaped by the event itself. Unless that makeup is anticipated or followed at the onset, the film will reflect the filmmaker's structure more than that of the event. This approach often predominates when the action cannot be written about in a narration or determined in advance. Blank noted, "You have to imagine what you're going to get, and that's hard to do, because my films don't really have a script. I just shoot what I think will make a film and then lace them together in the editing process." A combination of both approaches is certainly possible and is a technique I used for *Tales of the*

*Supernatural,* which followed one event but which I pastiched together in the editing room to reflect my attitudes about the content.

Frequently, the film seems to impose its own structure, leading the filmmaker to an unanticipated breakthrough. For example, Davenport talked about his experience with the process of following the twists and turns that the structure of a film might take:

> A film always seems to me to have a certain kind of logic in the material that you sort of discover. It's kind of an interface between yourself and the material, but what usually happens is you go and have these great ideas about what you're going to do and then somehow it doesn't work out, and the film's here and you're over there and you're thinking it should be this way, and the film is basically what it is. You have to make an adjustment between the two and then discover what the film wants itself to be in the process.
>
> It's a process of discovery. We never went to any of these projects with a script. We had an idea that it would be a film about "this," but none of these ideas turned out to be what the film ended up to be. The idea was usually very simpleminded and we'd say, "We'll go in there and do it and it will be real easy and we'll finish it up." But it always turned out to be much, much different.

Often the film acquires unity and direction only after the filmmaker recognizes that a shift is vital. To let the film unfold, seemingly "on its own," is disturbing because of the filmmaker's expectations about what will occur and how it will be shot. Filmmakers do begin with a hypothesis, although many believe they do not. As is true in any fieldwork situation, something about a particular subject intrigues the filmmaker. The idea may seem vague and perhaps not yet verbalized or visualized clearly, but it does underlie the rationale, both for fieldworkers and for filmmakers. When this hypothesis changes because unexpected traditional behaviors or issues are encountered in fieldwork, the filmmaker must rethink the direction of the project. The film sometimes forces the filmmaker to reassess and adjust it.

The Prelorans looked at the footage they had shot for their film project in Ecuador, but were unable to see a pattern. Jorge's filmic approach was to follow the activities and ideas of one person as representative of the culture at large, but the usual click with a subject did not occur easily for *Zulay.* The Prelorans were searching for the path the film would take. They ascertained that the film they had shot of daily activities, rituals, and festivities in Otavalo was quite ordinary. "It was probably beautiful," Jorge said, "but to me it had no dramatic content. . . . You need a strong dramatic thread and there was nothing there. So anthropologists liked it, they were looking at little details, but an audience would have been bored to death after a while." Like Cohen, Preloran had long recognized that film has its own structure, which leads the filmmaker. In the case of *Zulay,* the film took eight years to cohere. Jorge remarked, "I think this film is quite original."

6.1 Zulay's aunt performs a ritual to cast out evil spirits in *Zulay*.

I've never seen anything like it. But the point is, I think that I'm a filmmaker. I'm not an ethnographic filmmaker or anything. I'm just a film-maker. And eventually the theme starts to tell you what to do. And this film was such a mess. . . .

The structure is not something that you impose. The imposition of structure is for documentaries that have an issue. You editorialize. You go in with an idea and then you shoot specifically to get your ideas across. Ethnographic and folklore is exactly opposite. It's learning as you film, which is wonderful. The idea that you're learning something, and you're digging in, you're shooting at the same time. And you don't know what you're looking for.

I made a film called *Zerda's Children*, which started out being a film about a woodsman . . . but it turned out that the man had ten children and four had left, and I started looking, by radio, for those children who had left. I'd try to get them in cities, and others were in school, and little by little the whole film started to turn on me that education was the only way out. This was Zerda's concern. He wanted his children to be educated so they wouldn't be the same as he. So the film now is a film about education, and it's based on the woodsman. . . . You start to try to see a structure. The structure is going to come very, very slowly.

Mabel Preloran explained that Zulay's aunt had a dream that made the creation of the film acceptable to Zulay's family. The dream also became the basis for a "re-created" scene in the finished film. The scene followed the dream's structure. Mabel explained the dream's significance:

These people believed very strongly in dreams. And we were lucky because Zulay was living at that moment with her aunt. Her aunt is a person who, they believe, has some kind of supernatural powers. She's like a seer. And the day that we asked Zulay to be part of the film and she said yes, we said, "What happened to your family?" She said that we could visit them and ask. That night her aunt had had a dream. . . . She told Zulay that she saw a couple of white people sweeping the living room, kitchen, and family room. Very, very clean—her aunt was clean—and it was perfect. Spotless! And three grains of wheat were shining from the kitchen corner. And that was very good. That was very good because in a dream, for them, cleanliness meant honesty, and the maize meant fortune. And they thought that we could film with honesty, and fortune, and we were welcome.

The filmmaker structures the film to make sense of the experience both personally and for the viewers. For example, Ken Thigpen was seen in his own Halloween film as an expert appearing on television, and he decided to use the studio's cues for his structure. I asked why he had taken this approach and had cut this film so differently than his others. He responded,

We'd never done it before and we've never done it since. We might do it for another film—well, there will be phoenix-like recombinations of some of these films one day possibly. But we felt we needed subtitles to say something like why we're doing this, so that it came up and I didn't say it on a camera in a way that we could use to say why we were doing a film in State College. In fact, we wanted to say, "State College has a very strong celebration of Halloween." Well, that sounded very pedantic. So we said, "That's not the tone of the thing that's evolving. So we should do it in a different structure." I was thinking in the back of my mind also how Mook had structured his Halloween film very carefully. And it was a play on structure, too. I mean, for me, it was sort of an ironic structure, since being in the midst of it was overwhelming; it was more difficult to understand the structure of the thing from within it as a participant, as a real participant in it. So I thought, "Well, why don't we just do these '1, 2, 3, on your mark, get set, go' kinds of things?" Because it started out with the camera, and I said, "Why don't we do 'on your mark,' because that's what they say in the studio. And then Hornbein says, "Yeah, then we can say, 'Get set,' and then we can say, 'Go.'" And we could develop the pace of it so that it ends up with this frenzy of the haunted house . . . at the end.

With this structure, Thigpen was able to combine all of the elements normally associated with Halloween. Drawing on the pacing of the event itself, the insights gained from being a participant, and his knowledge of Mook's film, Thigpen shifted away from the vérité style with which he had shot and edited his other film projects.

This type of stylistic expansion adds variety to the corpus of each filmmaker. The filmmaker is continually maturing as an artist. Cohen explained that being engaged in film creates a dialogue. "You're always in a state of development and the only thing that's consistent is that I make the films and that I make films about music, but that I feel very much in dialogue with many things. The issues of filmmaking . . . I'm in dialogue with and, even though I set out to film a certain way, perhaps, if the situation doesn't allow it to happen, then I'm willing to change it because I'm never stuck by a format." For Cohen, film is a dialogue on another level. He has used his camera as the eye for himself and has participated in conversation and in actions through the lens by melding with his camera and becoming part of the scene.

> At moments it is vérité, but the vérité is a dialogue between me and them. Two things have emerged from that filming approach because I realize I use it a lot. In *Mountain Music of Peru* [1984], there's a place where a kid's having a little haircut, a little Indian kid, Quechua Indian kid, and a woman comes out. I'm filming my hand cutting the kid's hair with one hand and the other hand is holding the camera and then the woman comes out and embraces me—still while I'm holding the camera—she leans right into the camera and embraces me. And the camera is running away. They're looking slightly off into space and the camera's running. Really what's happening is that my right eye is against the viewfinder which then goes a little bit to the right at the prism which then goes to the lens which is another inch over, so the camera eye is about two or three inches more to the right and they're addressing my left eye, they're addressing my living human eye. They're addressing the flesh and being recorded by the lens so that they don't look like they're talking into the camera, and it's partly because I'm using a wide-angle lens that it exaggerates it a little bit 'cause I'm not close. So this happens quite a bit in the films now.
>
> The cameraman in the right situation can also be the ethnographer, and the editor, and the camera eye, and observer, and almost participant at the same time. Your relationship with the people you're filming at that moment is very important, and if it's worked right, it can be an incredible moment where the people who are doing their ritual also know who you are, so they're neither shunning you nor putting on a pose, but they sometimes acknowledge you and dance with you, or allow you to be there, giving you a lot of permission, and you have a lot of responsibility as you film it. But it's a very interactive moment. It's different from the cameraman or somebody stepping in [and saying], "We are now filming so and so. Tell me your thoughts." But their acknowledgment of the camera is part of the scene.
>
> In a Greek wedding I was filming in Athens [for *Pericles in America*], I was in the circle inside the inner circle of the dancers and I was really dancing with the lead dancer. And he knew I was there. I was undeniable. But he still was doing it and it was, to me, one of the most thrilling things. You would never go there if you were an observer. You don't have that permission. But the camera gave you that permission and you weren't turning the people into clowns or into performers, but you were just allowed in there.

> Like you were the camera involved with your work. They were doing a
> dance, and they knew you were there. And I was so close. When the guy
> got down on the floor, I got down on the floor, and when he got up, I got
> up. So it was very, very special. It means so much when you can get to a
> moment of understanding.

How filmmakers achieve an understanding with the people they are filming is
as individual as the filmmaker and the situation. Cohen became an insider in
the dance for *Pericles;* for others, he communicated by playing well-known traditional music; and for *Carnival,* he engaged in a barter process on screen.
Each film project presents situations that create further stylistic shifts.

Similarly, with *Zulay,* Preloran made a radical style shift, one that led him
and Mabel "into" the film themselves and brought their subject "out" of the film
to construct her own image as a filmmaker. Preloran used sync-sound for this
project, and he was shooting in Ecuador instead of Argentina, which was in a
state of political turmoil. In a new setting, he was open to a change in style. Not
only did *Zulay* become a means of communication for the filmmakers—all
three of them—it also became a means of communicating through film, on film.
*Zulay* begins and ends with a letter Zulay is seeing, sent via camera, from her
mother. The film is the vehicle for dialogue. Jorge described the process:

> Zulay was in L.A., and that's when the film starts, by giving her a letter,
> and we shot the letter. That is something we did on purpose. We took the
> letter Zulay sent to Otavalo and we set it down, and we set the camera all
> up, and then I gave the family the letter and they started to open it. That
> was real. And then, I thought, "Wouldn't it be extraordinary if the mother
> answered Zulay through film and she would see it for the first time on the
> flatbed [film editing table]." So I tried it, and the son told her, "Look, you
> just talk to Mabel, and then after a while just turn to the camera and say,
> "Well, now that they're shooting, I might as well talk to you." She did it!
> She did it like a pro! I mean, she was there talking to Zulay and it was ex-
> traordinary what she said! I mean, I couldn't believe it when they
> translated. So, when we came back——

Mabel interjected, "In a way, Zulay was prepared, because when we wrote the
letter she said to me, 'I'd like to answer, but they don't write. They don't have a
cultural writing.' And I said, 'Well, I can record for you, tape record for you.' She
said, 'Fantastic.' And after a while, Jorge said, 'If you like, you can say the letter
in the camera.' And she said, 'Oh! Okay!'" Jorge continued, "By then they knew
what we were doing. It was very cute. And so we set up the Moviola [editing
table] and we put Zulay there, and I showed her the letter [from her mother]
and I got her first reaction." The film begins and ends with these letters, indicating that it is all, in a sense, a flashback. Following the unfolding relationship
established with Zulay, and baring the self of all three filmmakers on the screen,
the film took unexpected turns and fundamentally altered Preloran's style.

Filmmakers change as their own sense of what is significant changes. As an inner stylistic process, filmmaking reflects the personal, ethical, and aesthetic evolution of the filmmaker as he or she works out a sense of self.

For example, Peiser has shifted her film structure from "portraits" such as Fannie Belle Chapman and Ray Lum to a larger framework. What is different, she remarked, is "putting the portraits together. It's putting the people together." In *All Day and All Night*, Peiser featured many of the musicians who worked on Beale Street. These portraits were a reflection of her day-to-day experiences after the Center for Southern Folklore moved to Beale Street and became part of the community.

Wagner also recognized the changes, or style shifts, he had made in his work. He remarked that his changes from one film to another were positive ones: "I think it's both a problem for me and an advantage, but unlike a lot of filmmakers, I am not interested in focusing on a particular style. You could probably name any number of filmmakers who have focused much more stylistically from film to film. A lot of my interest in film is in the potential of the medium, exploring the different ways in which it can be manipulated."

Wagner agreed with my observation that he had made films that document events happening in front of the camera as well as ones structured around oral history.

> That's absolutely true. Well, in a way, *Stone Carvers*, I guess, is sort of a combination of the two and literally a combination of the two in that there are two principal scenes in the first two-thirds of the film, one of which is oral history and one of which is a carving scene. So it literally combines the two. I think that's the strength of it actually, that you're able to see the craft as it's happening, but your understanding of it is sort of confused by the broader understanding of the cultural context that it comes out of or in which it exists.
>
> But that's right. The other two one-hour films are fundamentally oral history. In *Free Show Tonite* we re-create a medicine show so there is a temporal event, if you will, and I think that helps that film to intercut between the two [event and oral history]. And with *Miles*, we do something that I've done in other things, which is to try to do oral histories, but energize them by using archival footage and stills and by making the interviews or the interactions with the interviewees a little more physical—like in the case of *Miles of Smiles*, having the porters make a bed.

*The Grand Generation* marks a strong departure from Wagner's other films in that it presents people static and isolated against a plain background; each verbalizes the major events in his or her life to the camera, and the film then moves to the next individual and begins a new film segment. The elders continue their monologues in voice-over, while still photos and other visuals depict them engaging in their former pursuits. Yet they are oral history films. Wagner observed,

> It's similar to the other films in that it grew out of research done by a folk-
> lorist in a particular subject area, but it certainly cuts folklore in a different
> direction. Rather than looking at a particular community or group of
> people, or particular occupation, it looks at more of a theoretical concept as
> played out in a variety of people and places. But the similarity is that all of
> them were programs at the [Smithsonian Festival of American Folklife on
> the Mall in Washington, D.C.] in various formulations, and all of them led
> to different films.
>
> That particular one, you're right, there was a Grand Generation program
> at the folklife festival in the summer of '84. And while people were in town,
> we filmed them. We set up a little studio intentionally. A no context look,
> which incidentally we were aware was something probably folklorists
> wouldn't like. Which again to me, I don't care. I had this idea that we do it
> around a thematic core rather than a particular locality and person.

Wagner responded to my suggestion that the film consists of several topics and intertitles indicate what the topics are.

> We tried to guide people. Those were all subgroups around this whole issue
> of the culture of aging. Those were all ideas developed by Steve Zeitlin and
> Marjorie Hunt conceptually and that had been field-tested in the sense that
> they had used those to develop questionnaires for interviewing older
> people. The film grew out of that basis. I mean, my contribution was to try
> to come up with a visual approach that expressed those concepts. For me,
> because it was more of an intellectual exercise I have to say, I hope not in a
> bad way, but the film is much more of an intellectual exercise than the
> others because it is cutting material in a conceptual way rather than in the
> way a fieldworker would do it. Plus, just the practical thing that we didn't
> have the money to go around the country to visit, so it was not going to be
> a compilation film of little mini–stone carver films where we'd go to New
> Mexico and film Cleophus out in the fields and then do an interview with
> him on his front porch—you know, sort of the format of the chicken
> scratching cutaways during the interview. This is the format of the folklore
> film that most people are comfortable with. Our idea was that maybe
> there's another way to think about this. We're gonna have 'em in Washing-
> ton. We have all these great people, a great resource to do interviews with.
> What if we didn't worry so much about the context because, after all, the
> film is not about Spanish-American farming or watermen or whatever.

Indeed, the film is not about the Grand Generation exhibit in Washington, nor is it a series of in-depth films on various folk artists or individuals. But a thread still exists—in this case, the folklore associated with aging. "It's about aging and the nature of aging, and the folklore of aging, and the relationship to the communities and all those kinds of things. So we thought, 'Why not be a little radical here and put them in a more contextless situation, cutting in, using stills and that sort of thing,' context as we chose to." As Wagner created a film out of the vignettes of people's lives and the way they face aging, he shifted his style to reflect his own ideas as a filmmaker. The nonfolklore films Wagner has produced have received little notice from folklorists.

Wagner still draws on folklore, despite his change in style to one that is less folklore oriented and more filmic. For example, a video about mail recalls a documentary classic with which most filmmakers are familiar: Basil Wright and Harry Watt's 1936 film *Night Mail.* Made for the Smithsonian Institution, Wagner's video, *Mail by Rail* (1993), documents railway post office clerks who sorted mail on the train cars as they traveled from town to town. They were an elite group; they were postal, not train, employees.

Wagner explained that the film was made entirely without a collaborator: "not a folklorist in sight." In contrast with the lengthy *Miles of Smiles,* this film is only four minutes long. Obviously, the film looks at an occupation and is a topic that folklorists would find fascinating. The connection to *Miles of Smiles* is strong, but the pull of the filmmaker to the image of *Night Mail* may be greater, and Wagner used it as a referent, from one filmmaker to another, when he described the film. Filmmakers trained in film history often explore different styles by experimenting with filmic modes learned in film school.

Style shifts occur for diverse reasons. They transpire because of funding, because filmmakers look at their previous work in a new way, because of the subjects in the film, because of technical problems or opportunities that alter the film's direction, and ultimately because the filmmaker is constantly evolving.

## Ethical Problems and Negotiated Films; or, Is Everybody Happy?

Some filmic changes are the consequences of negotiation between filmmaker and subjects. Often, in published sources and archival materials, the names of informants are not printed to protect their identities. With filmmaking, obviously, such restrictions cannot be applied, for the informant is visually depicted. Most filmmakers use a standard release form that subjects sign before the filming begins. Nevertheless, those appearing in the film are often unaware of how the material will be used, the specific audiences who might view the film, or the ways in which audiences might perceive them. The final film might cast an informant in an unfavorable light not anticipated while shooting was in progress. Narrated films may make statements that the film subject believes are false and misleading.

Two prevailing approaches address the problem of ethical standards in documenting the unstaged behavior of film participants. The first solution is to have informants sign release papers so that the filmmaker cannot be sued if those filmed are unhappy with the results. The filmmaker thus has absolute control over the editing and shapes the film according to his or her own perception of the individuals and events. If informants are displeased, they have little recourse. Release forms are also signed for the second alternative, but the filmmaker allows those filmed to see the raw footage or the roughly edited workprint before the final print is prepared. If informants believe certain scenes or narrative comments falsify the events or invade their privacy, the filmmaker then either corrects or deletes the material. This approach can create enormous problems for the filmmaker, who may disagree with the informants, but if the filmmaker represents his informants *honestly and with dignity,* such conflicts are likely to be rare.

Cohen ensures that the people in the film structure it. He informs them in advance what *he* wishes to do and then finds out *their* wishes: "The concerns for the people who are in the film are very important, and sometimes those concerns are expressed and explored even before the film is made. Or even before they allow you to film or before you start. It's not even 'allow.' This contract is an explanation unless you're really deceptive. If you're really open, then I think people will edit themselves."

Ferrero echoes the idea of subjects editing themselves: "I don't believe in catching people off guard around something as intimate as the meaning of their lives. I feel that's a collaboration, that people choose what they want to say. They don't say everything, and the more they understand the larger meaning of what you're trying to say, the more they can choose to disclose or not disclose."

Ferrero also pointed out that the unexpected is occasionally disclosed to everyone's delight. The Miller sisters of *Quilts in Women's Lives* repeat each other's words constantly: "I don't know that the Miller sisters would have said out loud that they were sibling rivals. And yet they're wonderful, and that whole element of their interaction was certainly essential to capture. And, in fact, the first time I filmed it, I didn't get it in the camera the way I wanted, and I actually went back and reshot in order to have it on camera. What I didn't have on camera was their echoing each other in a way that people would believe it. And I didn't want the audience to think that I had constructed that in the editing." Being on the scene for a while, the filmmaker learns what behavior generally occurs and then tries to film it. Most people do edit themselves in the process. People who become comfortable with the filming situation and establish a relationship with the filmmaker become collaborators reenacting what they think the filmmaker might be searching for.

Compromising in some instances is a matter of catching what happens but downplaying it. For example, the men in *Buck Season at Bear Meadow* didn't want Thigpen to show how heavily they were drinking. They also requested that Thigpen ignore a controversy in the camp. Thigpen agreed but still caught the camp's flavor. "We showed them drinking and playing cards, and they drank a lot more than we showed. But we went along with that." Sensitive to the image the men wished to portray, Thigpen negotiated with them to meet both his needs and their requirements.

Negotiating with the subjects sometimes means allowing them to "direct" the action, as Les Blank did while shooting *Živeli*. Because he was less acquainted with the people, and the film was not his idea, how would Blank know what should be shot?[1] He noted, "They might make suggestions. They might say, 'Well, we're going to be doing a concert over here. Do you want to come shoot that?' And then we ask for photographs from their scrapbooks and they might comment on them."

Because, to him, the Serbs were the Other, Blank had problems with the film. Of *Živeli* Blank explained,

> I can't say I like it as much as some of the others. I don't dislike it. I guess I had a hard time getting connected with it. . . . The Serbian film, we're all over the place. We're in someone's store one afternoon and someone's bar at night, and the people, I guess we didn't know them very well. We were also trying to show a culture, a Serbian culture, and the Serbian culture is not that easy to lay out. There are a lot of complexities and conflicts, and at that time there was a split in the church, and this made it difficult because there were people who wouldn't speak to other people during the film.

In some cases, negotiation is not possible and the filmmaker must eliminate entire scenes after the film is shot.

> There were a couple of people who told great stories, and one lady on her deathbed asked that we remove a story. I don't think she asked it, but one of her friends did, who thought she'd be remembered better if she was not in the film talking about her relationship with Al Capone, and how they used to smuggle hooch across the borders, using these nice little old ladies who would hide the bathtub gin under their shawls and in the back seat of the convertible. And I thought it was a great story, and she, as she told the story, thought it was a great memory too—how he had protected these ladies. I guess their husbands had died in the factories and they used their cellars to make the gin and it had gotten them through hard times, and they were grateful. I guess one lady appointed herself to watch the moral lessons of the film and asked for it to be struck from the film. With great reluctance, we took it out.

Blank agreed to the woman's request. Eliminating a scene which may have taken hours to arrange and shoot is difficult. The filmmaker has already paid for the film stock, its development, and a workprint. In terms of time, energy, and money, removing material is frustrating. But trust between the filmmaker and those being filmed is strengthened, and the filmmaker will not have to "second-guess" the decision later.

Just as Blank experienced problems with the Serbian film because of division in the group, Davenport had to negotiate with a community that had splintered into two groups because of religious differences. They no longer communicated with one another, which put Davenport in a quandary for shooting *The Shakers*.

> And what happened was when we went to the Shakers and said, "Well, we've got this money. We'd like to come and film you," one group said absolutely no, and the other group said yes. Well, the two groups happened to be in a terrible schism. They were divided in a very desperate situation. And the one group that said yes, we filmed. And then the one that didn't allow themselves to be filmed said, "Well, you've got to hear our point of view." So they allowed us to film."

The saga of making *A Singing Stream* is one that includes the many ethical pitfalls encountered in documentary film projects. Not only did Davenport, Patterson, and Tullos face technical problems, but the murder of one of the participants caused a subject shift. The story of their predicament is symbolic of the kinds of issues that arise in documentary film projects. In separate interviews, Davenport and Patterson spoke at length about the negotiation process and other challenges. Davenport recalled,

> Dan and Allen went to an anniversary concert, and they saw the Golden Echoes, which was a black group there. And they said that they thought this was a good subject because they sang traditional black songs, but they also sang songs from country western, "Dust on the Bible," and things like that. And so I listened to the tape that they sent up and I thought it sounded pretty good, and I said, "Well, let's go down and talk to them." So I went down and met the family and did some interviews and it seemed like it was a good idea. But as we worked on this film, it became clear that the idea to do a film on gospel singing, black gospel quartet singing, was such a limited idea, and what was really interesting was this woman, Bertha Landis, the mother. We had some really nice scenes with her. So after our second or third trip down there . . . I suddenly realized that we should switch the subject all around to this Landis family.
>
> Now this caused Dan a lot of problems. . . . We had told this gospel group that we were going to do it about them and we'd already given all the members of the gospel group an honorarium to be participants and most of the members of the gospel group weren't of the Landis family. And so by changing it, and saying, "Heck, we're not going to deal with the gospel group anymore. We're switching to the family," Dan felt—and probably this was something that was pretty touch and go at the time—the gospel group would say, "Why are they doing it on the family now? They're supposed to be doing it about us. What's wrong with us? Why is the Landis family

better? Why don't they do it on our family instead of their family?" and so on. Dan was very reticent to change. So we said, "It's going to be a film in which we're going to feature the Golden Echoes, but it's really going to be about the Landis family." . . . And I don't know, I think it did create some hard feelings, but we kind of left that up to John Landis, who was one of the main figures in the film, and he was very, very diplomatic, and I think he basically ironed things out in the gospel group. He was the lead singer there and was the real dynamic force behind the Golden Echoes. . . .

We spent lots and lots of money on a couple of shoots and everything went wrong. The Golden Echoes didn't perform well, they couldn't hear; we had new audio systems; the musicians couldn't hear the singers and everything was out of key, and we spent about a third of our budget on one shoot of that, twenty-five thousand dollars, just on the shoot, and we didn't get anything because it was so poorly done. And, in fact, in the film, the only piece that's there is when they sing "The Old Rugged Cross," and the only way we were able to do that is that we dubbed all of the sound in there. We went to the studio and redid the whole thing and dubbed the sound in. Kept a little bit of track for the applause and stuff like that. But dubbed it in—essentially watched it and dubbed it. It's hard to tell that that's dubbed in, but in other sections you can tell that it's dubbed in. So those are the kind of situations you have to deal with for a lot of folklore films—if you're changing the subject, and then you've told some people that the film's going to be about them—*that* was a very difficult switch to make, but there was no way to make the film with the original idea we had.

The film team encountered several catastrophic moments and incidents over the course of shooting the film. Patterson remembered the technical problems and how they were overcome:

One of the problems was trying to film an anniversary concert, a black gospel event, community event—large scale for anything we had attempted—you know, four or five hundred people in a combination gymnasium/school auditorium. Lighting problems, miking problems, and we tried it, I think, about three different years. The first year the musicians were not on somehow. We had some very expensive equipment, thousands of dollars on that one night. And the musicians somehow just weren't on that night. You know, it was one of those freak things. Another time, one member of the group . . . had been murdered shortly before. . . . And it was under unfortunate circumstances and the community was upset about it, and the musicians were deeply moved, and this man's memory was in the presence of everybody's mind. But instead of destroying the performance, they were kind of making it a tribute to him and they rose through this. That's not mentioned in the film, but it was a fact that night. The performances were really on. . . .

In the crucial moment, in the best performance that we've got, "Going Up to Meet Him in the Air," the one that closes that scene, Tom Rankin's camera jammed. . . . And Tom Davenport was alerted to that, and did most of that thing as a . . . single take. And I think that showed Tom's great strength—his intuitive sense of where the motion of this thing's going to go. And so he's trying, he's catching John Landis as he lays the mike down, and he's trying to catch the band, the backup. And then suddenly in the middle of this piece, the niece gets up and takes the mike. There was just no warning—she didn't know John Landis laid the mike down as he often did; it was part of his way of doing the song. . . . He lays down the microphone and just goes away shaking his head, he's overcome, he can't sing anymore. She took the microphone and started singing, and then he joyfully came back over and put his arm around her and they start doing the rest of this spontaneously. . . . And then a man on the stage saw and motioned to her backup group, which is named Echoes of Heaven—there's a link there that's intentional, I'm sure. And . . . so the girls came up on the stage and took the microphones, and John Landis and his niece stepped back and just kept with that beat, with the hands, but let the women in her group take the microphones and bend the song in their own direction. And they have a different refrain, set of lines, a different response pattern. So it was a wonderful moment, and Tom got it all somehow.

The frozen second camera almost caused the scene to be lost. But Tom Davenport continued shooting with his handheld camera and did get the climactic scene. Everyone was relieved. "And when we saw the footage, we realized that it was some of the most powerful we had," Patterson said.

I asked Patterson about the thrust of the film: "It seems to me that the film is really about many things—about family and family lore, and narratives about what it was like being black during a certain time period—so there's a whole film of the Landis family and a political statement as well. And then there's the reunion. You could just take the reunion as one whole topic. And, of course, the significance of gospel music in people's lives."

Dan responded, "Where it started was on the Golden Echoes. There again it was going to be a limited film on the Golden Echoes. We said, `The last films we've done are about lore, like the tall tale, that's not really an alive tradition any longer.'"

The film team shifted its attention to "something that was really vital and ongoing and a rich tradition. And gospel music is as rich a tradition as we have in the whole area." After looking at a number of groups and consulting with colleagues who studied black traditional music, they focused on a group that folklorist George Holt had written about in a term paper for Dan Patterson years before when Holt was an undergraduate. Eventually, the film team decided to document the Golden Echoes—their music, their performances, their aesthetic, and their lives. But two different groups formed the Golden Echoes: the Landis group and a group from another town. Once the two groups had merged, they changed their name to the Golden Echoes and began describing themselves not from either of the towns but from the town halfway in between. Patterson observed,

> And this was beginning to get a very sizable cast of characters. And then the murder took place, and the murdered man was the most articulate person of the group. . . . And Mr. Landis was very verbal. And so it looked like it would be harder to do the whole group, and then as I began to talk with the Landises, Mrs. Landis emerged as a dominant figure in it. Everything went back to Mamma. "Mamma taught us this music." "Mamma really inspired us to do these things." She was very musical, and she mentioned this singing stream that she felt came from her father, down through her and to them and now their grandchildren, and she began to emerge as the central figure—for which there was a parallel in the other family, the guitarist in the other family, but we couldn't interview them as well. And there are too many characters. So we said, "Well, look, this is a representative thing. It looks like in several of these families, it's a family heritage, and so if we take one of these families it can stand for the whole." We talked to other people who had interviewed in the neighborhood for other purposes. Sociologists who'd worked there, and there was another family that had gotten land at the same time the Landises did in the same way, and they said that the key thing in this was the parents' determination. And they went to a family reunion that was held in a Holiday Inn and all of the family came back and it was essentially a tribute to their mother and father. . . . Here was something that had happened in the same neighborhood [as that of the Landis family]. . . . And then we began to see the patterns in the family reunion weekend, when there's a family reunion at the home house, and all the immediate family, and then it broadens to the church with five families of their reunion which Mrs. Landis helped to establish, and then the Golden Echoes concert for the wider community of many people like these people.

Thus, the film captures music that moves from a small family community into a much larger one. Patterson and Davenport believed the Landis family's experience was typical and one to which people in the area would relate and which folklorists could study as a model in terms of gospel singing families and family reunions.

Nonetheless, cutting out the other family presented an ethical problem. The Golden Echoes included members of that family. Patterson was hesitant about making such a change. He described his dismay:

> Since we had gone to the group originally as wanting to do a film about the Golden Echoes, this gave us a moral crisis and gave Mr. Landis, I think, in particular, a diplomacy crisis. . . . We recognized that other members of the group that were not in the Landis family might feel offended. Before we made that change, we got representatives from the Landis family and showed them the footage and said, "This is what we've got, and here are

the problems. This man is dead now. We cannot go any further in that direction." He was the person who could talk best, and they understood that. They're performers themselves. They know that certain people can present and other people have to play the guitar. And so they saw it . . . the situation and the problem, and agreed themselves that this change seemed advisable. They knew it was going to be a difficult one, and they had sessions. . . . Other members of the group did have a hard time accepting this change. Not all of them, but certain ones probably. And I think that in making the shift, I was the one who dragged the feet the longest. Tom felt early that it was aesthetically going to be necessary to simplify, and Mrs. Landis was the key figure, and he was wanting to go on. I was saying, "Oh, but we can't do this, we can't do this. They expect this thing to happen." So it took me the longest to become convinced that was a change that we had to make because I felt anxiety for the feelings of other people. I felt anxiety for the difficult situation Mr. Landis and the other Landis brothers might find themselves in. I think it was the right way to make the film. Certainly for the black community as a whole it was the right way to go. I still have qualms about it for the members in the Echoes who were not in the Landis family. I think I'll never probably get to feel wholly right about it. It's just one of the burdens that I am just going to have to have on my conscience—that somehow it would have been better if we had known not to set it up in quite as fixed an expectation when we started.

Despite all the planning, a film is designed piece by piece.[2] Ethical decisions will propel the content and structure of film to create waves of decisions that filmmakers cannot foresee.

Ferrero also found herself confronted with an ethical question, though different in nature. When offered some footage of katchina ceremonies, she declined. Her knowledge of the sacredness and secrecy of the rituals made her sensitive to the explosiveness of the material:

It's footage most filmmakers would die for. But, for me, I knew that it was more important that I be able to return to the community and maintain relationships with the people I was working with. . . . You know, it's years later, and there are other Pueblo communities. There's something in the film; I think it's because people chose to give me material that would endure. That is not to say that the film isn't in a particular time and place. It is. But what people talk about holds.

When Ferrero was filming *Hopi*, the major issue in the area was a struggle between the Hopi and the Navaho at Big Mountain, Arizona. She resisted the temptation to make a film about it, because a film on political issues connected to specific events quickly becomes dated. She preferred producing a film about Hopi that would have impact long after it was shot.

The range of people that use it is very wide: it's used in the schools; it's used in the public health sector; it's used by the government office. So it's used in both traditional and progressive and in-between communities. . . . And I always wanted the film to be something that bridged those communities, because when filmmakers go to Hopi, they tend to go to what's considered the traditional and, for those filmmakers, the only "true" community. And often those filmmakers are representing some very timely political controversy and they're advocacy filmmakers. They're often accepted into the community because they will provide a public forum for an issue. And I was very clear that I wanted to do something that cut across what I came to see as one level of division within a community, but something that individuals in their lives might go through all phases—they might be traditional at one point, progressive at another, and then traditional again. And families often had all those people from all those various factions in their families. So, at Hopi, people had to negotiate those boundaries within their own families and villages and communities, and something tied them together that transcended those differences. And I wanted the film to be about that aspect of the culture that essentially united them.

Folkloric films are often shown in the communities where they were shot. For example, Ferris negotiates and meets ethical standards by showing the raw footage first and giving the community a final print: "We try to express, as much as possible, our concern and desire to have a film be part of the community's life." For Ferrero, the value of the film to the community is paramount. Although Preloran screens his films for the community, he often needs a generator to show the films in the outlying communities where they were made. His films also serve the community in an uncommon way. He has stated that his films are made for those being filmed; the films give a voice to those who are not heard otherwise and thus may promote change by making others recognize that we are all very similar, although our traditions may differ. Preloran discussed his philosophy of filmmaking: "Because films are a very strong means of mass communication, I should use them for something purposeful. . . . I think that philosophically I've come to the conclusion that I would like to make films for the people, for them, because in that way I could help a community that has never had any access to mass communication, much less film, which is perhaps the most sophisticated medium of communication we have. . . . If the films could be an instrument of change, to better the people that I film would be the best use for film I could find" (1976). By presenting communities that have been little recognized, including local groups whose artistic endeavors have gone unnoticed, filmmakers are able to give the community a sense of pride and to foreground the value of their traditional practices.

Films that satisfy community or individual needs at the same time that they fulfill the filmmaker's purposes demonstrate the filmmaker's respect for the people in the film. It may be assumed that such filmmakers are not confronted by claims that they were unethical in the handling of the film data.

Peiser, for example, considers herself an insider on Beale Street. She commented that she shows the "rushes" (unedited film) to the community.

> We've always worked with the community. When we did *All Day and All Night*, we brought in people throughout the making of the film—the musicians who were in it. . . . You get a lot of feedback just by being there and knowing it's not something that you have to do as a film editor coming in. I mean, we're there. . . . I think that the more you work with a community, or with people, the more you know what that relationship is. . . . The Beale Street stuff, I'm intimately related. I mean, I know these men and women. Rufus Thomas stops by the Center all the time. It's like his home. B. B. King is there. It's a relationship.

Wagner remarked that he came to each folk community from the opposite position, as an outsider, but nonetheless was responsive to the people being portrayed on film. He accounted for the informants' ideas as he shot the film, rather than relying on feedback as he edited:

> Clearly we are filmmakers from outside, with our own ideas about the subject matter and what's interesting, and making the film about that community, not with that community. Now having said that, I think we probably exercise a lot more sensitivity and we're more forthcoming in terms of trying to get the input of people we're working with in terms of what they thought, but that's more in the nature of the way a folklorist always works. . . . It's just sort of a given. There's a deference paid by the researcher or the fieldworker toward the people in the community, occupation, whatever it is. . . . We were always interested in what they had to say, but we shot the film and went back and edited, and in none of those cases did the subjects of the film come into the editing room and even see it before it was finished.

Wagner's method is characteristic of most filmmakers; Jean Rouch is exceptional for asking for feedback before the film is in final print and then making changes (although video tends to encourage videographers to draw feedback because of its instant feedback capability). For all folklore fieldwork, community input is considered as the project is being directed, and for outsiders such input is essential.

Zulay Saravino was both an outsider and an insider, shifting from one role to the other as she became involved in making the film about herself. The Prelorans discovered that making *Zulay* gave Saravino a powerful self-image as she traveled in Los Angeles and abroad. Because she always wore her Otavaleño clothing, she looked, Mabel says, "like a princess" wherever she went. In her own society she was considered a deviant. "She's somebody who didn't follow the rules, and that is very risky in a traditional society." Jorge explained that leaving society as a young unmarried and unaccompanied woman set a bad example. Yet, Zulay's parents gave her their blessings as she departed.

Her success enabled her to send money to her family in Ecuador. Mabel pointed out that her parents and family "loved that because she was really the main supporter, the main income producer in that moment." Eventually, the film brought her reacceptance by her village.

Les Blank found that his subjects also were empowered by film:

> It reinforces their positive feelings toward their community and their traditions. . . . The non-Cajun French didn't like *Spend It All* at all. They got me disinvited from going to France to represent the French-American culture over there at one of their big expositions. But Marc Savoy was delighted with the film. In his music store, the day after it was broadcast on local TV, all the young Cajun boys were coming in and speaking Cajun French, and it was the first time he'd ever seen them speaking it, and buying Cajun instruments and Cajun records, and starting up Cajun bands. By seeing their culture on TV, it made them feel like it must be okay to be a Cajun. . . . And the Mexican-Americans, a similar thing happened. I had some static [about *Chulas Fronteras*] from the middle-class Americans who were trying to ignore their roots. But the people who were in it were very proud to be in it.

The notion of a culture, or those filmed as "Other," set apart and thus denigrated by its difference from the filmmaker's culture, is rarely an issue in folklore film, which not only confirms but reifies tradition and identity.

In the negotiation process, confrontation is linked to compromise. In shifting from the folklorist looking *at* someone else to the folklorist making a film *with* someone else, lengthy debates are to be expected. Once the Prelorans comprehended that *Zulay* was really about transculturation, Mabel and Zulay discussed what was on the screen while Jorge shot them talking. Jorge feared that the interview with Mabel would reenact all the stereotypes of ethnographic research: "Immediately there was this sense of, 'gosh, an anthropologist with a subject'—it's so passé. So what about a conversation between two people who are in the ongoing state of emigrating? And the relationship was of *equals,* not somebody asking questions, but rather a conversation about what happened. And right away, that struck a chord. That was wonderful." Mabel's observations about Zulay's culture and the similarities of their experiences as émigrés were often countered by Zulay. Mabel said, "I don't know if it is noticeable in the film, but I like that Zulay doesn't say yes to my comments. She is always questioning me, and that I think is very important." Jorge continued, "So they would argue these things and Mabel would say, 'Well, but, you know, in my opinion,' but Zulay would say, 'Well, in our place, it's different.' So that kind of, not confrontation, but of disagreement." Mabel noted, "We knew what we were going to say." Jorge continued, "Because they were clearly thought out and they were concepts that had to be boiled down, they couldn't be talked about at length. They had to be very concise." Mabel recalled that

Zulay made her own decisions about what to include in the film: "Sometimes she says, 'Oh, I would like to say so and so, but I won't say it in the film.' And I say, 'Well, it's okay,' because it was her choice. That means that it was a kind of control of decision, no?"

Zulay was concerned with the unseen audience. Jorge pointed out that she was "very careful about talking about other people and maybe hurting feelings and things like that. It was very conscious and, in fact, she was very conscious of how this would be seen in her community. So it was very carefully plotted out; it's a thought-out film, it's not just off the cuff." Although the Prelorans were working outside Argentina, they were—like Zulay—caught between worlds. Zulay related to the culture she was now making a film about, with Los Angeles as the foreign culture, and the Prelorans, now somewhat at home in Los Angeles, saw Zulay's culture as distinct from their own.

In contrast, most folklore filmmakers cling to their own circles, inspired by what is familiar. Pat Ferrero, for example, was from the Southwest and she returned to New Mexico often. Her initial contacts for the Hopi film developed out of her ties in Hopi country. *Hopi* was in production for four years with a dozen production trips and five major shoots.

> I had been going back to that community for almost a decade. . . . Actually it didn't start out as a film. It started out as going back and just reconnecting with people there, and it began when a group of women asked me to do a film on piki [a thin blue bread made on a hot stone]. I actually brought the quilt film and showed it to them. And they really loved it, and said, "You know, piki's unique to us." Essentially I was invited to do a film on that process, which again was women's work. And I shot the film and they really liked it, and they said, "But it's not the whole story. You have to go into the field." And I said, "Well, take me out into the field." And so the film evolved over a period of time out of collaboration with a variety of extended families who were willing to work with me. And I brought the footage back, showed it, screened it, so people really had a sense of participating in the film as it unfolded.

When I said, "So, they saw pieces of it, and then they could make suggestions," Ferrero responded, "Right, *they* made decisions about whether they wanted to be in the film, because there is still a tremendous tension around bringing a camera to Hopi."[3] Ferrero's fieldwork methodology ensured a strong relationship. Some films are the result of years of feedback.

This feedback occurs, in a sense, "behind the screen." The audience rarely sees the interaction and negotiation process that leads to a film. For *A Singing Stream*, Davenport and Patterson sought input from the Landis brothers and were conscientious about sharing the editing process with them. To a query about how much say the people in the film had, Patterson replied,

> We tried to be really careful that way. Even the very first footage, Tom [came] down, got a room at the University of North Carolina and invited

Mr. Landis and anybody he wanted to bring with him to come on over and "just show you what we've got." So they could see some evidence of the work in progress from the very beginning. They'd look at it and we'd talk about what they'd think the best things were, and what we thought the best things were. Then as Tom later began to edit it together, we'd show sections so they'd get a sense of how things worked. And I think as a matter of fact that they understood better than most people would because they put [song] pieces together. . . . I think the aesthetics of filming were probably more natural to them at the grasp than they would be to many a person. And so I think they could see the issue and the problem. I think Mr. Landis's driving impulse was to get the best film out of this that they could. And I think he trusted Tom to be wanting to do that. So if Tom had a feeling it was going to work better this way—Tom knowing all about film that he did—Mr. Landis said, "Let's trust his judgment and go that way."

In this interactive setting, both the filmmaker and the subjects of the film worked to create a vision that characterized the documented events as each saw them.

Regardless of the reasons one creates a film—to use for personal research, to show folkloric processes for classroom discussion, or to test certain hypotheses about folkloric behavior—informants' wishes and suggestions must be respected. Those filmed recognize that they speak to a greater audience than the film crew and are portraying themselves as they wish to be seen.[4] If filmmakers believe that the informant's desires to delete (or include) certain materials conflict with the demands of the film and that the data must be deleted (or included) despite objections, they may reach a moral impasse. Although a filmed comment could be added at the end as the informant's rejoinder, the filmmaker's own ethical standards will most likely cause acquiescence to the informant's objections. Suggestions of the informants that should be determining factors for reediting consist of inaccuracies, omissions, or scenes that might cause embarrassment for the informant. These details should be thoroughly discussed in advance with those to be filmed so that informants are aware of their rights. The basic rule of thumb is never to produce a film that one fears to show to those appearing in the film. Feedback becomes a special consideration with video, since the tape can be played back immediately and those who were taped can comment on the footage. A project that pleases both the filmmaker and the filmed results from a blend of feedback, ethics, and honesty.

## Funding—For Love or Money or Both

Filmmaking is an expensive endeavor that usually requires either academic or grant support. Funding may determine the film's direction if the filmmaker is obligated to satisfy the funding agencies or donors. Sometimes the views of those underwriting the film conflict with the original vision of the film and the views of those appearing in it.

Few filmmakers are able to finance their own films, although they periodically add out-of-pocket monies in the completion stages. Folkloric filmmakers have approached the problems of financing their work in several ways, although many are now bypassing film and shooting in video to save on expenses as well as to increase portability. Cohen and Blank are both independent filmmakers who have had some grant assistance but who have also partially funded their own films. Cohen commented, "Initially my film projects were financed by myself, largely from the meager proceeds from New Lost City Ramblers' concerts. Recently I have received grants, although I have had to add my own funds to finish these films. I have never had university or academic support" (1975). Blank's films, the cost of which varied widely depending on the subject matter and approach, were each financed by different means. His early films serve as an example of how he gained funds:

> On *The Blues Accordin' to Lightnin' Hopkins* I ran into someone who was interested in filmmaking, and he borrowed $5,000 to get it started. I ran up debts for the rest—I worked as a freelance cameraman and editor to pay off the rest, which took a period of several years. And I got most of the money back by distribution through European television sales and selling the prints of the film to libraries and schools. *The Sun's Gonna Shine* was made from the outtakes of *The Blues Accordin' to Lightnin' Hopkins* and the same thing applies to that. *Spend It All* I financed on $4,000 that I'd saved from working as an industrial filmmaker—enough to buy a used camera. I paid rental for a tape recorder and I quickly spent all that money and ran up a lab bill which took about three years to pay off. And *A Well-Spent Life* on Mance Lipscomb was shot on the same trip as *Spend It All*, and it was shot in just one week because it was more or less an afterthought. I had an industrial job lined up starting a week after I had finished shooting the Cajun film, and John Lomax Jr. . . . was interested in my documenting Mance. He paid the lab costs for the film. So I went and shot that—just as much as I could get within the week I had, and I was doing it just for a documentary record. But as it turns out, I was able to edit it into a complete film. *Dry Wood* and *Hot Pepper* were financed . . . by working in industrial films. And Chris Strachwitz of Arhoolie Records had loaned me $1,500 on that one, too. For *Dry Wood* and *Hot Pepper* I received a $15,000 grant from the National Endowment for the Arts and public media. And I borrowed $5,000 from John Lomax Jr. and Chris Strachwitz. And the actual costs are something I'm not too sure of, but roughly I'd say that *The Blues* was around $10,000; *Sun's Gonna Shine*, probably $2,000; *Spend It All*, probably close to $10,000; *Well-Spent Life* was around about $8,000 to $9,000. *Dry Wood* and *Hot Pepper* probably cost $23,000. [1975]

Blank's growing reputation and illustrious career eventually created new sources of backing for his films. Likewise, his grant approvals increased.

6.2 Tom Davenport leading a seminar on filmmaking at the
South Carolina Media Arts Center

Davenport has created a series of films, based on the Grimm tales, which
are particularly popular with those who purchase films for their libraries or
public schools. Because children prefer a visual medium, these films expose
them to tales that are rarely read to them; rather, they learn through print and
media, often via Disney films. Folklorists have criticized Disney for his bas-
tardization of traditional tales. Davenport, on the other hand, is sensitively
adapting traditional tales, using regional actors. Although "updated" in terms
of setting, the tales have that same universal underpinning which has always

6.3 *Hansel and Gretel* from Tom Davenport's Brothers Grimm film series

made the Grimm tales so memorable. For example, *Bearskin* (1983), set in the South following the Civil War, is about endurance and spiritual transformation; *Rapunzel, Rapunzel* (1978) maintains its theme of the struggle for independence and evokes the romance of the Victorian era; *Hansel and Gretel* (1975) looks at loyalty and how to deal with fear against the background of southern Appalachia during the Depression. Accompanied by bibliographic references and comments from Davenport as the publisher, *From the Brothers Grimm* is a study guide series that accompanies the films. Funded by the Corporation for Public Broadcasting, the Arthur Vining Davis Foundations, and the Virginia Commission on the Arts, the Grimm films received no funding from the National Endowment for the Arts, although that foundation has supported other Davenport films, which are aimed at adult audiences and thus are seen as more important. Because of their mass appeal and distribution, the Brothers Grimm films, in a sense, underwrite Davenport's other productions, which attract a smaller audience.

Preloran has also had to seek various means of support for his work, but nevertheless he has managed to complete seventy-seven films. He laughed when I asked in 1976 how he financed his projects.

> That's a good one. Well, I'll tell you. I look back on my *curriculum vitae* and I can't believe that I made so many films. It really doesn't seem right. . . . Some films were done with $3,000, $5,000. I really don't know because I sometimes buy film that has been dated, so it brings it down 50 percent. I make my workprint on positive black-and-white film that's pushed into reversal, and in doing so, the contrast is so big that many times you can't tell in the reds, or in the skin, what the man is doing on his face. You can't see expressions. Many times I've even hitchhiked to where I was going because I didn't have any money. I film very, very economically because I shoot sometimes 2 to 1, or 2.5 to 1, or 3 to 1, but more than that, never. In other words, I know exactly what I am shooting and how I am going to use it—which by the way cannot be done with sync-sound. Sync-sound—you shoot much more because you have to. And also you have to transfer all that quarter-inch tape to 16mm magnetic, which means that your budget goes way up. So I don't have those problems. And I am generally my own sound man, so I don't use up much sound either. I record the sounds I need and go in, generally, with one assistant who is also a photographer, and he does sound, too. I put the sound in and I mix it. . . . So the budget is really very, very low, and my time is worth nothing. . . . Because of economic conditions in Argentina—well, I was stopped many times. Films have been in the can one or two years before I could put the sound to them or mix and much less make a print. But I've been able to do it because I had grants. I had two Guggenheim Fellowships and a $5,000 grant from a folklore society. . . . And then you find ways, you know. You find ways of cutting corners. The thing is that I've never worked in anything but film. . . . I've been lucky in that sense. I've never had to work at something else to be able to earn a living to be able to make films.

Although Preloran has been able to cut corners because of his skill as a filmmaker and his use of sound-over rather than sync-sound, costs can also be cut if the filmmaker does most of the technical work, as Preloran notes. For my film *Tales of the Supernatural,* I did the sound transfer, sound mix, and all editing and negative cutting. Even though the film was shot in sync, the shooting ratio was 4 to 1. By keeping the ratio low and doing the technical work myself, the film was produced for just under $2,000, a very low figure even in 1970. The equipment was provided by the UCLA Ethnographic Film Program. I produced *Kathleen Ware, Quiltmaker* for $30,000 in 1979 and was funded, in part, with a National Endowment for the Arts grant.

Most folkloric films are made with grants or in conjunction with local television stations. For example, the Center for Southern Folklore is supported by grants, both public and private, and Fleischhauer's films were made under the auspices of WWVU-TV in Morgantown, West Virginia.

The Folk Arts Division of the National Endowment of the Arts, the National Endowment for the Humanities, state arts commissions, and private agencies such as the Rockefeller Foundation have financed folkloric films. Individuals who construct film project proposals that prove both a knowledge of the complexities of filmmaking and the benefits to be derived from a film that will advance folklore scholarship and increase public awareness of folklore should be able to receive assistance from foundations. Generally, folklore filmmakers also have the advantage of academic support, and matching funds required by some granting agencies can be provided by university sponsorship.

Sometimes, however, filmmakers face problems in obtaining such grants. As a case in point, Ferrero discovered that her ideas were in conflict with prevailing ideas about history, which made procuring grant funds difficult. To create the script for *Hearts and Hands,* she had already raised the research money to pay research assistants to gather the diary material, the photographs, and the quilts. She recalled, "Raising the production money to make it was a big undertaking. And it took me a long time to write a proposal to the National Endowment for the Humanities that convinced them that I could do history using primary material. The hardest problem I had was convincing them that quilts could be a proper historical device for telling history, that material culture could function that way."

In contrast, the Folk Arts program of the National Endowment for the Arts supplied some of the funds for Ferrero's film *Hopi: Songs of the Fourth World.* The idea of metaphor and the aesthetics of *alltägsleben,* or everyday life, met the goals of that agency: "I was interested in looking at an aspect of the culture that was more subtle, and that bridged a particular interest I had—not only in women again, but in that boundary of the sacred and the secular, of art and daily life—and relooking at those boundaries. Those were questions I looked at on many levels. So I was able to get some funding from Folk Arts, because I was looking at foodways. I mean, they were willing to trust me broadly with looking at corn." But Ferrero actually had to refuse money from another agency to maintain her principles for making the Hopi film.

The pacing of the film matched that of Hopi life; Ferrero believed that, to correlate with Hopi culture, the timing in the film was critical. The Corporation for Public Broadcasting asked her to recut the film:

My horror story about that was when I was desperately looking for production money. I was recommended for a CPB grant, for a significant amount of money—$100,000. And they came out to look at the footage and said to me, "It's too slow." And essentially required me to either cut it faster or they would take the money away. And they took the money away. In other words, I refused to compromise on the pacing.

That was the lowest point in my career as a professional filmmaker, to turn down money. And, as a result, I never got back to Hopi for the last production shoot I wanted, and I cut the film on a shoestring, and I was in debt for years, but it was more important to me that the film have the pace that it had.

Most agencies are concerned with content, not pacing, so the request to change the film came as a great surprise to Ferrero. To be true to herself and the Hopi, Ferrero suffered a great setback because of the pacing issue. Different film topics suggest distinct pacing. For example, *Kathleen Ware, Quiltmaker* is slowly paced to match the rhythm of quiltmaking, whereas *Spirits in the Wood* has a rapid editing style to correspond with the quickness of the chainsaw.

## Distribution, or, Getting It Out There

Distribution is the part of funding that occurs after the film is completed. For some, the funds replace out-of-pocket costs, help start a new project, or provide basic income. Generally, when filmmakers get together, they spend 90 percent of their time talking about funding and distribution rather than critically analyzing film. Obtaining funds and getting the films out to audiences is a serious issue. For instance, Thigpen has a small company set up for distribution, but as an academic with a full-time job, he has no time to actively distribute the films. Pat Ferrero has advertised her films by attending conferences and screening her films there, sending out flyers to pertinent mailing lists, and having the films shown on PBS. As an independent filmmaker, Les Blank distributes his and others' films to support his production company. He sells a number of his films to video stores and to those who initially have rented one. On the back of each cassette, Blank prints a notice that he has other films, and a catalog is available. Blank also appears at some screenings:

> They sell it in theaters. Very often, I would be there in person and hand out catalogs, and I sell T-shirts and now videotapes. And some of these people who will buy a videotape realize they can watch it over and over, and it's something they like and they want more of it. . . . And they're shown on TV, and people . . . call up halfway through—on the Discovery Channel, the Learning Channel—they'll want to know what happened. And if it's not being reprogrammed, they'll get my address and contact me and then buy a tape over the phone and want to know what else I have, and I'll send them a catalog.

6.4 Les Blank eating crawfish and wearing an advertisement for one of his films on his T-shirt. Photo by Chris Simon

In addition to T-shirts advertising the film, Blank also produces postcards and other tie-in materials to entice purchasers.

Distributing film in video format is now common. Few media outlets (such as libraries, universities, and museums) will buy a 16mm film. Cohen and Davenport both lamented the loss that results from miniaturizing what was meant to be shown on a large screen. "The 16mm market, as far as purchase of prints or showing the prints, is very dead," Davenport said. "It's probably never going to come back. What will happen is that there will be video formats that are finer and finer and high definition, and you'll be able to project them just like film."

Blank's distribution methods highlight the many ways in which film becomes an experience, not only for the filmmaker who shoots, edits, and releases and distributes it, but for the audience as well:

> When I did the garlic film, I made my first T-shirt and I enjoyed seeing the design on the shirt and I enjoyed seeing people walking around in it. And from a practical point of view, it's good advertising for the films. And the title and the design have an element of expression, just like a film does or a song. And I like going beyond just presenting images on a screen with sound for people to watch and listen. I like giving them clothing to wear out of the theater and, on occasions, to give them food to eat when they're in the theater. So they get the film going in their stomachs and on their skin and in their brains and their ears and their eyes.

Although most films are not screened and presented with the panache of Les Blank, film transcends text to both record and become a holistic experience.

## Film as Text, Film as Experience

Like folklore, film is communicative. Similarly, it is not a text but an event. The process of filmmaking is an event, the content may cover an event, and the filmmaker's examination of his or her own behavior in that event causes reflexivity. Thus, scholars who have sought to analyze film as text by reducing it to language fail to recognize how different are the forms, conventions, and processes of language and film. If they looked at filmmaking as a behavior, they would note the obvious difference. For Sol Worth, lack of negation and of the dialogue that corresponds with language behaviors mark the differences. In "Pictures Can't Say Ain't," Worth remarks, "What is communicated by pictures . . . is the way picture makers structure their dialogue with the world" (1982:108).

Inherent in that structuring is a dimension that cannot be adequately described by, or as, language. In "Perceptual Ethics," Nico Bogaart discusses this breach: "Where the facts used to be translated into words, nowadays the visual element is increasingly regarded as indispensable and, in some cases, the only way. However succinctly words might evoke an image, language always loses out against what is visible" (1983:18). To analyze film as language is reductive. Words fall back upon language. Film, on the other hand, is the opening to a different perception, the filmmakers' communication with and visualization of humanity.

The idea of film as a text has created whole schools of thought on how to critically analyze film. Looking at film as a text allows semioticians to examine filmic elements for signification. But film may also be seen as a text in terms of representing a documented experience. Moreover, it may seem to serve as a substitute for it. Filmmakers and subjects may also treat films as texts, physical entities that they can cart about to replace what they might have said if no film existed. For example, Skip Armstrong pops the videotape about his sculpturing into the VCR and uses it at demo shows to explain his work. Indeed, as Thigpen noted, the screening of *Salamanders* replaced the actual event for a number of years, and the film became a "cult" film for some students at Penn State. Their responses led him to see how this documented occasion could be "read" in ways he had not anticipated. During the filming, the unforeseen occurred. "The transspecies people around became very concerned about what we were doing, if we were going to be promoting this. We said, 'No, we're documenting something that is actually going on, will go on whether or not we do it, will not go on to any greater extent because we do it.'" Ironically, after the film was made, it replaced the event. "For a number of years after that, the fraternity tended to show the film rather than to do the thing. Now that was an unexpected consequence for us." Thigpen's daughter "experienced" the ritual that her father had documented years before from the perspective of a child and then as a college student.

> My daughter, who's a sophomore at Penn State now, said that they're starting to do it again, and, of course, the film became sort of a cult object within the university among the fraternities. And everybody seems to know about it and that one of these rituals that they do was actually filmed once. It becomes sort of the romantic past. Because now, here it is ten years later, and ten years is a long time within the tradition of academe. And so, you know, it seems like only yesterday in some ways, but it's become a historical icon for people who were involved in that and, to a certain extent, eventually their children. I mean, my daughter was, you know, at the time about nine years old, and now she's there and I hear the reports coming back to her, so that was an interesting project, an interesting process that came up.

As he reflected on his experience, Thigpen began to analyze what *Salamanders* represented not only to him but to those who were the subjects and to those who were the audience.

My videotape *Passover, a Celebration* also became a reference point, in this case for me as filmmaker and for the family whom I documented. For a few years, it was shown before the Passover Seder, especially so that those who had not been there during the taping could see it. Over the years, those who had participated would make remarks about the tape in the midst of the current year's seder. "That's not the way we did it in the tape," they would argue. The videotape also allowed participants to analyze their own behavior on another level. For example, the women noticed that only men washed their hands before certain prayers. This practice was traditional in Conservative and Orthodox Jewish homes and was an established ritual for this family. Nevertheless, the tape highlighted this gender split, and the women insisted that all at the table who wished to do so should be offered the opportunity to wash their hands. This change has now become integrated into the Seder.

Films or videotapes also freeze a moment in time and may serve as a point of reference for narratives. "Remember what happened at the Seder when Mikey was only three years old?" or "That was the year when the family . . ." might be such openers. In this manner, the tape acts precisely like a text, a fixed entity that changes only in the minds of the viewers. Thus, using film as a means of not reducing an event to a verbal representation of that event on paper becomes, instead, a "text" that preserves the event on multiple levels.

Because of these multiple levels, film or videotape is a different way of understanding and conceptualizing the world. Rather than a text, it is an experience, part of which is created by the very act of participating in the event, with all its possible anxieties and transformations, and part of which occurs with sharing the viewing of the film. Both of these acts create a small world for the participants—a world that is often a model of a larger world (for example, one individual Passover Seder to represent a concurrent worldwide celebration; or a wedding video to mark a ritual that is mirrored throughout the world; and the viewing of the film as yet another event reproduced by successive audiences). "Experience" may refer to the experience of the individual, in the empirical sense, or it may refer to one experience—a remembered event that has significance.[5] Filmmakers document both behaviors; folklore filmmakers generally study those behaviors which are expressive and have been shared. Thus, the idea of documenting (and becoming part of) an event experience motivates the folklorist.

The act of shooting and constructing a film is also an experience and one that often becomes a driving creative passion. The *process* is more vital than the celluloid (or video-recorded) product or "text." Filmmakers tend to be consumed by the means rather than the ends (much like folk artists). Jorge Preloran stated, "The thing about me is I like the process, I don't care about the film. I think the process is important. And the making of the film is what really is exciting."

Cohen spoke to me about how film transcends text in its *figurative* meaning. "A text is a text. It talks about what it can talk about, and to write a good sentence is sometimes as hard as to make a good scene and edit a good scene or film one. So it's the attitude of who's reporting and from what viewpoint." Anthropologist Billie Jean Isabel gave Cohen a copy of a book in which she had discussed his work. She explained how Cohen's films conveyed all the things that scholars "try inadequately to do in their texts," Cohen said. "I'm dealing with the same questions that they are, but through my own terms. So that the 'ist' that I end up being, the way I settle it on myself, is I'm an artist— back to my very beginning." Those who work with words and those who work with film are all artists, experiencing the creative process, albeit in a dissimilar way. By encountering the world visually, the filmmaker creates an art form that is complementary to a text, but surpasses it by unveiling levels of experience for which words are insufficient.

Jorge Preloran believes that film as experience is paramount, but for him, the vital issue is the experience lived by the persons in his films. Addressing students in a film and folklore class, he explained:

> Anything that comes from experience is much stronger than what comes through the brain. So that if you make films about experiences, about people, dealing with society with problems and things, and you make a very convincing emic approach—you know what emic is, from the inside?—that's indelible. In Eugene, about ten years ago, I showed a film here, *Imaginero.* Somebody came up to me and said, "I saw that film twelve years ago, and I remembered it to this day." Can you imagine? I mean, that's astounding. Think of all the films you've seen and how many stand out in your mind as something that suddenly clicked. I'll tell you, somebody who had a divorce will remember *Kramer vs. Kramer* [1987] vividly. And anything that had something to do with your own experience clicks. Suddenly it becomes a major thing that you'll remember; it may even change your life. Art is an extraordinary thing. If you can convince us through the soul, it is a great and powerful tool.

The experiences of the filmmaker, those appearing in the film, and those in the audience unite to make film a primary art form.

## Film: The Vehicle for Event and Performance

Once a film is made, it acquires a life of its own. The filmmaker may share that life, accompanying the film and offering interpretations for some screenings. But usually the film presents itself to viewers for analysis. Viewers can examine its structure to determine the fieldwork approach (whether a folklorist appears in the film or not). Moreover, the filmmaker's presuppositions and theoretical assumptions become evident when viewers compare the content focus and filmmaking techniques. Romanticism, textual preoccupations, context concerns, and event orientations, for example, can be perceived by noting how narration, sync-sound, and sound-over are used, in addition to the format the filmmaker uses to present the visuals, such as animation, vignette, montage, cinéma vérité, or observational film.

Folklorists constantly gather data by observing the interactions of those with whom they come in contact or by observing their own behavior. Because all persons narrate, sing, or play games, we need not search for "other" people in order to conduct fieldwork. We can engage in research within our own environments and can illustrate folkloric processes by analyzing our own actions and reactions when such processes as narrating and singing occur. Yet, because studying one's own behavior is difficult, film allows viewers to see the events of others more completely than those in which they themselves are directly involved. In addition, because not everyone is engaged in similar events, film exposes viewers to those events or persons whose behavior they might not be able to observe directly.[6]

By documenting, analyzing, and presenting the events and interactions of people in motion, the folkloric film or videotape opens up new realms. Most significantly, and simultaneously, film displays the similarities of our common experiences, the ways in which tradition is shaped, the ways we are constantly transforming, and the ways we wish to present and view ourselves.

The pieces of the filmic puzzle shift with every new film project. The primary concerns of one project become minor for another. But as the puzzle coheres anew each time, each film imparts new meanings, new messages, new knowledge, and new experiences for the filmmaker, the subjects, and the viewers; each film creates a fresh picture. All of the filmmakers quoted here saw each project as a new chance to communicate, through folklore, the essentials of what it is to be human. These filmmakers are almost heroic in their efforts to create films. Working on shoestring budgets, they tend to conduct fieldwork alone, seeking the beauty of life. Most seem somewhat alienated by, or dissatisfied with, the contemporary world. They either reject it or try to understand it, using tradition as their guide. Motivated by an artistic drive, they have a fascination for documenting others. The people they document are also artists whose work offers the filmmakers a way to see themselves. A sense of loss, of a world rapidly changing, triggers a driving desire to film and sometimes to videotape, not to preserve the past but to understand the present.

# 7

# Visions of Ourselves

*If your life was on video tape*
*Wouldn't everything be all right?*
*When your head hurts the morning after,*
*You could roll it back to late last night.*
*You could replay all the good parts*
*And cut out what you don't like.*
*Oh, wouldn't you be in good shape*
*If your life was on video tape.*

*If everybody had ESP*
*Everything would be ok,*
*We could see trouble coming*
*And we could step out of the way.*
*When that grim reaper comes to call*
*Then we could arrange to be out of town,*
*It would be the great escape*
*And you could put it on video tape.*
*—Steve Goodman, "Video Tape"*

These words written by Steve Goodman (before the video boom) express the desire to control events in our lives by controlling images on videotape. Goodman laments that he can't predict the future, but in terms of today's video user, he did. Today the videotape is becoming as commonplace in fieldwork as the tape recorder. The focus on events and reflexively oriented fieldwork naturally leads from film to video. As more of us make home videos, we become accustomed to the added capabilities of instant feedback. These experiences pose new research questions about ourselves and others, and video data are exponentially affecting our field.

In today's world, life does seem to be on videotape. Monitors reflect faces as shoppers walk along department store aisles. Videotaping is a common sight at children's soccer and baseball games and at weddings, bar mitzvahs, and birthday parties. The prevalence of video in our lives has steadily expanded. We can document our own lives as we perceive them, and we can record our vision of events. At the heart of the video explosion is the desire not only to record oneself and one's family but to present that view of the self back to the self after documentation.

Camcorders have blurred the line between the professionals and amateurs. Television networks may air "home" video (which does not have enough lines of resolution for broadcast according to FCC regulations) when their own coverage is lacking and they consider the amateur footage newsworthy. To maintain their technological mystique, the networks report that such excerpts were shot by amateurs—hence the lack of "quality" and the studio's inability to edit the tape into polished form, since amateurs don't shoot for the same style of editing (establishing shot, long shot, medium shot, close-up) used by the stations. Still, more and more of this footage *is* broadcast, and viewers are beginning to see how news shows, those they thought were "objective," have manipulated them. Likewise, their own shooting experiences have taught them enough about the process to question what content the networks select and why, and how that content is technically presented.[1] The ideological implications of the power, finances, and control of the networks over the reporting of events are clear, and the folk take up cameras and document their own news in their own way. When the Berlin Wall fell and Europe once more shifted its ephemeral borders, amateur videographers captured the "unofficial" news and smuggled their tapes to the West as testimonies of injustice. A good part of that news is within the purview of folklorists.

## Mass Media, Folklore, and Popular Culture

Television causes some videographers to adjust their visions to the specifications of mass media. For the scholars of the Frankfurt school of critical theory, mass culture serves the interests of capitalism by underscoring the status quo. The Frankfurt school values traditional culture, or folklore, but believes that it is being undermined and subsumed by mass culture.[2] Mass culture had become so widespread that it could not offer "revolutionary potential," that is, Marxist potential. Popular art was created by the people; mass art was created "from the top" by the institutions of capitalism to maintain power and gain profit. The notion of mass art created "from above" also became the manifesto of popular culture critics such as Dwight Macdonald, who saw the "tepid ooze" of what he called "mass cult" (since it was not really *culture*) creeping everywhere and, like raspberry jam, spreading high culture out too thin to satisfy anyone (1962:54).

In contrast, the Birmingham school of scholars looked at audiences to see if they were brainwashed into accepting what was thrown at them. They showed how complex audience response is. Tania Modleski explains how one of the leading members of the Birmingham school viewed responses to a filmic "text":

According to [Stuart] Hall, the dominant reading of a mass cultural text accepts the text's messages at face value; the negotiated response might dispute a particular claim while accepting the overall system; and an oppositional response rejects the capitalist system in the interests of the subordinate class. The way a particular message is received, then, obviously depends not only on the text or the medium in question, but on the audience's political beliefs and general social experience. It follows from such a premise that critics should study this social experience rather than examine texts in isolation from the people who consume them. [1986: xi]

Analogous to the way in which folklorists analyze the backgrounds, beliefs, and responses of their subjects, Hall suggests studying the audience's responses in relation to its experience, which must be contextualized socially and historically.[3] Influenced by Gramsci, his work marks a shift in ways of thinking about the Marxist concept of ideology. Hall's request that critics not study texts [films] in isolation parallels folklorists' pleas with regard to folklore texts. In this respect, folklorists share much in common with cultural studies, especially with the Birmingham school.

Another meaning of popular culture, according to Raymond Williams, "takes up that whole range which never got recognized as culture at all within an old dispensation: that of a very active world of everyday conversation and exchange. Jokes, idioms, characteristic forms not just of everyday dress but occasional dress, people consciously having a party, making a do, marking an occasion" (Heath and Skirrow 1986:5). Television uses these forms of folklore, says Williams. Although he does not label them as folklore, the forms of which he speaks obviously are folklore, and his use of the term *popular culture* to describe these acts harkens back to such terms as *popular antiquities* and *popular ballad*—that which people held to be traditional and which was popular in the broad sense of being generated and received by many.

Williams believes that television and "this active world," or folklore, of which he speaks have been depreciated:

I think this area has been very seriously undervalued, and it isn't only that it is undervalued in itself. We're not yet clear about the relation of those things to certain widely successful television forms. There is a sense in which everyday gossip passes straight into a certain kind of serial. And there's an obvious relation between the whole joke world and certain kinds of comedy, and the question then would be whether such television forms are articulating those areas, or whether they're simply latching onto them and in fact displacing, manipulating, redirecting them. But "popular" means all those things, I think. [Heath and Skirrow 1986:5]

Thus, folklore is intertwined with mass culture; television manipulates folklore and reproduces it (cf. Benjamin 1968), but it does not displace it (although, as both Blank and Wagner have pointed out, it does have an effect). For mass culture to have appeal, it turns to folklore; producers of mass culture know traditional materials will resonate with audiences. Drawing on the plotlines of traditional narratives, using urban legends to create episodes, incorporating jokes, and using folksongs, television grabs the audience's attention by speaking to an inner plane of deeply felt knowledge and familiarity that is recognized, in some cases on an unconscious level.

What happens when art is created from the "bottom up"? Video, as art, explores that possibility. For scholars of folklore whose studies cut across social and economic class lines, this question is moot or insignificant. Like folk art, folklore video is created by the individual working within what has become an evolving "tradition." Unlike television producers who merely draw on folklore to create their worlds, folklore videographers document folklore directly.

## Folklore Films and Documentary Modes

Folklore films and videos differ from the documentary as defined by film critic and historian Paul Rotha (1963) and subsequent film scholars who insist that documentary provide social analysis that will lead to social change. Folklore film usually does not ask directly how we might lobby for tenants' rights, change big business, create a union, overthrow a dictatorship, or champion any one of many causes. Rather, folklore films ask viewers to look at their own lives and find resemblances to what is seen in the filmic record. How do their rites of passage, material culture, foodways, and ethnicity function for them and correlate with that depicted on film or video? Folklore film authenticates the folk practices and events that people perform, and viewers search to find themselves mirrored or shattered by the images. How do our traditions compare with those on the screen? Thus, folklore films and videos offer an interpretive window for comprehending ourselves.

For the most part, folklore films are not trying to change the world, as film critic Thomas Waugh (1984) suggests committed documentaries do. Instead, folklore films explain our traditional behavior, which may then lead to an understanding of change. The notion of "us" and "them" disappears. For example, Davenport points out that part of the purpose of making *A Singing Stream* was to understand cultural similarities and differences: "We were white southerners making a film about this black family and trying to see it through our eyes. If multiculturalism means an increase in tolerance and understanding, that was part of the purpose of making the film, and that was our experience as filmmakers."

Folklore film has its own community of filmmakers, a set of discursive practices, and, like all documentary film, produces an expectation "that its sounds and images bear an indexical relation to the historical world" (Nichols 1991:27). Film theorist Bill Nichols has identified five modes used in documentary film for structuring its representation of events: expository, observational, interactive, reflexive (1991:33-75), and performative (1994:95). Each is created out of a dialectic with an earlier mode, which has come to be conventionalized and stale. The changes occur historically, but each mode remains, affecting the others—either as a mode to be reacted against or as one to be incorporated in a new manner. This progression has remarkable parallels with the shifts in folklore paradigms.

The *expository* mode, which grows out of the work of Flaherty, offers a solution to a problem or moves toward a needed conclusion. As noted in chapter 1, such films often employ a voice of God narrator. One example is *Dead Birds*, in which Robert Gardner orders the images to fit his argument about warfare. Another is the nightly news, which draws on this expository mode. The text controls the witnesses. The effect may be subtle if the filmmaker uses voices who speak for others (who ultimately speak for the filmmaker) to convey the argument, as does Ken Burns for *The Civil War* (1989). Folklore films do not build a problem/solution argument, but those folklore films which emphasize texts or artifacts may utilize a narrator or call upon vocal witnesses to fit a prearranged filmic text. Thus, we might create a category named the *folklore text* film. For example, similar in structure to *The Civil War*, *Hearts and Hands* argues that quilts are artifacts that reveal history and uses women's voices reconstructed from written documents. *Pizza Pizza Daddy-O* imposes a narrator who places the emphasis on children's singing games. *Folk Housing in Kentucky* strings together clips and demonstrations to explain house types. *I Ain't Lying* uses vignettes and narration to detail different types of folktales told in the Mississippi Delta.

The *observational* mode (cf. MacDougall 1975; Nichols 1991; Young 1975) employs sync-sound and long camera takes. It first appeared in the 1960s when technology produced portable sync-sound equipment capable of long takes. The emphasis in this mode is on the individual, a process, a crisis, or other "present tense" experience. *High School* and *Primary*, which explore individuals in an institutional setting and a political race, respectively, typify this mode. Unlike "slice of life" films, these films take time to develop; they seem to follow "real" time. The viewer is unhampered by a sense of the presence of the filmmaker and allowed to observe the lives of "social actors" who represent themselves to others "as a performance" (Nichols 1991:42). The *folklore process film* uses this style to emphasize individuals and processes. Examples include *How to Make Sorghum Molasses, Ray Lum, Spirits in the Wood,* and *It Ain't City Music* (which addresses many individuals engaged in the process of a contest).

*Interactive* films, according to Nichols, are derived from Dziga Vertov's *kino-pravda* and Jean Rouch's direct cinema. The filmmaker negotiates the interaction. Barbara Kopple stands on the picket line in *Harlan County, U.S.A.*, and the camera becomes a casualty of the violence ensuing there. Bonnie Klein appears in her film *Not a Love Story* as she questions those involved in pornography. Ted Koppel controls and participates in the action on *Nightline*. The point of this mode is the drama of interaction as in Deborah Hoffmann's *Complaints of a Dutiful Daughter* (1994), in which Hoffmann interacts with her mother, or *The Tourist* (1991), in which filmmaker Rob Moss travels as a tourist, both in his professional life as a cameraman on the road and in his personal life as a husband. "Actors" may address the camera as folklorist Pat Turner does in *Ethnic Notions*, or they may provide oral histories for the filmmaker. In some ethnographic films, the intertitles represent the filmmaker, as in *Wedding Camels* by the MacDougalls or the Balinese films from Tim and Patsy Asch and Linda Connor. Folklore filmmakers Jorge and Mabel Preloran present their growing relationship with their "informant," Zulay, and Les Blank is heard interacting with his subjects, while the viewer "in the know" watches for a glimpse of him. These interactive films, such as *Zulay, Facing the Twenty-first Century* and *Halloween '85*, and oral history films such as *Free Show Tonite* and *Miles of Smiles*, are *folklore context films*.

The *reflexive* mode identified by Nichols calls attention to itself by examining the problems of representation. Related to the work of Vertov, the films question their own conventions. The filmmaker unmasks the film itself in a metacommentary about how the world is presented by film. In *Man with a Movie Camera*, Vertov shows how the film is edited. How "realism" is constructed becomes the major issue. An enhanced recognition of the limitations of film and the creation of a "subject" underscore the subjectivity of film in the reflexive mode. A folklore film parallel that bridges categories is *Zulay*, where the filmmakers move to and from the editing table as Zulay is cutting the film in which both she and the Prelorans appear. Reflexivity is heralded by Nichols as evidence of the maturity of documentary film. It has resisted analysis because it does not lend itself well to current theoretical debate; rather, it turns back to modernism as an approach. In addition to form, these films are reflexive in terms of the political. Drawing on the work of Julia Lesage (1978), Nichols comments that feminist film calls attention to ideology and is thus reflexive (on this level, *Hearts and Hands* might be seen as reflexive). Nichols's theories on reflexivity join those advanced by folklorists and anthropologists. Indeed, Nichols remarks that the reflexive mode is most often found in anthropological films.

Obviously, the interactive film and the reflexive film are connected. In one, the filmmaker interacts with the subjects; in the other, the filmmaker may detail how the film affects her. Whereas the interactive film literally shows the filmmaker, the reflexive mode shows the film as a construct, but it may also show the filmmaker as part of that construction, as does *Man with a Movie*

*Camera.* For folklore, such a mode might include questions about how all aspects of folklore fit together (at the "expense" of any one "item," for example, a story). These films might be labeled *folklore event films,* such as *Tales of the Supernatural,* which makes the filmic construction noticeable and which cuts out portions of tales to detail the event rather than specific narratives ("Why did she cut into the middle of those tales?" some textualists asked at its first screening), *Passover,* which condenses a five-hour ritual into 28 minutes and documents the filmmaker's own family, and *Buck Season at Bear Meadow Sunset,* which is more about a weekend gathering than it is about hunting or stories. When the emphasis is placed more on film construction than on a single folklore event (*Carnival in Q'eros,* for example), we might call such films the *folklore reflexive* film. Many of these will appear as videos that unveil subjectivity and reveal construction through feedback seen on camera.

In *Blurred Boundaries* (1994) Nichols adds yet another category: the *performative* mode, which lacks the historical referent that viewers associate with documentary. In the performative mode, the poetic, the expressive, and the rhetorical overshadow the historical domain. Just as folklorists looked at performative events, this filmic mode asks for and receives multiple interpretations. Evocation reigns over representation, subjectivity over objectivity, and montage over the linear or vérité. These films ask the viewer to see in a different way, to "read" the film as an almost fictional offspring of its documentary parent. As one example, Nichols includes *Tongues Untied,* by Marlon Riggs, a lyrical treatment of homosexuality that uses subjectivity to create a dialectic with a larger conceptual issue such as homophobia. The affective and the subjective also merge in *Dear America: Letters Home from Vietnam* (1987), which relies on the emotion engendered by the individuals' stories read by actors and combined with historical footage and the popular songs of the era. The letters evoke fear, anxiety, and a longing for home. The film is thus less about the war and more about the emotion created by the war experience. Here again, folk history, rather than the dry military news, views the war from within. *Common Threads: Stories from the AIDS Quilt* (1989) uses a similar tactic by narrating the subjective experiences of those who have lost loved ones to heighten awareness of the personal effects of the AIDS virus.

The performative mode requires the viewer to create the larger message that the film's emotions trigger: "Performative texts thus avoid both the reductionism inherent to theory and the vacuous obsession with detail inherent to formalism and contextualism" (Nichols 1994:104). The folklore film *Clotheslines* exemplifies the performative mode. Laundry represents familial relationships, especially between mothers and daughters but also between mother and child, husband and wife. Repression and freedom hang on the clotheslines. Cantow sets the viewers in a dreamlike state of a woman speaking as the visuals present a woman's dream of laundry. At times, the laundry giggles as it is placed in drawers. A woman tosses a sheet in the air and it waves onto a bed. The scene repeats as a voice-over matches the action, exclaiming, "Every day. Every day." Cantow relies on the subjective and on art as her method. Another folklore film that might easily be called performative is *Style Wars* (1983). The film begins with the operatic strains of Richard Wagner's *Die Götterdämmerung* and the sight of vivid graffiti passing the camera on subway cars slowly snaking out on a journey. Tony Silver and Henry Chalfant uncover the history and artistic value of these "outlaw" art forms through the creation of their own filmic art form. They match music and rap with the ever moving subway cars to create a performative presentation of New York's hip-hop culture. *Paris Is Burning* (1990) also uses a message greater than that which appears on the surface in its documentation of transvestite competitions. Categories are taken directly from the "straight" world: town and country, schoolgirl, and executive, for example. The performance of these men on runways at elaborate balls and the narratives of their lives unfold in ball scenes and evocative interviews, as Jennie Livingston presents history and the continuity of a tradition woven into the larger fabric of life and death. Consumerism is glorified by those unable to obtain it, by those who have a lifestyle that is anything but "realness" (a performance category for those who prance down the runway). Rather, the film points to the subjectivity of the "real," which the men seek but which is unattainable in a society that shuts them out of white middle-class heterosexual America. The film addresses the "real" of class consciousness and the play between what is real for the men in the film and what is real for the filmmaker or viewer.

To avoid the complications which the term *performance* might have as a referent solely to content, "performative" works for folklore films on both content and construction levels. Yet, in keeping with the historical progression that matches these filmic types to stylistic and technological changes, the term *folklore postvérité film* defines films about performance and expressive behavior as well as films *as* performance.

Folklorists might easily add the *folklore family film* or *folklore home movie mode,* an "inside-out film." Akin to the observational mode, the camera follows passages of life and meaningful events in a family, usually that of the filmmaker. Interaction with the camera is overt, as in the Beatles' *A Hard Day's Night* (1964) or *Benji's Family on Wheels* (1991), a film made by skateboarders. In the home movie, couples wave as they depart by car after their wedding and children make faces at the camera and blow out birthday candles on a prearranged signal from the cameraperson. Others smile openly.

The modes proposed as film categories are not mutually exclusive for folklore or for documentary. Likewise, filmmakers might easily challenge both the boundaries and the names of the categories themselves, asking that cinéma vérité, for example, be substituted as a more tightly constructed and appropriately signifying term for what Nichols dubs "observational" or what I call the "folklore process film" and that it be added as a separate but related category. However, no matter which categories are used, film modes overlap; certain portions of one film may fall into more than one mode. For example, Blank's *Sprout Wings and Fly* (1983), which documents the tales and music of fiddler Tommy Jarrell, fits into a folklore text film mode because of its vignette style, yet it also overlaps with the interactive or folklore context mode for some scenes; *Halloween '85* might be a context film yet also be an event film; and both *Passover* and *Tales of the Supernatural* will neatly fit into folklore event and folklore reflexive film modes.

Other filmic modalities similar to the folklore film modes described might easily be drawn. Peter Loizos (1992) and Peter Ian Crawford (1992) have both devised different sets of modalities. Crawford labels films as perspicuous, experiential, or evocative. The experiential matches what Loizos calls "experience," and the evocative is the same as Nichols's performative mode and my *postvérité.* Because of the constructed nature of film and a history of development that has established certain forms and approaches that replicate themselves (regardless of what they are called), and that are always creating (or re-creating) new ones as technology changes (witness television and hypertext channels of distribution, which will further alter form), all documentary filmic categories or modalities share commonalities.

Using these modes, combined with those categories presented in chapters 2 and 3 that look at content focus and style, will help define/describe a particular folklore film. For example, in a film about community shot in montage, the style and content focus determine the mode. In some instances the correlation is direct, for example, for text, event, and process films. In others, such as community and region films, the filmic categories overlap: the event film is the process, the reflexive is the negotiated, and the subjective becomes postvérité. The modes offer a way to discuss style on more general grounds as well as on editing and exegesis as revelatory of the filmmaker's intent. As demonstrated, folklorists might take these categories and modes as a starting point for creating a new set of discourses regarding folklore films and videos.

The desire to recognize the self, whether the filmmakers appear in the film or not, has made both the evocative film and the reflexive film doorways to discovery; the folklore film may hold the key that unlocks the doors. Reflexivity explores what the experience of fieldwork has done to transform the fieldworker (and the documentary filmmaker). Anthropologist and filmmaker Jay Ruby began to address the issue of reflexivity and documentary films in the 1970s. Ruby asserts that the philosophy of positivism blinded us into thinking that we could achieve objectivity. Structuralism and Marxism led us to see otherwise, as did cultural manifestations of self-awareness. Once we recognize that we construct our own world, then we can develop a method for revealing the self. Ruby's remarks are especially relevant for folklorists and anthropologists. He points to the problem of the western middle class documenting the Other, those who differ most from the filmmaker politically, financially, or culturally—those without access to power. "Documentary films dealing with the rich and powerful or even the middle class are as sparse as are social science studies of these people. The documentary film has not been a place where people explored themselves or their own culture" (Ruby 1988:71-72). Although Ruby does note that the home movie and the avant-garde film do so, he overlooks the folklore film, which explores the self and one's own culture.

The influences of reflexivity and home videos on folklorists blend to provide a new approach to performance and events in which we place ourselves in the frame and tell our own stories about our families and our ethnic and regional backgrounds. When we tell someone else's story, we still appear in the frame and make the content our story as well. As Barbara Myerhoff and Jay Ruby have pointed out, "Reflexive . . . describes the capacity of any system of signification to turn back upon itself, to make itself its own object by referring to itself: subject and object fuse" (1982:2).

## Video Reflections

In reaction to my questions about their own uses of video, filmmakers addressed issues of image size, training, and the influence of the video camera for recognizing the importance of everyday life. Video is one of the media by which we define ourselves; all of the filmmakers I interviewed have considered the dynamic possibilities of video as the gap narrows between the discrepancy in quality and cost of film versus video. Preloran remarked on the changes wrought during his lifetime:

> I grew up when 8mm was the camera of choice for tourists. Nobody else was doing it. And then I started shooting 16mm. . . . And I've never shot video. Until this day I've shot 16mm. Very expensive, very costly, but it's professional. . . . Then came Super 8. That was quite interesting, and many of my friends in Argentina did Super 8 as a profession. Then three-quarter-inch video, half-inch video [VHS]. And a camcorder now is the camera of choice. Now you can become a professional with very cheap equipment. . . . So now there's no excuse.
>
> Every generation finds a way of expressing itself with the equipment that's available. It gets easier and easier because when there is a technological explosion, equipment becomes easier to use and faster and cheaper.

> 16mm was very expensive and I had to shoot one-to-one in order to
> become a professional and a Third World filmmaker in a Third World
> country. . . . Everybody's going to find his own way, and hopefully they'll
> find in this new tool [video] a great medium. My students go to film school
> to make 16mm films, but there are those . . . that have done documentaries
> with camcorders, Hi-8 video . . . and you can't tell the difference.

As the technology changes, new methods are built upon the older approaches.
Relying on an established foundation, the filmmaker (or videographer) combines the old methodology with the new technology to create a fresh image of
the world.

Video is the result of constantly improving formats in a tradition of visualizing that started with still photography. At each stage of development, the
users of the previous formats generally continue to document as they always
have. Preloran noted that it was too late for him to change formats. Cohen re-
iterated that reluctance. Cohen echoes Thomas Kuhn's idea in *The Structure of
Scientific Revolutions* (1962) that paradigms do not become extinct until their
advocates die; the 16mm filmmaker becomes a dinosaur resisting the change
to video: "I used 16mm from the outset. And I wouldn't advise it to anyone
who's starting right now because the video technology is so much more flexi-
ble and accessible. So, in a certain sense, I'm admitting my willingness to be a
dinosaur." Cohen believes a few future dinosaurs will arrive because of the
quality and image size of 16mm.

> If you can't give students that experience ever, if they don't know what
> 16mm looks like, if they don't know the quality it looks like, then in a
> strange way video has reduced filmmaking back to information. And
> mostly you look at it for information and not necessarily for quality, or you
> have to film video or use the camera in a different way in order to get a
> sense of quality. Video is so dependent on close-ups, just like the television
> experience is built on close-ups, and I love long shots where you can see the
> whole panorama and a small individual in it. . . . I still conceive of my films
> being seen communally in a dark theater, with other people sitting along-
> side, and breathing and sighing, and influencing each other, and the
> common experience of viewing.

Distribution defeats these purposes. Cohen states, "In a strange way, I'm doing
that odd thing, making 16mm because I believe in it even though the distributors don't particularly want it."

Les Blank is also hesitant to change formats, partly because he is so profi-
cient in 16mm. The drawback is the expense of 16mm, which causes the
filmmaker to be cautious about wasting film.

> With video, people tend to be not so careful when they're gathering their
> images. Unlike with film, which is so expensive that you have to have your

brain connected to the cost per frame as it's running through the camera. So you're always waiting. You wait too long, or you might turn the camera off too soon for fear of spending too much money on the shoot, and you miss a lot of good things. The videographer picks up those scenes that just happened out of nowhere and can afford to waste a lot of tape to get it. But they don't always strive for the best dynamic angle like a film photographer might.

Wagner also talked about the beauty of film and its large screen projection format. Without grant money, he uses videotape, which gives him that freedom mentioned by Blank. More of an editor than a cameraman, Wagner feels unfettered by videotape. He may shoot without thinking about the cash running through the gate of a 16mm camera. Similarly, Thigpen switched to video when he realized that, financially, shooting in 16mm was "going to be an uphill battle."

Thigpen also pointed out that videotape had changed who was behind the camera. Years ago, Thigpen said, "If you came out and said, 'I want to film your family on a certain occasion,' people were going to talk to you. But they're doing it more and more for themselves." Video erases the line between the Other and the self. Amateurs or professionals, the filmmaker/videographer is drawn to the self that resonates within. Both portray the self. The professional does so through subject choice, style, and structure; the amateur does so through selection (what to shoot, when, and how much). Each has been influenced by the other, having seen the products of each other's work. The amateur has watched television and thousands of films in his or her lifetime, and the professional has sat through screenings of family films and videos, whether from his or her own family or the families of others. Although amateurs will make videos of their families and communities, few will engage in editing (as was also true for the 8mm and Super 8mm filmmaker), because editing videotape is more complex than film. But the techniques will become ever simpler with the linkage of the computer and the video recorder. The effects of economics have irretrievably altered aesthetic practices.

Video has forever changed folklore documentaries while unremittingly changing our vision of the world. Mabel Preloran reminded me, "Don't forget that Zulay is part of the TV generation. She knows what films need, and that makes a difference." As Tom Davenport, who works in both film and video formats, observed, videotape has made the camera easily accessible. What people record will, like the professional film, have lasting value:

> There's a ton of people out there with video cameras now who are recording things right and left. . . . It's an interesting archive. Whatever anybody will do with it, you don't know. And maybe in the long run it will be more significant than the work of so-called sophisticated filmmakers because it's

done naively, simply because you want to record what you thought was important in your family's life. And maybe that will be more revealing than any kind of sense of what sophisticated filmmakers are doing. Eventually, it will have to be edited and put into some form, I suppose, but who knows what that archive will mean.

When you look at old family albums, they're very interesting things. And then you look at pictures of the so-called art photography—a little boat in the sunset, and it looks like a thousand other boats in the sunset—it's not at all interesting. But the album is a picture of 1920 snapshots—what people wore, and the houses they owned, and the kind of pets they had, and what they wanted you to see about their house and all those kinds of things.

What once seemed commonplace becomes "rare" and vice versa, as one looks back through another window to find the self immortalized within the frame.

Both amateurs and professionals look at the events in which that content is displayed to reveal how those events function in the lives of the people on screen. Preloran records the event as an organizing principle to discover meaning: "You want to record in different times. For instance, in a big festivity, the person is happy and full of life and excitement and explaining and things like that, and what is a ceremony? I don't care about whether they go around twice and then they yell, 'Hee, hee.' That's just form. You shoot that, but what I want to know is why they do it, what does it mean, and how do they feel." Rather than document one event, Preloran extends his focus to explore personal and public events as well as calendrical ones to construct his ethnobiographies. These events, taken together, speak to meaning on a more complex level than content and structure.

Borrowing from Dell Hymes's idea of event (1962, 1964), Richard Chalfen has suggested that "film communication can be . . . studied as the creation, manipulation, and interpretation of symbolic events that occur in, and as, a series of social 'performances.'" He then breaks film communication "into four kinds of 'events,' namely: (1) planning events, (2) filming events (which necessarily include the two subcategories of 'on-camera' events and 'behind-camera' events), (3) editing events, and (4) exhibition events" (1975:87). Thus, film communication becomes a performance event with a recognizable pattern of behavior—much like folklore. The contents of these performance events, or films, are "patterned," especially in the home movie, whose content is "distinguished by a limited number of people participating in a continued array of places and events" (Chalfen 1982:129). The consensus among home moviemakers on what to include or how to structure their world might thus be seen as analogous to how narratives and rituals are structured (a point Worth and Adair make in *Through Navajo Eyes* [1972]).

With home movies, the act of watching the films becomes a reflexive event. Likewise, films about the self may give rise to stories about the filming process as well as create new exhibition modes of behavior. My film on Kathleen Ware is regularly shown at Ware family gatherings. In home movies, *the filmmaker* wants to be in the movie whenever possible. As Chalfen has stated, we also have a basic drive "to see ourselves performing, either in terms of doing something . . . or in some form of interpersonal interaction" (1975:99). We want to be in the audience watching our *own* interactions and performances.

In *Home Movie: An American Folk Art* (1975), Steve Zeitlin and Ernst Edward Star visibly illustrate how we choose to present ourselves. The recorded rites of passage, Sunday picnics, babies in rubber pools, and vacations become the ideal, the "golden age." We remember our lives via the films and become actors in the drama of life. At the same time, we create a folk art of home movies by using the same content and structure and the same conventions and behaviors of home moviemakers.

The home movie mode also makes us aware of how many people see life as a series of events and indicates why event-oriented films are successful. For example, *A Singing Stream* succeeds because of Davenport's excellent technical skills and his focus on one family and event. Its tales, remembrances, beliefs, and music are all part of the family experience and are revealed within the framework of a family reunion. Dan Patterson's article about this same group, "'Going Up to Meet Him': Songs and Ceremonies of a Black Family's Ascent" (1988), is not as effective as the film in depicting how family members tell their own stories and communicate the strength of their relationships.

People believe what they see in documentaries. Home movies reinforce this belief because of their seeming "mistakes" (out-of-focus shots, rapid pans, jump cuts) and their general lack of editing. An example is the Zapruder footage of John F. Kennedy's assassination, which set a precedent for amateur footage representing "the truth" via the accidental recording of an event. Thirty years later, video served a similar function with the capture on videotape of the Rodney King beating. The desire for "truth" and the realization that "truth" is manufactured by the media, as evidenced by docudramas and reenactments, have made us want to regain control over how we might perceive ourselves. As an outgrowth of the home movie, video creates that opportunity and at the amateur level it democratizes the process as a low-cost, readily available medium whose technology improves with startling rapidity.

Video raises the old question of whether art imitates life or life imitates art. The question surfaced, for instance, when *Bad Influence* (1990), a feature film starring Rob Lowe, made headline news for mirroring Lowe's private indiscretions with a fictional scene in which the actor videotapes his bedroom exploits. In *Broadcast News* (1987), the plot turns on an incident in which "reality" is faked with editing. The news story looks good, but can we trust it? Can we still say, as John Fogarty does in a popular song, "I Know It's True

'Cause I Saw It on TV"? Home movie style seems to transcend these questions. Patricia Erens, in "Home Movies in Commercial Narrative Film," has pointed out that when home footage is included in features it functions "as the bearer of truth. As if their existence created another level of reality (a separate diegetic world), home movies are coded as documentaries, images which document real events, images which don't lie" (1986:99). Video grants the same sense of objectivity conferred by home movies. One of television's biggest hits, *America's Funniest Home Videos*, has people all over the country watching other people just like them. Columnist Ellen Goodman notes that this America is the one we want to see—wholesome and family oriented and "real." The program receives as many as 1,800 tapes per day (De Atley 1990); the $10,000 prize undoubtedly causes videographers to stage events for the camera. The half-hour program becomes a "packaged, edited, marketed version of other Americans' 'real life'" (Goodman 1990:3c).

Although the Super 8mm home movie of the 1960s seemed objective, with people watching a soundless track while the person showing the film merely identified people or explained events, the filmmaker/narrator actually used the medium as a platform for making jokes and personal comments (Camper 1986). He was the insider describing the family to itself as audience members (men shot most of the home movies.) With video, this reflexive platform changes. The "commentator" changes from the filmmaker to those being filmed. Sound is synchronous, and the "highlights" are extended to long takes that require less explanation. Video has also leveled the gender distinction of who operates the camera.

Videotape doesn't have to be as selective as film. Two-hour video cassettes have replaced three-minute 8mm film rolls, and time constraints have disappeared. In "Some Notes on the Home Movie," Fred Camper observes that video "is even better suited, in short, to become continuous with the life it depicts." Events can be viewed while they are occurring: "Those images become a real-time part of our daily lives" (Camper 1986:13). Instant feedback becomes the new mode of reflexivity and allows for an instant change of image or sound. The event as a whole may be represented—including our simultaneous evaluation of it, visibly demonstrating its workings in a way no ethnographic writing ever can. The viewer and the subject unite. Heavy-voiced narrations become outmoded, and a candor and believability emerge.

In his 1988 presidential address to the American Folklore Society, Alan Jabbour praised folklorists for having "been at the vanguard of the dawning late-twentieth-century realization that observation changes that which is observed, and thus that engagement must replace objectivity as the model for our relationship with those whom we study" (1989:296-97). Folklorists often study those like themselves. Unlike the ethnographic researcher or filmmaker carrying out the "urgent film anthropology" requested by the Institut für den Wissenschaftlichen Film to document cultures changing rapidly, folklorists have heeded the admonition of such scholars as Rolf Husman: "We must not forget also to turn our attention to modern aspects of culture life" (1983:97). Although they do not often face the problems of cross-cultural research, folklore filmmakers do need to analyze and reflect on their roles and the effect of those roles on the people they document.

Community member status determines access to information. This is true not only in a cross-cultural sense but for any insider/outsider dichotomy. The role within the group (not just as a member, but the type of member) is also relevant. The importance of role is underscored by John Cohen, who recalled the failure of communication between himself and the Q'eros. Even though he had filmed them previously and was godfather to an informant's child, he was an outsider. Six months after a successful shoot in 1984, Cohen returned to Peru and was attacked by the Q'eros when he attempted to film their carnival (as noted in chapter 3).

More and more of us are now writing and filming as insiders. We recognize our "engagement" and no longer fear studying ourselves. For example, for *Passover, a Celebration,* I videotaped my own family and later wrote about how I overcame the problems of being an insider (Sherman 1986). Gayla Jamison's video production, *Living in America: One Hundred Years of Ybor City* (1987), points to how folklorists have embraced an insider's stance. The video is personalized by Jamison's "references to her own family history. . . . [Jamison moves] back and forth between the personal and the communal" (Saltzman 1989:318). Sheila Chamovitz explores *Murray Avenue* (1983), her own Jewish neighborhood in Pittsburgh, and friends and relatives appear in the normal course of their day on the street. In a similar way, films made by "outsiders" work well when insiders talk about themselves. For example, in *Every Island Had Its Own Songs* (1988), produced by the Bureau of Florida Folklife Programs about Nikitas Tsimouris, a Greek bagpipe maker/musician and his family, the family scenes have a genuine quality because family members describe their actions and feelings to the camera. We feel the family's warmth. The presence of outsiders flaws this wonderful film by interrupting the viewers' connection to the family: the narrator and "experts" ponder the possible future problems of ethnic identity and place their scholarly "stamp of importance" on such activities as making a bagpipe and celebrating Epiphany.

In *A Singing Stream,* which also focuses on the family, insiders bring us into that family. Viewers associate directly with those they see. Davenport remarked,

> The trick in a folklore film, I think, is to make it both universal and particular. Universal in the sense that anybody that watches it can feel their own

empathy toward the people in the film. . . . So the audience has to be brought in to say, "Hey, that could be my life," or "I'd like to be a member of that family." But then the particular things are all the particular ways they sing songs or tell stories, or their particular circumstances in their lives, but it's always threaded on a universal story. . . . You look at *A Singing Stream.* The audience will say, "I think that's a great family. I wish my family was like that. I'd like to be a family. This is a wonderful bunch of people."

Folklore strikes a chord of recognition because of its universality. Despite differences in their own traditional behavior, the viewers relate the folklore on the screen to that manifested in their own families or lives. This association gives folklore film its reverberant quality.

*Roger and Me* (1989), the documentary megahit, breaks the more routine outsider mold by using an insider's format. The tale of the destruction of Flint, Michigan, caused by the layoff of 35,000 General Motors workers (while GM was opening a new plant in Mexico) is told from filmmaker Michael Moore's perspective. The film portrays an ideological class struggle between the workers and the GM bureaucracy; emphasizes the questionable ethics of its chairman, Roger Smith; and juxtaposes the poor workers facing foreclosures on their homes the day before Christmas with the GM gala Christmas banquet. Moore also documents the town's ludicrous attempts, via parades and the building of Auto-World, to recover emotionally and economically. But the film is a personal saga.

Moore opens with shots of his family members, many of whom worked at GM. He tells us about his own expectations of continuing the tradition. The film is often shot "handheld," and it has a vérité feel and a home movie style. Shooting over a period of two years, Moore gives us a sense of being there when anything significant happens, as he takes us along on his struggles to interview Roger Smith. At the film's end, the viewer cheers because certain GM officers are also laid off. Moore thus succeeds in bringing the audience "inside."

Just as Moore's film suggests a new model, feminist film and video provide new ways to view the self. In one such film, to make sense of her own changing relationship with her aging mother, Deborah Hoffmann records the metamorphic mother/daughter patterns wrought by her mother's struggle with Alzheimer's disease. Although particular to Hoffmann's own story, it is also the universal story of mother/daughter bonds and shifting roles. Women have taken this filmic form of self-examination to new heights. *Clotheslines* speaks directly to the female self. A film on the folk art inherent in one of life's routines—laundry—it is by women and about women. Lauren Rabinovitz has commented that female video artists have "pursued self-examination in relationship to how culture shapes sexual identity" (1986:115).

Likewise, when women tell the stories of other women, they tell themselves their own history. For example, Luci Arnez, with her husband Lawrence Luckinbill, compiled and broadcast home movie footage of her parents in *Lucy and Desi: A Home Movie* (1994) to make sense of their lives, not only to television viewers but to herself. Ten years of soundless footage from the 1950s relies on Arnez's recollections and voice for construction. Similarly, filmmaker Pat Ferrero uses the voices and quilts of nineteenth-century women to create a female social history in *Hearts and Hands* (1987), and Amalie Rothschild's *Nana, Mom, and Me* (1974) covers three generations of women. Rothschild notes that she made the film originally for herself and her family as a record: "I felt I had really pushed back barriers as far as I could in terms of delving into intensely personal and private matters in real people's lives" (1980:425). Zulay Saravino also was able to break the boundaries set for women in her culture by depicting herself and her community to the community.

These reflexive styles proclaim a new model for the folklore film. Folklore films and videotapes will shift from implicitly showing theories by the "objective" structuring of "reality" to the explicitly subjective filming of events that reveal the self. For portions of *Zulay*, Jorge Preloran has a photographer shooting him shooting the film. In *A Country Auction* (1984), Robert Aibel, Ben Levin, Chris Musello, and Jay Ruby let their presence as filmmakers and ethnographers become part of the story. These styles mirror reality: videotape has become a common occurrence in daily life and in film and television. Think, for example, of Max Whiteman, the son in *Down and Out in Beverly Hills* (1986), making a videotape throughout the film as his father shouts, "Stop wasting time with the camera"; of *Drugstore Cowboy,* which Gus Van Sant opens and closes with a home movie style "documenting" the actors in the skid row section of Portland to show that these young addicts are "ordinary" kids; or Van Sant's *My Own Private Idaho,* which uses a home movie style as a flashback to a former life held in memory only by a video dream; or of *The Wonder Years* (1988-93), which opens with a "home movie," to place the viewers nostalgically "there" in the late 1960s; or Bob Saget exclaiming, "America, this is you," on *America's Funniest Home Videos.*[4]

Professional filmmakers are now following amateur home moviemakers by focusing on the family, often their own families. Pat Ferrero, for example, purchased a Hi-8 video camera. She spoke of the freedom video offers and a project she was considering, one in which she would look at intercultural contact on the overland trial, commenting, "It's partly a film about my family and about my family in New Mexico." Family, place, and personal history blend as topics in her search for self.

Each of the interviewed filmmakers has touched on a part of the self. Cohen, an artist and musician, has examined the function of art and music.

Jorge Preloran looks for the loner he sees in himself and in Argentina. An artist, he taps into the artistic qualities of the individuals he documents. I respond to teenagers telling the horror stories that fascinated me in my own youth and have turned to my family as a way of examining ethnicity. In a parallel with filmmaking, like Preloran, I identify with artists in my own locale who love the artistic process more than the product. Ken Thigpen presents his family and himself, his students, and the male-centered communities of rural Pennsylvania. Peiser documents the people of Beale Street and, like Ferrero, is looking at ways to document her family. Ferris films his native Mississippians. The daughter of folklorist John Lomax, Hawes follows in his footsteps by documenting song texts and unusual musicians. Wagner re-creates the past and has looked into his own ethnic and historical background for inspiration. Davenport follows his interest in religion and photography, and his rural roots match those he documents. Blank uses the exotic and unusual, perhaps vicariously trying to be, or at least understand, the Other. Yet he frequently does so in his own California backyard. He correlates his experience as a filmmaker in making a film about a filmmaker. Ferrero taps into the political issues raised by gender and ethnicity.

By drawing on the self of the filmmaker, film and videotape can become a reflexive means of capturing folkloric performances, processes, or events. Like home movies, they "provide people with a means of presenting themselves through the mediation of symbolic visual forms, with a means of showing what they *want* to show *about* themselves *to* themselves" (Chalfen 1982:134). Video allows ordinary people to illustrate their own insider's idea of society in a culturally acceptable manner. The home video style, reflexivity, and a process/performance/ event focus will combine with the accessibility of this new video technology and its instant feedback capacity to change our perception of ourselves and the Other to a perception of "all of us."

Videotape and film are bound up in changing theoretical debates. Filmmakers and videographers, as they represent folklore, convey their own attitudes and theories about cultural processes. Cultural and social change combined with technological innovation have propelled folklore film from a mere fieldwork tool to a means of representing and revealing the self.

# Filmography

*Afghan Nomads* (1974), 21 min. David Hancock and Herb DiGioia
*An Afghan Village* (1974), 44 min. David Hancock and Herb DiGioia
*Afro-American Worksongs in a Texas Prison* (1966), 29 min. Pete and Toshi Seeger
*All Day and All Night: Memories from Beale Street Musicians* (1990), 30 min. Robert
    Gordon, Louis Guida, and Judy Peiser
*All Hand Work* (1974), 15 min. Carl Fleischhauer
*Altar of Fire* (1976), 58 min. Robert Gardner
*Always for Pleasure* (1978), 58 min. Les Blank
*America's Funniest Home Videos* (1990-). An ABC-TV series. Vin Di Bona
*Araucanians of Ruca Choroy: Summer* (1971), 52 min. Jorge Preloran
*At the Time of Whaling* (1974), 38 min. Sarah Elder and Lenny Kamerling
*At the Autumn River Camp* (1967), 59 min. Asen Balikci, Guy Mary-Rousseliére, and
    Quentin Brown. Netsilik Eskimo Series
*At the Caribou Crossing Place* (1967), 59 min. Asen Balikci, Guy Mary-Rousseliére, and
    Quentin Brown. Netsilik Eskimo Series
*At the Winter Sea Ice Camp* (1967), 4 parts: 36, 36, 30, and 35 min. Asen Balikci, Guy
    Mary-Rousseliére, and Quentin Brown. Netsilik Eskimo Series
*Bad Influence* (1990), 35 mm, 99 min. Steve Tisch
*A Balinese Trance Seance* (1980), 36 min. Timothy Asch and Linda Connor
*Bathing Babies in Three Cultures* (1952), 9 min. Gregory Bateson and Margaret Mead
*The Battle of San Pietro* (1944-45), 39 min. John Huston
*BBC: The Voice of Britain* (1934-35). Stuart Legg
*Bearskin* (1983), 20 min. Tom Davenport
*Being a Joines: A Life in the Brushy Mountains* (1980), 55 min. Tom Davenport and
    Dan Patterson
*Benji's Family on Wheels* (1991), video, 31 min. DCTV Youth with Dennison Joyce
*Berlin: The Symphony of a Great City* (1927), 60 min. Walter Ruttman
*Bitter Melons* (1971), 30 min. John Marshall
*Black Delta Religion* (1973/1968), 15 min. Bill and Josette Ferris
*The Blues Accordin' to Lightnin' Hopkins* (1969), 31 min. Les Blank
*Born for Hard Luck: Sam Peg Leg Jackson* (1976), 29 min. Tom Davenport and Dan
    Patterson
*Broadcast News* (1987), 35mm, 132 min. James L. Brooks
*Buck Dancer* (1974/1966), 6 min. Edmund Carpenter, Bess Lomax Hawes, and Alan
    Lomax

*Buck Season at Bear Meadow Sunset* (1983), 28 min. Ken Thigpen and George Hornbein

*Burden of Dreams* (1982), 94 min. Les Blank

*Cannibal Tours* (1987), 70 min. Dennis O'Rourke

*Carnival in Q'eros: Where the Mountains Meet the Jungle* (1990), 32 min. John Cohen

*Chang* (1927), 72 min. M. C. Cooper and E. B. Schoedsack

*Childhood Rivalry in Bali and New Guinea* (1952/ 1936-38), 17 min. Gregory Bateson and Margaret Mead

*Chulas Fronteras [Beautiful Borders]* (1976), 58 min. Les Blank

*The Children Were Watching* (1960), 30 min. Richard Leacock

*Chronique d'un été,* (*Chronicle of a Summer,* 1960), 90 min. Jean Rouch and Edgar Morin

*The Civil War* (1989), 11 hours, 21 min. Ken Burns

*Clotheslines* (1981), 31 min. Roberta Cantow

*Coal Face* (1936), 400 ft. Alberto Cavalcanti

*Cochengo Miranda* (1975), 58 min. Jorge Preloran

*Common Threads: Stories from the AIDS Quilt* (1989), 79 min. Robert Epstein, Jeffrey Friedman, and Bill Couterié. HBO Video

*Complaints of a Dutiful Daughter* (1994), 44 min. Deborah Hoffmann

*A Country Auction: The Paul V. Leitzel Estate Sale* (1984), 58 min. Robert Aibel, Ben Levin, Chris Musello, and Jay Ruby

*The Country Fiddle* (1959), 28 min. Pete and Toshi Seeger

*Dancing with the Incas: Huayno Music of Peru* (1991), 58 min. John Cohen

*Dead Birds* (1963), 83 min. Robert Gardner

*Dear America: Letters Home from Vietnam* (1987), 170 min. Bill Couterié. PBS Video

*Deep Hearts* (1981), 58 min. Robert Gardner

*Delta Blues Singer: James "Sonny Ford" Thomas* (1970), 45 min. Bill Ferris

*The Divine Horsemen* (1977), 54 min. Maya Deren

*Doc Watson: Rare Performances, 1963-1981* (1995), 60 min. Vestapol Videos

*Doc Watson: Rare Performances, 1982-1993* (1995), 60 min. Vestapol Videos

*Don't Look Back* (1967), 90 min. Donn Alan Pennebaker

*Down and Out in Beverly Hills* (1986), 35mm, 103 min. Paul Mazursky

*Drugstore Cowboy* (1989), 102 min. Gus Van Sant

*The Drums of Winter [Uksuum Cauyai]* (1988), 90 min. Sarah Elder and Lenny Kamerling

*Dry Wood* (1973), 37 min. Les Blank

*Duke Tritton, Australian Sheep-Shearer* (1963), 10.5 min. Pete and Toshi Seeger

*Earl Collins* (1974), 24 min. Steve Weiner

*Echoes from the Hills* (1970), 51 min. Jim Young and John Burrison

*Elephant Boy* (1937), 82 min. Robert Flaherty

*Emperor Jones* (1933), 72 min. Dudley Murphy

*The End of an Old Song* (1970), 27 min. John Cohen

*Enough to Eat* (1936). Edgar Anstey

*Ethnic Notions* (1987), 58 min. Marlon Riggs

*Every Island Had Its Own Songs* (1988) 28 min. Linda Basset and Ken Cherry. Bureau of Florida Folklife Programs

*Eyes on the Prize* (1987), 14 cassettes, 60 min. each. PBS Video
*Faces* (1968), 125 min. John Cassavetes
*Fannie Bell Chapman: Gospel Singer* (1975), 42 min. Bill Ferris and Judy Peiser
*The Feast* (1968), 29 min. Timothy Asch and Napoleon Chagnon
*The Fight for Life* (1941), 70 min. Pare Lorentz
*Finger Games* (1957), 10 min. Pete and Toshi Seeger
*Fishing at the Stone Weir* (1967), 30 min. Asen Balikci, Guy Mary-Rousseliére, and
   Quentin Brown. Netsilik Eskimo Series
*The Five-String Banjo* (1958), 40 min. Pete and Toshi Seeger
*Fitzcarraldo* (1982), 158 min. Werner Herzog
*Folk Housing in Kentucky* (1969-70), 20 min. Lynwood Montell
*Forest of Bliss* (1985), 90 min. Robert Gardner
*Four Families* (1960), 60 min. Ian McNeill, Guy Glover, and Margaret Mead
*Free Show Tonite* (1983), 60 min. Paul Wagner and Steve Zeitlin
*From Inuit Point of View* (1987). Zach Kunuk
*From the First People* (1977), 45 min. Sarah Elder and Lenny Kamerling
*Garlic Is as Good as Ten Mothers* (1980), 51 min. Les Blank
*Gap-Toothed Women* (1987), 31 min. Les Blank, Maureen Gosling, Chris Simon, and
   Susan Kell
*The Georgia Sea Island Singers* (1974/1963), 12 min. Edmund Carpenter, Bess Lomax
   Hawes, and Alan Lomax
*Gimme Shelter* (1970), 90 min. Albert Maysles, David Maysles, and Charlotte Zwerin
*The Girl in the Pullman* (1927). Erle C. Kenton
*Give My Poor Heart Ease: Mississippi Delta Bluesmen* (1975), 20 min. Bill Ferris
*Glass* (1956), 12 min. Bert Haanstra
*God Respects Us When We Work, but Loves Us When We Dance* (1968), 22 min. Les Blank
*God's Mother Is the Morning Star: The Life and Art of Joseph Mender* (1990), 20 min.
   Karen Lux and Peter Biella
*The Gods Must Be Crazy* (1984), 109 min. Jamie Uys
*The Grand Generation* (1993), 30 min. Paul Wagner, Marjorie Hunt, and Steve Zeitlin
*Grass: A Nation's Battle for Life* (1925), 70 min. M.C. Cooper and E.B. Schoedsack
*Gravel Springs Fife and Drum* (1971), 10 min. Bill Ferris, David Evans, and Judy Peiser
*Halloween '85* (1986), 26 min. Ken Thigpen and George Hornbein
*Hansel and Gretel* (1975) 16 min. Tom Davenport
*Happy Mother's Day* (1963), 26 min. Richard Leacock
*A Hard Day's Night* (1964), 108 min. Richard Lester
*Harlan County, U.S.A.* (1976), 103 min. Barbara Kopple
*Harmonize: Folklore in the Lives of Five Families* (1976), 21 min. Paul Wagner and
   Steve Zeitlin
*Harvest of Shame* (1960), 55 min. Edward R. Murrow
*Hearts and Hands: A Social History of Nineteenth-Century Women and Quilts* (1987),
   63 min. Pat Ferrero
*High School* (1968), 75 min. Frederick Wiseman
*High School II* (1995), 200 min. Frederick Wiseman
*The High Lonesome Sound* (1963), 29 min. John Cohen
*The Holdup of the Rocky Mountain Express* (1906), 569 ft. Wallace McCutcheon

*Home Economics: A Documentary of Surburbia* (1994), 47 min. Jenny Cool
*Home Movie: An American Folk Art* (1975), 25 min. Steve Zeitlin and Ernst Edward Star
*Hopi: Songs of the Fourth World* (1983), 58 min. Pat Ferrero
*Hospital* (1970), 84 min. Frederick Wiseman
*Hot Pepper* (1973), 54 min. Les Blank
*Housing Problems* (1935), 17 min. Arthur Elton and Edgar Anstey
*How to Make Sorghum Molasses* (1971), 20 min. Carl Fleischhauer
*The Hunters* (1958), 73 min. John Marshall
*Husbands and Wives* (1992), 108 min. Woody Allen
*I Ain't Lying: Folktales from Mississippi* (1975), 20 min. Bill Ferris
*Ika Hands* (1988), 60 min. Robert Gardner
*Imaginero* (1969), 52 min. Jorge Preloran
*Imrat Khan Demonstrates the Sitar* (1963), 11.5 min. Pete and Toshi Seeger
*In Heaven There Is No Beer?* (1984), 51 min. Les Blank
*In Her Own Time: The Final Fieldwork of Barbara Myerhoff* (1985), 60 min. Lynne Littman
*In the Land of the War Canoes: Kwakiutl Indian Life on the Northwest Coast* (1914), 47 min. Edward S. Curtis
*It Ain't City Music* (1973), 14 min. Tom Davenport
*Italian Folk Songs* (1964), 10 min. Pete and Toshi Seeger
*Itam Hakim, Hopiit* (1984), 58 min. Victor Masayesva Jr.
*Jaguar* (1967/1954), 93 min. Jean Rouch
*J'ai Été au Bal (I Went to the Dance): The Cajun and Zydeco Music of Louisiana* (1989), 84 min. Les Blank
*Jero on Jero: A Balinese Trance Seance Observed* (1981), 47 min. Timothy Asch, Patsy Asch, and Linda Connor
*Jero Tapakan: Stories from the Life of a Balinese Healer* (1983), 25 min. Timothy Asch, Patsy Asch, and Linda Connor
*Kathleen Ware, Quiltmaker* (1979), 33 min. Sharon Sherman
*The Kennedys* (1992), 231 min. David Espar, PBS Video
*King Kong* (1933), 95 min. M.C. Cooper and E.B. Schoedsack
*Kramer vs. Kramer* (1987), 105 min. Nestor Al Mendros
*The Land* (1941), 44 min. Robert Flaherty
*Law and Order* (1969), 81 min. Frederick Wiseman
*Legends of Old Time Music* (1995), 60 min. Vestapol Videos
*Les Maîtres Fous (Mad Masters*, 1955), 30 min. Jean Rouch
*Living in America: One Hundred Years of Ybor City* (1987), 53 min. Gayla Jamison
*Lonely Boy* (1961), 53 min. Wolf Koenig and Roman Kroiter
*Lorang's Way* (1979/1973–74), 69 min. David and Judith MacDougall
*Louisiana Story* (1948), 77 min. Robert Flaherty
*Lucy and Desi: A Home Movie* (1994), 111 min. Luci Arnez and Lawrence Luckinbill
*Luther Metke at 94* (1979), 27 min. Jorge Preloran and Steve Raymen
*Mail by Rail* (1993), video, 7 min. Paul Wagner
*Made in Mississippi: Black Folk Art and Crafts* (1975), 20 min. Bill Ferris
*Making Sense of the Sixties* (1991), 60 min. WETA-TV
*Man of Aran* (1934), 76 min. Robert Flaherty

*Man with a Movie Camera* (1928), 66 min. Dziga Vertov
*The Many Colored Paper* (1959), 13 min. Pete and Toshi Seeger
*Marc and Ann* (1991), 27 min. Les Blank
*Masters of American Traditional Music* series (1967-69): *Fred McDowell*, 15 min.; *Reverend Gary Davis*, 26 min.; *Jesse "Lone Cat" Fuller*, 26 min.; *Doc Watson with Clint Howard and Fred Price*, 25 min.; and *Buell Kazee*, 16 min. Seattle Folklore Society and KCTS-TV Seattle
*The McPeake Family of Ireland* (1964), 12 min. Pete and Toshi Seeger
*Meat* (1976), 120 min. Frederick Wiseman
*Medium Cool* (1969), 111 min. Haskell Wexler
*The Medium Is the Masseuse: A Balinese Massage* (1983), 35 min. Timothy Asch, Patsy Asch, and Linda Connor
*Meshes of the Afternoon* (1943), 20 min. Maya Deren
*Miles of Smiles, Years of Struggle: The Untold Story of the Black Pullman Porter* (1982), 60 min. Jack Santino and Paul Wagner
*Mississippi Delta Blues* (1974/1968-70), 18 min. Bill and Josette Ferris
*Moana: A Romance of the Golden Age* (1926), 85 min. Robert Flaherty
*Model* (1980), 132 min. Frederick Wiseman
*Mondo Cane* (1961), 90 min. Antonio Climati
*Monterey Pop* (1968), 79 min. Donn Alan Pennebaker, Albert Maysles, and Richard Leacock
*Mountain Music of Peru* (1984), 60 min. John Cohen
*Murray Avenue* (1983), 28 min. Sheila Chamovitz
*Murrow-McCarthy Debate* (1954). Televised news
*Music from Oil Drums* (1956), 15 min. Pete and Toshi Seeger
*My Aunt Nora* (1982), 90 min. Jorge and Mabel Preloran
*My Own Private Idaho* (1991), 105 min. Gus Van Sant
*N!ai: The Story of a !Kung Woman* (1980), 59 min. John Marshall
*Naim and Jabar* (1973), 70 min. David Hancock and Herb DiGioia
*Nana, Mom, and Me* (1974), 47 min. Amalie Rothschild
*Nanook of the North* (1922), 55 min. Robert Flaherty
*Navajo Silversmith* (1966), 20 min. Johnny Nelson
*A Navajo Weaver* (1966), 20 min. Susie Benally
*Night Mail* (1936), 25 min. Basil Wright and Harry Watt
*North Sea* (1938), 32 min. Harry Watt
*Not a Love Story: A Film about Pornography* (1981), 68 min. Bonnie Klein and Linda Lee Tracy
*The Nuer* (1970), 75 min. Hilary Harris, George Breidenbach, and Robert Gardner
*N/um Tchai: The Ceremonial Dance of the !Kung Bushmen* (1968), 20 min. John Marshall
*Nunaqpa [Going Inland]* (1991), 58 min. Zack Kunuk
*Olympiad* (1938), 200 min. Leni Riefenstahl
*On the Bowery* (1957), 65 min. Lionel Rogosin
*On the Spring Ice* (1975), 45 min. Sarah Elder and Lenny Kamerling
*'Oss 'Oss Wee 'Oss* (1971), 20 min. Alan Lomax
*Out of Ireland* (1994), 111 min. Paul Wagner
*Paris Is Burning* (1990), 76 min. Jennie Livingston

*Passover, a Celebration* (1983), 28 min. Sharon Sherman

*Pericles in America* (1988), 70 min. John Cohen

*Pizza Pizza Daddy-O* (1969), 18 min. Bess Lomax Hawes

*The Plow that Broke the Plains* (1936), 21 min. Pare Lorentz

*Point of Order!* (1963), 97 min. Emile de Antonio and Daniel Talbot

*Power and the Land* (1940), 105 min. Joris Ivens

*The Popovich Brothers of South Chicago* (1978), 60 min. Jill Godmilow

*Primary* (1960), 54 min. Drew Associates

*Q'eros: The Shape of Survival* (1979), 53 min. John Cohen

*Qaggiq* (1989), 58 min. Zach Kunuk

*Quilino* (1969), 14 min. Jorge Preloran

*Quilts in Women's Lives* (1980), 28 min. Pat Ferrero

*Rattlesnakes: A Festival at Cross Fork, PA* (1991), 28 min. Ken Thigpen and George
     Hornbein

*Rapunzel, Rapunzel* (1978), 50 min. Tom Davenport

*Ray Lum: Mule Trader* (1973), 18 min. Bill Ferris, Bobby Taylor, and Judy Peiser

*Record of a Sneeze* (1894), 169 ft. W.K.L. Dickson

*Releasing the Spirits: A Village Cremation in Bali Eastern Indonesia* (1990), 43 min.
     Timothy Asch, Patsy Asch, and Linda Connor

*Rien que les heures (Nothing but the Hours,* 1926), 35 min. Alberto Cavalcanti

*The River* (1937), 30 min. Pare Lorentz

*Rivers of Sand* (1974), 85 min. Robert Gardner

*Roger and Me* (1989), 100 min. Michael Moore

*Salamanders: A Night at the Phi Delt House* (1982), 12 min. Ken Thigpen and George
     Hornbein

*Salesman* (1969), 90 min. Albert Maysles

*Say, Old Man, Can You Play the Fiddle?* (1971) 20 min. Bess Lomax Hawes and
     Barbara Lapan Rahm

*The Shallow Well* (1966), 20 min. Johnny Nelsen

*The Shakers* (1970), 30 min. Tom Davenport and Dan Patterson

*Showman* (1962) 52 min. Frederick Wiseman

*The Silent World* (1956), 86 min. Jacques Cousteau

*The Singing Fishermen of Ghana* (1964), 15 min. Pete and Toshi Seeger

*A Singing Stream: A Black Family Chronicle* (1986), 50 min. Tom Davenport, Dan
     Patterson, and Allen Tullos

*Spend It All* (1970), 41 min. Les Blank

*Spirits in the Wood: The Chainsaw Art of Skip Armstrong* (1991), 28 min. Sharon
     Sherman

*Sprout Wings and Fly* (1983), 30 min. Les Blank, Cece Conway, Alice Gerrard, and
     Maureen Gosling

*The Stone Carvers* (1985), 29 min. Paul Wagner and Marjorie Hunt

*The Store* (1983), 119 min. Frederick Wiseman

*Style Wars* (1983), 59 min. Tony Silver and Henry Chalfant

*The Sun's Gonna Shine* (1969), 10 min. Les Blank

*Surname Viet Given Name Nam* (1989), 108 min. Trinh T. Minh-ha

*Tales of the Supernatural* (1970), 27 min. Sharon Sherman

*The Talking Drums of Nigeria* (1964), 17 min. Pete and Toshi Seeger

*This Is Spinal Tap* (1984), 82 min. Rob Reiner
*Three Songs of Leadbelly* (1945), 8 min. Pete Seeger, Blanding Sloan, and Wah Mong Chang
*Three Songs of Lenin* (1934), 62 min. Dziga Vertov
*Titicut Follies* (1967), 85 min. Frederick Wiseman
*To Die For* (1995), 107 min. Gus Van Sant
*To Live with Herds* (1972), 68 min. David and Judith MacDougall
*Tongues Untied* (1989), 55 min. Marlon Riggs
*The Tourist* (1991), 58 min. Rob Moss
*Trance and Dance in Bali* (1952), 20 min. Gregory Bateson, Margaret Mead, and Jane Belo
*Triumph of the Will* (*Triumph des Willens*, 1935), 110 min. Leni Riefenstahl
*Truth or Dare* (1991), 118 min. Alek Keshishian
*Tununeremiut: The People of Tununak* (1972), 35 min. Sarah Elder and Lenny Kamerling
*Two Black Churches* (1975), 20 min. Bill Ferris
*Union Maids* (1976), 48 min. James Klein, Julia Reichert, and Miles Mogulescu
*The Upperville Show* (1970), 9 min. Tom Davenport
*Valle Fertil* (1972), 90 min. Jorge Preloran
*The Village* (1967), 70 min. Mark McCarty and Paul Hockings
*War Comes to America* (1945), 67 min. Frank Capra
*The Warao* (1975), 54 min. Jorge Preloran
*Washington National Cathedral* (1993), 60 min. PBS Video
*A Well-Spent Life* (1971), 44 min. Les Blank
*"We Shall Overcome"* (1988), 58 min. Jim Brown, Ginger Brown, Harold Leventhal, and George Stoney
*The Wedding Camels* (1977/1973–74), 108 min. David and Judith MacDougall
*Welfare* (1975), 167 min. Frederick Wiseman
*A Wife among Wives* (1982), 68 min. David and Judith MacDougall
*Woman under the Influence* (1974), 147 min. John Cassavetes
*The Wonder Years* (1988–1993), an ABC-TV series, Neal Marlens and Carole Black
*Woodstock* (1970), 184 min. Michael Wadleigh
*Workers at the White House* (1994), 32 min. Marjorie Hunt
*Workers Emerging from a Factory* (1894), 1-2 min. Louis and Auguste Lumière
*Yanki No!* (1960), 53 min. Albert Maysles and Richard Leacock
*Yanomamö Myth of Naro as Told by Dedeheiwa* (1971), 25 min. Timothy Asch and Napoleon Chagnon
*Yanomamö Myth of Naro as Told by Kaobawa* (1971), 17 min. Timothy Asch and Napoleon Chagnon
*Years of Lightning, Day of Drums* (1966), 88 min. Bruce Herschensohn
*Yum, Yum, Yum! A Taste of Cajun and Creole Cooking* (1990), 31 min. Les Blank
*Zelig* (1983), 79 min. Woody Allen
*Zerda's Children* (1978), 51 min. Jorge Preloran
*Živeli: Medicine for the Heart* (1987), 50 min. Les Blank and Andrei Simic
*Zulay, Facing the Twenty-first Century* (1993), 108 min. Zulay Saravino, Jorge and Mabel Preloran

# Notes

## 1. Folklore, Film, and Video

1. The term *film*, as used in this work, refers to motion picture photography or the actual celluloid rolls of film used in such photography. Individual photographs will always be called *stills* or *still photography*, and the process used to create them will be referred to as *still photography*. I use the term *video* to encompass all formats, including but not limited to VHS, Beta, 8mm, Hi-8mm, S-VHS, and Beta SP.

2. The first films were used for photographic records. Early filmmakers in the biological sciences then began to analyze features of human motion and interaction (which have also been studied by folklorists). Some examined gesture and facial expressions. Others compared memory with repertoire and used their data for cross-cultural behavior pattern analyses. Documentary filmmakers who initially sought to create short records of interesting phenomena eventually constructed feature-length films that usually focused on a small group of people, their activities, and their concerns.

3. See, for example, Edward Curtis's *In the Land of the War Canoes: Kwakiutl Indian Life on the Northwest Coast* (1914).

4. The documentary genre may be classified in several ways to include travelogues, newsreels, training films, and industrial films, films whose purpose is to analyze social issues, and films whose goal is to present ethnographic data. Although all of these films are "documents" that can provide insights into human behavior (as, indeed, can the fiction film), the latter two are those generally regarded as constituting a type of factual film most suited to the "documentary" idiom and most closely studied by film historians and social scientists.

5. As film historian Paul Rotha notes, filmmaking that demands analysis—be it political, social, or economic—is essential for effective documentary style. The filmmaker can and should inform people about various aspects of their existence within the framework of society. For Rotha, "The plain descriptive pictures of everyday life (travel pictures, nature films, educationals and newsreels) . . . fall short of documentary requirements. . . . The creative dramatization of actuality and the expression of social analysis . . . are the first demand of the documentary method" (1959:357-58).

6. For example, Merian C. Cooper and Ernest Beaumont Schoedsack, well known for the classic Hollywood film *King Kong* (1933), followed the Flaherty tradition in their first film, *Grass* (1925), by portraying the hardship of the semiannual trek made over mountains and rivers by 50,000 Bakhtiari tribesmen of central Persia in search of

grazing land for their herds. *Grass* appealed to the viewers' increasing interest in remote places. In 1927, Cooper and Schoedsack re-created their formula with *Chang*, a view of family life that focused on the terrors of coexisting with ferocious beasts in the jungles of Siam.

7. See Louis D. Giannetti (1976:244) for an analysis of Vertov's editing and restructuring of chaos.

8. Examples include *Housing Problems* (1935), directed by Edgar Anstey and Arthur Elton (made for the British Commerical Gas Association); *North Sea* (1938), directed by Harry Watt; *BBC: The Voice of Britain* (1934–35), directed by Stuart Legg; *Coal Face* (1936) by Alberto Cavalcanti; *Enough to Eat* (1936), directed by Anstey for the Gas, Light, and Coke Company of London; and *Night Mail* (1936), directed by Basil Wright and Harry Watt.

9. The ideals and methodology of the cinéma vérité documentarians of the 1960s were preshadowed by the work of Grierson's film crews, who endeavored to capture unstaged situations with synchronous sound to reveal social problems. In 1939, Grierson founded the National Film Board of Canada and thus affected the development of documentary in Canada. Despite this move, Grierson's influence continued to be manifested by the British filmmakers and producers who succeeded him.

10. Cinéma vérité was made possible by the invention of a lightweight portable camera (the prototype of which had been developed for the armed services during World War II), matched with a tape recorder that maintained sound in synchronization with the moving image. Casting off the bulky cameras that motion picture studios relied on for sound movies, documentary filmmakers could now shoot an event with a two-person crew. Interference in the scene was minimized. (The development of the zoom or telephoto lens meant the cameraperson could stand back from the action while capturing close-ups.) Film magazines expanded from 100 to 400 feet, and camera takes as long as ten minutes in length gave a sense of being on the scene in "real time" as opposed to camera time. Filmmakers demanded a film stock that was more sensitive to light and hence "faster" in that the cameraperson could shoot without artificial light, using available lighting instead.

11. Interspersed with concert footage, *Spinal Tap* presents itself as the documentary of a "real" band. The parody has continued; the band released an album after the film was completed and has its own web page.

12. *Itam Hakim, Hopiit* won a Gold Hugo award at the 1984 Chicago International Film Festival.

13. Edward W. Said looks at a similar representation of the Orient as seen by the West in *Orientalism* (1978). Said observes the "Occident" studying the "Orient" as exotic, mysterious, and Other, an idea that reinforces political dominance. By contrast, Orientalism defines the West. Like anthropology, it uses an arbitrary geography to separate "us" from "them." Intellectuals from Aeschylus to Kissinger have perpetuated the abstract notion of the Orient as a complementary opposite.

14. Fiction films communicate information about the cultural background of the filmmaker and contain information about the culture being filmed. The members of the audience then interpret the scenes and the filmmaker's method of structuring such scenes according to their own cultural coding. Views internalize the filmmaker's ideas and blend them with their own perceptions. Films made by Americans may communicate ideas to Americans that they do not communicate to non-Americans. While

Americans may recognize the filmmaker's intent and the nuances in the film, foreign audiences may interpret the film differently. "Hollywood" films thus not only communicate something to us but they also say something about us. Although fictional, such films relate actual modes of behavior. In a like fashion, foreign "fiction" filmmakers communicate their behavioral and cultural perceptions to us. Fictional films may thus be "ethnographic" in certain respects.

15. At the time *Dead Birds* was shot (1961), the area was known as Netherlands New Guinea.

16. As with Mead and Bateson, Gardner's work was part of a larger anthropological research project. The Dutch government proposed that Gardner organize a scholarly team to conduct research in the highlands of central New Guinea (currently Indonesia). Seven scholars were selected to make up the Harvard Peabody Expedition: filmmaker/anthropologist Robert Gardner, still photographer and sound recordist Michael Rockefeller, sociologist Jan Broekhuijse, author and naturalist/historian Peter Matthiessen, still photographer Samuel Putnam, still photographer Eliot Elisofon, and anthropologist Karl Heider. As a result of the expedition, a book, a monograph, and a dissertation were written on the Dani, a photographic ethnography was published, and *Dead Birds* was produced.

Materials available include Peter Matthiessen, *Under the Mountain Wall: A Chronicle of Two Seasons in the Stone Age;* Robert Gardner and Karl G. Heider, *Gardens of War: Life and Death in the New Guinea Stone Age;* J. Th. Broekhuijse, *De Wiligaman-Dani: Een Cultural-Anthropologische Studie over Religie en Oorlogvoering in de Baliem-Vallei;* and Karl G. Heider, *The Dugum Dani: A Papuan Culture in the Highlands of West New Guinea.* In addition, Karl Heider produced a study guide module that included an ethnographic profile of the Dani, a statement by Gardner on the making of the film, and an annotated shot-by-shot analysis with Gardner's narration printed vertically alongside the shot descriptions (Heider 1972).

17. Karl Heider has somewhat rectified the problem of presenting the Dani solely as warriors by producing two films shot in 1963, two years after *Dead Birds. Dani Houses* (1974), a sixteen-minute film, shows the construction of two types of dwellings. *Dani Sweet Potatoes* (1974), a nineteen-minute film, treats the agricultural practice from planting to meal preparation. Also included are some sequences on rearing children.

18. Ruby (1991:14) makes a similar comment about Gardner's exoticizing the people in *Forest of Bliss* in the name of art. He notes that Gardner's North American Yankee Brahmin culture is a "tribe" that most of us would find exotic.

19. The term *participatory camera* was first used by filmmaker and film analyst Luc de Heusch to refer to Flaherty's work.

20. Many scholars have discussed *Les Mâitres Fous.* See, for example, Heider 1976; de Brigard 1975; de Heusch 1962; Muller 1971; and Nichols 1991.

21. Marcus Banks (1992:124) addresses this issue in reference to why certain films are considered ethnographic.

22. See Paul Stoller's discussion of Rouch for a further development of this idea (1992).

23. Bill Nichols (1991) goes so far as to compare ethnographic films to pornographic films, saying that they objectify and degrade the Other and are no longer tenable.

## 2. The Folkloric Film

1. In the area of folklore per se, the first call for film reviews in the *Journal of American Folklore* does not appear until 1974, and Carl Fleischhauer's review of the Appalshop films marks the first discussion in that journal (vol. 87, no. 345). The next review does not appear until 1976 (vol. 89, no. 353). Despite this somewhat late acknowledgment of the importance of film, these reviews demonstrate the growing interest in film among folklorists during the 1970s when new theories about performance began to gain acceptance.

2. Definitions of folklore vary. Twenty-one definitions appear in the *Funk and Wagnalls Standard Dictionary of Folklore, Mythology, and Legend* (Leach 1949-50:398-403). Alan Dundes defines folklore by listing the forms (or genres) that folklorists study (1965:1-3). For Barre Toelken, folklore comes "directly from dynamic interactions among human beings in communal-traditional performance contexts rather than through the more rigid lines and fossilized structures of technical instruction or bureaucratized education, or through the relatively stable channels of the classical traditions" (1979:28-29).

3. The opening and closing scenes are of the churchyard where Leadbelly is buried in Mooringsport, Louisiana. Each song performance is a separate scene. In the first, Leadbelly wears work clothes and is outdoors. In the second, he wears a suit and the background is unlit. The third scene shows him once again in work clothes but on a stage.

4. Film Images advertisement for "The Folklore Research Films of Peter and Toshi Seeger."

5. For a review of the five-film series, see David Evans, *Journal of American Folklore* 90 (1977):111-13.

6. Bess Lomax Hawes, taped interview, 2 November 1974. Hawes pointed out that *The Georgia Sea Island Singers* was originally entitled *Bright Star Shining in Glory,* but references have also been made to it as *Yonder Comes Day.* Hawes calls this "a minor historical detail which might be of some help to people who try to keep things unscrambled in the area of film. Dr. Carpenter took all the outs from this first film of the Sea Islanders singing religious material and slapped a title on it and put it in our A-V department simply to have some way to refer to it, and the title of that is *Yonder Comes Day.* But it is not a completed film; it's just the two chunks of their singing that we could not use in the final finished film. So every once and a while someone comes up and asks me about the film. They've heard of a film called *Yonder Comes the Day,* and it really isn't one. There've never been any other copies made of it or anything, just the workprint and some stuff left over."

7. Although other filmmakers such as Ron Finne, Craig Hinde, Lucyann Kerry, Pat Mire and Charles Bush, Barry Dornfeld, and the Appalshop film group have created folklore films, I have tried to select those who have had the greatest influence on the film movement in folklore. See Ron Finne, *Natural Timber Country* (1972), 53 min., color, distributed by Audiovisual Instruction, Oregon Division of Continuing Education; W. Craig Hinde, *The Birch Cane Builder* (1971), 23 min., color, distributed by ACI Media; W. Craig Hinde and Robert Davis, *Maple Sugar Farmer* (1972), 29 min., color, distributed by ACI Media; Lucyann Kerry, *Basket Builder* (1974), 12 min., color, dis-

tributed by Blue Ridge Films; Pat Mire and Charles Bush, *"Anything I Catch..." The Handfishing Story* (1990), 28 min., color, distributed by Attakapas Productions; and Barry Dornfeld and Maggie Holtzberg-Call, *Gandy Dancers* (1994). Dornfeld also served as cameraman for *A Singing Stream* (which is discussed here) and has collaborated on films with Tom Rankin and Jeff Titon.

Appalshop concentrates on the coalfields of the southern Appalachians. A brochure is available from the Appalachian Film Workshop, Whitesburg, Kentucky.

Many public-sector folklorists, including the Florida Folklife Council, have made excellent films with television production houses. See, for example, *Fishing All My Days: Florida Shrimping Traditions* (1986), by Peggy Bulgar and David Taylor, with WUFT-TV, Gainesville.

I have also omitted creators of 8mm films from the discussion in chapters 2 and 3 because of the limited distribution of such visuals. One of the most notable is Patricia Mastick Young's Super 8mm film *The Quiltmakers*, 17 min., color, distributed by the filmmaker, c/o Lourdes Regional Health Services, Paducah, Kentucky (or c/o Folklore and Mythology, UCLA). The film documents quiltmaking by Mormon women in Los Angeles.

I have, no doubt, left out films that others consider important. My method of analyzing films may easily be applied to any folklore film.

8. The two most famous practitioners of using film to analyze movement are Raymond Birdwhistell and Alan Lomax. Birdwhistell produced the film *Microcultural Incidents in Ten Zoos* and has detailed his approach to the study of gestures, facial expressions, and body shifts in two books, *Introduction to Kinesics* (1952) and *Kinesics and Context* (1970). He concentrates on the nonverbal aspects of interaction and uses film as a method for conducting microcultural analyses of patterns he finds repeated. Lomax has used film for choreometrics (see Lomax 1975). Defined as "dance as a measure of culture," choreometrics involves the construction of profiles of redundant patterns that exist in daily activities and that reinforce culture.

9. The textual nature of Hawes's film is most evident when compared with *Earl Collins* (1974), made by Steve Weiner of the University of Southern California. The film follows Collins to concerts and to a party where he performs. Whereas *Say, Old Man* is a situation staged for the camera, *Earl Collins* portrays the significance of Collins's music for him, his audiences, and his fellow musicians.

10. A companion book, *Hearts and Hands: The Influence of Women and Quilts on American Society* (Ferrero, Hedges, and Silber 1987), contains photographs, an extensive bibliography, and additional materials.

11. See, for example, Abrahams (1970:50, 60-62) and Jacobs, Landau, and Pell (1971).

12. See William Bascom (1954) for a discussion of some of the ways in which folklore functions.

13. Les Blank's Flower Films is in El Cerrito, California, next to Berkeley.

14. Marjorie Hunt (1986) has discussed the stone carvers of the Washington Cathedral in *Folklife Annual 1985*. Hunt has also looked at occupational folklore elsewhere in Washington, D.C. She documents the narratives and traditions of "ordinary" people in her video *Workers at the White House* (1994), based on the 1992 Festival of American Folklife presented by the Smithsonian Institution.

15. Despite the decline of the Shakers, they remain a popular topic. Filmmaker Ken Burns used much of the same material for his own version, *The Shakers: Hearts to God, Hands to Work* (1985).

16. The other films are *The Shakers, Born for Hard Luck: Peg Leg Sam Jackson*, and *Being a Joines: A Life in the Brushy Mountains*.

## 3. Documentation

1. To alleviate this problem and to suggest how folk art is really a process and an act of communication, Michael Owen Jones (1995) has suggested the term *material behavior*.

2. Jan Brunvand has used the term *modern urban legend* in four popular books to refer to tales such as these (1981, 1984, 1986, 1989). Other possible terms for these tales are *contemporary legend, proto-legend, urban belief tale, rumor,* and *legend* (see Hand 1971). *Ghost tale* is yet another such term. Because of the shifting nature of "contemporary" (the "vanishing hitchhiker" was contemporary when she rode off in a horse and buggy, but that was many years ago) and urban (many of the tales have nothing to do with the city per se), I prefer the unadorned term *legend.* The tales in the film also belong to the genre of legend that specifically plays upon horror for intensity; thus, *horror tales* is another way to describe the stories. *Ghost tales* is limiting because monsters and supernatural beings other than ghosts appear as the central characters in many of the tales.

3. Mailed response from Les Blank, 14 February 1975.

4. On request, the Center for Southern Folklore will provide a film transcript for *Ray Lum.* It employs columns of sound-over and sync dialogue with stills from the film. An essay on aspects of Lum's storytelling is also available. For a detailed discussion of Lum's storytelling, see *"You Live and Learn, Then You Die and Forget It All": Ray Lum's Tales of Horses, Mules, and Men* (Ferris 1992).

5. Taped interview with Jorge Preloran, 23 August 1976.

6. A journey is used to illustrate the economic hardship and environmental isolation of the protagonist in *Imaginero* and *Cochengo Miranda*. A journey is also a theme in *Zerda's Children*. While hitchhiking to the school party, Zerda is picked up by the governor, but he returns on foot, four leagues. Preloran's depiction of the journey, as with all of these filmic journeys, is unusual. In Zerda's journey, no car appears. The sound of a car approaching and stopping combines with a pan down an empty road following the unseen car's arrival, wait, and departure. Television coverage of the party serves to document Zerda's presence, and a shot of the empty road indicates his walk home.

Throughout the film, radio melodramas dominate as the family gathers to eat. Because of the radio, Zerda and his children are very much aware of life outside the brush. As he did in *Valle Fertil* and *Cochengo Miranda*, Preloran shows how radio supplies isolated families with a knowledge of urban events.

7. By cutting from one shot to another with the intervening action that occurred between shots omitted, the film editor creates a "jump." Often, filmmakers will edit together a long shot, a medium shot, and a close-up to preserve continuity in action. With jump cutting, we lose some of the data. As Metke cuts down a tree with a chainsaw, for example, we do not see the whole process because of the filmmaker's editing technique.

8. Despite the film's success, Luther Metke was not pleased with the results. After the film's release, Metke became a local celebrity and the Eugene *Register Guard* interviewed him several times. He stated that parts of the film that he thought most important—primarily his comments about timber management and forest preservation in the Northwest—were left on the cutting room floor. As is sometimes the case in filmmaking (and fieldwork), the filmmakers (or researchers) and their subjects may have different "visions" of what is significant.

9. The shared human identity that exists between fieldworkers and those they study has been explored by Georges and Jones (1980).

## 4. A Search for Self

1. In academic writing it has become de rigueur to cite others briefly to support the ideas presented. Academicians do not generally quote others at length except in a strict interview format. I shall break from this tradition for this chapter and the following ones, and blend the voices of filmmakers addressing similar topics.

2. Most folklorists would agree on a basic definition of folklore, yet each might have a different emphasis. Cohen's recognition of this problem is echoed by the existence of so many scholarly as well as amateur definitions (see chap. 2, note 2). See also Robert Georges and Michael Owen Jones for a definition based on behavior rather than genre in *Folkloristics: An Introduction* (1995:1). These differing definitions, although complementary, add to non-folklorists' common problem with defining folklore.

3. John Cohen, taped interview, Los Angeles, 22 February 1992. All subsequent comments by Cohen are taken from the transcription of the tape, unless otherwise noted. Quoted material cited as 1975 is taken from a communication by personal letter, 4 August 1975.

4. Judy Peiser, taped interview at the American Folklore Society meeting, Jacksonville, Florida, 10 October 1992. All subsequent quotations are taken from this interview unless otherwise noted. Remarks from an interview conducted on 25 October 1975 will be so noted as 1975.

5. Bill Ferris, taped interview at the American Folklore Society Meeting, Portland, Oregon, 4 November 1974. Subsequent comments are taken from the transcription of this tape.

6. Les Blank, taped interview, 22 March 1993, at Flower Films, El Cerrito, California. All subsequent comments are from the transcriptions of this interview unless otherwise noted. Blank's comments from a taped mailed response, 14 February 1975, will be noted as 1975 in the text.

7. Bess Lomax Hawes, taped interview at the American Folklore Society meeting, Portland, Oregon, 2 November 1974. Subsequent comments are taken from the transcription of this tape.

8. Jorge Preloran, taped classroom discussion and taped interviews, Eugene, Oregon, March 1992. All subsequent remarks are from the transcription of these tapes, unless otherwise noted. Remarks from an interview conducted 23 August 1976 are noted as 1976.

9. Ken Thigpen, taped interview at the American Folklore Society Meeting, Jacksonville, Florida, 18 October 1992. Further comments are from the transcription of the tape.

10. Tom Davenport, taped interview, 17 May 1993, at Davenport Films, Delaplane, Virginia. Subsequent comments are from the transcription of the tape.

11. Paul Wagner, taped interview, 15 May 1993, at American Focus Films, Charlottesville, Virginia. Further remarks are from the transcription of this tape.

12. Carl Fleischhauer, taped interview, at the American Folklore Society Meeting, Portland, Oregon, 2 November 1974. Subsequent comments are from the transcription of the tape.

13. Pat Ferrero, taped interview, 22 March 1993, at Ferrero Films, San Francisco. Further remarks are from the tape transcription.

14. Michael Owen Jones has also addressed the issue of folk versus "high" art in *Exploring Folk Art: Twenty Years of Thought on Craft, Work, and Aesthetics* (1987). Most folklorists ignore art that doesn't neatly fit their definition rather than try to explain what folk art is or isn't. Art that is considered unusual and somewhat crude, created by such idiosyncratic artists as Grandma Moses or Watts tower builder Simon Rodía, often becomes "folk" even though the art has little connection to tradition. Sometimes a distinction is made, and such idiosyncratic art is labeled "outsider" art, a term some accept as synonymous with "folk." Art that is learned by those who are not part of the group that "normally" creates it (i.e., occupational groups, families) may be imitative of that art. When learned through apprenticeships, such art will represent folk art if it replicates and continues a tradition. For definitions of folk art, see, for example, Simon J. Bronner, *Grasping Things: Folk Material Culture and Mass Society in America* (1986); Henry Glassie, *The Spirit of Folk Art* (1989); Suzi Jones, *Oregon Folklore* (1977); and John Vlach and Simon J. Bronner, eds., *Folk Art and Art Worlds: Essays Drawn from the Washington Meeting on Folk Art* (1986). See also Sherman, *Chainsaw Sculptor: The Art of J. Chester "Skip" Armstrong* (1995), for a discussion of Armstrong's work as both folk and fine art and how definitions change according to various contexts. See also Michael D. Hall, *Stereoscopic Perspective: Reflections on American Fine and Folk Art* (1987).

15. Viewer response has been addressed. See, for example, "Part Two: Image, Audience and Aesthetics," in Crawford and Turton (1992:83-161). The study of viewer reactions and their variance from the filmmaker's intention is paralleled in literature by reader-response theory, which assumes that the text is different for each reader and may have little resemblance to that which the author meant. See, for example, Stanley Fish 1980; Janice Radway 1984; and Jane Tompkins 1980.

16. Dan Patterson, taped interview, 17 October 1992, at the American Folklore Society meeting, Jacksonville, Florida. All further remarks are from the tape transcription. My gratitude to Dan.

17. I was pleased to have my film, *Kathleen Ware, Quiltmaker,* also included in the Oakland quilt exhibit.

18. Filmmaker Peter Biella, who has worked with numerous cultural specialists, including folklorist Karen Lux for the film *God's Mother Is the Morning Star* (1990), discusses some of the unanticipated difficulties encountered by academics and filmmakers who choose to collaborate. His "Guideline for Collaboration" details potential conflicts and how to overcome them (1989).

## 5. Projecting the Self

1. Jay Ruby has pointed out that "the camera creates a photographic realism re-

flecting the culturally constructed reality of the picture-taker and is not a device that can somehow transcend the photographer's cultural limitations" (1982b:125).

2. Kirsten Hastrup (1992) argues for the use of text over photography in her account of the problems she had documenting a ram exhibition in Iceland. A male ritual exuded sexual tension which her camera could not capture.

## 6. Structure Shifts and Style

1. The films Blank made for or with others reflect their interests rather than Blank's. Perhaps that is why they have less appeal. They are competently done, but they lack the immediacy present in his other work.

2. Tom Rankin, who was a cameraman for *A Singing Stream,* recalls the film team's need to respond quickly when the unexpected occurs (1989). While shooting the reunion church service, the film crew took a break outside. The emotional tenor of the service swelled, and the film team quickly returned to the sanctuary to shoot what later would become a powerful scene in the film.

3. Many peoples believe that a camera captures one's soul. Furthermore, Ferrero might have been referring to the Hopi reaction concerning fieldwork. The Hopi have been studied excessively by anthropologists for decades.

4. This knowledge of another audience is not limited to those who appear in folklore film (and who generally have access to the media), but applies equally to those in ethnodocumentary film. David MacDougall addresses the issue of the influence of the subjects in "Whose Story Is It?" (1994). Annette B. Weiner realized that the Trobriand Islanders whom she was filming had "not only appropriated the filmmakers' presence but how long they had adapted capitalistic ideologies and technologies to their own advantages" (1994:57). Further, the phrasing of their answers to questions indicated their sophisticated awareness of how to meet the demands of the camera and editing.

5. Bill Goldsmith and I have discussed this idea of experience with reference to his work on celebration.

6. For these notions regarding direct observations versus film observations, I am indebted to communications with Robert A. Georges.

## 7. Visions of Ourselves

1. Many filmmakers and film theorists have dismissed documentary video because of its most common means of presentation: television. The assumption is that television is unscrupulous. Consequently, television documentaries and, by extension, video have no place in serious discourse.

2. For example, Frankfurt scholar Theodor Adorno's main criticism is that culture has become commodified. Likewise, for Fredric Jameson, culture is "the very element of consumer society itself" (1990:22); the only "authentic cultural production" is that which issues from marginal pockets of society not yet affected by the market (1990:23). In many respects, these pockets might be called folk. Yet Walter Benjamin believed that even though mass culture destroyed the aura of folk culture by mechanically reproducing folk art, it also made such art available to many and had the potential to produce resistant possibilities (1968). Thus such mechanical art was dialectical; it did damage

to the traditional, yet had the potential to provide insight into social relations because it could be used democratically, not just by capitalists.

3. Folklorists recognize that viewers comprise diverse folk groups and identify themselves in many ways. The notion of one immense audience, all responding to television in a similar way, is fatuous (Nielsen ratings notwithstanding). Critics tell us that television may produce lethargic, passive consumers. It runs counter to that movie theater "audience breathing together" of which Cohen spoke. On the other hand, television may also create a different kind of audience, an associative one in which people interact. Unlike film, its manner of communicating is both intimate and close up.

4. Van Sant continued to play with documentary in *To Die For* (1995): the main character films a documentary, believes she is only "alive" when appearing on television, addresses the camera as if she were being interviewed, and records her own story.

# References

Abrahams, Roger D. 1968. Introductory Remarks to a Rhetorical Theory of Folklore. *Journal of American Folklore* 81:143-58.

—————. 1976. The Complex Relations of Simple Forms. *Folklore Genres,* ed. Dan Ben-Amos, 193-214. Austin, Tex.: Publications of the American Folklore Society, Bibliographical and Special Series 26. First published in *Genre* 2 (1969):104-28.

—————. 1970. *Positively Black.* Englewood Cliffs, N.J.: Prentice-Hall.

—————. 1971. Personal Power and Social Restraint in the Definition of Folklore. *Journal of American Folklore* 84:16-30.

Anderson, Jervis. 1972. *A. Philip Randolph: A Biographical Portrait.* New York: Harcourt Brace Jovanovich.

Arnold, James. 1979. The Present State of the Documentary. 1968. In *The Documentary Tradition,* 2d ed., ed. Lewis Jacobs, 483-91. New York: W.W. Norton.

Asch, Timothy. 1972. Making Ethnographic Films for Teaching and Research. *Program in Ethnographic Film Newsletter* 3:6-10.

—————. 1975. Using Film in Teaching Anthropology: One Pedagogical Approach. In *Principles of Visual Anthropology,* ed. Paul Hockings, 385-420. The Hague: Mouton.

—————. 1988. Collaboration in Ethnographic Filmmaking: A Personal View. In *Anthropological Filmmaking,* ed. Jack R. Rollwagen, 1-29. Chur: Harwood Academic.

Austin, J. L. 1962. *How to Do Things with Words.* Cambridge: Harvard University Press.

Babcock, Barbara. 1980. Reflexivity: Definitions and Discriminations. *Semiotica* 30: 1-14.

Balikci, Asen. 1970. *The Netsilik Eskimo.* Garden City, N.Y.: Natural History Press for the American Museum of Natural History.

—————. 1975. Reconstructing Cultures on Film. In *Principles of Visual Anthropology,* ed. Paul Hockings, 191-200. The Hague: Mouton.

Banks, Marcus. 1992. Which Films Are the Ethnographic Films? In *Film as Ethnography,* ed. Peter Ian Crawford and David Turton, 116-29. Manchester: Manchester University Press.

Barsam, Richard. 1988. *The Vision of Robert Flaherty: The Artist as Myth and Filmmaker.* Bloomington: Indiana University Press.

Bascom, William R. 1954. Four Functions of Folklore. *Journal of American Folklore* 67:333-49.

Bateson, Gregory, and Margaret Mead. 1942. *Balinese Character: A Photographic Analysis.* New York: Academy of Sciences.

Bauman, Richard. 1977. *Verbal Art as Performance.* Prospect Heights, Ill.: Waveland Press.

———. 1986. *Story, Performance, and Event: Contextual Studies of Oral Narrative.* Cambridge Studies in Oral and Literate Culture 10. Cambridge: Cambridge University Press.

Bausinger, Hermann. 1990. *Folk Culture in a World of Technology.* Translated by Elke Dettmer. 1961. Reprint, Bloomington: Indiana University Press.

Ben-Amos, Dan. 1969. Analytical Categories and Ethnic Genres. *Genre* 2:275-301.

———. 1971. Toward a Definition of Folklore in Context. *Journal of American Folklore* 84:3-15.

———. 1975. *Sweet Words: Storytelling Events in Benin.* Philadelphia: Institute for the Study of Human Issues.

———. 1993. "Context" in Context. *Western Folklore* 52:209-26.

Benjamin, Walter. 1968. The Work of Art in the Age of Mechanical Reproduction. In *Illuminations,* ed. Hannah Arendt, 219-53. New York: Harcourt, Brace, and World.

Biella, Peter. 1989. Trouble Shooting: Overcoming Problems of Colloboration in Film Production. *New York Folklore* 15:47-67.

Birdwhistell, Ray L. 1952. *Introduction to Kinesics.* Louisville, Ky.: University of Louisville Press.

———. 1970. *Kinesics and Context: Essays on Body Motion Communication.* Philadelphia: University of Pennsylvania Press.

Blank, Les. 1975. Taped mailed responses to a letter. 14 February.

———. 1993. Taped interview. 22 March. El Cerrito, Calif.

Blumenreich, Beth, and Bari Polansky. 1974. Re-evaluating the Concept of Group: ICEN as an Alternative. *Folklore Forum,* Bibliographic and Special Series 12: 12-18.

Boas, Franz. 1916. *Tsimshian Mythology.* Thirty-first Annual Report of the Bureau of American Ethnology. Washington: Government Printing Office.

———. 1935. *Kwakiutl Culture as Reflected in Mythology.* New York: Publications of the American Folklore Society, Memoir Series 28.

———. 1940. *Race, Language, and Culture.* New York: Macmillan.

Bogaart, Nico C.R. 1983. Perceptual Ethics. In *Methodology in Anthropological Filmmaking,* ed. Nico C.R. Bogaart and Henk W.E.R. Ketelaar, 11-23. Papers of the International Union of Anthropological and Ethnological Sciences Intercongress, Amsterdam 1981. Göttingen: Herodot.

Brazeal, Brailsford. 1946. *The Brotherhood of Sleeping Car Porters.* New York: Harper and Brothers.

Broekhuijse, J.Th. 1967. *De Wiligaman-Dani: Een Cultural-Anthropologische Studie over Religie en Oorlogvoering in de Baliem-Vallei.* Tilburg: H. Gianotten.

Bronner, Simon. 1986. *Grasping Things: Folk Material Culture and Mass Society in America.* Lexington: University Press of Kentucky.

Brunvand, Jan Harold. 1981. *The Vanishing Hitchhiker: American Urban Legends and Their Meanings.* New York: W.W. Norton.

————. 1984. *The Choking Doberman and Other "New" Urban Legends.* New York: W.W. Norton.

————. 1986. *The Mexican Pet: More "New" Urban Legends and Some Old Favorites.* New York: W.W. Norton.

————. 1989. *Curses Broiled Again! The Hottest Urban Legends Going.* New York: W.W. Norton.

Buchan, David. 1985. Performance Contexts in Historical Perspectives. *New York Folklore* 11:61-78.

Calder-Marshall, Arthur. 1963. *The Innocent Eye: The Life of Robert J. Flaherty.* London: W. H. Allen.

Camper, Fred. 1986. Some Notes on the Home Movie. *Journal of Film and Video* 38: 9-14.

Carpenter, Edmund. 1972. *Oh, What a Blow That Phantom Gave Me!* New York: Holt, Rinehart and Winston.

Chagnon, Napoleon. 1968. *Yanomamö: The Fierce People.* New York: Holt, Rinehart and Winston.

Chalfen, Richard. 1975. Cinéma Naiveté: A Study of Home Moviemaking as Visual Communication. *Studies in the Anthropology of Visual Communication* 2:87-103.

————. 1982. Home Movies as Cultural Documents. In *Film/Culture: Explorations of Cinema in Its Social Context,* ed. Sari Thomas, 126-38. Metuchen, N.J.: Scarecrow Press.

Clifford, James, and George E. Marcus, eds. 1986. *Writing Culture: The Poetics and Politics of Ethnography.* Berkeley: University of California Press.

Cohen, John. 1975. Personal letter. 4 August.

————. 1987. Among the Q'eros: Notes from a Filmmaker. In *Folklife Annual 1986,* ed. Alan Jabbour and James Hardin, 22-41. Washington: Library of Congress.

————. 1990. Musical Documents. *Visual Anthropology* 3:457-78.

————. 1992. Taped interview. 22 February. VITAS Film Festival, Los Angeles.

Collier, John Jr. 1986. *Visual Anthropology: Photography as a Research Method.* Revised and expanded with Malcolm Collier. Albuquerque: University of New Mexico Press.

Coleman, Edwin L. 1982. "Yassah, Right This Way": Recurring Themes in the Oral Tradition of Porters. Paper presented at the American Folklore Society meeting, Minneapolis.

Connor, Linda H. 1988. Third Eye: Some Reflections on Colloboration for Ethnographic Film. In *Anthropological Filmmaking,* ed. Jack R. Rollwagen, 97-110. Chur: Harwood Academic.

Connor, Linda H., and Patsy Asch and Timothy Asch. 1986. *Jero Tapakan: Balinese Healer.* New York: Cambridge University Press.

Crawford, Peter Ian. 1992. Film as Discourse: The Invention of Anthropological Realities. In Peter Ian Crawford and David Turton, *Film as Ethnography,* 66-82. Manchester: Manchester University Press.

Crawford, Peter Ian, and David Turton. 1992. *Film as Ethnography.* Manchester: Manchester University Press.

Crowdus, Gary. 1979. Harlan County, U.S.A. 1977. In *The Documentary Tradition,* 2d ed., ed. Lewis Jacobs, 563-68. New York: W. W. Norton.

Crowley, Dan. 1966. *I Could Talk Old-Story Good: Creativity in Bahamian Folklore.* Folklore Studies 17. Berkeley: University of California Press.

Davenport, Tom. 1993. Taped interview. 17 May. Delaplane, Va.

De Atley, Richard. 1990. TV Viewers Enjoy Watching Themselves. *Register-Guard,* March 30, 11E. Eugene, Ore.

de Brigard, Emilie Rahman. 1975. The History of Ethnographic Film. In *Principles of Visual Anthropology,* ed. Paul Hockings, 13-43. The Hague: Mouton.

de Heusch, Luc. 1962. *The Cinema and Social Science: A Survey of Ethnographic and Sociological Films.* Paris: UNESCO.

Dégh, Linda. 1969. *Folktales and Society: Story-Telling in a Hungarian Peasant Community.* Trans. Emily M. Schossberger. Bloomington: Indiana University Press.

Devereaux, Leslie. 1995. Experience, Re-presentation, and Film. In *Fields of Vision: Essays in Film Studies, Visual Anthropology, and Photography,* ed. Leslie Devereaux and Roger Hillman, 56-73. Berkeley: University of California Press.

Dorson, Richard M. 1952. *Bloodstoppers and Bearwalkers: Folk Traditions of the Upper Peninsula.* Cambridge: Harvard University Press.

———. 1964. *Buying the Wind: Regional Folklore in the United States.* Chicago: University of Chicago Press.

———, ed. 1972a. *Folklore and Folklife: An Introduction.* Chicago: University of Chicago Press.

———. 1972b. History of the Elite and History of the Folk. In *Folklore: Selected Essays,* ed. Richard M. Dorson, 225-59. Bloomington: Indiana University Press.

———. 1972c. Introduction: Concepts of Folklore and Folklife Studies. In *Folklore and Folklife: An Introduction,* ed. Richard M. Dorson, 1-50. Chicago: University of Chicago Press.

———. 1972d. The Use of Printed Sources. In *Folklore and Folklife: An Introduction,* ed. Richard M. Dorson, 465-77. Chicago: University of Chicago Press.

———. 1981. *Land of the Millrats.* Cambridge: Harvard University Press.

———. 1983. Methods of Research. In *Handbook of American Folklore,* ed. Richard M. Dorson, 359-61. Bloomington: Indiana University Press.

Dundes, Alan. 1964. Texture, Text, and Context. *Southern Folklore Quarterly* 28:251-65.

———. 1965. What is Folklore? In *The Study of Folklore,* ed. Alan Dundes, 1-3. Englewood Cliffs, N.J.: Prentice-Hall.

Erens, Patricia. 1986. Home Movies in Commercial Narrative Film. *Journal of Film and Video* 38:99-101.

———. 1988. Women's Documentary Filmmaking: The Personal is Political. In *New Challenges for Documentary,* ed. Alan Rosenthal, 554-65. Berkeley: University of California Press.

Evans, David. 1977. Folk Music Film Review. *Journal of American Folklore* 90:111-13.

Ferrero, Pat, and Elaine Hedges and Julie Silber. 1987. *Hearts and Hands: The Influence of Women and Quilts on American Society.* San Francisco: Quilt Digest Press.

———. 1993. Taped interview. 22 March. San Francisco.

Ferris, William R. 1974. Taped interview. 4 November. American Folklore Society meeting, Portland, Ore.

————. 1983. Vision in Afro-American Folk Art: The Sculpture of James Thomas. In *Afro-American Folk Art and Crafts*, ed. William Ferris, 111-28. Jackson: University Press of Mississippi. Originally published in *Journal of American Folklore* 88 (1975): 115-31.

————. 1992. *"You Live and Learn, Then You Die and Forget It All": Ray Lum's Tales of Horses, Mules, and Men*. New York: Doubleday/Anchor Books.

Fish, Stanley. 1980. *Is There a Text in This Class?* Cambridge: Harvard University Press.

Flaherty, Robert. 1950. Robert Flaherty Talking. In *Cinema 50*, ed. Roger Manvell. London: Pelican.

————. 1979. Filming Real People. 1934. Reprinted in *The Documentary Tradition*, 2d ed., ed. Lewis Jacobs, 97-99. New York: W.W. Norton.

Fleischhauer, Carl. 1974a. A Short Essay to Accompany the Film *How to Make Sorghum Molasses*. Morgantown: Office of Radio, Television, and Motion Pictures, West Virginia University.

————. 1974b. Taped interview. 2 November. American Folklore Society meeting, Portland, Ore.

Freyer, Ellen. 1979. *Chronicle of a Summer*—Ten Years After. 1971. Reprinted in *The Documentary Tradition*, 2d ed., ed. Lewis Jacobs, 437-43. New York: W.W. Norton.

Gabriel, Teshome H. 1985. Towards a Critical Theory of Third World Film. In *Third World Affairs 1985*, 355-69.

————. 1988. Thoughts on Nomadic Aesthetics and the Black Independent Cinema: Traces of a Journey. In *Blackframes: Critical Perspectives on Black Independent Cinema*, ed. Mbye B. Cham and Claire Andrade-Watkins, 62-79. Cambridge: MIT Press.

————. 1989. Third Cinema as Guardian of Popular Memory: Toward a Third Aesthetics. In *Questions of Third Cinema*, ed. Jim Pines and Paul Willemen, 53-64. London: British Film Institute.

Gardner, Robert. 1957. Anthropology and Film. *Daedalus* 86:344-52.

————. 1972. On the Making of *Dead Birds*. In *The Dani of West Irian: An Ethnographic Companion to the Film "Dead Birds,"* ed. Karl G. Heider, 31-35. New York: Warner Modular.

————. 1975. Guest lecture and film screening of *Rivers of Sand*. February 16. Bloomington, Indiana.

————. 1979. A Chronicle of the Human Experience: *Dead Birds*. In *The Documentary Tradition*, 2d ed., ed. Lewis Jacobs, 430-36. New York: W.W. Norton.

Gardner, Robert, and Karl G. Heider. 1968. *Gardens of War: Life and Death in the New Guinea Stone Age*. New York: Random House.

Geduld, Harry M. 1967. *Filmmakers on Film Making*. Bloomington: Indiana University Press.

Geertz, Clifford. 1988. *Works and Lives: The Anthropologist as Author*. Stanford: Stanford University Press.

Georges, Robert A. 1968. Epilogue. In *Studies in Mythology*, ed. Robert A. Georges, 222-34. Homewood, Ill.: Dorsey Press.

————. 1969. Toward an Understanding of Storytelling Events. *Journal of American Folklore* 82:313-28.

———. 1976. From Folktale Research to the Study of Narrating. *Studia Fennica* 20:159-68.

Georges, Robert A., and Michael Owen Jones. 1980. *People Studying People.* Berkeley: University of California Press.

———. 1995. *Folkloristics: An Introduction.* Bloomington: Indiana University Press.

Gerbrands, Adrian. 1957. *Art as an Element of Culture.* Leiden: Mededelingen van de Ryksmuseum voor Volkenkunde 12.

Giannetti, Louis D. 1976. *Understanding Movies.* 2d ed. Englewood Cliffs, N.J.: Prentice-Hall.

Ginsberg, Faye. 1991. Indigenous Media: Faustian Contract or Global Village? *Cultural Anthropology* 6:94-114.

Glassie, Henry. 1968. *Pattern in the Material Folk Culture of the Eastern United States.* Philadelphia: University of Pennsylvania Press.

———. 1989. *The Spirit of Folk Art: The Girard Collection at the Museum of International Folk Art.* New York: Abrams.

Goldschmidt, Walter. 1972. Ethnographic Film: Definition and Exegesis. *Program in Ethnographic Film Newsletter* 3:1-3.

Goldstein, Kenneth S. 1967. The Induced Natural Context: An Ethnographic Field Technique. In *Essays in the Verbal and Visual Arts,* ed. June Helm, 1-6. Seattle: University of Washington Press.

Goodman, Ellen. 1990. TV Wants Us to Believe It's Showing Us Real Life. Eugene, Ore., *Register-Guard,* 15 April, 3C.

Goodman, Steve. 1977. Video Tape. From the album *Say It in Private.* Los Angeles: Big Ears Music/Red Pajamas Music (ASCAP).

Grierson, John. 1979. Flaherty's Poetic *Moana.* 1926. Reprinted in *The Documentary Tradition,* 2d ed., ed. Lewis Jacobs, 25-26. New York: W.W. Norton.

Griffith, Richard. 1963. The Use of Films by the U.S. Armed Services. In *Documentary Film,* ed. Paul Rotha, Sinclair Road, and Richard Griffith, 344-45. London: Faber and Faber.

Hall, Michael D. 1987. *Stereoscopic Perspective: Reflections on American Fine and Folk Art.* Ann Arbor: UMI Research Press.

Hardy, Forsyth, ed. 1966. *Grierson on Documentary.* New York: Praeger.

Hastrup, Kirsten. 1992. Anthropological Visions: Some Notes on Visual and Textual Authority. In *Film as Ethnography,* ed. Peter Ian Crawford and David Turton, 8-25. Manchester: Manchester University Press.

Hawes, Bess Lomax. 1974. Taped interview. 2 November. American Folklore Society meeting, Portland, Ore.

Heath, Stephen, and Gillian Skirrow. 1986. An Interview with Raymond Williams. In *Studies in Entertainment: Critical Approaches to Mass Culture,* ed. Tania Modleski, 3-17. Bloomington: Indiana University Press.

Heider, Karl G. 1970. *The Dugam Dani: A Papuan Culture in the Highlands of West New Guinea.* Chicago: Aldine Press.

———, ed. 1972. *The Dani of West Irian: An Ethnographic Companion to the Film "Dead Birds."* New York: Warner Modular.

———. 1976. *Ethnographic Film.* Austin: University of Texas Press.

Hufford, Mary, Marjorie Hunt, and Steve Zeitlin. 1987. *The Grand Generation:*

*Memory, Mastery, Legacy.* Washington: Smithsonian Institution; Seattle: University of Washington Press.

Hunt, Marjorie. 1986. "Born into the Stone": Carvers at the Washington Cathedral. In *Folklife Annual 1985,* ed. Alan Jabbour and James Hardin, 120-41. Washington: American Folklife Center at the Library of Congress.

Husman, Rolf. 1983. Film and Fieldwork: Some Problems Reconsidered. In *Methodology in Anthropological Filmmaking,* ed. Nico C.R. Bogaart and Henk W.E.R. Ketelaar, 93-111. Papers of the International Union of Anthropological and Ethnological Sciences Intercongress, Amsterdam, 1981. Göttingen: Herodot.

Hymes, Dell. 1962. The Ethnography of Speaking. In *Anthropology and Human Behavior,* ed. T. Gladwin and W. C. Sturtevant, 13-53. Washington: Anthropological Society of Washington.

———. 1964. Introduction: Toward Ethnographies of Communication. In *The Ethnography of Communication,* ed. John Gumperz and Dell Hymes. *American Anthropologist* 66:1-34.

Jabbour, Alan. 1989. On the Values of American Folklorists. *Journal of American Folklore* 102:292-98.

Jackson, Bruce. 1972. *Wake Up Dead Man: Afro-American Worksongs from Texas Prisons.* Cambridge: Harvard University Press.

———. 1987. *Fieldwork.* Urbana: University of Illinois Press.

Jacobs, Lewis, ed. 1979. *The Documentary Tradition.* 2d ed. New York: W.W. Norton.

Jacobs, Paul, and Saul Landau and Eve Pell. 1971. *To Serve the Devil,* vol. 1, *Natives and Slaves.* New York: Random House.

Jameson, Fredric. 1990. *Signatures of the Visible.* New York: Routledge.

Jones, Michael Owen. 1987. *Exploring Folk Art: Twenty Years of Thought on Craft, Work, and Aesthetics.* Ann Arbor: UMI Research Press.

———. 1995. Why "Material Behavior"? Paper presented at the American Folklore Society meeting, Lafayette, La.

Jones, Suzi. 1977. *Oregon Folklore.* Eugene: Randall V. Mills Archives of Northwest Folklore, University of Oregon.

Kirshenblatt-Gimblett, Barbara. 1975. A Parable in Context: A Social Interactional Analysis of Storytelling Performance. In *Folklore: Performance and Communication,* ed. Dan Ben-Amos and Kenneth Goldstein, 105-30. The Hague: Mouton.

Kuhn, Thomas S. 1962. *The Structure of Scientific Revolutions.* Chicago: University of Chicago Press.

Leach, Maria, ed. 1949-50. *Funk and Wagnalls Standard Dictionary of Folklore, Mythology, and Legend.* 2 vols. New York: Funk and Wagnalls.

Lesage, Julia. 1978. The Political Aesthetics of the Feminist Documentary Film. *Quarterly Review of Film Studies* 3:507-23.

———. 1982. For Our Urgent Use: Films on Central America. *Jump-Cut* 27:15-20.

Lévi-Strauss, Claude. 1969. *The Raw and the Cooked.* Translated by John and Doreen Weightman. New York: Harper and Row. Originally published as *Le Cru et le Cruit.* Paris: Plon, 1964.

Levin, G. Roy. 1971. *Documentary Explorations: Fifteen Interviews with Filmmakers.* Garden City, N.Y.: Doubleday.

Loizos, Peter. 1992. Admissible Evidence? Film in Anthropology. In *Film as Ethnography*, ed. Peter Ian Crawford and David Turton, 50-65. Manchester: Manchester University Press.

Lomax, Alan. 1975. Audiovisual Tools for the Analysis of Culture Style. In *Principles of Visual Anthropology*, ed. Paul Hockings, 303-22. The Hague: Mouton.

Lux, Karen D. 1989. The Making of "God's Mother Is the Morning Star": A Case Study in Videotaping an Elderly Folk Artist. *New York Folklore* 15:33-46.

MacCann, Richard Dyer. 1979. World War II: Armed Forces Documentary. In *The Documentary Tradition*, 2d ed., ed. Lewis Jacobs, 213-23. New York: W. W. Norton.

Macdonald, Dwight. 1962. Mass Cult and MidCult. In *Against the American Grain*, 3-75. New York: Random House.

MacDougall, David. 1970. Prospects of the Ethnographic Film. *Film Quarterly* 23:16-30.

———. 1975. Beyond Observational Cinema. In *Principles of Visual Anthropology*, ed. Paul Hockings, 109-24. The Hague: Mouton.

———. 1994. Whose Story Is It? In *Visualizing Theory*, ed. Lucien Taylor, 27-36. New York: Routledge.

———. 1995. The Subjective Voice in Ethnographic Film. In *Fields of Vision: Essays in Film Studies, Visual Anthropology, and Photography*, ed. Leslie Devereaux and Roger Hillman, 217-55. Berkeley: University of California Press.

Malinowski, Bronislaw. 1961. *Argonauts of the Western Pacific*. 1922. Reprint, New York: Dutton.

———. 1954. Myth in Primitive Psychology. 1926. Reprinted in *Magic, Science and Religion and Other Essays*, ed. Robert Redfield, 93-148. Garden City, N.Y.: Anchor.

March, Richard. 1978. "How I Became the TV Man": Video Fieldwork in the Calumet Region. *Folklore Forum* 11:254-64.

Marshall, John, and Emilie de Brigard. 1975. Idea and Event in Urban Film. In *Principles of Visual Anthropology*, ed. Paul Hockings, 133-45. The Hague: Mouton.

Matthiessen, Peter. 1962. *Under the Mountain Wall: A Chronicle of Two Seasons in the Stone Age*. New York: Viking Press.

McCarty, Mark. 1975. McCarty's Law and How to Break It. In *Principles of Visual Anthropology*, ed. Paul Hockings, 45-51. The Hague: Mouton.

Mead, Margaret. 1972. *Blackberry Winter: My Earlier Years*. New York: William Morrow.

Mills, Nicolaus. 1977. Harlan County, U.S.A. *Dissent* 24:307.

Minh-ha, Trinh T. 1989. *Woman, Native, Other: Writing Postcoloniality and Feminism*. Bloomington: Indiana University Press.

Modleski, Tania. 1986. Introduction. In *Studies in Entertainment: Critical Approaches to Mass Culture*, ed. Tania Modleski, ix-xx. Theories of Contemporary Culture 7. Bloomington: Indiana University Press.

Moore, Rachel. 1994. Marketing Alterity. In *Visualizing Theory: Selected Essays from V.A.R., 1990-1994*, ed. Lucien Taylor, 126-39. New York: Routledge.

Morris, Peter. 1987. Re-thinking Grierson: The Ideology of John Grierson. *Dialogue: Canadian and Quebec Cinema* 3:21-56.

Morrison, Vonie, and Johnny Russell. 1985. Act Naturally. Sony Music (BMI).

Muller, Jean Claude. 1971. Review of *Les Maîtres Fous. American Anthropologist* 73:1471-73.

Mulvey, Laura. 1985. Visual Pleasure and Narrative Cinema. In *Movies and Methods,* vol. 2, ed. Bill Nichols, 303-15. Berkeley: University of California Press.

Myerhoff, Barbara, and Jay Ruby. 1982. Introduction to *A Crack in the Mirror: Reflexive Perspectives in Anthropology,* ed. Jay Ruby, 1-35. Philadelphia: University of Pennsylvania Press.

Nichols, Bill. 1991. *Representing Reality: Issues and Concepts in Documentary.* Bloomington: Indiana University Press.

———. 1994. *Blurred Boundaries: Questions of Meaning in Contemporary Culture.* Bloomington: Indiana University Press.

Paredes, Américo and Richard Bauman, eds. 1972. Austin, Tex.: Publications of the American Folklore Society, Bibliographic and Special Series 23. Originally published in *Toward New Perspectives in Folklore,* special issue of *Journal of American Folklore* 84 (1971).

Patterson, Daniel W. 1979. *The Shaker Spiritual.* Princeton: Princeton University Press.

———. 1988. "Going Up to Meet Him": Songs and Ceremonies of a Black Family's Ascent. In *Diversities of Gifts,* ed. Ruel Tyson Jr., James L. Peacock, and Daniel Patterson, 91-102. Urbana: University of Illinois Press.

———. 1992. Taped interview. 17 October. American Folklore Society meeting, Jacksonville, Fla.

Peiser, Judy. 1975. Taped interview. 25 October. American Folklore Society meeting, New Orleans, La.

———. 1992. Taped interview. 10 October. American Folklore Society meeting, Jacksonville, Fla.

Porter, James. 1976. Review of *Italian Folk Songs* and *The McPeake Family of Ireland. Journal of American Folklore* 189:519-20.

Preloran, Jorge. 1975. Documenting the Human Condition. In *Principles of Visual Anthropology,* ed. Paul Hockings, 103-7. The Hague: Mouton.

———. 1976. Taped interview. 23 August. Los Angeles.

Preloran, Jorge, and Mabel Preloran. 1992. Taped interview. 8 March. Eugene, Ore.

Propp, Vladimir. 1968. *Morphology of the Folktale.* Rev. ed. Translated by Laurence Scott. 1928. Reprint, Austin, Tex.: Publications of the American Folklore Society, Bibliographic and Special Series 9.

Rabinovitz, Lauren. 1986. College Course File: History of American Video Art. *Journal of Film and Video* 38:111-22.

Rabinow, Paul. 1977. *Reflections on Fieldwork in Morocco.* Berkeley: University of California Press.

Radway, Janice. 1984. *Reading the Romance: Women, Patriarchy, and Popular Literature.* Chapel Hill: University of North Carolina Press.

Rankin, Tom. 1989. The Folklorist as Filmmaker. In *Time and Temperature: A Centennial Publication of the American Folklore Society,* ed. Charles Camp, 32-34. Washington: American Folklore Society.

Ricoeur, Paul. 1974. *The Conflict of Interpretations: Essays in Hermeneutics.* Evanston, Ill.: Northwestern University Press.

Rotha, Paul. 1959. Some Principles of Documentary. In *Film: An Anthology,* ed. Daniel Talbot, 357-69. New York: Simon and Schuster.

Rotha, Paul, Sinclair Road, and Richard Griffith, eds. 1963. *Documentary Film.* 3d ed. London: Faber and Faber.

Rothschild, Amalie. 1980. *It Happens to Us* and *Nana, Mom, and Me.* In *The Documentary Conscience: A Casebook in Film Making,* ed. Alan Rosenthal, 415-25. Berkeley: University of California Press.

Rouch, Jean. 1974. The Camera and Man. Translated by Steve Feld. *Studies in the Anthropology of Visual Communication* 1:37-44.

Ruby, Jay. 1971. Toward an Anthropological Cinema. *Film Comment* 7:35-40.

———, ed. 1982a. *A Crack in the Mirror: Reflexive Perspectives in Anthropology.* Philadelphia: University of Pennsylvania Press.

———. 1982b. Ethnography as *Trompe l'Oeil:* Film and Anthropology. In *A Crack in the Mirror: Reflexive Perspectives in Anthropology,* ed. Jay Ruby, 121-31. Philadelphia: University of Pennsylvania Press.

———. 1988. The Image Mirrored: Reflexivity and the Documentary Film. In *New Challenges for Documentary,* ed. Alan Rosenthal, 64-77. Berkeley: University of California Press. First published in *Journal of the University Film Association* 29 (1977).

———. 1991. An Anthropological Critique of the Films of Robert Gardner. *Journal of Film and Video* 43:3-17.

———. 1992. Speaking for, Speaking about, Speaking with, or Speaking alongside: An Anthropological and Documentary Dilemma. *Journal of Film and Video* 44: 42-66.

Said, Edward. 1978. *Orientalism.* New York: Pantheon.

Saltzman, Rachelle H. 1989. Review of *One Hundred Years of Ybor City. Journal of American Folklore* 102:318-20.

Savoy, Ann Allen. 1988. *Cajun Music: A Reflection of a People,* vol. 1. 1984. Reprint, Eunice, La.: Bluebeard Press.

Sherman, Sharon R.

———. 1983. Rank and File: The Visualization of Occupational Folklore and Union History. *Western Folklore* 42:78-84.

———. 1985. Human Documents: Folklore and the Films of Jorge Preloran. *Southwest Folklore* 6:17-61.

———. 1986. "That's How the Seder Looks": A Fieldwork Account of Videotaping Family Folklore. *Journal of Folklore Research* 23:53-70.

———. 1995. *Chainsaw Sculptor: The Art of J. Chester "Skip" Armstrong.* Jackson: University Press of Mississippi.

Simon, Paul. 1973. Kodachrome. From the album *There Goes Rhymin' Simon.* New York: Paul Simon Music (ASCAP).

———. 1986. The Boy in the Bubble. From the album *Graceland.* New York: Paul Simon Music (ASCAP).

Sontag, Susan. 1979. *On Photography.* Harmondsworth, U.K.: Penguin.

Stoller, Paul. 1992. *Cinematic Griot: The Ethnography of Jean Rouch.* Chicago: University of Chicago Press.

Suber, Howard. 1971. Jorge Preloran. *Film Comment* 7:43-51.

Sufrin, Mark. 1979. Filming Skid Row. 1955-56. Reprinted in *The Documentary Tradition,* 2d ed., ed. Lewis Jacobs, 307-15. New York: W.W. Norton.

Sussex, Elizabeth. 1975. *The Rise and Fall of British Documentary: The Story of the Film Movement Founded by John Grierson.* Berkeley: University of California Press.

Thigpen, Kenneth. 1992. Taped interview. 18 October. American Folklore Society meeting, Jacksonville, Fla.

Toelken, J. Barre. 1976. The 'Pretty Language' of Yellowman: Genre, Mode, and Texture in Navajo Coyote Narratives. In *Folklore Genres*, ed. Dan Ben-Amos, 145-70. Austin, Tex.: Publications of the American Folklore Society, Bibliographical and Special Series 26. First published in *Genre* 2 (1969):211-35.

———. 1979. *The Dynamics of Folklore.* Boston: Houghton Mifflin.

Toelken, J. Barre, and Tacheeni Scott. 1981. Poetic Retranslation and the 'Pretty Language' of Yellowman. In *Traditional Literatures of the American Indian: Texts and Interpretations*, ed. Karl Kroeber, 65-116. Lincoln: University of Nebraska Press.

Tompkins, Jane, ed. 1980. *Reader-Response Criticism: From Formalism to Post-Structuralism.* Baltimore: Johns Hopkins University Press.

Tullos, Allen, Daniel W. Patterson, and Tom Davenport. 1989. Special Issue: *A Singing Stream: A Black Family Chronicle:* Background and Commentary. *North Carolina Folklore* 36 (1):1-37.

Vlach, John, and Simon J. Bronner, eds. 1986. *Folk Art and Art Worlds: Essays Drawn from the Washington Museum on Folk Art.* Ann Arbor: UMI Research Press.

Wagner, Paul. 1993. Taped interview. 15 May. Charlottesville, Va.

Waugh, Thomas. 1984. Introduction: Why Documentary Filmmakers Keep Trying to Change the World, *or* Why People Changing the World Keep Making Documentaries. In *"Show Us Life": Toward a History and Aesthetics of the Committed Documentary*, ed. Thomas Waugh, xi-xxvii. Metuchen, N.J.: Scarecrow Press.

Weiner, Annette B. 1994. Trobrianders On Camera and Off: The Film That Did Not Get Made. In *Visualizing Theory: Selected Essays from V.A.R., 1990-1994*, ed. Lucien Taylor, 54-59. New York: Routledge.

Wolfenstein, Martha, and Nathan Leites. 1950. *Movies: A Psychological Study.* New York: Free Press of Glencoe.

Worth, Sol. 1972. Toward the Development of a Semiotic of Ethnographic Film. *Program in Ethnographic Film Newsletter* 3:8-12.

———. 1982. Pictures Can't Say Ain't. In *Film/Culture: Explorations of Cinema in Its Social Context*, ed. Sari Thomas, 97-109. Metuchen, N.J.: Scarecrow Press.

Worth, Sol and John Adair. 1972. *Through Navajo Eyes: An Exploration in Film Communication and Anthropology.* Bloomington: Indiana University Press.

Young, Colin. 1975. Observational Cinema. In *Principles of Visual Anthropology*, ed. Paul Hockings, 65-80. The Hague: Mouton.

# Index

Abrahams, Roger, 149
Abrego, Eugenio, 103
Abshire, Nathan, 98, 108
Academe, folklore of, 137-38, 171, 178
Acuff, Roy, 136, 137, 143, 218
Adair, John, 26, 51-54, 58, 204
Adorno, Theodor, 293 n 7.2
*Afghan Nomads*, 51
*Afghan Village*, 51
African Americans, films on: crafts, 70-71, 86-87; occupation, 81-84; music, 71, 84-87, 92-93, 99-102, 120-23, 131, 143-46, 149, 151; games, 131-32, ; narrative, 71, 73; religion, 131, 151
*Afro-American Worksongs in a Texas Prison*, 65
Aibel, Robert, 274
Alaskan Native Heritage Project, 50
*All Day All Night: Memories from Beale Street Musicians*, 92-93, 229, 240
*All Hand Work*, 129, 131
Allen, Woody, 22
Alltägsleben, 248. *See also* everyday life
*Altar of Fire*, 45
*Always for Pleasure*, 181
*America's Funniest Home Videos*, 271, 274
Ames, Ruth "Blues," 144
Ancelet, Barry Jean, 108, 217
Andean music. *See* music
"Another Man Done Gone," 76
Antczak, Jerzey, 205
*Antelope Lake*, 53

anthropological documentaries, 33, film, 32-33, 159, 169, 262; and folklore film compared, 169, 173.
anthropology, shared, 46-48, 56; visual, 191. *See also* ethnodocumentary film
*Araucanians of Ruca Choroy*, 93-96, 125, 164
architecture, folk, 71, 95, 156-57
Ardoin, Alphonse "Bois Sec," 99
Armstrong, Skip, 146-48, 175, 218, 219, 252
Arnez, Luci, 274
Asch, Patsy, 55-56, 58, 262
Asch, Timothy, 38-39, 51, 55-56, 58, 61, 62, 68, 165, 168-69, 262
*At the Autumn River Camp*, 49
*At the Caribou Crossing Place*, 49
*At the Time of Whaling*, 50
*At the Winter Sea Ice Camp*, 49
auctions, 151, 155, 274
audience, 149, 183-89
Austin, J. L., 19
authority of filmmaker, 13, 55, 59, 162, 210-11

*Bad Influence*, 270
Baez, Joan, 74, 75, 76, 77, 109
Balfa Brothers, The, 98, 105, 108, 194
Balfa, Dewey, 99
Balikci, Asen, 48-50, 70, 74, 99, 137
*Balinese Trance Seance, A*, 55
ballads, 7, 89, 187, 259
Banks, Marcus, 287 n 21
baptism, 131, 146

## DATE DUE